OXFORD WORLD'S CLASSICS

LEAVES OF GRASS

WALT WHITMAN was born into a working-class family in West Hills, Long Island on 31 May 1819, the second of nine children. Forced to leave school aged 11 due to his father's financial troubles, Walt began working as a printer's apprentice and compositor for a variety of Brooklyn and New York newspapers. Over the next years, he wrote journalism, took on a number of editorial positions, and tried his hand at long fiction, publishing the popular temperance novel *Franklin Evans; or The Inebriate* (1842). Sometime in the later 1840s, Whitman read Ralph Waldo Emerson's essay 'The Poet' (1844), which argued that the time had come for a distinctively American poet to step forward. With the self-funded publication of *Leaves of Grass* in 1855, Whitman answered that call, styling himself as the self-proclaimed bard of his democracy. The book is widely regarded as a watershed in the history of Anglo-American poetry, constituting a radical new vision of the body, same-sex love, and marking the inception of what became known as 'free verse'. Whitman revised, expanded, and republished *Leaves* a further seven times during his lifetime: in 1856, 1860, 1867, 1870, 1871–2, 1876, 1881–2, and 1891–2. A temporary break from the project came with *Drum-Taps* (1865), a collection of Civil War poetry that drew on his experiences volunteering as a nurse in the Washington hospitals. Whitman's service during the war permanently affected his health, but he continued to write and publish throughout the 1870s and 1880s—his prose works *Democratic Vistas* and *Memoranda During the War* appearing in 1870 and 1875–6 respectively. His fame steadily grew during these later years, and he gained a devoted circle of supporters and followers on both sides of the Atlantic. He died in 1892 in Camden, NJ.

PETER RILEY is Senior Lecturer in Nineteenth-Century American Literature at the University of Exeter. He is the author of *Against Vocation: Whitman, Melville, Crane, and the Labors of American Poetry* (Oxford University Press, 2019) and *Strandings: Confessions of a Whale Scavenger* (2022), which won the Ideas Prize for non-fiction. He organized the International Walt Whitman Week in 2016 and has served as faculty for it twice.

OXFORD WORLD'S CLASSICS

For over 100 years Oxford World's Classics have brought
readers closer to the world's great literature. Now with over 700
titles—from the 4,000-year-old myths of Mesopotamia to the
twentieth century's greatest novels—the series makes available
lesser-known as well as celebrated writing.

The pocket-sized hardbacks of the early years contained
introductions by Virginia Woolf, T. S. Eliot, Graham Greene,
and other literary figures which enriched the experience of reading.
Today the series is recognized for its fine scholarship and
reliability in texts that span world literature, drama and poetry,
religion, philosophy, and politics. Each edition includes perceptive
commentary and essential background information to meet the
changing needs of readers.

OXFORD WORLD'S CLASSICS

WALT WHITMAN

Leaves of Grass

With an Introduction and Notes by
PETER RILEY

OXFORD
UNIVERSITY PRESS

OXFORD
UNIVERSITY PRESS

Great Clarendon Street, Oxford, OX2 6DP,
United Kingdom

Oxford University Press is a department of the University of Oxford.
It furthers the University's objective of excellence in research, scholarship,
and education by publishing worldwide. Oxford is a registered trade mark of
Oxford University Press in the UK and in certain other countries

Published in the United States of America by Oxford University Press
198 Madison Avenue, New York, NY 10016, United States of America

British Library Cataloguing in Publication Data

Data available

Library of Congress Control Number: 2023920388

ISBN 978-0-19-289444-1

Printed and bound in the UK by
Clays Ltd, Elcograf S.p.A.

CONTENTS

Introduction   vii

Note on the Text   xxxiii

Select Bibliography   xxxvi

A Chronology of Walt Whitman   xxxviii

LEAVES OF GRASS

LEAVES OF GRASS (1855)   11

from LEAVES OF GRASS (1856)   121

from LEAVES OF GRASS (1860–1861)   191

from DRUM-TAPS (1865)   275

from SEQUEL TO DRUM-TAPS (1865–1866)   303

from LEAVES OF GRASS (1867)   319

from LEAVES OF GRASS (1871–1872)   325

from PASSAGE TO INDIA (1871)   331

from AS A STRONG BIRD ON PINIONS
   FREE (1872)   355

from TWO RIVULETS (1876)   369

from LEAVES OF GRASS (1881–1882)   379

from NOVEMBER BOUGHS (1888)   383

from LEAVES OF GRASS (1891–1892)   391

Appendix A: Selected Prefaces and Letters   399

Appendix B: 'Song of Myself' from *Leaves of Grass*
   (1891–1892)   452

Explanatory Notes   509

Index of Titles   521

INTRODUCTION

I spring from the pages into your arms

AT heart, Walt Whitman's poetry is a celebration of the body: how that body relates to the world, to others; the way it senses, suffers, loves, labours, desires, reproduces, and dies. He spent his career as a poet exploring the ways in which the physical immediacy—the electricity—of lived experience might in some way be translated into book form. Strange as it may sound, *Leaves of Grass*, the project Whitman repeatedly revised, expanded, and republished from 1855 until his death in 1892, is an extended fantasy of the self circulating as a book. What new intimacies and communities, Whitman repeatedly asks, become possible if the poet could somehow transform his body into codex? Where, and by whom, might this book be carried, cherished, and possessed? Can a book of poems, he asks, make a material difference to our world?

In book form, *as his own book*, Whitman imagined himself sitting in (usually men's) laps; being carried in breast pockets; handled in sweating palms—even hatching through the page so as to reach out and 'come closer' to his beloved 'you', the reader. In his third 1860 edition of *Leaves of Grass*, on the eve of the American Civil War, he wrote: 'This is no book, | Who touches this, touches a man, | (Is it night? Are we here alone?) | It is I you hold, and who holds you, | I spring from the pages into your arms' (p. 274). The poet of America, Whitman believed, could be 'no stander above men and women or apart from them' (p. 36). On the contrary, such a poet needed to be in contact—in a position to experience his nation's shocks and triumphs as part of the demos, the people. The opening line of the 1855 *Leaves of Grass*, 'I CELEBRATE myself' (p. 15), was a new eucharist: a celebration or secular consecration of the inextricable relationship between poet, book, and republic. It is a trinity based on solidarity and shared material experience: 'And what I assume you shall assume, | For every atom belonging to me as good belongs to you' (p. 15).

Leaves of Grass is an evolving body of work. After the book's initial appearance in June 1855, Whitman revised the project a further seven times—in 1856, 1860, 1867, 1870–1, 1876, 1881–2, and 1891–2. With each new outing, he not only included new poems but also reworked what had gone before, experimenting with line length, format, punctuation, titles, numbering systems, book layout, and illustrations. Each version was a provisional response to, and attempt to keep up with, the extraordinary years that in his own words, 'trembled and reel'd beneath' him (p. 299). His poems are included here chronologically, as they first appeared in print in his various editions. To flick through these pages is to witness Whitman's extended labour of renewal—how and when he accumulated his poems over time. One immediate effect of this editorial arrangement is to get a sense of just how prolific Whitman was in the immediate years leading up to the American Civil War. The majority of his most well-known works found initial form in those first three editions—in 1855, 1856, and 1860—as the United States grappled with mortal existential questions concerning the future of slavery, labour, and capitalism. This is in no way to diminish the many important works that emerged during and after the Civil War, but rather to recognize the extent to which his vision altered after his experiences of this conflict, which famously culminated in his volunteering as a self-styled 'wound dresser' in Washington DC's field hospitals. After 1865, and as his health began to deteriorate, Whitman was increasingly occupied with questions of mortality, reputation, public image, legacy—of looking back, revising and consolidating what had gone before. Many of those subsequent revisions have had an undeniable impact on his reputation—several of his most unforgettable titles were formulated later in his career, 'Song of Myself' (first titled 'Leaves of Grass') and 'Out of the Cradle Endlessly Rocking' (first, 'A Child's Reminiscence') among them. However, many of his alterations and redactions also tempered the audacity of his earlier poems. An arresting line from 1860 for example—'I take for my love some prostitute' (p. 234)—goes missing by 1881. Some of the apparently more personal 'Calamus' poems are deleted after their initial appearance in 1860. The present edition aims to shift focus away from the more frequently reprinted 'end' of each poem's journey in 1892, and back onto the immediacy of their time-sensitive inception.

Beginnings

Walter Whitman Jnr. was born in 1819 into an aspirational working-class family on Long Island, New York. His father, Walter Whitman

Snr., made a living as a sometime housebuilder and farmer, and moved his young family from West Hills to Brooklyn when Walt was 4, hoping to profit from the city's latest property boom. When things didn't go to plan, the 11-year-old Walt was forced to finish school and help support his family financially, taking a job as an office boy at a local law firm. Auspiciously, he soon switched positions, becoming a printer's apprentice, or 'printer's devil' at the *Long-Island Patriot* newspaper. Barely a teenager, Whitman began developing an intimate knowledge of the printing process that he would carry with him for the rest of his life: the setting of type, composition on the page, the required consistency of ink, the workings of the printing press, keeping to deadlines, developing an eye for a headline. Every single one of these skills would come to determine the shape of the various books this poet would eventually put together.

Walt happened to be working at the *Long-Island Star* when his family decided to move back to rural Long Island in 1835. Already so bound up with this trade and the lifestyle it afforded, this now 16-year-old veteran of the printing trade decided to remain behind in Brooklyn. When the Great Fire of New York largely destroyed the city's printing district, he was temporarily forced to seek alternative employment, and after unhappy spells teaching at various Long Island schools, Whitman seized an opportunity to move to Huntington where he founded his own newspaper, *Long-Islander* in 1838. Although this endeavour was short-lived (he took it upon himself to edit, write, print, distribute, and advertise the publication himself), it signalled his general direction of travel. Throughout the 1840s, Whitman contributed countless editorials, commentary pieces, short stories, and even early poems to several New York and Brooklyn newspapers. In 1842, he tried his hand at long fiction, publishing the novel *Franklin Evans; or The Inebriate* in a special issue of the *New World*. It is still something of a critical conundrum that the first serious literary outing of the eventual author of *Leaves of Grass* was a temperance novel—and a popular one at that—a cautionary tale of a young man drawn to alcohol and the pursuit of pleasure.[1]

---

[1] See Michael Warner, 'Whitman Drunk', in Betsy Erkkila and Jay Grossman (eds.), *Breaking Bounds: Whitman and American Cultural Studies* (Oxford: Oxford University Press, 1996), 30–43, for a discussion of Whitman's temperance activism and *Franklin Evans* as an inverse exploration of the themes that would emerge in *Leaves*. This text reputedly sold 20,000 copies, making it the bestselling thing Whitman wrote during his lifetime.

By the late 1840s and early 1850s, Whitman was operating as a jack of all trades, a class migrant trying out different personae and performing a variety of labours. There was the lover of opera and New York dandy-journalist Whitman, who, according to one of his colleagues, often 'wore a frock coat and high hat, carried a small cane, and the lapel of his coat was almost invariably ornamented with a boutonniere'.[2] There was also the political Whitman who steadily aligned himself with the 'free soilers', a single-issue movement that opposed slavery on the grounds of its potential westward expansion and threat to white working-class interests (rather than on any abolitionist or humanitarian grounds). In 1848, Whitman joined the newly formed Free Soil Party and was elected as delegate to its convention in Buffalo, New York. He was reportedly dismissed from his position as editor of the *Brooklyn Daily Eagle* because of this political affiliation, with the paper's pro-slavery Democrat publisher Isaac Van Anden unhappy with the direction his paper was taking. Then there was also (perhaps most surprisingly) the real-estate dealer Whitman, who bought, renovated, and sold several houses in and around Brooklyn between 1848 and 1855. A variety of business-related documents from Whitman's archive shows him not only contributing manually to these projects, but also taking an administrative role in these transactions. Such materials further suggest how integrated this work was with Whitman's early poetic production. Buying and selling a house on Skillman Street helped fund his initial print run of *Leaves* (some lines were even drafted on the back of wallpaper samples). Bound up with the restless rhythms of his city, and complicit in its early mercantile capitalist economy, it's perhaps no wonder that a hustling, transacting voice would come to structure and balance so many of his most famous lines: 'take the best I possess, | Yield closer and closer and give me the best you possess' (p. 71). He spoke this language fluently, and saw in it a new economy of intimacy and loving touch.

Emerson and 'The Poet'

Thinking back to these early years, the older Whitman claimed that as a poet he had been 'simmering, simmering, simmering'—and that it

---

[2] William Cauldwell, quoted in Ed Folsom and Kenneth M. Price, *Re-Scripting Walt Whitman: An Introduction to His Life and Work* (Oxford: Blackwell, 2005), 10.

had been Ralph Waldo Emerson who eventually brought him 'to the boil'. What he quite meant by this is still up for debate.[3] By the 1850s, Emerson was the celebrated figurehead of 'American Transcendentalism', a nationally inflected adaptation of European, and particularly British, Romanticism. A former Unitarian minister and variously an essayist, poet, and sometime abolitionist, Emerson made the bulk of his living on the Lyceum Lecture circuit, a popular adult-education programme that flourished in New England throughout the nineteenth century. Whitman was likely in the audience to hear him give a version of his 1844 essay 'The Poet', which to this Brooklynite at least, sounded like something of a job description:

> I look in vain for the poet whom I describe [. . .] We have yet had no genius in America, with tyrannous eye, which knew the value of our incomparable materials [. . .] Our logrolling, our stumps and their politics, our fisheries, our Negroes, and Indians, our boasts, and our repudiations, the wrath of rogues, and the pusillanimity of honest men, the northern trade, the southern planting, the western clearing, Oregon, and Texas, are yet unsung. Yet America is a poem in our eyes; its ample geography dazzles the imagination, and it will not wait long for metres.[4]

Before outlining Whitman's response to these sentiments and ideas, a few caveats. First, it is impossible to ignore in these sentences the absolutist language of empire and exceptionalism. Those collective possessive pronouns with their sweeping confidence are breathtaking in their entitlement, and in their seemingly cursory treatment of slavery and Native American genocide. Whitman and Emerson were very different writers, but any engagement with either will always have to navigate this troubling ideological terrain. Second, to reproduce this paragraph of Emerson's is to also risk falling into a somewhat conventional retelling of the classic American literary nativity story—with Whitman hearing Emerson's prophetic words about the lack of an American original, a genius, and thinking to himself: 'I could do that!' This story gained literary-historiographical traction

---

[3] Quoted in John Townsend Trowbridge, 'Reminiscences of Walt Whitman', *Atlantic Monthly*, 89 (Feb. 1902), 163–75. Jay Grossman has pointed out the ambiguity of this comment—does it express provocation, or maybe even exasperation with the 'Bard of Concord'? (Grossman, *Reconstituting the American Renaissance: Emerson, Whitman, and the Politics of Representation* (Durham, NC: Duke University Press, 2003), 76).

[4] Ralph Waldo Emerson, *Essays: Second Series* (Boston: James Munroe & Company, 1844), 40–1.

in the first half of the twentieth century, with a group of scholars (and particularly the influential Americanist F. O. Matthiessen) looking back to the middle of the previous century and identifying the flourishing of an 'American Renaissance'.[5] From their vantage point, and bristling with Cold War anxieties about America's place in the world, the mid-nineteenth century was the pivotal moment when the nation stopped imitating Europe and found its exceptional, unique voice; when America's literary founding fathers—Emerson and Thoreau, Melville, Hawthorne, and Whitman—stepped forward and started articulating the 'American condition'. As the discipline of American Studies emerged over the following decades, new generations of scholars not only sought to identify and incorporate further voices into this canon but also were at pains to point out that the marking of a cultural 'renaissance' is always implicitly a claim to power, the self-confirmation of an exceptional 'great nation' asserting its place among other 'great nations'.[6] Any retelling of a literary beginning needs to be accompanied by an awareness of how and why the story has been passed down; how in this case it was inevitably fashioned according to the liberal fictions of manifest destiny, individual creative genius, and self-reliance—the extent to which it is laden with imperial anxieties concerning America's cultural standing. Ultimately, you need to decide how much critical distance ought to be placed between you and this nation's self-mythologizers in chief.

These caveats in mind, Emerson's argument nevertheless gave voice to a prominent contemporary anxiety: how could the United States claim its place on the world stage—how could it fulfil its own destiny—without a national bard to speak of? Ancient Greece had Homer, England had Shakespeare, Germany Goethe—what about the United States? To be reckoned with, a nation needed its poets just as much as it needs its industrialists, lawyers, and politicians. Not that these giants of literature could be directly emulated, but rather the American poet needed to channel their state of inspiration, their attitude. Get this right—become equal to the present—and the new

---

[5] See F. O. Matthiessen, *American Renaissance: Art and Expression in the Age of Emerson and Whitman* (Oxford: Oxford University Press, 1941).

[6] See Donald Pease's introduction to *The American Renaissance Reconsidered* (Baltimore: Johns Hopkins University Press, 1985), 3.

poetic form would surely follow: 'For it is not metres,' Emerson argued, 'but a metre-making argument, that makes a poem,— a thought so passionate and alive, that, like the spirit of a plant or an animal, it has an architecture of its own, and adorns nature with a new thing.'[7] In his earlier essay 'Nature' (1836), he outlined what this passionate 'thought' might look and feel like in an American context:

In the woods, we return to reason and faith. There I feel that nothing can befall me in life,—no disgrace, no calamity, (leaving me my eyes,) which nature cannot repair. Standing on the bare ground,—my head bathed by the blithe air, and uplifted into infinite space,—all mean egotism vanishes. I become a transparent eye-ball; I am nothing; I see all; the currents of the Universal Being circulate through me; I am part or particle of God. The name of the nearest friend sounds then foreign and accidental: to be brothers, to be acquaintances,—master or servant, is then a trifle and a disturbance. I am the lover of uncontained and immortal beauty.[8]

'In the woods': in such a location, according to Emerson, it is possible to return to a state of ultimate self-potential. All codes and customs, tensions and hierarchy, formal precedents, bodily limitations fall away. In the woods, the 'I' can cultivate 'an original relation to the universe'.[9] Don't look to others—even if those others are your siblings or friends—rely on yourself; transform into a refractive, disembodied transparent I/eye-ball and watch as your trivial material problems and your society's problems become resolved within a transcendent unity. If this supposedly 'new' American thinking happened to resemble the basic tenets of European Romanticism, so be it—'a foolish consistency is the hobgoblin of little minds'.[10] Aim for a free-flowing equivalence and harmony in which even the relationship between 'master or servant' becomes a 'trifle and a disturbance'—a line that is just as surprising and disturbing now as it was to his abolitionist contemporaries.

Whitman absorbed and weighed Emerson's thinking throughout the 1840s and early 1850s. With *Leaves*, he departed ways: his relationship to the woods, to society, the city—the body—would be

---

[7] Emerson, *Essays: Second Series*, 41.

[8] Emerson, *Nature* (Boston: James Monroe & Company, 1836), 12.

[9] Emerson, *Nature*, 1.

[10] 'Self-Reliance', in Emerson, *Essays: First Series* (Boston: Philips, Sampson & Co., 1854), 50.

different. At boiling point (the nativity story continues), Whitman approached a small Brooklyn printing firm, the Rome Brothers, and put together *Leaves* in a promethean fever-dream—inventing 'free verse' in the process, a new form of poetic expression or 'metre-making argument' uncontained by the metrical formalities of the past and suddenly spilling out across the page. He soon sent a copy directly to Emerson, speculatively attempting to establish a connection between himself and one of the most famous American intellectuals of the age. Astonishingly, given this was an unsolicited submission from a largely unknown writer, Emerson replied: 'I am not blind to the worth of the wonderful gift of "Leaves of Grass." I find it the most extraordinary piece of wit and wisdom that America has yet contributed [. . .] I greet you at the beginning of a great career.' These words of acknowledgement and praise have understandably attained the status of secular scripture in US culture, endlessly reproduced by subsequent generations of commentators—and not least of all by Whitman himself, who was never averse to publicizing and mythologizing his own unlikely emergence. On the spine of his second 1856 edition, and without seeking Emerson's permission, he stamped 'I greet you at the beginning of a great career' (coincidentally this was also the invention and first-known use of the book blurb). In an annex, and alongside Emerson's letter and his extended response, he also appended a selection of the decidedly mixed reviews he'd received for the first edition. It turns out that three of the more positive assessments were written by Whitman himself, partly to offset a recent review (also included by Whitman) in the *Boston Intelligencer*: 'The beastliness of the author is set forth in his own description of himself, and we can conceive no better reward than the lash for such a violation of decency as we have before us.' Yet to several people who mattered, this was something exciting and new. Henry David Thoreau, colleague of Emerson's and author of *Walden* (1854), wrote: 'We rejoice greatly in Walt Whitman. . . . You can't confound him with the other inhabitants of Brooklyn or New York. How they must shudder when they read him! He is awfully good.'[11]

---

[11] Henry David Thoreau, *Familiar Letters*, ed. F. B. Sanborn (Boston and New York: Houghton, Mifflin & Company, 1894), 346.

The First Leaves of Grass

Intoxicating as such an account of Whitman's emergence might be (and Emerson's often-overstated influence aside), a much more complicated and in some ways precarious picture of the first edition of *Leaves of Grass* has emerged in recent years. New Yorkers would have been highly unlikely to encounter a copy of this book when it first appeared in June 1855. If they'd been readers of the local paper, the *Brooklyn Daily Eagle*, they might have passed over a small notice— 'WALT WHITMAN'S POEMS. "LEAVES OF GRASS." 1 vol. small quarto: price $2'—sandwiched between the offer of a $3 reward for the safe return of a 'lady's gold breastpin' and a notice of real-estate ordinance. Some might have heard the local gossip about an odd new book being distributed by a local eccentric and sometime journalist, editor, printer, obscure novelist, real-estate dealer, and occasional writer of light verse—the now 36-year-old Walter Whitman Jnr. Far more likely, however, is that the appearance of this eventual lodestar of American literature would have initially gone unnoticed. In its first year, the 1855 *Leaves* probably sold fewer than twenty copies (the initial print run was 795); by comparison, Henry Wadsworth Longfellow's 1855 epic long poem *The Song of Hiawatha*, published a few months later in November (and written in strict trochaic tetrameter), shifted 50,000 copies in its first two years. Whitman's poetry never got anywhere near this figure during his lifetime.

Not that those who first came across *Leaves* would have necessarily been able to discern what kind of writing this was; or for that matter, who had written it. Whitman's name does not appear on the front, back, or spine of this first edition. Embossed on the cover of this oddly oversized, relatively slim volume are the gilt words 'Leaves of Grass', with each letter taking its cue from the season (late spring, early summer) by sprouting leaves and spreading roots. You'd also forgive a casual browser of a local Brooklyn bookshop for simply assuming it was the latest offering of another writer entirely. Fanny Fern, a friend and early supporter of Whitman's, had only recently published the incredibly successful *Fern Leaves from Fanny's Portfolio* (1853) and *Fern Leaves, Second Series* (1854). With its vegetative design and dark green cover, Whitman's *Leaves* bore a striking resemblance to Fern's. Her *Leaves*, collections of journalistic and commentary pieces, sold enough copies within the first months of their appearance to make them one of the most popular American books of the nine-teenth century (and make Fern financially independent for the rest of her life). Always attentive to the latest trends in the marketplace, and acutely aware of the risk he was taking by funding and publishing the book himself, Whitman may even have wanted to encourage the resemblance.

Open a copy of Whitman's *Leaves*, though, and that's where most resemblances stop. The first thing you come to is a smallish engraving of a day labourer, an image of Whitman in working man's clothing, staring out with cocked-hat, open-top-button, hands-on-hip attitude—right at you. Establishing his white, working-class 'free soil' credentials—immediately drawing attention to his own body—Whitman mixes a street-smart 'Bowery B'hoy' confidence with a 'where do you think you're going' defiance. A title page, 'Leaves of Grass. Brooklyn, New York: 1855', makes no reference to poems or poetry, and provides no further clue as to who might have put this together. In tiny lettering, over the page, you find out that this was 'Entered according to Act of Congress in the year 1855, by WALTER WHITMAN, in the Clerk's office of the District Court of the United States for the Southern District of New York' (p. 13). A lengthy prefatory essay, appearing like two newspaper columns, heralds the news of what has just dropped: a bold new American poetry that will not conform to the formal or intel-lectual precedents of the past, but rather shape itself according to the energies of the sensuous present:

> I CELEBRATE myself,
> And what I assume you shall assume,
> For every atom belonging to me as good belongs to you.
>
> I loafe and invite my soul,
> I lean and loafe at my ease . . . . observing a spear of summer
> grass.
>
> Houses and rooms are full of perfumes . . . . the shelves are
> crowded with perfumes,
> I breathe the fragrance myself, and know it and like it,
> The distillation would intoxicate me also, but I shall not let it.
>
> The atmosphere is not a perfume . . . . it has no taste of the
> distillation . . . . it is odorless,

> It is for my mouth forever . . . . I am in love with it,
> I will go to the bank by the wood and become undisguised and
>   naked,
> I am mad for it to be in contact with me.

(p. 15)

In this retelling of the Genesis story, a body wakes up to itself, extends and relaxes into space, realizes its sensory capacities as if for the first time, and thrills at the material fact of being alive. Observing, touching, tasting, smelling, listening—present-participle living. The expansive lines and dotted ellipses traverse as much of the page as they require—uncontained temporal and visual enactments of leaning and loafing and observing. This 'self' demands contact with the 'atmosphere', rather than any prefabricated 'perfume' or 'distillation' (pleasing as those can be). Whitman's speaker celebrates a sensory openness which participates in the miracle of the present.

'Free verse' is a term that often gets associated with Whitman's innovations here, and while this moniker captures something of this writing's immediacy, it can also often be unhelpful. Undoubtedly, his poetry did signal a departure from the verse forms that had up to this point defined Anglophone culture, but this does not mean they were now formless or unstructured:

> Through me the afflatus surging and surging . . . . through me the
>   current and index.
>
> I speak the password primeval . . . . I give the sign of democracy;
> By God! I will accept nothing which all cannot have their
>   counterpart of on the same terms.
>
> Through me many long dumb voices,
> Voices of the interminable generations of slaves,
> Voices of prostitutes and of deformed persons,
> Voices of the diseased and despairing, and of thieves and dwarfs,
> Voices of cycles of preparation and accretion,
> And of the threads that connect the stars   and of wombs, and
>   of the fatherstuff,
> And of the rights of them the others are down upon,
> Of the trivial and flat and foolish and despised,
> Of fog in the air and beetles rolling balls of dung.

Through me forbidden voices,
Voices of sexes and lusts . . . . voices veiled, and I remove the veil,
Voices indecent by me clarified and transfigured.

(p. 36)

'Through', 'of', 'by', 'and': Whitman saturates his lines with preposi-
tions and conjunctions, little facilitative words serving as grammat-
ical hinges that continually give way to new inclusions; allowing his
speaker to pass freely from perspective to perspective. Molly McGarry
has pointed out that this writing in part draws inspiration from the
occult world of trance mediumship, a practice that Whitman was
familiar with at the time of writing.[12] Instead of channelling spirits
from an above or beyond, though, the aim here was to give voice to
what surged from below: 'Through me forbidden voices'. In other
words, this free verse is governed by alternative structuring prin-
ciples. In his classic 1953 essay 'Some Lines from Walt Whitman',
Randall Jarrell memorably characterized Whitman as

the poet of parallel present participles, of twenty verbs joined by a single
subject: all this helps to give his work its feeling of raw hypnotic reality, of
being that world which also streams over us joined only by ands, until we
supply the subordinating conjunctions; and since as children we see the
ands and not the becauses, this method helps to give Whitman some of the
freshness of childhood. How inexhaustibly interesting the world is in
Whitman! . . . They might have put on his tombstone WALT WHITMAN:
HE HAD HIS NERVE. He is the rashest, the most inexplicable and
unlikely—the most impossible, one wants to say—of poets.[13]

The 'nerve' of this poetry, according to Jarrell, is that it forces us to
inhabit a grammar of attentiveness and wonder. Whitman supplies a suc-
cession of interconnected independent clauses that largely go unencum-
bered by a subordinate clause—a clause that would seek to explain,
justify, or complicate the thing being described. So while Whitman's
poetry invests heavily in coordinating conjunctions such as 'both/and',
'so', 'either/or', 'neither/nor', 'not only', 'whether/or', 'so/as', com-
pletely absent from 'Song of Myself' are the common, qualifying words:
'although', 'unless', 'provided', 'in case', 'even if', 'however', 'otherwise',

[12] Molly McGarry, *Ghosts of Futures Past: Spiritualism and the Cultural Politics of
Nineteenth-Century America* (Berkeley and Los Angeles: University of California Press,
2012), 169.

[13] Randall Jarrell, 'Some Lines from Walt Whitman', in Jarrell, *Poetry and the Age*
(London: Vintage, 1953), 118.

'thus' (one temporal usage: 'thus far'), 'instead'. What this means is that the words that would otherwise perform an act of explaining away, or seeing through, go missing. More startling is Whitman's sparing use of the two most common subordinating conjunctions: 'because' (which Jarrell associates with an adult's critical consciousness) and 'though' (a word that might hinder or qualify the confidence of a particular proclamation). Each is used only once in the entirety of Whitman's first 1855 poem—what would eventually become 'Song of Myself':

because:
'And do not call the tortoise unworthy *because* she is not something else' (pp. 25, 463; emphasis added)

though:
'The young fellow drives the express-wagon . . . . I love him *though* I do not know him' (pp. 26, 464; emphasis added)

In Whitman's hands, a line about a tortoise can transform into a meditation on the grammatical dismissiveness that the overly familiar word 'because' might inflict. A tortoise is worthy—she simply is. Similarly, in glimpsing a young driver in New York, the speaker's love and admiration agitates against the need for further clarification. In 1860, such fleeting, metropolitan encounter found exhilarating expression in 'City of My Walks and Joys' (later 'City of Orgies'): 'O Manhattan! your frequent and swift flash of eyes offering me love' (p. 254).

Zoom out, and you can see how Whitman's grammar of immediacy begins to determine the material dimensions of his book. Ed Folsom, one of the most influential Whitman scholars of the last three decades, has shown how many of the distinctive features of the 1855 *Leaves* actually came about by chance, as responses to immediate circumstances rather than any strictly preconceived artistic vision. He suggests, for example, that the unusual oversized formatting of *Leaves* was the result of the Rome Brothers printing house only having legal paper to hand when Whitman approached them. Since most of their commissions were business contracts, this was the only paper size they had in stock—and he just went with it. What better way to showcase his longer, contractually structured lines of this new giving and taking?[14] Amazing to think that this landmark literary intervention

[14] Ed Folsom, *Whitman Making Books/Books Making Whitman: A Catalog and Commentary* (Iowa City: Obermann Center for Advanced Studies, University of Iowa, 2005), <https://whitmanarchive.org/criticism/current/anc.00150.html>.

was precipitated by a Brooklyn paper shortage. Folsom also contends that, strapped for cash and with extensive knowledge and experience of the printing process, Whitman fussed over the print run itself, revising particular lines and correcting typos as he went. For many years, scholars and students debated the absence of a period (full point) at the end of the poem that would become 'Song of Myself': 'I stop some where waiting for you[.]' (p. 71). Was this another act of daring experimentation, with Whitman declining to end-stop a line about waiting and stopping? No, it turns out that the missing period was a misprint, with the typeface slipping during the print run, jamming up against the final vowel 'u' (making it impossible to read as a separate entity in some copies), and then falling out completely.

Step back still further, and you can also begin to apprehend how this loving presentism collapses clear distinctions between book and body. Intimately involved in the labour of producing his *Leaves*, Whitman imagined himself dissolving into its pages. At one juncture in the first edition, the speaker directly calls up from the reader's lap:

Listener up there! Here you . . . . what have you to confide to me?
(pp. 70, 507)

By holding the physical object, Whitman suggests, you are holding a manifestation of the poet himself. Across the Atlantic, Karl Marx had begun describing the commodity form as 'congealed labour'— a physical embodiment of the work that had gone into its making. Even as such a commodity gets circulated in the marketplace, severed or 'alienated' from its maker, converted into capital, it still in some sense retains a trace of that initial human contact, the work that made it. While Marx wanted to disturb his readers with this thought, Whitman fantasized about the other erotic and gendered possibilities of this economy. 'WHOEVER you are holding me now in hand' (p. 239), Whitman writes again in the 'Calamus' cluster of 1860—thrilling at the idea of being able to promiscuously circulate as a book; pressing up against a citizen of his beloved America. His second 1856 edition seems to have been reshaped with exactly this priority in mind. Culling numerous conjunctions in an attempt to force his existing lines (and new poems) into a smaller page space, he conceived of this new edition as a kind of pocketbook—a volume designed to be kept close to the body of his readers. The earliest known image of a Whitman reader (and for that matter, a Whitman book) is a startling

picture of a young, relatively affluent woman posing for a daguerro-
type in the 1850s. No one knows who she was, but she's displaying
a copy of this 1856 pocketbook *Leaves* suggestively in her lap, having
smuggled it into an otherwise conventional portrait (at first glance
you assume she's holding a bible). With her subtle smile and direct
gaze, the image feels like a conscious staging of Whitmanic intimacy
between book and reader: she gets it; she is in touch.[15]

'Calamus' and the Eve of War

Given the political volatility of the United States during the 1850s, it
might seem surprising, shocking even, that Whitman felt able to put
forward his tactile, celebratory vision when he did. *Leaves* appeared
just six years before the outbreak of what is still the bloodiest war in the
nation's history. By 1855, debates as to whether or not the newly
colonized western territories ought to be 'slave' or 'free' states had
already broken out into open civil conflict, particularly in borderland
states such as Kansas and Missouri. Set against this fractured, rapidly
deteriorating situation, *Leaves of Grass* feels like Whitman reaching for
a compensatory language of renewed contact; an attempt to mitigate or
even remedy impending catastrophe. The recent discovery of a previ-
ously unknown prose work provides a fascinating snapshot of
Whitman's conflicted mindset in the years immediately preceding the
outbreak of war. In late 1858, writing under the pen name Mose Velsor,
Whitman serialized a 50,000-word fitness guide, 'Manly Health and
Training', in the *New York Atlas*. Aside from being another excellent
opportunity to focus once more on the (male) physique, the project
also speaks to his intense anticipatory anxieties concerning the nation's
potential state of preparedness—the need for the body politic, in the
face of potential violence, to be at the ready, trained.

Faced with the imminent possibility of war, Whitman began to
temper the exuberance and surety that had defined his first two edi-
tions. When he published his third *Leaves* in 1860, many of the newly
included poems suddenly gave voice to a more pensive persona. What
would eventually become 'As I Ebb'd with the Ocean of Life' included
the line (unthinkable in either 1855 or 1856): 'I have not once had the

---

[15] See Ed Folsom, 'The Sesquicentennial of the 1856 Leaves of Grass: A Daguerreotype
of a Woman Reader', *Walt Whitman Quarterly Review*, 24 (Summer 2006), 33–4.

least | idea who or what I am' (p. 211). This said (and we have to just
add another contradiction to the pile), the 1860 *Leaves* was also in
some senses an intensification of his previous convictions. The closer
the nation came to tearing itself apart, the closer men needed to come
together. Whitman's 'Calamus' cluster, consisting of forty-five new
poems, was an extraordinary call for 'comrades' to unite:

> WE two boys together clinging,
> One the other never leaving,
> Up and down the roads going—North and South
>   excursions making,
> Power enjoying—elbows stretching—fingers clutching,
> Armed and fearless—eating, drinking, sleeping, loving,
>   (p. 258)

Elsewhere, he began describing this passionate clinging together as
'adhesiveness'. Borrowed from phrenology (a pseudoscience that
claimed an individual's personality could be assessed by measuring
the contours of their skull), adhesiveness was the propensity to form
close attachments to others. Contemporary commentators generally
viewed it as a decidedly feminine trait, or an 'organ most pronounced
in women', as one practitioner put it.[16] Offset by (and legitimized
within) the militaristic tone of preparedness and solidarity—'armed
and fearless'—Whitman's writing now expanded the sexual and gen-
dered horizons he'd prised open in 1855. The third 'Calamus' poem,
'WHOEVER you are holding me now in hand', included the lines: 'put
your lips upon mine I permit you, | With the comrade's long-dwelling
kiss, or the new | husband's kiss, | For I am the new husband, and
I am the comrade' (p. 240). If there are any lingering doubts about the
erotic excitements and erect penises Whitman was fantasizing about
here, just look up an image of the calamus plant (also commonly
known as 'sweet flag').[17]

---

[16] *OED*, 'adhesiveness', quoted from *Chambers's Encyclopædia: A Dictionary of
Universal Knowledge for the People*, 10 vols. (1st edn., London: W. and R. Chambers,
1860–8).

[17] Ed Folsom was the first scholar to notice that the decorative finials on the title page
of the 1860 edition are not just arbitrary flourishes, but individual sperms inseminating
the letters that make up 'Leaves of Grass'. See Folsom, '"A Spirt of My Own Seminal
Wet": Spermatoid Design in Walt Whitman's 1860 *Leaves of Grass*', *Huntington Library
Quarterly*, 73/4 (2010), 585–600.

By the late 1850s, Whitman had begun frequenting Pfaff's, a restaurant at the centre of New York's bohemian and literary scene. Here he became affiliated with the 'Fred Grey Association', a group of men interested in exploring same-sex relationships.[18] It was also around this time that he likely fell in love with a young Manhattan stagecoach driver called Fred Vaughan, the first (that we know of) in a line of young men to whom Whitman would form close attachments. Though the precise nature of the relationship is unknown, it does seem to have been intense, short-lived, and painful. There are poems in the 'Calamus' cluster that dramatize a deep sense of personal anguish (Whitman expurgated the following from all future editions of his work):

> Sullen and suffering hours! (I am ashamed—but it
>   is useless—I am what I am;)
> Hours of my torment—I wonder if other men ever
>   have the like, out of the like feelings?
> Is there even one other like me—distracted—his
>   friend, his lover, lost to him?
>
> (p. 248)

Several scholars have gently cautioned against too quickly assuming this to be the language of the closet and gay shame (understandable though such a reading is). Written at a point in time when the familiar labels of sexual identity were not yet in circulation, what we instead have access to here is something much richer and stranger: a language of same-sex desire that spills beyond our current epistemological categories, and allows us to think more expansively about the loving we do, or might do.[19] To read *Leaves of Grass* is to glimpse the contours of a world that predates and simultaneously exceeds our sexological present, giving way to all sorts of alternative queer universes: weird nation-states, surrogacies, gender roles, friendships, polyamories.

In one unforgettable scene (first published in the 1855 edition), Whitman's speaker initially inhabits the perspective of a woman who

[18] See Stephanie M. Blalock, '"Tell What I Meant by Calamus": Walt Whitman's Vision of Comradeship from Fred Vaughan to the Fred Gray Association', in Joanna Levin and Edward Whitley (eds.), *Whitman Among the Bohemians* (Iowa City: University of Iowa Press, 2014), 155–71.

[19] See Jonathan Katz, *Love Stories: Sex Between Men before Homosexuality* (Chicago: University of Chicago Press, 2001), 165–7. Or Jay Grossman, 'Walt Whitman and Sexuality', in Edward Whitley and Joanna Levin (eds.), *Walt Whitman in Context* (Cambridge: Cambridge University Press, 2018), 227–38.

is looking longingly out of her window at a group of young men frolicking together in a body of water:

> Twenty-eight young men bathe by the shore,
> Twenty-eight young men, and all so friendly,
> Twenty-eight years of womanly life, and all so lonesome.
>
> She owns the fine house by the rise of the bank,
> She hides handsome and richly drest aft the blinds of the window.
>
> Which of the young men does she like the best?
> Ah the homeliest of them is beautiful to her.
>
> Where are you off to, lady? for I see you,
> You splash in the water there, yet stay stock still in your room.
>
> Dancing and laughing along the beach came the twenty-ninth bather,
> The rest did not see her, but she saw them and loved them.
>
> The beards of the young men glistened with wet, it ran from their long hair,
> Little streams passed all over their bodies.
>
> An unseen hand also passed over their bodies,
> It descended tremblingly from their temples and ribs.
>
> The young men float on their backs, their white bellies swell to the
>   sun . . . . they do not ask who seizes fast to them,
> They do not know who puffs and declines with pendant and bending arch,
> They do not think whom they souse with spray.

(p. 23)

So many proliferating possibilities in these lines: the sustained ambiguity of exactly whose trembling unseen hand starts passing over these bodies; the passionate acknowledgement of a woman's masturbatory desire; the celebration of beautiful bodies; the visionary trans pregnancies of men as their 'white bellies' begin swelling to the sun in what ends up becoming a gender-fluid surrogate birthing pool. In giving voice to this multiverse, Whitman also inevitably interposes himself in our present struggles around sexual and gender identity, holding out solidarity and kinship to those who are currently fighting for recognition.

* * *

Before we get too excited by this representation of gender play, same-sex love, and transition, however, we must again face the complications and cross-currents. In close proximity to these affirmations are some deeply discomforting questions concerning Whitman's attitude to race and particularly slavery. His ongoing affiliation with the Free Soil Party requires further scrutiny in this regard, because it reveals the racialized dimensions of the bodies he fantasizes about. 'Free soil, free speech, free labour, and free men' was the campaign slogan that had secured Martin Van Buren's nomination for the presidency back in 1848. In yet another guise, Whitman had actively campaigned under this banner, and again, it ought not be confused with the abolitionist call to end slavery on ethical grounds. Much to the disappointment of many of his subsequent followers, Whitman did not take an unequivocal stand on the great issue of his age. Indeed, his thinking about slavery seems never to have untangled itself from its role in delineating the dimensions of an ideal free white body politic; never was he quite able to separate the black body from its association with bondage and subjection.

Granted, there are some extraordinary passages in the first editions of *Leaves* that indicate sympathetic leanings. At one point in the poem that would become 'Song of Myself', the speaker imagines providing shelter for a runaway, implicating this self in the 'underground railroad', the network of secret routes and safe houses designed to facilitate a passage north. Whitman's roving 'I' even goes so far as to briefly inhabit the first-person perspective of the suffering enslaved: 'I am the hounded slave . . . . I wince at the bite of the dogs, | Hell and despair are upon me . . . . crack and again crack the marksmen' (pp. 49, 487). Such passages, however, tend to be defined by an uneasiness and distance—the speaker remembers the man's 'revolving eyes and his awkwardness' (pp. 23, 460), apparently drawing inspiration from the tradition of blackface minstrelsy rather than any lived experience. He also invites the fugitive to sit with him 'at table', a statement qualified with 'my firelock leaned in the corner' (pp. 23, 460)—a line that seems at once to encompass both trust and mistrust. There are also certain comments that have been attributed to Whitman the journalist and editor. Roy Morris Jnr., a biographer of the Civil War years, is unflinching in his presentation of Whitman's racist attitudes, and attributes the following to him from a *Brooklyn Daily Times* editorial of 1858 (Whitman was then working as an editor at the newspaper): 'Who believes that

Whites and Blacks can ever amalgamate in America? Or who wishes it to happen? Nature has set an impassable seal against it. Besides, is not America for the Whites? And is it not better so?'[20] Whether or not he wrote these lines is up for debate, but he would have known his paper was publishing them, and it would be remiss not to draw attention to this significant strand in the complicated, often irreconcilable, weave of his outlook.

Whitman's War and Drum-Taps

In December 1862, Whitman was at home in Brooklyn, anxiously scanning a list of dead and wounded from the latest major military engagement—the Battle of Fredericksburg. He came across the name 'G. W. Whitmore'. His brother George had enlisted in April 1861, at the war's very beginning, and it was likely that he'd been caught up in the latest fighting. Fearing the worst (misprints were common at this time), he made his way to Washington DC, a city now just 50 miles from the front. George, it turned out, had received only a minor facial injury, but the carnage Whitman saw during that trip, particularly in the makeshift field hospitals, changed the course of his life. In a diary entry collected in his 1876 prose work *Memoranda During the War*, the poet of clinging-together love describes coming across a scene that constitutes a kind of nightmare inversion of *Leaves*: 'a heap of amputated feet, legs, arms, hands, &c., a full load for a one-horse cart'.[21] In the vicinity, corpses lay scattered on the frozen earth, each barely covered over with a brown woollen blanket.

It's sometimes difficult to maintain critical distance from the three years that followed, such was the extraordinary nature of Whitman's conduct and service. From Christmas 1862 to the end of the war and even beyond, he visited the casualties, tending to thousands (possibly tens of thousands) of wounded and dying soldiers. In his collection of war poetry *Drum-Taps*, published in 1865, the Whitmanic self now transformed into 'The Dresser' (later 'The Wound-Dresser'):

---

[20] Quoted in Roy Morris Jnr., *The Better Angel: Walt Whitman in the Civil War* (Oxford: Oxford University Press, 2000), 80.

[21] *Memoranda During the War* (Camden, NJ: Printed for the Author by New Republic Print, Federal St., 1875–6), 60.

I am faithful, I do not give out;
The fractur'd thigh, the knee, the wound in the abdomen,

These and more I dress with impassive hand—(yet
    deep in my breast a fire, a burning flame.)

(p. 289)

'Faithful' to the men he looked after, but also to the promise of his books. Extending a critical tradition that has read Whitman's Civil War service as an attempt to live up to—embody—the promise of *Leaves*, Peter Coviello writes that Whitman resolved now to '*enact* that fantasy of self-manufactured cohesion, bed by bed, soldier by wounded soldier'.[22] Aside from tending to the immediate medical needs of patients, he made sure that these men were not alone when they died; handed out small gifts to raise spirits; transcribed countless letters home for illiterate soldiers; delivered stationery to those who wanted to communicate with their loved ones. *Through me many long dumb voices*. Whitman consciously attempted to make manifest his poetry, to turn words into deeds. In *Memoranda*, he also describes tending to African American soldiers who were most often placed in separate, segregated facilities: 'among the black soldiers, wounded or sick, and in the contraband camps, I also took my way whenever in their neighbourhood, and did what I could for them'.[23] In so many of the decisions that Whitman made during his Washington years, the poetry of 'through', 'of', and 'by' steadily walked its talk. One letter he wrote for a young Union soldier called Nelson Jabo recently came to light in 2017 (during an episode of the PBS's *Antiques Roadshow*): 'I hope it is God's will that we shall yet meet again'; 'I send you all of my love'. After signing the soldier's name, he wrote: 'By Walt Whitman, a friend.'[24] No one knows how many of these 'through me/ by me' letters exist in family archives, but they too can be counted as extensions, real-life applications, of *Leaves*.

To support his voluntary work in the capital, the poet initially took a position as a part-time clerk in the Army Paymaster's Office. The

---

[22] Peter Coviello, 'Introduction: Whitman at War', in *Memoranda During the War*, ed. Coviello (New York: Oxford University Press, 2004), p. xlii.

[23] *Memoranda* (1875–6), 56.

[24] Walt Whitman Civil War Letter, The Civil War Years Preview, *Antiques Roadshow* (PBS), broadcast 18 January 2017.

schedule was relentless and all-consuming. In January 1865, after a six-month period of sick leave due to exhaustion, he was appointed to a more permanent clerkship at the Bureau of Indian Affairs. According to legend, he was then fired from this position because his boss, Cabinet Secretary James Harlan, discovered a copy of the 1860 *Leaves* in his desk and thought it obscene. With the support of his slowly expanding circle of friends and admirers—particularly the writer William D. O'Connor and naturalist John Burroughs—Whitman then managed to secure work as a copyist in the Attorney General's Office, a job he kept until 1873. Such details are significant because, by undertaking this labour, he also served as the medium of the broader political 'current and index'. In a remarkable discovery, Kenneth M. Price recently brought to light 3,000 documents in Whitman's hand that had been stored at the National Archives in Maryland. Between 1865 and 1873, he took down dictations and copied the communications of successive attorneys general. Inhabiting the voices of senior politicians, doing his rounds in the hospitals, he managed to position himself at the epicentre of his nation's existential drama. It was a routine that even brought him into the orbit of the President: 'I see very plainly ABRAHAM LINCOLN'S dark brown face,' he wrote in *Memoranda*, 'with the deep cut lines, the eyes, &c., always to me with a deep latent sadness in the expression. We have got so that we always exchange bows, and very cordial ones.'[25] News of Lincoln's assassination broke only a few days after the poet had sent his *Drum-Taps* manuscript off to the printers. Too late to stop the press and incorporate the poems that now came to him—'When Lilacs Last in the Dooryard Bloom'd' and 'O Captain, My Captain' among them—he was moved to put together *Sequel to Drum-Taps*. When finally in possession of both printed texts, he reportedly spent that 1865 summer with needle and thread, physically stitching the two collections together, beginning the work (in his mind at least), of national healing and reconciliation.

The Good Grey Poet

Those who saw the emotional and physical toll that Whitman's time in Washington had taken felt increasingly compelled to come to his

---

[25] *Memoranda* (1875–6), 23.

aid. In 1866, William O'Connor published a pamphlet entitled *The Good Grey Poet: A Vindication*, an attack on what he saw as Whitman's unjust treatment by Harlan at the Bureau of Indian Affairs. He followed this up with a short story, 'The Carpenter: A Christmas Story', which he contributed to *Putnam's Monthly Magazine* in 1868. The narrative centres around the appearance of a Christ-like figure (a thinly veiled representation of Whitman in the hospitals) who moves

with a sort of measured alertness among the group, paying his simple and affectionate addresses to each person, with the air of being already on familiar terms with them, and of knowing all about them; thus establishing himself in close *rapport* with every one, as only a man of powerful intuitions, vivid impressions, and great magnetic force and dignity could have done, and leaving them with a sense as if something electric and very sweet had swept through them.[26]

This representation of electric Whitmanic sociability was subsequently expanded upon by the poet himself in his 1868 essay 'Personalism', which then became one of the central parts of his extended prose work *Democratic Vistas* (1870). In its preoccupation with economic expansion and self-interest, Whitman argued, America was in danger of not learning key lessons of the war. To move forward, to fulfil its promise, the nation needed to temper the forces of business, reform its institutions 'saturated in corruption, bribery, falsehood, maladministration', and get back to the first principles of democratic rapport.[27] On the question of how the United States might go about enfranchising the four million people who had been freed by the 1863 Emancipation Proclamation, however (and by the passage of the Constitutional amendments outlawing slavery at the war's end), Whitman was almost completely silent—a silence that is impossible to reconcile with the scope and ambition of these 'vistas' (and these *Leaves*).

Regaining a sense of purpose and vision, however, Whitman reaffirmed his commitment to *Leaves*, incorporating his war poetry into a new 1867 edition. Further celebratory assessments were soon forthcoming—this time from the other side of the Atlantic and particularly

[26] William Douglas O'Connor, 'The Carpenter: A Christmas Story', *Putnam's Monthly Magazine*, 1 (1868), 55–90.

[27] 'Democratic Vistas', in Whitman, *Complete Prose Works* (Philadelphia: David McKay, 1892), 210.

in Britain, where his reputation was outpacing his American reception. Having contributed a highly favourable article to the *London Chronicle*, William Michael Rossetti (brother of Dante Gabriel and Christina Georgina) reached out to Whitman and suggested an English edition. After some difficult conversations regarding the navigation of British censorship laws, *Poems of Walt Whitman* appeared in London in 1868. This edition greatly enhanced Whitman's literary standing, both at home and abroad. In 1870, the English writer Ann Gilchrist, one of the poet's earliest and most vocal woman supporters, published the enthusiastic and sharply observed 'A Woman's Estimate of Walt Whitman' in the *Boston Radical* (1870). A year later, he received a salutary poem of praise from Algernon Swinburne, followed by birthday greetings from the then British Poet Laureate Alfred Lord Tennyson. Others were steadily drawn into the orbit of this increasingly mythic figure. In portraits from the era, you can see Whitman adopt a further persona, 'The Good Grey Poet', replete with full white bardic beard, and in one iconic image, a (model) butterfly perched on his extended finger.

Whitman suffered his first paralytic stroke in 1873, and, unable to continue with his job in Washington, he moved to Camden, NJ, to be closer to his brother's family. Increasingly preoccupied with questions of legacy and reputation, he put out a further 'Centennial Edition' of *Leaves* in 1876, alongside his prose work *Memoranda During the War*. Ever the self-promoter, he accompanied these publications with the unsigned article 'Walt Whitman's Actual American Position', which provoked further international debate concerning his relative neglect at home (and an uptick in sales and donations). However it was only really with the sixth 1882 edition of *Leaves*, published by David McKay in Philadelphia, that Whitman finally secured favourable copyright terms—as well as an opportunity to rework, revise, and reorder what he now thought of as his final, definitive book (though he also continued to contribute new poems). The edition also benefited from being subject to a complaint by the Boston District Attorney on the grounds of obscenity, which hugely increased the book's visibility. Coincidentally, 1882 was the year that Oscar Wilde decided to pay his respects on his way through Philadelphia—the international celebrity describing Whitman to the press as 'the grandest man [he had] ever seen'.[28] No one quite knows what passed

---

[28] 'Oscar Wilde', *Boston Herald* (29 Jan. 1882), 7.

between these two great queer icons, but one (the best) retelling of the encounter has them passionately kissing one another.

With the royalties from the 1882 book contract, Whitman was able to purchase a house on Mickle Street in Camden, an address that became a centre of gravity for what scholars have subsequently described as his 'disciples'.[29] When he suffered a further serious stroke in 1888, such men provided round-the-clock care and company, presented him with a mobility horse and cart to get around town, and—in the case of Horace Traubel—kept a detailed record of nearly daily conversations with the poet in his last years.[30] Whitman died on 26 March 1892 at the age of 72, just a few months after publishing the final 'Deathbed' edition of *Leaves*. According to Elizabeth Keller (another close friend and follower), his last words were spoken to Frederick Warren Fritzinger, a 25-year-old former sailor who had nursed him through his final days. A request to be moved in his bed: 'shift, Warry'.[31]

Afterlives

Wherever the poetic and political avant-garde has gone, Whitman has insisted on accompanying. In the April 1913 issue of *Poetry: A Magazine of Verse*, Ezra Pound contributed a poem calling for a 'truce' with his 'detested' 'pig-headed father', before begrudgingly acknowledging that it was Whitman who 'broke the new wood'. Pound positioned his 'Imagist' poem 'In a Station of the Metro' immediately after his 'pact', a work so formally dissimilar to Whitman's writing that it must be regarded as being inversely sculpted by it. A hundred years later, in the era-defining *Citizen: An American Lyric* (2014), Claudia Rankine begins her long poem with the pronoun 'you'. Sustaining this unsettling, disembodied second-person persona throughout, Rankine voices the experiences of those subjects who are still not able to identify or speak with Whitman's confident, celebratory 'I'. African American poets have long signalled

[29] See Michael Robertson, *Worshipping Walt: The Whitman Disciples* (Princeton, NJ: Princeton University Press, 2010).

[30] See Traubel, *With Walt Whitman in Camden* (1906–96). Three volumes appeared during Traubel's lifetime; a further six posthumously.

[31] Elizabeth Leavitt Keller, *Walt Whitman in Mickle Street* (New York: Mitchell Kennerley, 1921), 204.

their ambivalence towards this lyric tradition, with Langston Hughes especially getting to the heart of the matter with his 1923 'I, too, sing America'.

Not that this poem was an outright dismissal. Dismissal is never quite possible. Hughes was also expressing his admiration and solidarity, not least because *Leaves of Grass* has served, and continues to serve, as a centre of gravity for generations of LGBTQIA+ poets, writers, and activists—from Hughes to Hart Crane to Federico García Lorca to June Jordan to Allan Ginsberg (and the rest). For Jordan, Whitman was the 'weird white father', a figure who at once exemplified all the traits of American exceptionalism and exclusion, and yet whose queer vision of comradeship is redemptive enough to still require our attention.[32]

Responses to Whitman's achievements are so sprawling, conflicted, and varied as to be impossible to catalogue. They extend into the histories of film, television, music, painting, dance, and architecture, across multiple languages, and have helped determine the course of numerous socialist and progressive causes.[33] Whitman continues to populate the world with queer new forms and persons. *Leaves* shows us another way through. Suspend the default grammar of subordination and judgement—learn to love an experience you might otherwise pass by—learn to love a person you might be tempted to look straight through. Always reach out. Prefigure the world to come. *Leaves* stops somewhere waiting for us.

[32] June Jordan, *Some of Us Did Not Die: New and Selected Essays* (New York: Basic Books, 2009), 245.

[33] See Kirsten Harris's work on, Whitman's influence on British socialism, and particularly the thinking of Edward Carpenter and his circle.

NOTE ON THE TEXT

MOST currently available Whitman texts reproduce the poetry from the 'Deathbed' edition of *Leaves of Grass*, first published by David McKay in Philadelphia in 1892. Whitman's own note to his final book endorsed this editorial policy: 'As there are now several editions of L. of G.,' he wrote, 'different texts and dates, I wish to say that I prefer and recommend the present one, complete, for future printing, if there should be any.' His health declining, Whitman was understandably concerned with questions of legacy. He'd also done continual battle with pirated editions of his work and was keen to properly back this 'complete' one, at last protected by satisfactory copyright and royalty terms.

Often obscured by the near-ubiquitous reprinting of the 1892 poems, however, is the elaborate fluidity of the various editions of *Leaves of Grass*. After the book's initial publication in June 1855, Whitman revised and expanded *Leaves* a further seven times, with subsequent editions appearing in 1856, 1860 (known as 1860–1), 1867, 1870 (known as 1871–2), 1876 (technically, a reprinting of the 1871–2 *Leaves*: no new setting of type but rather minor interpolations, little glued-on poems making use of available white space in that earlier edition), 1881–2, and 1891–2. His revisions to particular poems were often substantial, and the addition of new poems to each successive edition so extensive that the book's dimensions radically altered. Whitman began with twelve poems in 1855; expanding this to thirty-two in 1856, and 154 by 1860. The final 1892 book contained over 400 poems—not to mention his continual experimentation with varieties of prose prefaces, afterwords, and 'Annexes'.

This Oxford World's Classics edition showcases (as far as possible) Whitman's ongoing labour of renewal. Beginning with the first edition of 1855, it moves chronologically, selecting and including the most substantial poems and 'clusters' as Whitman included them. In most cases, the present edition reprints the published beginning, rather than the more frequently reproduced, fully-revised 'end' of a particular poem's journey (though it should be noted that some poems found their first published form in magazines—see the Walt Whitman Archive's 'Periodicals' section for further details). It thereby provides a portrait of a poet whose extensive knowledge of the printing process allowed him to personally shape and reshape his books and poetic forms in tandem with some of the most tumultuous decades in American history. While it would be impossible to reproduce Whitman's typological accidentals of each edition exactly, the present text aims to introduce general readers to his successive *mises-en-page* (or process of 'putting on the page'). As with nearly all posthumous editions that reproduce the earlier *Leaves*, it should be noted that Whitman's extended lines of 1855 have had to be adapted here to fit the spec of this book. As discussed in the Introduction, he printed his first edition on oversized paper (normally used for legal contracts), which allowed his lines to flow across the page. The present edition does, however, maintain Whitman's line lengths for each of his subsequent editions.

The source texts for most editions of *Leaves* (at least on the level of individual poems) are relatively stable, with the one glaring exception being the 1855 *Leaves* (discussed further in the Introduction). The present edition selects as its source the relatively well-known 'Copy 3' from the Feinberg Collection held at the Library of Congress. Those interested in the multitude of 1855 variations and manuscript drafts should consult the *Leaves of Grass* (1855) 'Variorum', readily available on the Walt Whitman Archive.

After the Civil War, Whitman experimented with diverging from his main *Leaves of Grass* project. This was most obviously the case in 1865: uneasy about the confidence that had defined his early *Leaves*, he struck out in a different direction, collecting his Civil War poetry under the new title of *Drum-Taps*. Such publications inform some exceptions to the general editorial rule here: in order to highlight his creative byways, the present volume reprints the war poetry from the 1865 *Drum-Taps* and its *Sequel*, rather than when he decided to fold these works back into the 1867 *Leaves*. There are also four further projects from which I take my source texts, all variously added by Whitman as annexes and companion volumes to *Leaves* (before then being incorporated back into later editions): with *Passage to India* (1871) he contemplated embarking on a major new emphasis, but did not have the energy to see this through; in 1872, he published *As a Strong Bird on Pinions Free*, a pamphlet which included a poem he had recited at Dartmouth College; in 1876 he printed *Two Rivulets*, a separate companion volume (an experimental mixture of prose and poetry) to the 1876 'Centennial' *Leaves*; and in 1888, he issued the companion volume *November Boughs*, soon incorporating this into the 1891–2 *Leaves* as the 'Sands at Seventy' annex. Although technically separate publications, Whitman saw each of these texts as part of a whole. In the preface to *As a Strong Bird*, he wrote that 'the present and any future pieces from me are really but the surplusage forming after that Volume [*Leaves of Grass*], or the wake eddying behind it.'

Whitman's various prefaces, along with Emerson's 1855 letter of praise (and Whitman's response) are included in the present volume as Appendix A. So that readers can see how far a poem eventually travelled, the final 1892 version of 'Song of Myself' makes up Appendix B. Whitman's own notes are given numerical callouts and appear as footnotes, as per Oxford World's Classics style. Editorial notes are cued with an asterisk in the text and gathered together in a section at the end. These Explanatory Notes recognize that modern readers have increased access to information, and thus focus on references not readily found online. Occasionally, they indicate the significance of a particular typographical error or misprint—as with the well-known (apparent) omission of the final period (full point) at the end of the poem that would become 'Song of Myself'. In the main, however, this edition silently corrects obvious errors (see Gary Schmidgall's thought-provoking discussion of Whitman's mistakes and misprints in *Walt Whitman: A Gay Life* (New York: Plume, 1998)).

The headnotes to several of the poems in the Explanatory Notes, outlining its subsequent evolution, are designed to facilitate further exploration of where a particular work went next. Anyone interested in following these stages of development and revision, often from the first manuscript jottings through to 1892, ought to pick up the trail at the Walt Whitman Archive, which has virtually every version of every poem free to access: https://whitmanarchive.org. I wish to express my deep gratitude to the scores of scholars, students, and enthusiasts who have worked on that outstanding resource, without whom this edition would have been impossible. Readers interested in an extended account of the publication history of *Leaves* should consult Ed Folsom's essential *Whitman Making Books/Books Making Whitman: A Catalog and Commentary* (Iowa City: Obermann Center for Advanced Studies, University of Iowa, 2005). I also want to acknowledge Gary Schmidgall's pathbreaking *Walt Whitman: Selected Poems 1855–1892: A New Edition* (New York: St Martin's Press, 1999), a precursor and touchstone for the present volume, and Kenneth M. Price and Jay Grossman for their guidance, expertise, and generosity. All mistakes are my own.

SELECT BIBLIOGRAPHY

Biographies

Genoways, Ted, *Walt Whitman and the Civil War: America's Poet During the Lost Years of 1860–1862* (Berkeley and Los Angeles: University of California Press, 2009).

Kaplan, Justin, *Walt Whitman: A Life* (New York: Simon and Schuster, 1980).

Loving, Jerome, *Walt Whitman: The Song of Himself* (Berkeley and Los Angeles: University of California Press, 2000).

Morris, Ray, Jnr., *The Better Angel: Walt Whitman in the Civil War* (Oxford: Oxford University Press, 2000).

Reynolds, David S., *Walt Whitman's America: A Cultural Biography* (New York: Alfred A. Knopf, 1995).

Critical Studies

Belasco, Susan, Folsom, Ed, and Price, Kenneth M. (eds.), *Leaves of Grass: The Sesquicentennial Essays* (Lincoln, NE: University of Nebraska Press, 2007).

Bennett, Jane, *Influx and Efflux: Writing Up with Walt Whitman* (Durham, NC: Duke University Press, 2020).

Cohen, Matt (ed.), *Whitman's Drift: Imagining Literary Distribution* (Iowa City: Iowa University Press, 2017).

Coviello, Peter, *Tomorrow's Parties: Sex and the Untimely in Nineteenth-Century America* (New York: New York University Press, 2013).

Doty, Mark, *What Is the Grass: Walt Whitman in My Life* (London: Jonathan Cape, 2020).

Erkkila, Betsy, *Whitman the Political Poet* (Oxford: Oxford University Press, 1997).

Erkkila, Betsy, and Grossman, Jay (eds.), *Breaking Bounds: Whitman and American Cultural Studies* (Oxford: Oxford University Press, 1996).

Folsom, Ed, *Whitman Making Books/Books Making Whitman: A Catalog and Commentary* (Iowa City: Obermann Center for Advanced Studies, University of Iowa, 2005).

Fretwell, Erica, 'Haptic Feelings', in Matt Cohen (ed.), *The New Walt Whitman Studies* (Cambridge: Cambridge University Press, 2020), 144–60.

Grossman, Jay, *Reconstituting the American Renaissance: Emerson, Whitman, and the Politics of Representation* (Durham, NC: Duke University Press, 2003).

Harris, Kirsten, *Walt Whitman and British Socialism: 'The Love of Comrades'* (Abingdon: Routledge, 2016).

Miller, Matt, *Collage of Myself: Walt Whitman and the Making of* Leaves of Grass (Lincoln, NE: University of Nebraska Press, 2010).

Moon, Michael, *Disseminating Whitman: Revision and Corporeality in* Leaves of Grass (Cambridge, MA: Harvard University Press, 1991).

Pollak, Vivian R., *The Erotic Whitman* (Berkeley and Los Angeles: University of California Press, 2000).

Price, Kenneth M., *To Walt Whitman, America* (Chapel Hill, NC: University of North Carolina Press, 2004).

Schmidgall, Gary, *Walt Whitman: A Gay Life* (New York: Plume, 1998).

Thomas, M. Wynn, *The Lunar Light of Whitman's Poetry* (Cambridge, MA: Harvard University Press, 1987).

Trethewey, Natasha, 'On Whitman, Civil War Memory, and My South', in Ivy G. Wilson (ed.), *Whitman Noir: Black America and the Good Gray Poet* (Iowa City: University of Iowa Press, 2014), 163–71.

Warner, Michael, *Publics and Counterpublics* (New York: Zone Books, 2002).

Wilson, Ivy G., *Specters of Democracy: Blackness and the Aesthetics of Politics in the Antebellum U.S.* (Oxford: Oxford University Press, 2011).

Further Reading in the Oxford World's Classics Series

Douglass, F., *Life and Times of Frederick Douglass*, ed. Celeste-Marie Bernier and Andrew Taylor.

Parkman, F., Jnr., *The Oregon Trail*, ed. Bernard Rosenthal.

Thoreau, H. D., *Walden*, ed. Stephen Allen Fender.

Whitman, W., *Specimen Days*, ed. Max Cavitch.

A CHRONOLOGY OF WALT WHITMAN

1819 (31 May) Walter Whitman Jnr. (known as Walt) born at West Hills, Huntington Township, Long Island, New York, to Louisa Van Velsor and Walter Whitman Snr., housebuilder and farmer. The second of nine children, his parents name three of their sons after US presidents: Andrew Jackson, George Washington, and Thomas Jefferson.

1823 Walter Whitman Snr. moves his family to Brooklyn, hoping to prosper from New York City's rapid expansion.

1825 Walt attends public school in Brooklyn.

1830–5 Completes formal education and begins work as an office boy; becomes a printer's apprentice ('printer's devil') at the *Long-Island Patriot*. Works as a compositor at the *Long-Island Star*. Family moves back to rural Long Island. Walt remains in Brooklyn.

1835–8 The 1835 Great Fire of New York devastates printing district, temporarily forcing Walt out of work. Begins teaching at various schools on Long Island. Becomes associated with the Democratic Party and campaigns for Martin Van Buren's successful presidential candidacy.

1838–9 Founds and edits weekly newspaper *Long-Islander* (Huntington), but this folds within a year.

1840–1 Teaches school again on Long Island. Moves to New York City and works as a compositor for the *New World*. Addresses Democratic Party rally in City Hall Park (July). Publishes short story 'Death in the School-Room (a Fact)' in *Democratic Review* (August).

1842–4 Continues writing journalism, short fiction, and conventional short poems for various newspapers in New York City. Tries hand at longer fiction; publishes temperance novel *Franklin Evans; or The Inebriate* in a special issue of *New World* (November 1842). Ralph Waldo Emerson publishes *Essays: Second Series* (1844), including 'The Poet', 'Nature', and 'Experience'.

1845–8 Returns to Brooklyn; works for *Brooklyn Evening Star* and edits *Brooklyn Daily Eagle*. Becomes lifelong fan of the opera.

1848–9 Quits *Daily Eagle* (or is fired) by the paper's pro-slavery Democrat publisher Isaac Van Anden (Whitman had been steadily leaning the paper towards 'free-soil' stance, which opposed slavery and its westward expansion on the grounds that it threatened white working-class interests). With brother Jeff, goes to New Orleans to edit *Daily Crescent* (February). Resigns position after three months and returns to Brooklyn. Founds and edits *Freeman*, a 'free-soil' newspaper. Office burns down after first issue.

1849–54 In notebooks, begins working up recognizable ideas and style associated with *Leaves of Grass*. Runs job-printing office, continues writing journalism, and speculates in real estate. Organizes purchase, renovation, and sale of at least five houses in Brooklyn. Anonymously serializes second novel, *Life and Adventures of Jack Engle* in *Sunday Dispatch* (March–April 1853). Fellow Brooklyn writer and friend Sara Payson Willis (known as 'Fanny Fern'), publishes *Fern Leaves from Fanny's Portfolio* (1853) and *Fern Leaves*, second series (1854).

1855 (15 May) Takes out copyright on the first edition of *Leaves of Grass*. During first week of July, 795 copies of the book printed by the Rome brothers in Brooklyn. The book contains twelve poems, a preface, and an engraving of the poet by Samuel Hollyer (copied from a daguerreotype by Gabriel Harrison). (11 July) Father dies. Sends Emerson unsolicited copy of *Leaves*; receives reply on 21 July: 'I greet you at the beginning of a great career'.

1856 Phrenologist publisher Fowler and Wells prints revised and expanded 'pocket-book' second edition of *Leaves of Grass*. Book contains thirty-two poems. Appendix (entitled 'Leaves Droppings') includes Emerson's reply, an open letter in response, along with several reviews of the 1855 edition (some positive, some negative—three by the poet himself). Writes unpublished prose polemic, 'The Eighteenth Presidency!'.

1857–9 (Spring 1857–Summer 1859) edits *Brooklyn Daily Times*; under the pen name Mose Velsor writes *Manly Health and Training*, a 47,000-word serialized fitness guide. Frequents Pfaff's restaurant, centre of New York's literary bohemia; joins the 'Fred Gray Association,' a group of men exploring new possibilities of same-sex love. Lives through some kind of heartbreak, possibly the result of a breakdown in his relationship with young Irish stagecoach driver Fred Vaughan. Writes 'Live Oak, with Moss', a group of manuscript poems that will form the basis of the 1860 'Calamus' cluster.

1860 Publishes third edition of *Leaves of Grass* with Thayer and Eldridge in Boston. Urged by Emerson to 'expurgate' the 'Enfans d'Adam' ('Children of Adam') poems, though not the 'Calamus' cluster. Whitman refuses.

1861 (12 April) American Civil War begins. Visits the injured and sick at New York Hospital. Brother George enlists. Walt continues writing freelance journalism.

1862 Learns that George has been wounded (it turns out only slightly) at Battle of Fredericksburg (December); travels to military encampments in Washington DC.

1863–4 Settles in Washington DC. Works as part-time clerk in Army Paymaster's Office; becomes self-styled 'Dresser' in the military hospitals. Over the next three years, tends to thousands of Union and Confederate soldiers. Close associations formed with writer William D. O'Connor and naturalist John Burroughs (future 'disciples' of Whitman). (June 1864) Exhausted, returns to Brooklyn on sick leave.

1865 (Jan.) Returns to Washington; appointed to clerkship in Indian Bureau of Department of the Interior, Washington DC. (Mar.) Attends Lincoln's second inauguration. (14 Apr.) Lincoln assassinated. With *Drum-Taps* already in press, Whitman writes *Sequel to Drum-Taps*. Discharged from clerkship by Cabinet Secretary James Harlan in June (supposedly because Harlan found and read a copy of the 1860 *Leaves*); O'Connor secures him position in the Attorney General's Office. Begins relationship with 21-year-old Confederate horse-car conductor Peter Doyle.

1866 O'Connor publishes *The Good Grey Poet: A Vindication* in response to the poet's dismissal by Harlan. Walt takes leave of absence and returns to New York; arranges next printing of poems.

1867 Fourth (and most chaotically arranged) edition of *Leaves of Grass* printed in New York. Publishes 'Democracy' (*Galaxy*), which will form the first part of *Democratic Vistas* (1871). John Burroughs's supportive *Notes on Walt Whitman as Poet and Person*; William Michael Rossetti's appreciation of 'Walt Whitman's Poems' (*London Chronicle*).

1868 The influential *Poems of Walt Whitman*, selected and edited by Rossetti (in dialogue with Whitman), published in London. 'Personalism' (*Galaxy*), second part of *Democratic Vistas*.

1870 Begins printing fifth edition of *Leaves of Grass* (known as the 1871–2 edition because of the varying dates on title pages) Anne Gilchrist publishes celebratory 'An Englishwoman's Estimate of Walt Whitman' in *Boston Radical*.

1871 Prints extended prose pamphlet *Democratic Vistas* and poetry collection *Passage to India* (variously appends both works to the 1871–2 *Leaves*). Receives poem of praise from Swinburne; birthday greetings from Tennyson. Reads 'After All, Not to Create Only' (later called 'Song of the Exposition') at American Institute Exhibition in New York City.

1872 Publishes the poetry pamphlet *As a Strong Bird on Pinions Free*, which included a poem he had recently recited at Dartmouth College after he had been invited by a group of Dartmouth students to deliver a commencement address (June).

1873 (Jan.) First paralytic stroke. (May) Mother dies. Leaves Washington for Camden, NJ; lives with brother George Whitman and family.

1874 Discharged from his position in Washington. Publishes 'Song of the Redwood-Tree' and 'Prayer of Columbus' in *Harper's Magazine*. Receives laudatory letter from Edward Carpenter.

1876 Publishes sixth 'Centennial' or 'Author's Edition' of *Leaves* (a reprint of 1871–2), along with *Two Rivulets*, and *Memoranda During the War* (all in Camden, NJ).

1877 Lectures on Thomas Paine in Philadelphia. Visited by Edward Carpenter and Richard Maurice Bucke in Camden.

1879 Gives first lecture on Lincoln in New York. Travels west as far as Colorado; falls ill again, stays with brother Jeff in St Louis (–Jan. 1880).

1881 Sixth edition of *Leaves* published in Boston by James R. Osgood and Co. dated 1881–2; visits Emerson in Concord, MA (who dies the following year).

1882 Publisher Osgood withdraws edition of *Leaves* after complaint from Boston District Attorney (lobbied by the Anthony Comstock's Society for the Suppression of Vice). Whitman refuses suggested redactions. Rees Welsh (and later David McKay) reprints Osgood edition in Philadelphia and issues prose counterparts *Specimen Days* and *Collect*.

1883 McKay publishes Bucke's biography of Whitman, written in close collaboration with poet.

1884–5 With the royalties from the 1881–2 *Leaves*, buys a house on Mickle Street in Camden. Becomes friends with Horace Traubel. Followers present him with horse and buggy to aid mobility.

1886 Campaign in *Pall Mall Gazette* raises and gifts the poet £80. Boston supporters send $800 for purchase of summer cottage (Walt uses most of this money to fund his own granite tomb).

1887 Delivers Lincoln lecture at Madison Square Theatre (New York), followed by reception at Westminster Hotel. Painted by Herbert Gilchrist, J. W. Alexander, and Thomas Eakins; sculpture made of Whitman's bust by Sidney Morse.

1888 Suffers further paralytic stroke. Draws up new will naming Bucke, Thomas B. Harned, and Traubel as literary executors. Traubel becomes Whitman's primary carer; they begin conversations that would form the basis of his nine-volume *With Walt Whitman in Camden*. McKay brings out *November Boughs*.

1889 Proceedings from seventieth birthday party published as *Camden's Compliment to Walt Whitman*, edited by Traubel and published by McKay.

1890 Delivers final Lincoln lecture in Philadelphia. Contracts his own $4,000 granite tomb to be erected in Harleigh Cemetery, Camden, NJ.

1891 Publishes *Good-Bye My Fancy* and final 'Deathbed' edition of *Leaves of Grass* (McKay, dated 1891–2). Prepares *Complete Prose Works* (McKay, 1892).

1892 (26 Mar.) Dies at home aged 72; more than 1,000 people pay their respects during a public viewing of his body. (30 Mar.) Interred at Harleigh Cemetery.

LEAVES OF GRASS

CONTENTS

Parentheticals refer to final titles

LEAVES OF GRASS (1855)

Frontispiece portrait, from daguerreotype by
Gabriel Harrison, copied by Samuel Hollyer on to
a lithographic plate   12

Leaves of Grass [Song of Myself]   15

Leaves of Grass [A Song for Occupations]   71

Leaves of Grass [To Think of Time]   80

Leaves of Grass [The Sleepers]   86

Leaves of Grass [I Sing the Body Electric]   95

Leaves of Grass [Faces]   102

Untitled [Song of the Answerer]   105

Untitled [Europe the 72d and 73d Years of These States]   108

Untitled [A Boston Ballad]   110

Untitled [There Was a Child Went Forth]   112

Untitled [Who Learns My Lesson Complete?]   114

Untitled [Great Are the Myths]   116

FROM LEAVES OF GRASS (1856)

2—Poem of Women [Unfolded Out of the Folds]   123

3—Poem of Salutation [Salut au Monde!]   124

5—Broad-Axe Poem [Song of the Broad-Axe]   137

9—Poem of Wonder at The Resurrection of The Wheat
[This Compost]   152

11—Sun-Down Poem [Crossing Brooklyn Ferry]   154

12—Poem of The Road [Song of the Open Road]   162

13—Poem of Procreation [A Woman Waits for Me]   175

15—Clef Poem [On the Beach at Night Alone]   177

21—Liberty Poem for Asia, Africa, Europe, America,
Australia, Cuba, and the Archipelagoes of the Sea
[To a Foil'd European Revolutionaire] 179

28—Bunch Poem [Spontaneous Me] 181

31—Poem of The Sayers of The Words of The Earth
[A Song of the Rolling Earth] 183

FROM LEAVES OF GRASS (1860–1861)

Proto-Leaf [Starting from Paumanok] 193

from CHANTS DEMOCRATIC AND NATIVE AMERICAN 208

14. [Poets to Come] 208
18. [Me Imperturbe] 209
20. [I Hear America Singing] 209

from LEAVES OF GRASS 210

1. [As I Ebb'd with the Ocean of Life] 210
16. [The World below the Brine] 214
17. [I Sit and Look Out] 214

Poem of Joys [A Song of Joys] 215

A Word Out of the Sea [Out of the
Cradle Endlessly Rocking] 223

from ENFANS D'ADAM 231

1. [To the Garden, the World] 231
2. [From Pent-up Aching Rivers] 232
8. [Native Moments] 234
9. [Once I Pass'd through a Populous City] 235
10. [Facing West from California's Shores] 235
14. [I Am He That Aches With Love] 236
15. [As Adam Early in the Morning] 236

The complete CALAMUS cluster 236

1. [In Paths Untrodden] 236
2. [Scented Herbage of My Breast] 237
3. [Whoever You Are Holding Me Now in Hand] 239
4. [These I Singing in Spring] 241
5. [For You O Democracy] 242
6. [Not Heaving From My Ribb'd Breast Only] 245
7. [Of the Terrible Doubt of Appearances] 245

  8. [excised from future editions]   246
  9. [excised from future editions]   247
 10. [Recorders Ages Hence]   248
 11. [When I Heard at the Close of the Day]   249
 12. [Are You the New Person Drawn toward Me?]   250
 13. [Roots and Leaves Themselves Alone]   251
 14. [Not Heat Flames up and Consumes]   251
 15. [Trickle Drops]   252
 16. [excised from future editions]   252
 17. [Of Him I Love Day and Night]   253
 18. [City of Orgies]   254
 19. [Behold This Swarthy Face]   254
 20. [I Saw in Louisiana a Live-Oak Growing]   255
 21. [That Music Always Round Me]   256
 22. [To a Stranger]   256
 23. [This Moment Yearning and Thoughtful]   257
 24. [I Hear it Was Charged against Me]   257
 25. [The Prairie-Grass Dividing]   258
 26. [We Two Boys Together Clinging]   258
 27. [O Living Always, Always Dying]   259
 28. [When I Peruse the Conquered Fame]   259
 29. [A Glimpse]   260
 30. [A Promise to California]   260
 31. [What Ship Puzzled at Sea & What Place is Besieged] 260
 32. [What Think You I Take My Pen in Hand?]   261
 33. [No Labor-Saving Machine]   261
 34. [I Dreamed in a Dream]   261
 35. [To the East and To the West]   262
 36. [Earth, My Likeness]   262
 37. [A Leaf for Hand in Hand]   262
 38. [Fast Anchor'd Eternal O Love!]   263
 39. [Sometimes with One I Love]   263
 40. [That Shadow My Likeness]   263
 41. [Among the Multitude]   264
 42. [To a Western Boy]   264
 43. [O You Whom I Often and Silently Come]   264
 44. [Here the Frailest Leaves of Me]   265
 45. [Full of Life Now]   265

from MESSENGER LEAVES   265
   To Him That Was Crucified   265
   To One Shortly to Die   266
   To a Common Prostitute   267
   Walt Whitman's Caution [To the States]   267
   To You   268

Mannahatta   268

A Hand-Mirror   269

So long!   270

FROM DRUM-TAPS (1865)

Drum-Taps [First O Songs For A Prelude]   277

Shut not your Doors to me proud Libraries [Shut not
   Your Doors]   279

Cavalry Crossing a Ford   280

Pioneers! O Pioneers!   280

Quicksand years that whirl me I know not whither
   [Quicksand Years]   286

The Dresser [The Wound-Dresser]   286

When I heard the learn'd Astronomer   289

Beat! Beat! Drums!   290

City of Ships   291

Vigil strange I kept on the field one night   291

A march in the ranks hard-prest, and the road unknown
   [A March in the Ranks Hard-Prest]   293

Give me the splendid silent Sun   294

Over the carnage rose prophetic a voice   296

Year of Meteors (1859–60)   298

Year that trembled and reel'd beneath me   299

Look down fair moon   299

Out of the rolling ocean, the crowd   300

I saw old General at bay   300

Not youth pertains to me   301

Contents

FROM SEQUEL TO DRUM-TAPS (1865–1866)

When Lilacs Last in the Door-Yard Bloom'd	305
O Captain! my Captain!	314
Chanting the Square Deific	315
As I lay with my head in your lap, Camerado	317
Reconciliation	318

FROM LEAVES OF GRASS (1867)

Inscription [Small the Theme of My Chant]	321
The Runner	321
2. [Tears]	321
When I Read the Book	322
The City Dead-House	322

FROM LEAVES OF GRASS (1871–1872)

One's-Self I Sing	327
For Him I Sing	327
To Thee, Old Cause!	327
The Base of all Metaphysics	328
Ethiopia Saluting the Colors	329

FROM PASSAGE TO INDIA (1871)

Passage to India	333
Proud Music of the Storm	343
Whispers of Heavenly Death	351
A Noiseless, Patient Spider	351
Sparkles from the Wheel	352
Gods	353

FROM AS A STRONG BIRD ON PINIONS FREE (1872)

One Song, America, before I go [in 1881, opening stanza of As a Strong Bird on Pinions Free]	357
Souvenirs of Democracy [My Legacy]	357

As a Strong Bird on Pinions Free [Thou Mother with
　　Thy Equal Brood]　　　　　　　　　　　　　　358
The Mystic Trumpeter　　　　　　　　　　　　　364

FROM TWO RIVULETS (1876)

Eidólons　　　　　　　　　　　　　　　　　　371
Prayer of Columbus　　　　　　　　　　　　　373
To a Locomotive in Winter　　　　　　　　　　376
The Ox Tamer　　　　　　　　　　　　　　　377

FROM LEAVES OF GRASS (1881–1882)

The Dalliance of the Eagles　　　　　　　　　　381
Spirit That Form'd This Scene *Written in Platte Cañon,
　　Colorado*　　　　　　　　　　　　　　　381
A Clear Midnight　　　　　　　　　　　　　　381

FROM NOVEMBER BOUGHS (1888)

Mannahatta　　　　　　　　　　　　　　　　385
A Font of Type　　　　　　　　　　　　　　　385
As I Sit Writing Here　　　　　　　　　　　　385
My Canary Bird　　　　　　　　　　　　　　385
Queries to My Seventieth Year　　　　　　　　386
America　　　　　　　　　　　　　　　　　386
Memories　　　　　　　　　　　　　　　　　386
Halcyon Days　　　　　　　　　　　　　　　386
Broadway　　　　　　　　　　　　　　　　　387
To Get the Final Lilt of Songs　　　　　　　　387
The Dead Tenor　　　　　　　　　　　　　　387
Thanks in Old Age　　　　　　　　　　　　　388
Life and Death　　　　　　　　　　　　　　389
Twilight　　　　　　　　　　　　　　　　　389
You Lingering Sparse Leaves of Me　　　　　　389
The Dismantled Ship　　　　　　　　　　　　389
After the Supper and Talk　　　　　　　　　　390

FROM LEAVES OF GRASS (1891–1892)

Good-Bye my Fancy	393
On, on the Same, ye Jocund Twain!	393
The Pallid Wreath	394
To the Sun-Set Breeze	394
A Twilight Song	395
L. of G.'s Purport	396
Unseen Buds	396
Good-Bye my Fancy!	397

LEAVES OF GRASS (1855)

Leaves of Grass*

I CELEBRATE myself,
And what I assume you shall assume,
For every atom belonging to me as good belongs to you.

I loafe and invite my soul,
I lean and loafe at my ease .... observing a spear of summer grass.

Houses and rooms are full of perfumes .... the shelves are crowded
    with perfumes,
I breathe the fragrance myself, and know it and like it,
The distillation would intoxicate me also, but I shall not let it.

The atmosphere is not a perfume .... it has no taste of the
    distillation .... it is odorless,
It is for my mouth forever .... I am in love with it,
I will go to the bank by the wood and become undisguised and
    naked,
I am mad for it to be in contact with me.

The smoke of my own breath,
Echos, ripples, and buzzed whispers .... loveroot, silkthread, crotch
    and vine,
My respiration and inspiration .... the beating of my heart .... the
    passing of blood and air through my lungs,
The sniff of green leaves and dry leaves, and of the shore and
    darkcolored sea-rocks, and of hay in the barn,
The sound of the belched words of my voice .... words loosed to the
    eddies of the wind,
A few light kisses .... a few embraces .... a reaching around
    of arms,
The play of shine and shade on the trees as the supple boughs wag,
The delight alone or in the rush of the streets, or along the fields
    and hillsides,
The feeling of health .... the full-noon trill .... the song of me rising
    from bed and meeting the sun.

Have you reckoned a thousand acres much? Have you reckoned the
    earth much?
Have you practiced so long to learn to read?
Have you felt so proud to get at the meaning of poems?

Stop this day and night with me and you shall possess the origin of
    all poems,
You shall possess the good of the earth and sun .... there are
    millions of suns left,
You shall no longer take things at second or third hand .... nor look
    through the eyes of the dead .... nor feed on the spectres in
    books,
You shall not look through my eyes either, nor take things from me,
You shall listen to all sides and filter them from yourself.

I have heard what the talkers were talking .... the talk of the
    beginning and the end,
But I do not talk of the beginning or the end.

There was never any more inception than there is now,
Nor any more youth or age than there is now;
And will never be any more perfection than there is now,
Nor any more heaven or hell than there is now.

Urge and urge and urge,
Always the procreant urge of the world.

Out of the dimness opposite equals advance .... Always substance
    and increase,
Always a knit of identity .... always distinction .... always a breed of
    life.

To elaborate is no avail .... Learned and unlearned feel that it is so.

Sure as the most certain sure .... plumb in the uprights, well
    entretied, braced in the beams,
Stout as a horse, affectionate, haughty, electrical,
I and this mystery here we stand.

Clear and sweet is my soul.... and clear and sweet is all that is not
   my soul.

Lack one lacks both.... and the unseen is proved by the seen,
Till that becomes unseen and receives proof in its turn.

Showing the best and dividing it from the worst, age vexes age,
Knowing the perfect fitness and equanimity of things, while they
   discuss I am silent, and go bathe and admire myself.

Welcome is every organ and attribute of me, and of any man hearty
   and clean,
Not an inch nor a particle of an inch is vile, and none shall be less
   familiar than the rest.

I am satisfied.... I see, dance, laugh, sing;
As God comes a loving bedfellow and sleeps at my side all night and
   close on the peep of the day,
And leaves for me baskets covered with white towels bulging the
   house with their plenty,
Shall I postpone my acceptation and realization and scream
   at my eyes,
That they turn from gazing after and down the road,
And forthwith cipher and show me to a cent,
Exactly the contents of one, and exactly the contents of two, and
   which is ahead?

Trippers and askers surround me,
People I meet..... the effect upon me of my early life.... of the
   ward and city I live in.... of the nation,
The latest news.... discoveries, inventions, societies.... authors old
   and new,
My dinner, dress, associates, looks, business, compliments, dues,
The real or fancied indifference of some man or woman I love,
The sickness of one of my folks   or of myself,.... or ill-doing....
   or loss or lack of money.... or depressions or exaltations,
They come to me days and nights and go from me again,
But they are not the Me myself.

Apart from the pulling and hauling stands what I am,
Stands amused, complacent, compassionating, idle, unitary,
Looks down, is erect, bends an arm on an impalpable certain rest,
Looks with its sidecurved head curious what will come next,
Both in and out of the game, and watching and wondering at it.

Backward I see in my own days where I sweated through fog with
    linguists and contenders,
I have no mockings or arguments.... I witness and wait.

I believe in you my soul.... the other I am must not abase itself to you,
And you must not be abased to the other.

Loafe with me on the grass.... loose the stop from your throat,
Not words, not music or rhyme I want.... not custom or lecture,
    not even the best,
Only the lull I like, the hum of your valved voice.

I mind how we lay in June, such a transparent summer morning;
You settled your head athwart my hips and gently turned over upon me,
And parted the shirt from my bosom-bone, and plunged your
    tongue to my barestript heart,
And reached till you felt my beard, and reached till you held my feet.

Swiftly arose and spread around me the peace and joy and
    knowledge that pass all the art and argument of the earth;
And I know that the hand of God is the elderhand of my own,
And I know that the spirit of God is the eldest brother of my own,
And that all the men ever born are also my brothers.... and the
    women my sisters and lovers,
And that a kelson* of the creation is love;
And limitless are leaves stiff or drooping in the fields,
And brown ants in the little wells beneath them,
And mossy scabs of the wormfence, and heaped stones, and elder
    and mullen and pokeweed.

A child said, What is the grass? fetching it to me with full hands;
How could I answer the child?.... I do not know what it is any more
    than he.

I guess it must be the flag of my disposition, out of hopeful green
    stuff woven.

Or I guess it is the handkerchief of the Lord,
A scented gift and remembrancer designedly dropped,
Bearing the owner's name someway in the corners, that we may see
    and remark, and say Whose?

Or I guess the grass is itself a child .... the produced babe of the
    vegetation.

Or I guess it is a uniform hieroglyphic,
And it means, Sprouting alike in broad zones and narrow zones,
Growing among black folks as among white,
Kanuck, Tuckahoe, Congressman, Cuff,* I give them the same,
    I receive them the same.

And now it seems to me the beautiful uncut hair of graves.

Tenderly will I use you curling grass,
It may be you transpire from the breasts of young men,
It may be if I had known them I would have loved them;
It may be you are from old people and from women, and from
    offspring taken soon out of their mothers' laps,
And here you are the mothers' laps.

This grass is very dark to be from the white heads of old mothers,
Darker than the colorless beards of old men,
Dark to come from under the faint red roofs of mouths.

O I perceive after all so many uttering tongues!
And I perceive they do not come from the roofs of mouths for
    nothing.

I wish I could translate the hints about the dead young men and
    women,
And the hints about old men and mothers, and the offspring taken
    soon out of their laps.

What do you think has become of the young and old men?
And what do you think has become of the women and children?

They are alive and well somewhere;
The smallest sprout shows there is really no death,
And if ever there was it led forward life, and does not wait at the end
    to arrest it,
And ceased the moment life appeared.

All goes onward and outward.... and nothing collapses,
And to die is different from what any one supposed, and luckier.

Has any one supposed it lucky to be born?
I hasten to inform him or her it is just as lucky to die, and I know it.

I pass death with the dying, and birth with the new-washed babe....
    and am not contained between my hat and boots,
And peruse manifold objects, no two alike, and every one good,
The earth good, and the stars good, and their adjuncts all good.

I am not an earth nor an adjunct of an earth,
I am the mate and companion of people, all just as immortal and
    fathomless as myself;
They do not know how immortal, but I know.

Every kind for itself and its own.... for me mine male and female,
For me all that have been boys and that love women,
For me the man that is proud and feels how it stings to be
    slighted,
For me the sweetheart and the old maid.... for me mothers and the
    mothers of mothers,
For me lips that have smiled, eyes that have shed tears,
For me children and the begetters of children.

Who need be afraid of the merge?
Undrape.... you are not guilty to me, nor stale nor discarded,
I see through the broadcloth and gingham whether or no,
And am around, tenacious, acquisitive, tireless.... and can never be
    shaken away.

The little one sleeps in its cradle,
I lift the gauze and look a long time, and silently brush away flies
    with my hand.

The youngster and the redfaced girl turn aside up the bushy hill,
I peeringly view them from the top.

The suicide sprawls on the bloody floor of the bedroom,
It is so.... I witnessed the corpse.... there the pistol had fallen.

The blab of the pave.... the tires of carts and sluff of bootsoles and
    talk of the promenaders,
The heavy omnibus, the driver with his interrogating thumb, the
    clank of the shod horses on the granite floor,
The carnival of sleighs, the clinking and shouted jokes and pelts of
    snowballs;
The hurrahs for popular favorites.... the fury of roused mobs,
The flap of the curtained litter—the sick man inside, borne to the
    hospital,
The meeting of enemies, the sudden oath, the blows and fall,
The excited crowd—the policeman with his star quickly working his
    passage to the centre of the crowd;
The impassive stones that receive and return so many echoes,
The souls moving along.... are they invisible while the least atom of
    the stones is visible?
What groans of overfed or half-starved who fall on the flags
    sunstruck or in fits,
What exclamations of women taken suddenly, who hurry home and
    give birth to babes,
What living and buried speech is always vibrating here.... what
    howls restrained by decorum,
Arrests of criminals, slights, adulterous offers made, acceptances,
    rejections with convex lips,
I mind them or the resonance of them.... I come again and again.

The big doors of the country-barn stand open and ready,
The dried grass of the harvest-time loads the slow-drawn wagon,
The clear light plays on the brown gray and green intertinged,
The armfuls are packed to the sagging mow:

I am there.... I help.... I came stretched atop of the load,
I felt its soft jolts.... one leg reclined on the other,
I jump from the crossbeams, and seize the clover and timothy,
And roll head over heels, and tangle my hair full of wisps.

Alone far in the wilds and mountains I hunt,
Wandering amazed at my own lightness and glee,
In the late afternoon choosing a safe spot to pass the night,
Kindling a fire and broiling the freshkilled game,
Soundly falling asleep on the gathered leaves, my dog and gun by
     my side.

The Yankee clipper is under her three skysails.... she cuts the
     sparkle and scud,
My eyes settle the land.... I bend at her prow or shout joyously
     from the deck.

The boatmen and clamdiggers arose early and stopped for me,
I tucked my trowser-ends in my boots and went and had a good
     time,
You should have been with us that day round the chowder-kettle.

I saw the marriage of the trapper in the open air in the far-west.... the
     bride was a red girl,
Her father and his friends sat near by crosslegged and dumbly
     smoking.... they had moccasins to their feet and large thick
     blankets hanging from their shoulders;
On a bank lounged the trapper.... he was dressed mostly in
     skins.... his luxuriant beard and curls protected his neck,
One hand rested on his rifle.... the other hand held firmly the wrist
     of the red girl,
She had long eyelashes.... her head was bare.... her coarse straight
     locks descended upon her voluptuous limbs and reached to her feet.

The runaway slave came to my house and stopped outside,
I heard his motions crackling the twigs of the woodpile,
Through the swung half-door of the kitchen I saw him limpsey and
     weak,
And went where he sat on a log, and led him in and assured him,

And brought water and filled a tub for his sweated body and bruised
    feet,
And gave him a room that entered from my own, and gave him some
    coarse clean clothes,
And remember perfectly well his revolving eyes and his
    awkwardness,
And remember putting plasters on the galls of his neck and ankles;
He staid with me a week before he was recuperated and passed north,
I had him sit next me at table .... my firelock leaned in the corner.

Twenty-eight young men bathe by the shore,
Twenty-eight young men, and all so friendly,
Twenty-eight years of womanly life, and all so lonesome.

She owns the fine house by the rise of the bank,
She hides handsome and richly drest aft the blinds of the window.

Which of the young men does she like the best?
Ah the homeliest of them is beautiful to her.

Where are you off to, lady? for I see you,
You splash in the water there, yet stay stock still in your room.

Dancing and laughing along the beach came the twenty-ninth
    bather,
The rest did not see her, but she saw them and loved them.

The beards of the young men glistened with wet, it ran from their
    long hair,
Little streams passed all over their bodies.

An unseen hand also passed over their bodies,
It descended tremblingly from their temples and ribs.

The young men float on their backs, their white bellies swell to the
    sun .... they do not ask who seizes fast to them,
They do not know who puffs and declines with pendant and bending
    arch,
They do not think whom they souse with spray.

The butcher-boy puts off his killing-clothes, or sharpens his knife at
　　the stall in the market,
I loiter enjoying his repartee and his shuffle and breakdown.*

Blacksmiths with grimed and hairy chests environ the anvil,
Each has his main-sledge .... they are all out .... there is a great heat
　　in the fire.

From the cinder-strewed threshold I follow their movements,
The lithe sheer of their waists plays even with their massive
　　arms,
Overhand the hammers roll—overhand so slow—overhand
　　so sure,
They do not hasten, each man hits in his place.

The negro holds firmly the reins of his four horses .... the block
　　swags underneath on its tied-over chain,
The negro that drives the huge dray of the stoneyard .... steady and
　　tall he stands poised on one leg on the stringpiece,*
His blue shirt exposes his ample neck and breast and loosens over
　　his hipband,
His glance is calm and commanding .... he tosses the slouch of his
　　hat away from his forehead,
The sun falls on his crispy hair and moustache .... falls on the black
　　of his polish'd and perfect limbs.

I behold the picturesque giant and love him .... and I do not stop
　　there,
I go with the team also.

In me the caresser of life wherever moving .... backward as well as
　　forward slueing,
To niches aside and junior bending.

Oxen that rattle the yoke or halt in the shade, what is that you
　　express in your eyes?
It seems to me more than all the print I have read in my life.

My tread scares the wood-drake and wood-duck on my distant and
　　daylong ramble,

They rise together, they slowly circle around.
.... I believe in those winged purposes,
And acknowledge the red yellow and white playing within me,
And consider the green and violet and the tufted crown intentional;
And do not call the tortoise unworthy because she is not something
    else,
And the mockingbird in the swamp never studied the gamut, yet
    trills pretty well to me,
And the look of the bay mare shames silliness out of me.

The wild gander leads his flock through the cool night,
Ya-honk! he says, and sounds it down to me like an invitation;
The pert may suppose it meaningless, but I listen closer,
I find its purpose and place up there toward the November sky.

The sharphoofed moose of the north, the cat on the housesill, the
    chickadee, the prairie-dog,
The litter of the grunting sow as they tug at her teats,
The brood of the turkeyhen, and she with her halfspread wings,
I see in them and myself the same old law.

The press of my foot to the earth springs a hundred affections,
They scorn the best I can do to relate them.

I am enamoured of growing outdoors,
Of men that live among cattle or taste of the ocean or woods,
Of the builders and steerers of ships, of the wielders of axes and
    mauls, of the drivers of horses,
I can eat and sleep with them week in and week out.

What is commonest and cheapest and nearest and easiest is Me,
Me going in for my chances, spending for vast returns,
Adorning myself to bestow myself on the first that will take me,
Not asking the sky to come down to my goodwill,
Scattering it freely forever.

The pure contralto sings in the organloft,
The carpenter dresses his plank.... the tongue of his foreplane
    whistles its wild ascending lisp,

The married and unmarried children ride home to their
    thanksgiving dinner,
The pilot seizes the king-pin,* he heaves down with a strong arm,
The mate stands braced in the whaleboat, lance and harpoon are ready,
The duck-shooter walks by silent and cautious stretches,
The deacons are ordained with crossed hands at the altar,
The spinning-girl retreats and advances to the hum of the big wheel,
The farmer stops by the bars of a Sunday and looks at the oats
    and rye,
The lunatic is carried at last to the asylum a confirmed case,
He will never sleep any more as he did in the cot in his mother's
    bedroom;
The jour printer* with gray head and gaunt jaws works at his case,
He turns his quid of tobacco, his eyes get blurred with the
    manuscript;
The malformed limbs are tied to the anatomist's table,
What is removed drops horribly in a pail;
The quadroon girl is sold at the stand . . . . the drunkard nods by the
    barroom stove,
The machinist rolls up his sleeves . . . . the policeman travels his
    beat . . . . the gate-keeper marks who pass,
The young fellow drives the express-wagon . . . . I love him though
    I do not know him;
The half-breed straps on his light boots to compete in the race,
The western turkey-shooting draws old and young . . . . some lean on
    their rifles, some sit on logs,
Out from the crowd steps the marksman and takes his position and
    levels his piece;
The groups of newly-come immigrants cover the wharf or levee,
The woollypates hoe in the sugarfield, the overseer views them from
    his saddle;
The bugle calls in the ballroom, the gentlemen run for their
    partners, the dancers bow to each other;
The youth lies awake in the cedar-roofed garret and harks to the
    musical rain,
The Wolverine sets traps on the creek that helps fill the Huron,
The reformer ascends the platform, he spouts with his mouth and
    nose,

The company returns from its excursion, the darkey brings up the
rear and bears the well-riddled target,

The squaw wrapt in her yellow-hemmed cloth is offering moccasins
and beadbags for sale,

The connoisseur peers along the exhibition-gallery with halfshut
eyes bent sideways,

The deckhands make fast the steamboat, the plank is thrown for the
shoregoing passengers,

The young sister holds out the skein, the elder sister winds it off in
a ball and stops now and then for the knots,

The one-year wife is recovering and happy, a week ago she bore her
first child,

The cleanhaired Yankee girl works with her sewing-machine or in
the factory or mill,

The nine months' gone is in the parturition chamber, her faintness
and pains are advancing;

The pavingman leans on his twohanded rammer—the reporter's
lead flies swiftly over the notebook—the signpainter is lettering
with red and gold,

The canal-boy trots on the towpath—the bookkeeper counts at his
desk—the shoemaker waxes his thread,

The conductor beats time for the band and all the performers
follow him,

The child is baptised—the convert is making the first professions,

The regatta is spread on the bay.... how the white sails sparkle!

The drover watches his drove, he sings out to them that would stray,

The pedlar sweats with his pack on his back—the purchaser higgles
about the odd cent,

The camera and plate are prepared, the lady must sit for her
daguerreotype,

The bride unrumples her white dress, the minutehand of the clock
moves slowly,

The opium eater reclines with rigid head and just-opened lips,

The prostitute draggles her shawl, her bonnet bobs on her tipsy and
pimpled neck,

The crowd laugh at her blackguard oaths, the men jeer and wink to
each other,

(Miserable! I do not laugh at your oaths nor jeer you,)

The President holds a cabinet council, he is surrounded by the great
    secretaries,
On the piazza walk five friendly matrons with twined arms;
The crew of the fish-smack pack repeated layers of halibut in the hold,
The Missourian crosses the plains toting his wares and his cattle,
The fare-collector goes through the train—he gives notice by the
    jingling of loose change,
The floormen are laying the floor—the tinners are tinning the
    roof—the masons are calling for mortar,
In single file each shouldering his hod pass onward the laborers;
Seasons pursuing each other the indescribable crowd is gathered....
    it is the Fourth of July.... what salutes of cannon and small arms!
Seasons pursuing each other the plougher ploughs and the mower
    mows and the wintergrain falls in the ground;
Off on the lakes the pikefisher watches and waits by the hole in the
    frozen surface,
The stumps stand thick round the clearing, the squatter strikes deep
    with his axe,
The flatboatmen make fast toward dusk near the cottonwood or
    pekantrees,
The coon-seekers go now through the regions of the Red river, or
    through those drained by the Tennessee, or through those of the
    Arkansas,
The torches shine in the dark that hangs on the Chattahoochee or
    Altamahaw;
Patriarchs sit at supper with sons and grandsons and great
    grandsons around them,
In walls of abode, in canvass tents, rest hunters and trappers after
    their day's sport.
The city sleeps and the country sleeps,
The living sleep for their time.... the dead sleep for their time,
The old husband sleeps by his wife and the young husband sleeps by
    his wife;
And these one and all tend inward to me, and I tend outward
    to them,
And such as it is to be of these more or less I am.

I am of old and young, of the foolish as much as the wise,
Regardless of others, ever regardful of others,

Maternal as well as paternal, a child as well as a man,
Stuffed with the stuff that is coarse, and stuffed with the stuff that
    is fine,
One of the great nation, the nation of many nations—the smallest
    the same and the largest the same,
A southerner soon as a northerner, a planter nonchalant and
    hospitable,
A Yankee bound my own way.... ready for trade.... my joints the
    limberest joints on earth and the sternest joints on earth,
A Kentuckian walking the vale of the Elkhorn in my deerskin
    leggings,
A boatman over the lakes or bays or along coasts.... a Hoosier,
    a Badger, a Buckeye,*
A Louisianian or Georgian, a poke-easy from sandhills and pines,
At home on Canadian snowshoes or up in the bush, or with
    fishermen off New-foundland,
At home in the fleet of iceboats, sailing with the rest and tacking,
At home on the hills of Vermont or in the woods of Maine or the
    Texan ranch,
Comrade of Californians.... comrade of free northwesterners,
    loving their big proportions,
Comrade of raftsmen and coalmen—comrade of all who shake
    hands and welcome to drink and meat;
A learner with the simplest, a teacher of the thoughtfulest,
A novice beginning experient of myriads of seasons,
Of every hue and trade and rank, of every caste and religion,
Not merely of the New World but of Africa Europe or Asia....
    a wandering savage,
A farmer, mechanic, or artist.... a gentleman, sailor, lover or
    quaker,
A prisoner, fancy-man, rowdy, lawyer, physician or priest.

I resist anything better than my own diversity,
And breathe the air and leave plenty after me,
And am not stuck up, and am in my place.

The moth and the fisheggs are in their place,
The suns I see and the suns I cannot see are in their place,
The palpable is in its place and the impalpable is in its place.

These are the thoughts of all men in all ages and lands, they are not
    original with me,
If they are not yours as much as mine they are nothing or next to
    nothing,
If they do not enclose everything they are next to nothing,
If they are not the riddle and the untying of the riddle they are
    nothing,
If they are not just as close as they are distant they are nothing.

This is the grass that grows wherever the land is and the water is,
This is the common air that bathes the globe.

This is the breath of laws and songs and behaviour,
This is the tasteless water of souls .... this is the true sustenance,
It is for the illiterate .... it is for the judges of the supreme court ....
    it is for the federal capitol and the state capitols,
It is for the admirable communes of literary men and composers and
    singers and lecturers and engineers and savans,
It is for the endless races of working people and farmers and seamen.

This is the trill of a thousand clear cornets and scream of the octave
    flute and strike of triangles.

I play not a march for victors only .... I play great marches for
    conquered and slain persons.

Have you heard that it was good to gain the day?
I also say it is good to fall .... battles are lost in the same spirit in
    which they are won.

I sound triumphal drums for the dead .... I fling through my
    embouchures* the loudest and gayest music to them,
Vivas to those who have failed, and to those whose war-vessels sank
    in the sea, and those themselves who sank in the sea,
And to all generals that lost engagements, and all overcome heroes,
    and the numberless unknown heroes equal to the greatest
    heroes known.

This is the meal pleasantly set .... this is the meat and drink for
    natural hunger,

It is for the wicked just the same as the righteous.... I make
    appointments with all,
I will not have a single person slighted or left away,
The keptwoman and sponger and thief are hereby invited.... the
    heavy-lipped slave is invited.... the venerealee is invited,
There shall be no difference between them and the rest.

This is the press of a bashful hand.... this is the float and odor of hair,
This is the touch of my lips to yours.... this is the murmur of yearning,
This is the far-off depth and height reflecting my own face,
This is the thoughtful merge of myself and the outlet again.

Do you guess I have some intricate purpose?
Well I have.... for the April rain has, and the mica on the side of
    a rock has

Do you take it I would astonish?
Does the daylight astonish? or the early redstart twittering through
    the woods?
Do I astonish more than they?

This hour I tell things in confidence,
I might not tell everybody but I will tell you.

Who goes there! hankering, gross, mystical, nude?
How is it I extract strength from the beef I eat?

What is a man anyhow? What am I? and what are you?
All I mark as my own you shall offset it with your own,
Else it were time lost listening to me.

I do not snivel that snivel the world over,
That months are vacuums and the ground but wallow and filth,
That life is a suck and a sell, and nothing remains at the end but
    threadbare crape and tears.

Whimpering and truckling fold with powders for invalids....
    conformity goes to the fourth-removed,
I cock my hat as I please indoors or out.

Shall I pray? Shall I venerate and be ceremonious?

I have pried through the strata and analyzed to a hair,
And counselled with doctors and calculated close and found no
    sweeter fat than sticks to my own bones.

In all people I see myself, none more and not one a barleycorn less,
And the good or bad I say of myself I say of them.

And I know I am solid and sound,
To me the converging objects of the universe perpetually flow,
All are written to me, and I must get what the writing means.

And I know I am deathless,
I know this orbit of mine cannot be swept by a carpenter's compass,
I know I shall not pass like a child's carlacue* cut with a burnt stick
    at night.

I know I am august,
I do not trouble my spirit to vindicate itself or be understood,
I see that the elementary laws never apologize,
I reckon I behave no prouder than the level I plant my house by
    after all.

I exist as I am, that is enough,
If no other in the world be aware I sit content,
And if each and all be aware I sit content.

One world is aware, and by far the largest to me, and that is myself,
And whether I come to my own today or in ten thousand or ten
    million years,
I can cheerfully take it now, or with equal cheerfulness I can wait.

My foothold is tenoned and mortised in granite,
I laugh at what you call dissolution,
And I know the amplitude of time.

I am the poet of the body,
And I am the poet of the soul.

The pleasures of heaven are with me, and the pains of hell are
    with me,
The first I graft and increase upon myself . . . . the latter I translate
    into a new tongue.

I am the poet of the woman the same as the man,
And I say it is as great to be a woman as to be a man,
And I say there is nothing greater than the mother of men.

I chant a new chant of dilation or pride,
We have had ducking and deprecating about enough,
I show that size is only developement.

Have you outstript the rest? Are you the President?
It is a trifle . . . . they will more than arrive there every one, and still
    pass on.

I am he that walks with the tender and growing night;
I call to the earth and sea half-held by the night.

Press close barebosomed night! Press close magnetic nourishing
    night!
Night of south winds! Night of the large few stars!
Still nodding night! Mad naked summer night!

Smile O voluptuous coolbreathed earth!
Earth of the slumbering and liquid trees!
Earth of departed sunset! Earth of the mountains misty-topt!
Earth of the vitreous pour of the full moon just tinged with blue!
Earth of shine and dark mottling the tide of the river!
Earth of the limpid gray of clouds brighter and clearer for my sake!
Far-swooping elbowed earth! Rich apple-blossomed earth!
Smile, for your lover comes!

Prodigal! you have given me love! . . . . therefore I to you give love!
O unspeakable passionate love!

Thruster holding me tight and that I hold tight!
We hurt each other as the bridegroom and the bride hurt each other.

You sea! I resign myself to you also.... I guess what you mean,
I behold from the beach your crooked inviting fingers,
I believe you refuse to go back without feeling of me;
We must have a turn together.... I undress.... hurry me out of
    sight of the land,
Cushion me soft.... rock me in billowy drowse,
Dash me with amorous wet.... I can repay you.

Sea of stretched ground-swells!
Sea breathing broad and convulsive breaths!
Sea of the brine of life! Sea of unshovelled and always-ready graves!
Howler and scooper of storms! Capricious and dainty sea!
I am integral with you.... I too am of one phase and of all phases.

Partaker of influx and efflux.... extoler of hate and conciliation,
Extoler of amies and those that sleep in each others' arms.

I am he attesting sympathy;
Shall I make my list of things in the house and skip the house that
    supports them?

I am the poet of commonsense and of the demonstrable and of
    immortality;
And am not the poet of goodness only.... I do not decline to be the
    poet of wickedness also.

Washes and razors for foofoos.... for me freckles and a bristling
    beard.

What blurt is it about virtue and about vice?
Evil propels me, and reform of evil propels me.... I stand indifferent,
My gait is no faultfinder's or rejecter's gait,
I moisten the roots of all that has grown.

Did you fear some scrofula out of the unflagging pregnancy?
Did you guess the celestial laws are yet to be worked over and
    rectified?

I step up to say that what we do is right and what we affirm is
    right.... and some is only the ore of right,

Witnesses of us.... one side a balance and the antipodal side
    a balance,
Soft doctrine as steady help as stable doctrine,
Thoughts and deeds of the present our rouse and early start.

This minute that comes to me over the past decillions,
There is no better than it and now.

What behaved well in the past or behaves well today is not such
    a wonder,
The wonder is always and always how there can be a mean man or
    an infidel.

Endless unfolding of words of ages!
And mine a word of the modern.... a word en masse.

A word of the faith that never balks,
One time as good as another time.... here or henceforward it is all
    the same to me.

A word of reality.... materialism first and last imbueing.

Hurrah for positive science! Long live exact demonstration!
Fetch stonecrop* and mix it with cedar and branches of lilac;
This is the lexicographer or chemist.... this made a grammar of the
    old cartouches,*
These mariners put the ship through dangerous unknown seas,
This is the geologist, and this works with the scalpel, and this is
    a mathematician.

Gentlemen I receive you, and attach and clasp hands with you,
The facts are useful and real.... they are not my dwelling....
    I enter by them to an area of the dwelling.

I am less the reminder of property or qualities, and more the
    reminder of life,
And go on the square for my own sake and for others' sakes,
And make short account of neuters and geldings, and favor men and
    women fully equipped,

And beat the gong of revolt, and stop with fugitives and them that
    plot and conspire.

Walt Whitman, an American, one of the roughs, a kosmos,
Disorderly fleshy and sensual.... eating drinking and breeding,
No sentimentalist.... no stander above men and women or apart
    from them.... no more modest than immodest.

Unscrew the locks from the doors!
Unscrew the doors themselves from their jambs!

Whoever degrades another degrades me.... and whatever is done or
    said returns at last to me,
And whatever I do or say I also return.

Through me the afflatus* surging and surging.... through me the
    current and index.

I speak the password primeval.... I give the sign of democracy;
By God! I will accept nothing which all cannot have their
    counterpart of on the same terms.

Through me many long dumb voices,
Voices of the interminable generations of slaves,
Voices of prostitutes and of deformed persons,
Voices of the diseased and despairing, and of thieves and dwarfs,
Voices of cycles of preparation and accretion,
And of the threads that connect the stars—and of wombs, and of
    the fatherstuff,
And of the rights of them the others are down upon,
Of the trivial and flat and foolish and despised,
Of fog in the air and beetles rolling balls of dung.

Through me forbidden voices,
Voices of sexes and lusts.... voices veiled, and I remove the veil,
Voices indecent by me clarified and transfigured.

I do not press my finger across my mouth,
I keep as delicate around the bowels as around the head and heart,
Copulation is no more rank to me than death is.

I believe in the flesh and the appetites,
Seeing hearing and feeling are miracles, and each part and tag of me
is a miracle.

Divine am I inside and out, and I make holy whatever I touch or am
touched from;
The scent of these arm-pits is aroma finer than prayer,
This head is more than churches or bibles or creeds.

If I worship any particular thing it shall be some of the spread of my
body;
Translucent mould of me it shall be you,
Shaded ledges and rests, firm masculine coulter,* it shall be you,
Whatever goes to the tilth of me it shall be you,
You my rich blood, your milky stream pale strippings of my life;
Breast that presses against other breasts it shall be you,
My brain it shall be your occult convolutions,
Root of washed sweet-flag,* timorous pond-snipe, nest of guarded
duplicate eggs, it shall be you,
Mixed tussled hay of head and beard and brawn it shall be you,
Trickling sap of maple, fibre of manly wheat, it shall be you;
Sun so generous it shall be you,
Vapors lighting and shading my face it shall be you,
You sweaty brooks and dews it shall be you,
Winds whose soft-tickling genitals rub against me it shall be you,
Broad muscular fields, branches of liveoak, loving lounger in my
winding paths, it shall be you,
Hands I have taken, face I have kissed, mortal I have ever touched,
it shall be you.

I dote on myself.... there is that lot of me, and all so luscious,
Each moment and whatever happens thrills me with joy.

I cannot tell how my ankles bend.... nor whence the cause of my
faintest wish,
Nor the cause of the friendship I emit.... nor the cause of the
friendship I take again.

To walk up my stoop is unaccountable.... I pause to consider if it
really be,

That I eat and drink is spectacle enough for the great authors and
    schools,
A morning-glory at my window satisfies me more than the
    metaphysics of books.

To behold the daybreak!
The little light fades the immense and diaphanous shadows,
The air tastes good to my palate.

Hefts of the moving world at innocent gambols, silently rising,
    freshly exuding,
Scooting obliquely high and low.

Something I cannot see puts upward libidinous prongs,
Seas of bright juice suffuse heaven.

The earth by the sky staid with.... the daily close of their junction,
The heaved challenge from the east that moment over my head,
The mocking taunt, See then whether you shall be master!

Dazzling and tremendous how quick the sunrise would kill me,
If I could not now and always send sunrise out of me.

We also ascend dazzling and tremendous as the sun,
We found our own my soul in the calm and cool of the daybreak.

My voice goes after what my eyes cannot reach,
With the twirl of my tongue I encompass worlds and volumes of worlds.

Speech is the twin of my vision.... it is unequal to measure itself.

It provokes me forever,
It says sarcastically, Walt, you understand enough.... why don't you
    let it out then?

Come now I will not be tantalized.... you conceive too much of
    articulation.

Do you not know how the buds beneath are folded?
Waiting in gloom protected by frost,

The dirt receding before my prophetical screams,
I underlying causes to balance them at last,
My knowledge my live parts.... it keeping tally with the meaning of
    things,
Happiness.... which whoever hears me let him or her set out in
    search of this day.

My final merit I refuse you.... I refuse putting from me the best I am.

Encompass worlds but never try to encompass me,
I crowd your noisiest talk by looking toward you.

Writing and talk do not prove me,
I carry the plenum* of proof and every thing else in my face,
With the hush of my lips I confound the topmost skeptic.

I think I will do nothing for a long time but listen,
And accrue what I hear into myself.... and let sounds contribute
    toward me.

I hear the bravuras of birds.... the bustle of growing wheat....
    gossip of flames ....clack of sticks cooking my meals.

I hear the sound of the human voice.... a sound I love,
I hear all sounds as they are tuned to their uses.... sounds of the
    city and sounds out of the city.... sounds of the day and night;
Talkative young ones to those that like them.... the recitative of
    fish-pedlars and fruit-pedlars.... the loud laugh of workpeople
    at their meals,
The angry base of disjointed friendship.... the faint tones of the sick,
The judge with hands tight to the desk, his shaky lips pronouncing
    a death-sentence,
The heave'e'yo of stevedores unlading ships by the wharves.... the
    refrain of the anchor-lifters;
The ring of alarm-bells.... the cry of fire.... the whirr of swift-
    streaking engines and hose-carts with premonitory tinkles and
    colored lights,
The steam-whistle.... the solid roll of the train of approaching
    cars;

The slow-march played at night at the head of the association,
They go to guard some corpse.... the flag-tops are draped with
    black muslin.

I hear the violincello or man's heart's complaint,
And hear the keyed cornet or else the echo of sunset.

I hear the chorus.... it is a grand-opera.... this indeed is music!

A tenor large and fresh as the creation fills me,
The orbic flex of his mouth is pouring and filling me full.

I hear the trained soprano.... she convulses me like the climax of
    my love-grip;
The orchestra whirls me wider than Uranus flies,
It wrenches unnamable ardors from my breast,
It throbs me to gulps of the farthest down horror,
It sails me.... I dab with bare feet.... they are licked by the
    indolent waves,
I am exposed.... cut by bitter and poisoned hail,
Steeped amid honeyed morphine.... my windpipe squeezed in the
    fakes* of death,
Let up again to feel the puzzle of puzzles,
And that we call Being.

To be in any form, what is that?
If nothing lay more developed the quahaug and its callous shell were
    enough.

Mine is no callous shell,
I have instant conductors all over me whether I pass or stop,
They seize every object and lead it harmlessly through me.

I merely stir, press, feel with my fingers, and am happy,
To touch my person to some one else's is about as much as I can
    stand.

Is this then a touch?.... quivering me to a new identity,
Flames and ether making a rush for my veins,

Treacherous tip of me reaching and crowding to help them,
My flesh and blood playing out lightning, to strike what is hardly
 different from myself,
On all sides prurient provokers stiffening my limbs,
Straining the udder of my heart for its withheld drip,
Behaving licentious toward me, taking no denial,
Depriving me of my best as for a purpose,
Unbuttoning my clothes and holding me by the bare waist,
Deluding my confusion with the calm of the sunlight and pasture
 fields,
Immodestly sliding the fellow-senses away,
They bribed to swap off with touch, and go and graze at the edges
 of me,
No consideration, no regard for my draining strength or my anger,
Fetching the rest of the herd around to enjoy them awhile,
Then all uniting to stand on a headland and worry me.

The sentries desert every other part of me,
They have left me helpless to a red marauder,
They all come to the headland to witness and assist against me.

I am given up by traitors;
I talk wildly .... I have lost my wits .... I and nobody else am the
 greatest traitor,
I went myself first to the headland .... my own hands carried me there.

You villain touch! what are you doing? .... my breath is tight in its
 throat;
Unclench your floodgates! you are too much for me.

Blind loving wrestling touch! Sheathed hooded sharptoothed touch!
Did it make you ache so leaving me?

Parting tracked by arriving .... perpetual payment of the perpetual
 loan,
Rich showering rain, and recompense richer afterward.

Sprouts take and accumulate .... stand by the curb prolific and vital,
Landscapes projected masculine full-sized and golden.

All truths wait in all things,
They neither hasten their own delivery nor resist it,
They do not need the obstetric forceps of the surgeon,
The insignificant is as big to me as any,
What is less or more than a touch?

Logic and sermons never convince,
The damp of the night drives deeper into my soul.

Only what proves itself to every man and woman is so,
Only what nobody denies is so.

A minute and a drop of me settle my brain;
I believe the soggy clods shall become lovers and lamps,
And a compend of compends is the meat of a man or woman,
And a summit and flower there is the feeling they have for each other,
And they are to branch boundlessly out of that lesson until it
      becomes omnific,
And until every one shall delight us, and we them.

I believe a leaf of grass is no less than the journeywork of the stars,
And the pismire* is equally perfect, and a grain of sand, and the egg
      of the wren,
And the tree-toad is a chef-d'ouvre for the highest,
And the running blackberry would adorn the parlors of heaven,
And the narrowest hinge in my hand puts to scorn all machinery,
And the cow crunching with depressed head surpasses any statue,
And a mouse is miracle enough to stagger sextillions of infidels,
And I could come every afternoon of my life to look at the farmer's
      girl boiling her iron tea-kettle and baking shortcake.

I find I incorporate gneiss and coal and long-threaded moss and
      fruits and grains and esculent* roots,
And am stucco'd with quadrupeds and birds all over,
And have distanced what is behind me for good reasons,
And call any thing close again when I desire it.

In vain the speeding or shyness,
In vain the plutonic rocks* send their old heat against my approach,

In vain the mastadon retreats beneath its own powdered bones,
In vain objects stand leagues off and assume manifold shapes,
In vain the ocean settling in hollows and the great monsters lying low,
In vain the buzzard houses herself with the sky,
In vain the snake slides through the creepers and logs,
In vain the elk takes to the inner passes of the woods,
In vain the razorbilled auk sails far north to Labrador,
I follow quickly .... I ascend to the nest in the fissure of the cliff.

I think I could turn and live awhile with the animals .... they are so
    placid and self-contained,
I stand and look at them sometimes half the day long.

They do not sweat and whine about their condition,
They do not lie awake in the dark and weep for their sins,
They do not make me sick discussing their duty to God,
Not one is dissatisfied .... not one is demented with the mania of
    owning things,
Not one kneels to another nor to his kind that lived thousands of
    years ago,
Not one is respectable or industrious over the whole earth.

So they show their relations to me and I accept them;
They bring me tokens of myself .... they evince them plainly in
    their possession.

I do not know where they got those tokens,
I must have passed that way untold times ago and negligently dropt
    them,
Myself moving forward then and now and forever,
Gathering and showing more always and with velocity,
Infinite and omnigenous and the like of these among them;
Not too exclusive toward the reachers of my remembrancers,
Picking out here one that shall be my amie,
Choosing to go with him on brotherly terms.

A gigantic beauty of a stallion, fresh and responsive to my caresses,
Head high in the forehead and wide between the ears,
Limbs glossy and supple, tail dusting the ground,

Eyes well apart and full of sparkling wickedness.... ears finely cut
    and flexibly moving.

His nostrils dilate.... my heels embrace him.... his well built limbs
    tremble with pleasure.... we speed around and return.

I but use you a moment and then I resign you stallion.... and do not
    need your paces, and outgallop them,
And myself as I stand or sit pass faster than you.

Swift wind! Space! My Soul! Now I know it is true what I guessed at;
What I guessed when I loafed on the grass,
What I guessed while I lay alone in my bed.... and again as I walked
    the beach under the paling stars of the morning.

My ties and ballasts leave me.... I travel.... I sail.... my elbows
    rest in the sea-gaps,
I skirt the sierras.... my palms cover continents,
I am afoot with my vision.

By the city's quadrangular houses.... in log-huts, or camping with
    lumbermen,
Along the ruts of the turnpike.... along the dry gulch and rivulet
    bed,
Hoeing my onion-patch, and rows of carrots and parsnips....
    crossing savannas... trailing in forests,
Prospecting.... gold-digging.... girdling the trees of a new
    purchase,
Scorched ankle-deep by the hot sand.... hauling my boat down the
    shallow river;
Where the panther walks to and fro on a limb overhead.... where
    the buck turns furiously at the hunter,
Where the rattlesnake suns his flabby length on a rock.... where the
    otter is feeding on fish,
Where the alligator in his tough pimples sleeps by the bayou,
Where the black bear is searching for roots or honey.... where the
    beaver pats the mud with his paddle-tail;
Over the growing sugar.... over the cottonplant.... over the rice in
    its low moist field;

Over the sharp-peaked farmhouse with its scalloped scum and
    slender shoots from the gutters;
Over the western persimmon.... over the longleaved corn and the
    delicate blue-flowered flax;
Over the white and brown buckwheat, a hummer and a buzzer there
    with the rest,
Over the dusky green of the rye as it ripples and shades in the
    breeze;
Scaling mountains.... pulling myself cautiously up.... holding on
    by low scragged limbs,
Walking the path worn in the grass and beat through the leaves of
    the brush;
Where the quail is whistling betwixt the woods and the wheatlot,
Where the bat flies in the July eve.... where the great goldbug drops
    through the dark;
Where the flails keep time on the barn floor,
Where the brook puts out of the roots of the old tree and flows to the
    meadow,
Where cattle stand and shake away flies with the tremulous
    shuddering of their hides,
Where the cheese-cloth hangs in the kitchen, and andirons straddle
    the hearth-slab, and cobwebs fall in festoons from the rafters;
Where triphammers crash.... where the press is whirling its
    cylinders;
Wherever the human heart beats with terrible throes out of its ribs;
Where the pear-shaped balloon is floating aloft.... floating in it
    myself and looking composedly down;
Where the life-car* is drawn on the slipnoose.... where the heat
    hatches pale-green eggs in the dented sand,
Where the she-whale swims with her calves and never forsakes
    them,
Where the steamship trails hindways its long pennant of smoke,
Where the ground-shark's fin cuts like a black chip out of
    the water,
Where the half-burned brig is riding on unknown currents,
Where shells grow to her slimy deck, and the dead are corrupting
    below;
Where the striped and starred flag is borne at the head of the
    regiments;

Approaching Manhattan, up by the long-stretching island,

Under Niagara, the cataract falling like a veil over my countenance;

Upon a door-step.... upon the horse-block of hard wood outside,

Upon the race-course, or enjoying pic-nics or jigs or a good game of
    base-ball,

At he-festivals with blackguard jibes and ironical license and
    bull-dances* and drinking and laughter,

At the cider-mill, tasting the sweet of the brown sqush*.... sucking
    the juice through a straw,

At apple-pealings, wanting kisses for all the red fruit I find,

At musters and beach-parties and friendly bees and huskings and
    house-raisings;

Where the mockingbird sounds his delicious gurgles, and cackles
    and screams and weeps,

Where the hay-rick stands in the barnyard, and the dry-stalks are
    scattered, and the brood cow waits in the hovel,

Where the bull advances to do his masculine work, and the stud to
    the mare, and the cock is treading the hen,

Where the heifers browse, and the geese nip their food with short
    jerks;

Where the sundown shadows lengthen over the limitless and
    lonesome prairie,

Where the herds of buffalo make a crawling spread of the square
    miles far and near;

Where the hummingbird shimmers.... where the neck of the
    longlived swan is curving and winding;

Where the laughing-gull scoots by the slappy shore and laughs her
    near-human laugh;

Where beehives range on a gray bench in the garden half-hid by the
    high weeds;

Where the band-necked partridges roost in a ring on the ground
    with their heads out;

Where burial coaches enter the arched gates of a cemetery;

Where winter wolves bark amid wastes of snow and icicled trees;

Where the yellow-crowned heron comes to the edge of the marsh at
    night and feeds upon small crabs;

Where the splash of swimmers and divers cools the warm noon;

Where the katydid works her chromatic reed on the walnut-tree over
    the well;

Through patches of citrons and cucumbers with silver-wired leaves,
Through the salt-lick or orange glade.... or under conical furs;
Through the gymnasium.... through the curtained saloon....
    through the office or public hall;
Pleased with the native and pleased with the foreign.... pleased with
    the new and old,
Pleased with women, the homely as well as the handsome,
Pleased with the quakeress as she puts off her bonnet and talks
    melodiously,
Pleased with the primitive tunes of the choir of the whitewashed
    church,
Pleased with the earnest words of the sweating Methodist preacher,
    or any preacher ....looking seriously at the camp-meeting;
Looking in at the shop-windows in Broadway the whole forenoon....
    pressing the flesh of my nose to the thick plate-glass,
Wandering the same afternoon with my face turned up to the clouds;
My right and left arms round the sides of two friends and I in the
    middle;
Coming home with the bearded and dark-cheeked bush-boy....
    riding behind him at the drape of the day;
Far from the settlements studying the print of animals' feet, or the
    moccasin print;
By the cot in the hospital reaching lemonade to a feverish patient,
By the coffined corpse when all is still, examining with a candle;
Voyaging to every port to dicker and adventure;
Hurrying with the modern crowd, as eager and fickle as any,
Hot toward one I hate, ready in my madness to knife him;
Solitary at midnight in my back yard, my thoughts gone from me
    a long while,
Walking the old hills of Judea with the beautiful gentle god by
    my side;
Speeding through space.... speeding through heaven and the stars,
Speeding amid the seven satellites and the broad ring and the
    diameter of eighty thousand miles,
Speeding with tailed meteors.... throwing fire-balls like the rest,
Carrying the crescent child that carries its own full mother in its belly;
Storming enjoying planning loving cautioning,
Backing and filling, appearing and disappearing,
I tread day and night such roads.

I visit the orchards of God and look at the spheric product,
And look at quintillions ripened, and look at quintillions green.

I fly the flight of the fluid and swallowing soul,
My course runs below the soundings of plummets.

I help myself to material and immaterial,
No guard can shut me off, no law can prevent me.

I anchor my ship for a little while only,
My messengers continually cruise away or bring their returns to me.

I go hunting polar furs and the seal.... leaping chasms with
    a pike-pointed staff .... clinging to topples of brittle and blue.

I ascend to the foretruck* .... I take my place late at night in the
    crow's nest.... we sail through the arctic sea.... it is plenty light
    enough,
Through the clear atmosphere I stretch around on the wonderful
    beauty,
The enormous masses of ice pass me and I pass them.... the
    scenery is plain in all directions,
The white-topped mountains point up in the distance.... I fling out
    my fancies toward them;
We are about approaching some great battlefield in which we are
    soon to be engaged,
We pass the colossal outposts of the encampments.... we pass with
    still feet and caution;
Or we are entering by the suburbs some vast and ruined city.... the
    blocks and fallen architecture more than all the living cities of
    the globe.

I am a free companion.... I bivouac by invading watchfires.

I turn the bridegroom out of bed and stay with the bride myself,
And tighten her all night to my thighs and lips.

My voice is the wife's voice, the screech by the rail of the stairs,
They fetch my man's body up dripping and drowned.

I understand the large hearts of heroes,
The courage of present times and all times;
How the skipper saw the crowded and rudderless wreck of the
    steamship,* and death chasing it up and down the storm,
How he knuckled tight and gave not back one inch, and was faithful
    of days and faithful of nights,
And chalked in large letters on a board, Be of good cheer, We will
    not desert you;
How he saved the drifting company at last,
How the lank loose-gowned women looked when boated from the
    side of their prepared graves,
How the silent old-faced infants, and the lifted sick, and the
    sharp-lipped unshaved men;
All this I swallow and it tastes good.... I like it well, and it becomes
    mine,
I am the man.... I suffered.... I was there.

The disdain and calmness of martyrs,
The mother condemned for a witch and burnt with dry wood, and
    her children gazing on;
The hounded slave that flags in the race and leans by the fence,
    blowing and covered with sweat,
The twinges that sting like needles his legs and neck,
The murderous buckshot and the bullets,
All these I feel or am.

I am the hounded slave.... I wince at the bite of the dogs,
Hell and despair are upon me.... crack and again crack the marksmen,
I clutch the rails of the fence.... my gore dribs thinned with the
    ooze of my skin,
I fall on the weeds and stones,
The riders spur their unwilling horses and haul close,
They taunt my dizzy ears.... they beat me violently over the head
    with their whip-stocks.

Agonies are one of my changes of garments;
I do not ask the wounded person how he feels.... I myself become
    the wounded person,
My hurt turns livid upon me as I lean on a cane and observe.

I am the mashed fireman with breastbone broken .... tumbling walls
    buried me in their debris,
Heat and smoke I inspired .... I heard the yelling shouts of my comrades,
I heard the distant click of their picks and shovels;
They have cleared the beams away .... they tenderly lift me forth.

I lie in the night air in my red shirt .... the pervading hush is for my
    sake,
Painless after all I lie, exhausted but not so unhappy,
White and beautiful are the faces around me .... the heads are bared
    of their fire-caps,
The kneeling crowd fades with the light of the torches.

Distant and dead resuscitate,
They show as the dial or move as the hands of me .... and I am the
    clock myself.

I am an old artillerist, and tell of some fort's bombardment .... and
    am there again.

Again the reveille of drummers .... again the attacking cannon and
    mortars and howitzers,
Again the attacked send their cannon responsive.

I take part .... I see and hear the whole,
The cries and curses and roar .... the plaudits for well aimed shots,
The ambulanza slowly passing and trailing its red drip,
Workmen searching after damages and to make indispensible repairs,
The fall of grenades through the rent roof .... the fan-shaped
    explosion,
The whizz of limbs heads stone wood and iron high in the air.

Again gurgles the mouth of my dying general .... he furiously waves
    with his hand,
He gasps through the clot .... Mind not me .... mind .... the
    entrenchments.

I tell not the fall of Alamo .... not one escaped to tell the fall of Alamo,
The hundred and fifty are dumb yet at Alamo.

Hear now the tale of a jetblack sunrise,
Hear of the murder in cold blood of four hundred and twelve
     young men.*

Retreating they had formed in a hollow square with their baggage
     for breastworks,
Nine hundred lives out of the surrounding enemy's nine times their
     number was the price they took in advance,
Their colonel was wounded and their ammunition gone,
They treated for an honorable capitulation, received writing and
     seal, gave up their arms, and marched back prisoners of war.

They were the glory of the race of rangers,
Matchless with a horse, a rifle, a song, a supper or a courtship,
Large, turbulent, brave, handsome, generous, proud and affectionate,
Bearded, sunburnt, dressed in the free costume of hunters,
Not a single one over thirty years of age.

The second Sunday morning they were brought out in squads and
     massacred.... it was beautiful early summer,
The work commenced about five o'clock and was over by eight.

None obeyed the command to kneel,
Some made a mad and helpless rush.... some stood stark and straight,
A few fell at once, shot in the temple or heart.... the living and
     dead lay together,
The maimed and mangled dug in the dirt.... the new-comers saw
     them there;
Some half-killed attempted to crawl away,
These were dispatched with bayonets or battered with the blunts of
     muskets;
A youth not seventeen years old seized his assassin till two more
     came to release him,
The three were all torn, and covered with the boy's blood.

At eleven o'clock began the burning of the bodies;
And that is the tale of the murder of the four hundred and twelve
     young men,
And that was a jetblack sunrise.

Did you read in the seabooks of the oldfashioned frigate-fight?*
Did you learn who won by the light of the moon and stars?

Our foe was no skulk in his ship, I tell you,
His was the English pluck, and there is no tougher or truer, and
    never was, and never will be;
Along the lowered eve he came, horribly raking us.

We closed with him.... the yards entangled.... the cannon touched,
My captain lashed fast with his own hands.

We had received some eighteen-pound shots under the water,
On our lower-gun-deck two large pieces had burst at the first fire,
    killing all around and blowing up overhead.

Ten o'clock at night, and the full moon shining and the leaks on the
    gain, and five feet of water reported,
The master-at-arms loosing the prisoners confined in the after-hold
    to give them a chance for themselves.

The transit to and from the magazine was now stopped by the sentinels,
They saw so many strange faces they did not know whom to trust.

Our frigate was afire.... the other asked if we demanded quarters? if
    our colors were struck and the fighting done?

I laughed content when I heard the voice of my little captain,
We have not struck, he composedly cried, We have just begun our
    part of the fighting.

Only three guns were in use,
One was directed by the captain himself against the enemy's
    mainmast,
Two well-served with grape and canister silenced his musketry and
    cleared his decks.

The tops alone seconded the fire of this little battery, especially the
    maintop,
They all held out bravely during the whole of the action.

Not a moment's cease,
The leaks gained fast on the pumps.... the fire eat toward the
    powder-magazine,
One of the pumps was shot away.... it was generally thought we
    were sinking.

Serene stood the little captain,
He was not hurried.... his voice was neither high nor low,
His eyes gave more light to us than our battle-lanterns.

Toward twelve at night, there in the beams of the moon they
    surrendered to us.

Stretched and still lay the midnight,
Two great hulls motionless on the breast of the darkness,
Our vessel riddled and slowly sinking.... preparations to pass to the
    one we had conquered,
The captain on the quarter deck coldly giving his orders through
    a countenance white as a sheet,
Near by the corpse of the child that served in the cabin,
The dead face of an old salt with long white hair and carefully
    curled whiskers,
The flames spite of all that could be done flickering aloft and below,
The husky voices of the two or three officers yet fit for duty,
Formless stacks of bodies and bodies by themselves.... dabs of flesh
    upon the masts and spars,
The cut of cordage and dangle of rigging.... the slight shock of the
    soothe of waves,
Black and impassive guns, and litter of powder-parcels, and the
    strong scent,
Delicate sniffs of the seabreeze.... smells of sedgy grass and fields
    by the shore... death-messages given in charge to survivors,
The hiss of the surgeon's knife and the gnawing teeth of his saw,
The wheeze, the cluck, the swash of falling blood.... the short wild
    scream, the long dull tapering groan,
These so.... these irretrievable.

O Christ! My fit is mastering me!
What the rebel said gaily adjusting his throat to the rope-noose,

What the savage at the stump, his eye-sockets empty, his mouth
    spirting whoops and defiance,
What stills the traveler come to the vault at Mount Vernon,
What sobers the Brooklyn boy as he looks down the shores of the
    Wallabout and remembers the prison ships,
What burnt the gums of the redcoat at Saratoga when he
    surrendered his brigades,
These become mine and me every one, and they are but little,
I become as much more as I like.

I become any presence or truth of humanity here,
And see myself in prison shaped like another man,
And feel the dull unintermitted pain.

For me the keepers of convicts shoulder their carbines and keep watch,
It is I let out in the morning and barred at night.

Not a mutineer walks handcuffed to the jail, but I am handcuffed to
    him and walk by his side,
I am less the jolly one there, and more the silent one with sweat on
    my twitching lips.

Not a youngster is taken for larceny, but I go up too and am tried
    and sentenced.

Not a cholera patient lies at the last gasp, but I also lie at the last gasp,
My face is ash-colored, my sinews gnarl.... away from me people
    retreat.

Askers embody themselves in me, and I am embodied in them,
I project my hat and sit shamefaced and beg.

I rise extatic through all, and sweep with the true gravitation,
The whirling and whirling is elemental within me.

Somehow I have been stunned. Stand back!
Give me a little time beyond my cuffed head and slumbers and
    dreams and gaping,
I discover myself on a verge of the usual mistake.

That I could forget the mockers and insults!
That I could forget the trickling tears and the blows of the
    bludgeons and hammers!
That I could look with a separate look on my own crucifixion and
    bloody crowning!

I remember.... I resume the overstaid fraction,
The grave of rock multiplies what has been confided to it.... or to
    any graves,
The corpses rise.... the gashes heal.... the fastenings roll away.

I troop forth replenished with supreme power, one of an average
    unending procession,
We walk the roads of Ohio and Massachusetts and Virginia and
    Wisconsin and New York and New Orleans and Texas and Montreal
    and San Francisco and Charleston and Savannah and Mexico,
Inland and by the seacoast and boundary lines.... and we pass the
    boundary lines.

Our swift ordinances are on their way over the whole earth,
The blossoms we wear in our hats are the growth of two thousand
    years.

Eleves* I salute you,
I see the approach of your numberless gangs.... I see you
    understand yourselves and me,
And know that they who have eyes are divine, and the blind and
    lame are equally divine,
And that my steps drag behind yours yet go before them,
And are aware how I am with you no more than I am with
    everybody.

The friendly and flowing savage.... Who is he?
Is he waiting for civilization or past it and mastering it?

Is he some southwesterner raised outdoors? Is he Canadian?
Is he from the Mississippi country? or from Iowa, Oregon or
    California? or from the mountains? or prairie life or bush-life? or
    from the sea?

Wherever he goes men and women accept and desire him,
They desire he should like them and touch them and speak to them
    and stay with them.

Behaviour lawless as snow-flakes.... words simple as grass....
    uncombed head and laughter and naivete;
Slowstepping feet and the common features, and the common
    modes and emanations,
They descend in new forms from the tips of his fingers,
They are wafted with the odor of his body or breath.... they fly out
    of the glance of his eyes.

Flaunt of the sunshine I need not your bask.... lie over,
You light surfaces only.... I force the surfaces and the depths also.

Earth! you seem to look for something at my hands,
Say old topknot! what do you want?

Man or woman! I might tell how I like you, but cannot,
And might tell what it is in me and what it is in you, but cannot,
And might tell the pinings I have.... the pulse of my nights and
    days.

Behold I do not give lectures or a little charity,
What I give I give out of myself.

You there, impotent, loose in the knees, open your scarfed chops* till
    I blow grit within you,
Spread your palms and lift the flaps of your pockets,
I am not to be denied.... I compel.... I have stores plenty and to
    spare,
And any thing I have I bestow.

I do not ask who you are.... that is not important to me,
You can do nothing and be nothing but what I will infold you.

To a drudge of the cottonfields or emptier of privies I lean.... on
    his right cheek I put the family kiss,
And in my soul I swear I never will deny him.

On women fit for conception I start bigger and nimbler babes,
This day I am jetting the stuff of far more arrogant republics.

To any one dying.... thither I speed and twist the knob of the door,
Turn the bedclothes toward the foot of the bed,
Let the physician and the priest go home.

I seize the descending man.... I raise him with resistless will.

O despairer, here is my neck,
By God! you shall not go down! Hang your whole weight upon me.

I dilate you with tremendous breath.... I buoy you up;
Every room of the house do I fill with an armed force.... lovers of
    me, bafflers of graves:
Sleep! I and they keep guard all night;
Not doubt, not decease shall dare to lay finger upon you,
I have embraced you, and henceforth possess you to myself,
And when you rise in the morning you will find what I tell you is so.

I am he bringing help for the sick as they pant on their backs,
And for strong upright men I bring yet more needed help.

I heard what was said of the universe,
Heard it and heard of several thousand years;
It is middling well as far as it goes.... but is that all?

Magnifying and applying come I,
Outbidding at the start the old cautious hucksters,
The most they offer for mankind and eternity less than a spirt of my
    own seminal wet,
Taking myself the exact dimensions of Jehovah and laying them
    away,
Lithographing Kronos and Zeus his son, and Hercules his
    grandson,
Buying drafts of Osiris and Isis and Belus and Brahma and Adonai,
In my portfolio placing Manito* loose, and Allah on a leaf, and the
    crucifix engraved,
With Odin, and the hideous-faced Mexitli, and all idols and images,

Honestly taking them all for what they are worth, and not a cent more,
Admitting they were alive and did the work of their day,
Admitting they bore mites as for unfledged birds who have now to
    rise and fly and sing for themselves,
Accepting the rough deific sketches to fill out better in myself....
    bestowing them freely on each man and woman I see,
Discovering as much or more in a framer framing a house,
Putting higher claims for him there with his rolled-up sleeves,
    driving the mallet and chisel;
Not objecting to special revelations.... considering a curl of smoke
    or a hair on the back of my hand as curious as any revelation;
Those ahold of fire-engines and hook-and-ladder ropes more to me
    than the gods of the antique wars,
Minding their voices peal through the crash of destruction,
Their brawny limbs passing safe over charred laths.... their white
    foreheads whole and unhurt out of the flames;
By the mechanic's wife with her babe at her nipple interceding for
    every person born;
Three scythes at harvest whizzing in a row from three lusty angels
    with shirts bagged out at their waists;
The snag-toothed hostler* with red hair redeeming sins past and to
    come,
Selling all he possesses and traveling on foot to fee lawyers for his
    brother and sit by him while he is tried for forgery:
What was strewn in the amplest strewing the square rod about me,
    and not filling the square rod then;
The bull and the bug never worshipped half enough,
Dung and dirt more admirable than was dreamed,
The supernatural of no account.... myself waiting my time to be
    one of the supremes,
The day getting ready for me when I shall do as much good as the
    best, and be as prodigious,
Guessing when I am it will not tickle me much to receive puffs out
    of pulpit or print;
By my life-lumps! becoming already a creator!
Putting myself here and now to the ambushed womb of the shadows!

....A call in the midst of the crowd,
My own voice, orotund sweeping and final.

Come my children,
Come my boys and girls, and my women and household and intimates,
Now the performer launches his nerve .... he has passed his prelude
    on the reeds within.

Easily written loosefingered chords! I feel the thrum of their climax
    and close.

My head evolves on my neck,
Music rolls, but not from the organ .... folks are around me, but
    they are no household of mine.

Ever the hard and unsunk ground,
Ever the eaters and drinkers .... ever the upward and downward
    sun .... ever the air and the ceaseless tides,
Ever myself and my neighbors, refreshing and wicked and real,
Ever the old inexplicable query .... ever that thorned thumb—that
    breath of itches and thirsts,
Ever the vexer's hoot! hoot! till we find where the sly one hides and
    bring him forth;
Ever love .... ever the sobbing liquid of life,
Ever the bandage under the chin .... ever the tressels of death.

Here and there with dimes on the eyes* walking,
To feed the greed of the belly the brains liberally spooning,
Tickets buying or taking or selling, but in to the feast never once
    going;
Many sweating and ploughing and thrashing, and then the chaff for
    payment receiving,
A few idly owning, and they the wheat continually claiming.

This is the city .... and I am one of the citizens;
Whatever interests the rest interests me .... politics, churches,
    newspapers, schools,
Benevolent societies, improvements, banks, tariffs, steamships,
    factories, markets,
Stocks and stores and real estate and personal estate.

They who piddle and patter here in collars and tailed coats .... I am
    aware who they are .... and that they are not worms or fleas,

I acknowledge the duplicates of myself under all the scrape-lipped
and pipe-legged concealments.

The weakest and shallowest is deathless with me,
What I do and say the same waits for them,
Every thought that flounders in me the same flounders in them.

I know perfectly well my own egotism,
And know my omniverous words, and cannot say any less,
And would fetch you whoever you are flush with myself.

My words are words of a questioning, and to indicate reality;
This printed and bound book.... but the printer and the printing-
office boy?
The marriage estate and settlement.... but the body and mind of
the bridegroom? also those of the bride?
The panorama of the sea.... but the sea itself?
The well-taken photographs.... but your wife or friend close and
solid in your arms?
The fleet of ships of the line and all the modern improvements....
but the craft and pluck of the admiral?
The dishes and fare and furniture.... but the host and hostess, and
the look out of their eyes?
The sky up there.... yet here or next door or across the way?
The saints and sages in history.... but you yourself?
Sermons and creeds and theology.... but the human brain, and
what is called reason, and what is called love, and what is
called life?

I do not despise you priests;
My faith is the greatest of faiths and the least of faiths,
Enclosing all worship ancient and modern, and all between ancient
and modern,
Believing I shall come again upon the earth after five thousand years,
Waiting responses from oracles.... honoring the gods.... saluting
the sun,
Making a fetish of the first rock or stump.... powowing with sticks
in the circle of obis,*
Helping the lama or brahmin as he trims the lamps of the idols,

Dancing yet through the streets in a phallic procession .... rapt and
    austere in the woods, a gymnosophist,*
Drinking mead from the skull-cup .... to shasta and vedas
    admirant .... minding the koran,
Walking the teokallis,* spotted with gore from the stone and
    knife—beating the serpent-skin drum;
Accepting the gospels, accepting him that was crucified, knowing
    assuredly that he is divine,
To the mass kneeling—to the puritan's prayer rising—sitting
    patiently in a pew,
Ranting and frothing in my insane crisis—waiting dead-like till my
    spirit arouses me;*
Looking forth on pavement and land, and outside of pavement and
    land,
Belonging to the winders of the circuit of circuits.

One of that centripetal and centrifugal gang,
I turn and talk like a man leaving charges before a journey.

Down-hearted doubters, dull and excluded,
Frivolous sullen moping angry affected disheartened atheistical,
I know every one of you, and know the unspoken interrogatories,
By experience I know them.

How the flukes splash!
How they contort rapid as lightning, with spasms and spouts of
    blood!

Be at peace bloody flukes of doubters and sullen mopers,
I take my place among you as much as among any;
The past is the push of you and me and all precisely the same,
And the day and night are for you and me and all,
And what is yet untried and afterward is for you and me and all.

I do not know what is untried and afterward,
But I know it is sure and alive and sufficient.

Each who passes is considered, and each who stops is considered,
    and not a single one can it fail.

It cannot fail the young man who died and was buried,
Nor the young woman who died and was put by his side,
Nor the little child that peeped in at the door and then drew back
    and was never seen again,
Nor the old man who has lived without purpose, and feels it with
    bitterness worse than gall,
Nor him in the poorhouse tubercled by rum and the bad disorder,
Nor the numberless slaughtered and wrecked.... nor the brutish
    koboo,* called the ordure of humanity,
Nor the sacs merely floating with open mouths for food to slip in,
Nor any thing in the earth, or down in the oldest graves of the earth,
Nor any thing in the myriads of spheres, nor one of the myriads of
    myriads that inhabit them,
Nor the present, nor the least wisp that is known.

It is time to explain myself.... let us stand up.

What is known I strip away.... I launch all men and women forward
    with me into the unknown.

The clock indicates the moment.... but what does eternity indicate?

Eternity lies in bottomless reservoirs.... its buckets are rising
    forever and ever,
They pour and they pour and they exhale away.

We have thus far exhausted trillions of winters and summers;
There are trillions ahead, and trillions ahead of them.

Births have brought us richness and variety,
And other births will bring us richness and variety.

I do not call one greater and one smaller,
That which fills its period and place is equal to any.

Were mankind murderous or jealous upon you my brother or my sister?
I am sorry for you.... they are not murderous or jealous upon me;
All has been gentle with me...... I keep no account with lamentation;
What have I to do with lamentation?

I am an acme of things accomplished, and I an encloser of things to be.

My feet strike an apex of the apices of the stairs,
On every step bunches of ages, and larger bunches between the steps,
All below duly traveled—and still I mount and mount.

Rise after rise bow the phantoms behind me,
Afar down I see the huge first Nothing, the vapor from the nostrils
    of death,
I know I was even there .... I waited unseen and always,
And slept while God carried me through the lethargic mist,
And took my time .... and took no hurt from the fœtid carbon.

Long I was hugged close .... long and long.

Immense have been the preparations for me,
Faithful and friendly the arms that have helped me.

Cycles ferried my cradle, rowing and rowing like cheerful boatmen;
For room to me stars kept aside in their own rings,
They sent influences to look after what was to hold me.

Before I was born out of my mother generations guided me,
My embryo has never been torpid .... nothing could overlay it;
For it the nebula cohered to an orb .... the long slow strata piled to
    rest it on .... vast vegetables gave it sustenance,
Monstrous sauroids* transported it in their mouths and deposited it
    with care.

All forces have been steadily employed to complete and delight me,
Now I stand on this spot with my soul.

Span of youth! Ever-pushed elasticity! Manhood balanced and florid
    and full!

My lovers suffocate me!
Crowding my lips, and thick in the pores of my skin,
Jostling me through streets and public halls .... coming naked to me
    at night,

Crying by day Ahoy from the rocks of the river.... swinging and
    chirping over my head,
Calling my name from flowerbeds or vines or tangled underbrush,
Or while I swim in the bath.... or drink from the pump at the
    corner.... or the curtain is down at the opera.... or I glimpse
    at a woman's face in the railroad car;
Lighting on every moment of my life,
Bussing my body with soft and balsamic busses,
Noiselessly passing handfuls out of their hearts and giving them to
    be mine.

Old age superbly rising! Ineffable grace of dying days!

Every condition promulges not only itself.... it promulges what
    grows after and out of itself,
And the dark hush promulges as much as any.

I open my scuttle at night and see the far-sprinkled systems,
And all I see, multiplied as high as I can cipher, edge but the rim of
    the farther systems.

Wider and wider they spread, expanding and always expanding,
Outward and outward and forever outward.

My sun has his sun, and round him obediently wheels,
He joins with his partners a group of superior circuit,
And greater sets follow, making specks of the greatest inside
    them.

There is no stoppage, and never can be stoppage;
If I and you and the worlds and all beneath or upon their surfaces,
    and all the palpable life, were this moment reduced back to
    a pallid float, it would not avail in the long run,
We should surely bring up again where we now stand,
And as surely go as much farther, and then farther and farther.

A few quadrillions of eras, a few octillions of cubic leagues, do not
    hazard the span, or make it impatient,
They are but parts.... any thing is but a part.

See ever so far…. there is limitless space outside of that,
Count ever so much…. there is limitless time around that.

Our rendezvous is fitly appointed…. God will be there and wait till
    we come.

I know I have the best of time and space—and that I was never
    measured, and never will be measured.

I tramp a perpetual journey,
My signs are a rain-proof coat and good shoes and a staff cut from
    the woods;
No friend of mine takes his ease in my chair,
I have no chair, nor church nor philosophy;
I lead no man to a dinner-table or library or exchange,
But each man and each woman of you I lead upon a knoll,
My left hand hooks you round the waist,
My right hand points to landscapes of continents, and a plain public
    road.

Not I, not any one else can travel that road for you,
You must travel it for yourself.

It is not far…. it is within reach,
Perhaps you have been on it since you were born, and did not know,
Perhaps it is every where on water and on land.

Shoulder your duds, and I will mine, and let us hasten forth;
Wonderful cities and free nations we shall fetch as we go.

If you tire, give me both burdens, and rest the chuff of your hand on
    my hip,
And in due time you shall repay the same service to me;
For after we start we never lie by again.

This day before dawn I ascended a hill and looked at the crowded
    heaven,
And I said to my spirit, When we become the enfolders of those orbs
    and the pleasure and knowledge of every thing in them, shall we
    be filled and satisfied then?

And my spirit said No, we level that lift to pass and continue
    beyond.

You are also asking me questions, and I hear you;
I answer that I cannot answer.... you must find out for yourself.

Sit awhile wayfarer,
Here are biscuits to eat and here is milk to drink,
But as soon as you sleep and renew yourself in sweet clothes I will
    certainly kiss you with my goodbye kiss and open the gate for
    your egress hence.

Long enough have you dreamed contemptible dreams,
Now I wash the gum from your eyes,
You must habit yourself to the dazzle of the light and of every
    moment of your life

Long have you timidly waded, holding a plank by the shore,
Now I will you to be a bold swimmer,
To jump off in the midst of the sea, and rise again and nod to me
    and shout, and laughingly dash with your hair.

I am the teacher of athletes,
He that by me spreads a wider breast than my own proves the width
    of my own,
He most honors my style who learns under it to destroy the teacher.

The boy I love, the same becomes a man not through derived power
    but in his own right,
Wicked, rather than virtuous out of conformity or fear,
Fond of his sweetheart, relishing well his steak,
Unrequited love or a slight cutting him worse than a wound cuts,
First rate to ride, to fight, to hit the bull's eye, to sail a skiff, to sing
    a song or play on the banjo,
Preferring scars and faces pitted with smallpox over all latherers and
    those that keep out of the sun.

I teach straying from me, yet who can stray from me?
I follow you whoever you are from the present hour;
My words itch at your ears till you understand them.

I do not say these things for a dollar, or to fill up the time while
    I wait for a boat;
It is you talking just as much as myself . . . . I act as the tongue of you,
It was tied in your mouth . . . . in mine it begins to be loosened.

I swear I will never mention love or death inside a house,
And I swear I never will translate myself at all, only to him or her
    who privately stays with me in the open air.

If you would understand me go to the heights or water-shore,
The nearest gnat is an explanation and a drop or the motion of
    waves a key,
The maul the oar and the handsaw second my words.

No shuttered room or school can commune with me,
But roughs and little children better than they.

The young mechanic is closest to me . . . . he knows me pretty well,
The woodman that takes his axe and jug with him shall take me with
    him all day,
The farmboy ploughing in the field feels good at the sound of my
    voice,
In vessels that sail my words must sail . . . . I go with fishermen and
    seamen, and love them,
My face rubs to the hunter's face when he lies down alone in his
    blanket,
The driver thinking of me does not mind the jolt of his wagon,
The young mother and old mother shall comprehend me,
The girl and the wife rest the needle a moment and forget where
    they are,
They and all would resume what I have told them.

I have said that the soul is not more than the body,
And I have said that the body is not more than the soul,
And nothing, not God, is greater to one than one's-self is,
And whoever walks a furlong without sympathy walks to his own
    funeral, dressed in his shroud,
And I or you pocketless of a dime may purchase the pick of the
    earth,

And to glance with an eye or show a bean in its pod confounds the
    learning of all times,
And there is no trade or employment but the young man following it
    may become a hero,
And there is no object so soft but it makes a hub for the wheeled
    universe,
And any man or woman shall stand cool and supercilious before
    a million universes.

And I call to mankind, Be not curious about God,
For I who am curious about each am not curious about God,
No array of terms can say how much I am at peace about God and
    about death.

I hear and behold God in every object, yet I understand God not in
    the least,
Nor do I understand who there can be more wonderful than myself.

Why should I wish to see God better than this day?
I see something of God each hour of the twenty-four, and each
    moment then,
In the faces of men and women I see God, and in my own face in the
    glass;
I find letters from God dropped in the street, and every one is
    signed by God's name,
And I leave them where they are, for I know that others will
    punctually come forever and ever.

And as to you death, and you bitter hug of mortality .... it is idle to
    try to alarm me.

To his work without flinching the accoucheur* comes,
I see the elderhand pressing receiving supporting,
I recline by the sills of the exquisite flexible doors .... and mark the
    outlet, and mark the relief and escape.

And as to you corpse I think you are good manure, but that does not
    offend me,
I smell the white roses sweetscented and growing,

I reach to the leafy lips.... I reach to the polished breasts of
    melons.

And as to you life, I reckon you are the leavings of many deaths,
No doubt I have died myself ten thousand times before.

I hear you whispering there O stars of heaven,
O suns.... O grass of graves.... O perpetual transfers and
    promotions.... if you do not say anything how can I say
    anything?

Of the turbid pool that lies in the autumn forest,
Of the moon that descends the steeps of the soughing twilight,
Toss, sparkles of day and dusk.... toss on the black stems that decay
    in the muck,
Toss to the moaning gibberish of the dry limbs.

I ascend from the moon.... I ascend from the night,
And perceive of the ghastly glitter the sunbeams reflected,
And debouch to the steady and central from the offspring great or small.

There is that in me.... I do not know what it is.... but I know it is
    in me.

Wrenched and sweaty.... calm and cool then my body becomes;
I sleep.... I sleep long.

I do not know it.... it is without name.... it is a word unsaid,
It is not in any dictionary or utterance or symbol.

Something it swings on more than the earth I swing on,
To it the creation is the friend whose embracing awakes me.

Perhaps I might tell more.... Outlines! I plead for my brothers and
    sisters.

Do you see O my brothers and sisters?
It is not chaos or death.... it is form and union and plan.... it is
    eternal life.... it is happiness.

The past and present wilt.... I have filled them and emptied them,
And proceed to fill my next fold of the future.

Listener up there! Here you.... what have you to confide to me?
Look in my face while I snuff the sidle of evening,
Talk honestly, for no one else hears you, and I stay only a minute longer.

Do I contradict myself?
Very well then.... I contradict myself;
I am large.... I contain multitudes.

I concentrate toward them that are nigh.... I wait on the door-slab.

Who has done his day's work and will soonest be through with his
　　supper?
Who wishes to walk with me?

Will you speak before I am gone? Will you prove already too late?

The spotted hawk swoops by and accuses me.... he complains of
　　my gab and my loitering.

I too am not a bit tamed.... I too am untranslatable,
I sound my barbaric yawp over the roofs of the world.

The last scud of day holds back for me,
It flings my likeness after the rest and true as any on the shadowed
　　wilds,
It coaxes me to the vapor and the dusk.

I depart as air.... I shake my white locks at the runaway sun,
I effuse my flesh in eddies and drift it in lacy jags.

I bequeath myself to the dirt to grow from the grass I love,
If you want me again look for me under your bootsoles.

You will hardly know who I am or what I mean,
But I shall be good health to you nevertheless,
And filter and fibre your blood.

Failing to fetch me at first keep encouraged,
Missing me one place search another,
I stop some where waiting for you.*

*Leaves of Grass**

COME closer to me,
Push close my lovers and take the best I possess,
Yield closer and closer and give me the best you possess.

This is unfinished business with me.... how is it with you?
I was chilled with the cold types and cylinder and wet paper
    between us.

I pass so poorly with paper and types.... I must pass with the
    contact of bodies and souls.

I do not thank you for liking me as I am, and liking the touch of
    me.... I know that it is good for you to do so.

Were all educations practical and ornamental well displayed out of
    me, what would it amount to?
Were I as the head teacher or charitable proprietor or wise
    statesman, what would it amount to?
Were I to you as the boss employing and paying you, would that
    satisfy you?

The learned and virtuous and benevolent, and the usual terms;
A man like me, and never the usual terms.

Neither a servant nor a master am I,
I take no sooner a large price than a small price.... I will have my
    own whoever enjoys me,
I will be even with you, and you shall be even with me.

If you are a workman or workwoman I stand as nigh as the nighest
    that works in the same shop,
If you bestow gifts on your brother or dearest friend, I demand as
    good as your brother or dearest friend,

If your lover or husband or wife is welcome by day or night, I must
    be personally as welcome;
If you have become degraded or ill, then I will become so for your sake;
If you remember your foolish and outlawed deeds, do you think
    I cannot remember my foolish and outlawed deeds?
If you carouse at the table I say I will carouse at the opposite side of
    the table;
If you meet some stranger in the street and love him or her, do I not
    often meet strangers in the street and love them?
If you see a good deal remarkable in me I see just as much
    remarkable in you.

Why what have you thought of yourself?
Is it you then that thought yourself less?
Is it you that thought the President greater than you? or the rich
    better off than you? or the educated wiser than you?

Because you are greasy or pimpled—or that you was once drunk, or
    a thief, or diseased, or rheumatic, or a prostitute—or are so
    now—or from frivolity or impotence—or that you are no
    scholar, and never saw your name in print.... do you give in that
    you are any less immortal?

Souls of men and women! it is not you I call unseen, unheard,
    untouchable and untouching;
It is not you I go argue pro and con about, and to settle whether you
    are alive or no;
I own publicly who you are, if nobody else owns.... aud see and hear
    you, and what you give and take;
What is there you cannot give and take?

I see not merely that you are polite or whitefaced.... married or
    single.... citizens of old states or citizens of new states....
    eminent in some profession ....a lady or gentleman in
    a parlor.... or dressed in the jail uniform.... or pulpit uniform,
Not only the free Utahan, Kansian, or Arkansian.... not only the
    free Cuban... not merely the slave.... not Mexican native, or
    Flatfoot, or negro from Africa,
Iroquois eating the warflesh—fishtearer in his lair of rocks and sand....

Esquimaux in the dark cold snowhouse.... Chinese with his
    transverse eyes ....Bedowee—or wandering nomad—or
    tabounschik at the head of his droves,
Grown, half-grown, and babe—of this country and every country,
    indoors and outdoors I see.... and all else is behind or through
    them.

The wife—and she is not one jot less than the husband,
The daughter—and she is just as good as the son,
The mother—and she is every bit as much as the father.

Offspring of those not rich—boys apprenticed to trades,
Young fellows working on farms and old fellows working on farms;
The naive.... the simple and hardy.... he going to the polls to
    vote.... he who has a good time, and he who has a bad time;
Mechanics, southerners, new arrivals, sailors, mano'warsmen,
    merchantmen, coasters,
All these I see.... but nigher and farther the same I see;
None shall escape me, and none shall wish to escape me.

I bring what you much need, yet always have,
I bring not money or amours or dress or eating.... but I bring as
    good;
And send no agent or medium.... and offer no representative of
    value—but offer the value itself.

There is something that comes home to one now and perpetually,
It is not what is printed or preached or discussed.... it eludes
    discussion and print,
It is not to be put in a book.... it is not in this book,
It is for you whoever you are.... it is no farther from you than your
    hearing and sight are from you,
It is hinted by nearest and commonest and readiest.... it is not
    them, though it is endlessly provoked by them.... What is there
    ready and near you now?

You may read in many languages and read nothing about it;
You may read the President's message and read nothing about it
    there,

Nothing in the reports from the state department or treasury
  department.... or in the daily papers, or the weekly papers,
Or in the census returns or assessors' returns or prices current or
  any accounts of stock.

The sun and stars that float in the open air.... the appleshaped earth
  and we upon it.... surely the drift of them is something grand;
I do not know what it is except that it is grand, and that it is
  happiness,
And that the enclosing purport of us here is not a speculation, or
  bon-mot or reconnoissance,
And that it is not something which by luck may turn out well for us,
  and without luck must be a failure for us,
And not something which may yet be retracted in a certain
  contingency.

The light and shade—the curious sense of body and identity—the
  greed that with perfect complaisance devours all things—the
  endless pride and outstretching of man—unspeakable joys and
  sorrows,
The wonder every one sees in every one else he sees.... and the
  wonders that fill each minute of time forever and each acre of
  surface and space forever,
Have you reckoned them as mainly for a trade or farmwork? or for
  the profits of a store? or to achieve yourself a position? or to fill
  a gentleman's leisure or a lady's leisure?

Have you reckoned the landscape took substance and form that it
  might be painted in a picture?
Or men and women that they might be written of, and songs sung?
Or the attraction of gravity and the great laws and harmonious
  combinations and the fluids of the air as subjects for the savans?
Or the brown land and the blue sea for maps and charts?
Or the stars to be put in constellations and named fancy names?
Or that the growth of seeds is for agricultural tables or agriculture
  itself?

Old institutions.... these arts libraries legends collections—and the
  practice handed along in manufactures.... will we rate them so
  high?

Will we rate our prudence and business so high?.... I have no objection,
I rate them as high as the highest.... but a child born of a woman
    and man I rate beyond all rate.

We thought our Union grand and our Constitution grand;
I do not say they are not grand and good—for they are,
I am this day just as much in love with them as you,
But I am eternally in love with you and with all my fellows upon the
    earth.

We consider the bibles and religions divine.... I do not say they are
    not divine,
I say they have all grown out of you and may grow out of you still,
It is not they who give the life.... it is you who give the life;
Leaves are not more shed from the trees or trees from the earth than
    they are shed out of you.

The sum of all known value and respect I add up in you whoever
    you are;
The President is up there in the White House for you.... it is not
    you who are here for him,
The Secretaries act in their bureaus for you.... not you here for them,
The Congress convenes every December for you,
Laws, courts, the forming of states, the charters of cities, the going
    and coming of commerce and mails are all for you.

All doctrines, all politics and civilization exurge from you,
All sculpture and monuments and anything inscribed anywhere are
    tallied in you,
The gist of histories and statistics as far back as the records reach is
    in you this hour—and myths and tales the same;
If you were not breathing and walking here where would they
    all be?
The most renowned poems would be ashes.... orations and plays
    would be vacuums.

All architecture is what you do to it when you look upon it;
Did you think it was in the white or gray stone? or the lines of the
    arches and cornices?

All music is what awakens from you when you are reminded by the
  instruments,
It is not the violins and the cornets .... it is not the oboe nor the
  beating drums—nor the notes of the baritone singer singing his
  sweet romanza .... nor those of the men's chorus, nor those of
  the women's chorus,
It is nearer and farther than they.

Will the whole come back then?
Can each see the signs of the best by a look in the lookingglass? Is
  there nothing greater or more?
Does all sit there with you and here with me?

The old forever new things .... you foolish child! .... the closest
  simplest things—this moment with you,
Your person and every particle that relates to your person,
The pulses of your brain waiting their chance and encouragement at
  every deed or sight;
Anything you do in public by day, and anything you do in secret
  betweendays,
What is called right and what is called wrong .... what you behold or
  touch .... what causes your anger or wonder,
The anklechain of the slave, the bed of the bedhouse, the cards of
  the gambler, the plates of the forger;
What is seen or learned in the street, or intuitively learned,
What is learned in the public school—spelling, reading, writing and
  ciphering .... the blackboard and the teacher's diagrams:
The panes of the windows and all that appears through them .... the
  going forth in the morning and the aimless spending of the day;
(What is it that you made money? what is it that you got what you
  wanted?)
The usual routine .... the workshop, factory, yard, office, store, or desk;
The jaunt of hunting or fishing, or the life of hunting or fishing,
Pasturelife, foddering, milking and herding, and all the personnel
  and usages;
The plum-orchard and apple-orchard .... gardening .. seedlings,
  cuttings, flowers and vines,
Grains and manures .. marl, clay, loam .. the subsoil plough .. the
  shovel and pick and rake and hoe .. irrigation and draining;

The currycomb . . the horse-cloth . . the halter and bridle and
  bits . . the very wisps of straw,
The barn and barn-yard . . the bins and mangers . . the mows and racks:
Manufactures . . commerce . . engineering . . the building of cities,
  and every trade carried on there . . and the implements of every
  trade,
The anvil and tongs and hammer . . the axe and wedge . . the square
  and mitre and jointer and smoothingplane;
The plumbob and trowel and level . . the wall-scaffold, and the work
  of walls and ceilings . . or any mason-work:
The ship's compass . . the sailor's tarpaulin . . the stays and lanyards,
  and the ground-tackle for anchoring or mooring,
The sloop's tiller . . the pilot's wheel and bell . . the yacht or
  fish-smack . . the great gay-pennanted three-hundred-foot
  steamboat under full headway, with her proud fat breasts and her
  delicate swift-flashing paddles;
The trail and line and hooks and sinkers . . the seine, and hauling
  the seine;
Smallarms and rifles . . . . the powder and shot and caps and
  wadding . . . . the ordnance for war . . . . the carriages:
Everyday objects . . . . the housechairs, the carpet, the bed and the
  counterpane of the bed, and him or her sleeping at night, and
  the wind blowing, and the indefinite noises:
The snowstorm or rainstorm . . . . the tow-trowsers . . . . the lodge-hut
  in the woods, and the still-hunt:
City and country . . fireplace and candle . . gaslight and heater and
  aqueduct;
The message of the governor, mayor, or chief of police . . . . the
  dishes of breakfast or dinner or supper;
The bunkroom, the fire-engine, the string-team, and the car or
  truck behind;
The paper I write on or you write on . . and every word we write . .
  and every cross and twirl of the pen . . and the curious way we
  write what we think . . . . yet very faintly;
The directory, the detector, the ledger . . . the books in ranks or the
  bookshelves . . . . the clock attached to the wall,
The ring on your finger . . the lady's wristlet . . the hammers
  of stonebreakers or coppersmiths . . the druggist's vials
  and jars;

The etui of surgical instruments, and the etui of oculist's or aurist's
    instruments, or dentist's instruments;
Glassblowing, grinding of wheat and corn . . casting, and what is
    cast . . tinroofing, shingledressing,
Shipcarpentering, flagging of sidewalks by flaggers . . dockbuilding,
    fishcuring, ferrying;
The pump, the piledriver, the great derrick . . the coalkiln and
    brickkiln,
Ironworks or whiteleadworks . . the sugarhouse . . steam-saws, and
    the great mills and factories;
The cottonbale . . the stevedore's hook . . the saw and buck of the
    sawyer . . the screen of the coalscreener . . the mould of the
    moulder . . the workingknife of the butcher;
The cylinder press . . the handpress . . the frisket and tympan* . .
    the compositor's stick and rule,
The implements for daguerreotyping . . . . the tools of the rigger or
    grappler or sail-maker or blockmaker,
Goods of guttapercha or papiermache . . . . colors and brushes . . . .
    glaziers' implements,
The veneer and gluepot . . the confectioner's ornaments . . the
    decanter and glasses . . the shears and flatiron;
The awl and kneestrap . . the pint measure and quart measure . . the
    counter and stool . . the writingpen of quill or metal;
Billiards and tenpins . . . . the ladders and hanging ropes of the
    gymnasium, and the manly exercises;
The designs for wallpapers or oilcloths or carpets . . . . the fancies for
    goods for women . . . . the bookbinder's stamps;
Leatherdressing, coachmaking, boilermaking, ropetwisting,
    distilling, signpainting, limeburning, coopering, cottonpicking,
The walkingbeam of the steam-engine . . the throttle and governors,
    and the up and down rods,
Stavemachines and plainingmachines . . . . the cart of the carman . .
    the omnibus . . the ponderous dray;
The snowplough and two engines pushing it . . . . the ride in the
    express train of only one car . . . . the swift go through a howling
    storm:
The bearhunt or coonhunt . . . . the bonfire of shavings in the open
    lot in the city . . the crowd of children watching;

The blows of the fighting-man . . the upper cut and one-two-three;
The shopwindows.... the coffins in the sexton's wareroom.... the
    fruit on the fruitstand.... the beef on the butcher's stall,
The bread and cakes in the bakery.... the white and red pork in the
    pork-store;
The milliner's ribbons . . the dressmaker's patterns.... the tea-table . .
    the home-made sweetmeats:
The column of wants in the one-cent paper . . the news by
    telegraph.... the amusements and operas and shows:
The cotton and woolen and linen you wear.... the money you make
    and spend;
Your room and bedroom.... your piano-forte.... the stove and
    cookpans,
The house you live in.... the rent.... the other tenants.... the
    deposite in the savings-bank.... the trade at the grocery,
The pay on Saturday night.... the going home, and the purchases;
In them the heft of the heaviest.... in them far more than you
    estimated, and far less also,
In them, not yourself.... you and your soul enclose all things,
    regardless of estimation,
In them your themes and hints and provokers . . if not, the whole
    earth has no themes or hints or provokers, and never had.

I do not affirm what you see beyond is futile.... I do not advise you
    to stop,
I do not say leadings you thought great are not great,
But I say that none lead to greater or sadder or happier than those
    lead to.

Will you seek afar off? You surely come back at last,
In things best known to you finding the best or as good as the best,
In folks nearest to you finding also the sweetest and strongest and
    lovingest,
Happiness not in another place, but this place . . not for another
    hour, but this hour,
Man in the first you see or touch.... always in your friend or brother
    or nighest neighbor.... Woman in your mother or lover or wife,
And all else thus far known giving place to men and women.

When the psalm sings instead of the singer,
When the script preaches instead of the preacher,
When the pulpit descends and goes instead of the carver that carved
    the supporting desk,
When the sacred vessels or the bits of the eucharist, or the lath and
    plast, procreate as effectually as the young silversmiths or bakers,
    or the masons in their overalls,
When a university course convinces like a slumbering woman and
    child convince,
When the minted gold in the vault smiles like the nightwatchman's
    daughter,
When warrantee deeds loafe in chairs opposite and are my friendly
    companions,
I intend to reach them my hand and make as much of them as I do
    of men and women.

*Leaves of Grass**

To think of time.... to think through the retrospection,
To think of today .. and the ages continued henceforward.

Have you guessed you yourself would not continue? Have you
    dreaded those earth-beetles?
Have you feared the future would be nothing to you?

Is today nothing? Is the beginningless past nothing?
If the future is nothing they are just as surely nothing.

To think that the sun rose in the east.... that men and women were
    flexible and real and alive.... that every thing was real and alive;
To think that you and I did not see feel think nor bear our part,
To think that we are now here and bear our part.

Not a day passes .. not a minute or second without an
    accouchement;
Not a day passes .. not a minute or second without a corpse.

When the dull nights are over, and the dull days also,
When the soreness of lying so much in bed is over,

When the physician, after long putting off, gives the silent and
 terrible look for an answer,
When the children come hurried and weeping, and the brothers and
 sisters have been sent for,
When medicines stand unused on the shelf, and the camphor-smell
 has pervaded the rooms,
When the faithful hand of the living does not desert the hand of the
 dying,
When the twitching lips press lightly on the forehead of the dying,
When the breath ceases and the pulse of the heart ceases,
Then the corpse-limbs stretch on the bed, and the living look upon
 them,
They are palpable as the living are palpable.

The living look upon the corpse with their eyesight,
But without eyesight lingers a different living and looks curiously on
 the corpse.

To think that the rivers will come to flow, and the snow fall, and
 fruits ripen . . and act upon others as upon us now . . . . yet not
 act upon us;
To think of all these wonders of city and country . . and others
 taking great interest in them . . and we taking small interest in
 them.

To think how eager we are in building our houses,
To think others shall be just as eager . . and we quite indifferent.

I see one building the house that serves him a few years . . . . or
 seventy or eighty years at most;
I see one building the house that serves him longer than that.

Slowmoving and black lines creep over the whole earth . . . . they
 never cease . . . . they are the burial lines,
He that was President was buried, and he that is now President shall
 surely be buried.

Cold dash of waves at the ferrywharf,
Posh and ice in the river . . . . half-frozen mud in the streets,

A gray discouraged sky overhead .... the short last daylight of
    December,
A hearse and stages .... other vehicles give place,
The funeral of an old stagedriver .... the cortege mostly drivers.

Rapid the trot to the cemetery,
Duly rattles the deathbell .... the gate is passed .... the grave is
    halted at .... the living alight .... the hearse uncloses,
The coffin is lowered and settled .... the whip is laid on the coffin,
The earth is swiftly shovelled in .... a minute . . no one moves or
    speaks .... it is done,
He is decently put away .... is there anything more?

He was a goodfellow,
Freemouthed, quicktempered, not badlooking, able to take his own
    part,
Witty, sensitive to a slight, ready with life or death for a friend,
Fond of women, . . played some . . eat hearty and drank hearty,
Had known what it was to be flush . . grew lowspirited toward the
    last . . sickened . . was helped by a contribution,
Died aged forty-one years . . and that was his funeral.

Thumb extended or finger uplifted,
Apron, cape, gloves, strap .... wetweather clothes .... whip carefully
    chosen .... boss, spotter, starter, and hostler,
Somebody loafing on you, or you loafing on somebody ....
    headway .... man before and man behind,
Good day's work or bad day's work .... pet stock or mean stock ....
    first out or last out .... turning in at night,
To think that these are so much and so nigh to other drivers . . and
    he there takes no interest in them.

The markets, the government, the workingman's wages .... to think
    what account they are through our nights and days;
To think that other workingmen will make just as great account of
    them . . yet we make little or no account.

The vulgar and the refined .... what you call sin and what you call
    goodness . . to think how wide a difference;

To think the difference will still continue to others, yet we lie beyond
    the difference.

To think how much pleasure there is!
Have you pleasure from looking at the sky? Have you pleasure from
    poems?
Do you enjoy yourself in the city? or engaged in business? or planning
    a nomination and election? or with your wife and family?
Or with your mother and sisters? or in womanly housework? or the
    beautiful maternal cares?

These also flow onward to others.... you and I flow onward;
But in due time you and I shall take less interest in them.

Your farm and profits and crops.... to think how engrossed you are;
To think there will still be farms and profits and crops .. yet for you
    of what avail?

What will be will be well—for what is is well,
To take interest is well, and not to take interest shall be well.

The sky continues beautiful.... the pleasure of men with women
    shall never be sated .. nor the pleasure of women with men ..
    nor the pleasure from poems;
The domestic joys, the daily housework or business, the building of
    houses—they are not phantasms .. they have weight and form
    and location;
The farms and profits and crops .. the markets and wages and
    government .. they also are not phantasms;
The difference between sin and goodness is no apparition;
The earth is not an echo.... man and his life and all the things of
    his life are well-considered.

You are not thrown to the winds .. you gather certainly and safely
    around yourself,
Yourself! Yourself! Yourself forever and ever!

It is not to diffuse you that you were born of your mother and
    father—it is to identify you,

It is not that you should be undecided, but that you should be
    decided;
Something long preparing and formless is arrived and formed in you,
You are thenceforth secure, whatever comes or goes.

The threads that were spun are gathered ̇.... the weft crosses the
    warp .... the pattern is systematic.

The preparations have every one been justified;
The orchestra have tuned their instruments sufficiently .... the
    baton has given the signal.

The guest that was coming .... he waited long for reasons .... he is
    now housed,
He is one of those who are beautiful and happy .... he is one of
    those that to look upon and be with is enough.

The law of the past cannot be eluded,
The law of the present and future cannot be eluded,
The law of the living cannot be eluded .... it is eternal,
The law of promotion and transformation cannot be eluded,
The law of heroes and good-doers cannot be eluded,
The law of drunkards and informers and mean persons cannot be
    eluded.

Slowmoving and black lines go ceaselessly over the earth,
Northerner goes carried and southerner goes carried .... and they
    on the Atlantic side and they on the Pacific, and they between,
    and all through the Mississippi country .... and all over the
    earth.

The great masters and kosmos are well as they go .... the heroes and
    good-doers are well,
The known leaders and inventors and the rich owners and pious and
    distinguished may be well,
But there is more account than that .... there is strict account of all.

The interminable hordes of the ignorant and wicked are not
    nothing,

The barbarians of Africa and Asia are not nothing,
The common people of Europe are not nothing.... the American
  aborigines are not nothing,
A zambo or a foreheadless Crowfoot or a Camanche is not nothing,
The infected in the immigrant hospital are not nothing.... the
  murderer or mean person is not nothing,
The perpetual succession of shallow people are not nothing as they go,
The prostitute is not nothing.... the mocker of religion is not
  nothing as he goes.

I shall go with the rest.... we have satisfaction:
I have dreamed that we are not to be changed so much.... nor the
  law of us changed;
I have dreamed that heroes and good-doers shall be under the
  present and past law,
And that murderers and drunkards and liars shall be under the
  present and past law;
For I have dreamed that the law they are under now is enough.

And I have dreamed that the satisfaction is not so much changed....
  and that there is no life without satisfaction;
What is the earth? what are body and soul without satisfaction?

I shall go with the rest,
We cannot be stopped at a given point.... that is no satisfaction;
To show us a good thing or a few good things for a space of
  time—that is no satisfaction;
We must have the indestructible breed of the best, regardless
  of time.

If otherwise, all these things came but to ashes of dung;
If maggots and rats ended us, then suspicion and treachery and death.

Do you suspect death? If I were to suspect death I should die now,
Do you think I could walk pleasantly and well-suited toward
  annihilation?

Pleasantly and well-suited I walk,
Whither I walk I cannot define, but I know it is good,

The whole universe indicates that it is good,
The past and the present indicate that it is good.

How beautiful and perfect are the animals! How perfect is my soul!
How perfect the earth, and the minutest thing upon it!
What is called good is perfect, and what is called sin is just as
     perfect;
The vegetables and minerals are all perfect . . and the imponderable
     fluids are perfect;
Slowly and surely they have passed on to this, and slowly and surely
     they will yet pass on.

O my soul! if I realize you I have satisfaction,
Animals and vegetables! if I realize you I have satisfaction,
Laws of the earth and air! if I realize you I have satisfaction.

I cannot define my satisfaction . . yet it is so,
I cannot define my life . . yet it is so.

I swear I see now that every thing has an eternal soul!
The trees have, rooted in the ground . . . . the weeds of the sea
     have . . . . the animals.

I swear I think there is nothing but immortality!
That the exquisite scheme is for it, and the nebulous float is for it,
     and the cohering is for it,
And all preparation is for it . . and identity is for it . . and life and
     death are for it.

*Leaves of Grass**

I WANDER all night in my vision,
Stepping with light feet . . . . swiftly and noiselessly stepping and
     stopping,
Bending with open eyes over the shut eyes of sleepers;
Wandering and confused . . . . lost to myself . . . . ill-assorted . . . .
     contradictory,
Pausing and gazing and bending and stopping.

How solemn they look there, stretched and still;
How quiet they breathe, the little children in their cradles.

The wretched features of ennuyees, the white features of corpses,
the livid faces of drunkards, the sick-gray faces of onanists,
The gashed bodies on battlefields, the insane in their strong-doored
rooms, the sacred idiots,
The newborn emerging from gates and the dying emerging from gates,
The night pervades them and enfolds them.

The married couple sleep calmly in their bed, he with his palm on
the hip of the wife, and she with her palm on the hip of the
husband,
The sisters sleep lovingly side by side in their bed,
The men sleep lovingly side by side in theirs,
And the mother sleeps with her little child carefully wrapped.

The blind sleep, and the deaf and dumb sleep,
The prisoner sleeps well in the prison.... the runaway son sleeps,
The murderer that is to be hung next day.... how does he sleep?
And the murdered person.... how does he sleep?

The female that loves unrequited sleeps,
And the male that loves unrequited sleeps;
The head of the moneymaker that plotted all day sleeps,
And the enraged and treacherous dispositions sleep.

I stand with drooping eyes by the worstsuffering and restless,
I pass my hands soothingly to and fro a few inches from them;
The restless sink in their beds.... they fitfully sleep.

The earth recedes from me into the night,
I saw that it was beautiful.... and I see that what is not the earth is
beautiful.

I go from bedside to bedside.... I sleep close with the other
sleepers, each in turn;
I dream in my dream all the dreams of the other dreamers,
And I become the other dreamers.

I am a dance.... Play up there! the fit is whirling me fast.

I am the everlaughing.... it is new moon and twilight,
I see the hiding of douceurs*.... I see nimble ghosts whichever way
    I look,
Cache and cache* again deep in the ground and sea, and where it is
    neither ground or sea.

Well do they do their jobs, those journeymen divine,
Only from me can they hide nothing and would not if they could;
I reckon I am their boss, and they make me a pet besides,
And surround me, and lead me and run ahead when I walk,
And lift their cunning covers and signify me with stretched arms,
    and resume the way;
Onward we move, a gay gang of blackguards with mirthshouting
    music and wildflapping pennants of joy.

I am the actor and the actress.... the voter . . the politician,
The emigrant and the exile . . the criminal that stood in the box,
He who has been famous, and he who shall be famous after today,
The stammerer.... the wellformed person . . the wasted or feeble
    person.

I am she who adorned herself and folded her hair expectantly,
My truant lover has come and it is dark.

Double yourself and receive me darkness,
Receive me and my lover too.... he will not let me go without him.

I roll myself upon you as upon a bed.... I resign myself to the dusk.

He whom I call answers me and takes the place of my lover,
He rises with me silently from the bed.

Darkness you are gentler than my lover.... his flesh was sweaty and
    panting,
I feel the hot moisture yet that he left me.

My hands are spread forth . . I pass them in all directions,
I would sound up the shadowy shore to which you are journeying.

Be careful, darkness.... already, what was it touched me?
I thought my lover had gone.... else darkness and he are one,
I hear the heart-beat.... I follow .. I fade away.

O hotcheeked and blushing! O foolish hectic!
O for pity's sake, no one must see me now!.... my clothes were
    stolen while I was abed,
Now I am thrust forth, where shall I run?

Pier that I saw dimly last night when I looked from the windows,
Pier out from the main, let me catch myself with you and stay....
    I will not chafe you;
I feel ashamed to go naked about the world,
And am curious to know where my feet stand.... and what is this
    flooding me, childhood or manhood.... and the hunger that
    crosses the bridge between.

The cloth laps a first sweet eating and drinking,
Laps life-swelling yolks.... laps ear of rose-corn, milky and just
    ripened:
The white teeth stay, and the boss-tooth advances in darkness,
And liquor is spilled on lips and bosoms by touching glasses, and
    the best liquor afterward.

I descend my western course.... my sinews are flaccid,
Perfume and youth course through me, and I am their wake.

It is my face yellow and wrinkled instead of the old woman's,
I sit low in a strawbottom chair and carefully darn my grandson's
    stockings.

It is I too.... the sleepless widow looking out on the winter
    midnight,
I see the sparkles of starshine on the icy and pallid earth.

A shroud I see—and I am the shroud.... I wrap a body and lie in
    the coffin;
It is dark here underground.... it is not evil or pain here.... it is
    blank here, for reasons.

It seems to me that everything in the light and air ought to be happy;
Whoever is not in his coffin and the dark grave, let him know he has
    enough.

I see a beautiful gigantic swimmer swimming naked through the
    eddies of the sea,
His brown hair lies close and even to his head .... he strikes out with
    courageous arms .... he urges himself with his legs.

I see his white body .... I see his undaunted eyes;
I hate the swift-running eddies that would dash him headforemost
    on the rocks.

What are you doing you ruffianly red-trickled waves?
Will you kill the courageous giant? Will you kill him in the prime of
    his middle age?

Steady and long he struggles;
He is baffled and banged and bruised .... he holds out while his
    strength holds out,
The slapping eddies are spotted with his blood .... they bear him
    away .... they roll him and swing him and turn him:
His beautiful body is borne in the circling eddies .... it is continually
    bruised on rocks,
Swiftly and out of sight is borne the brave corpse.

I turn but do not extricate myself;
Confused .... a pastreading .... another, but with darkness yet.

The beach is cut by the razory ice-wind .... the wreck-guns sound,
The tempest lulls and the moon comes floundering through the
    drifts

I look where the ship helplessly heads end on .... I hear the burst as
    she strikes . . I hear the howls of dismay .... they grow fainter
    and fainter.

I cannot aid with my wringing fingers;
I can but rush to the surf and let it drench me and freeze upon me.

I search with the crowd .... not one of the company is washed to us
    alive;
In the morning I help pick up the dead and lay them in rows in
    a barn.

Now of the old war-days . . the defeat at Brooklyn;*
Washington stands inside the lines . . he stands on the entrenched
    hills amid a crowd of officers,
His face is cold and damp .... he cannot repress the weeping
    drops .... he lifts the glass perpetually to his eyes .... the color is
    blanched from his cheeks,
He sees the slaughter of the southern braves confided to him by
    their parents.

The same at last and at last when peace is declared,
He stands in the room of the old tavern .... the wellbeloved soldiers
    all pass through,
The officers speechless and slow draw near in their turns,
The chief encircles their necks with his arm and kisses them on the
    cheek,
He kisses lightly the wet cheeks one after another .... he shakes
    hands and bids goodbye to the army.

Now I tell what my mother told me today as we sat at dinner
    together,
Of when she was a nearly grown girl living home with her parents on
    the old homestead.

A red squaw came one breakfasttime to the old homestead,
On her back she carried a bundle of rushes for rushbottoming
    chairs;
Her hair straight shiny coarse black and profuse halfenveloped her
    face,
Her step was free and elastic .... her voice sounded exquisitely as
    she spoke.

My mother looked in delight and amazement at the stranger,
She looked at the beauty of her tallborne face and full and pliant limbs,
The more she looked upon her she loved her,

Never before had she seen such wonderful beauty and purity;
She made her sit on a bench by the jamb of the fireplace .... she
    cooked food for her,
She had no work to give her but she gave her remembrance and
    fondness.

The red squaw staid all the forenoon, and toward the middle of the
    afternoon she went away;
O my mother was loth to have her go away,
All the week she thought of her .... she watched for her many
    a month,
She remembered her many a winter and many a summer,
But the red squaw never came nor was heard of there again.

Now Lucifer was not dead .... or if he was I am his sorrowful
    terrible heir;
I have been wronged .... I am oppressed .... I hate him that
    oppresses me,
I will either destroy him, or he shall release me.

Damn him! how he does defile me,
How he informs against my brother and sister and takes pay for their
    blood,
How he laughs when I look down the bend after the steamboat that
    carries away my woman.

Now the vast dusk bulk that is the whale's bulk .... it seems mine,
Warily, sportsman! though I lie so sleepy and sluggish, my tap is death.

A show of the summer softness .... a contact of something
    unseen .... an amour of the light and air;
I am jealous and overwhelmed with friendliness,
And will go gallivant with the light and the air myself,
And have an unseen something to be in contact with them also.

O love and summer! you are in the dreams and in me,
Autumn and winter are in the dreams .... the farmer goes with his
    thrift,
The droves and crops increase .... the barns are wellfilled.

Elements merge in the night.... ships make tacks in the dreams....
    the sailor sails.... the exile returns home,
The fugitive returns unharmed.... the immigrant is back beyond
    months and years;
The poor Irishman lives in the simple house of his childhood, with
    the wellknown neighbors and faces,
They warmly welcome him.... he is barefoot again.... he forgets he
    is welloff;
The Dutchman voyages home, and the Scotchman and Welchman
    voyage home . . and the native of the Mediterranean voyages home;
To every port of England and France and Spain enter wellfilled ships;
The Swiss foots it toward his hills.... the Prussian goes his way, and
    the Hungarian his way, and the Pole goes his way,
The Swede returns, and the Dane and Norwegian return.

The homeward bound and the outward bound,
The beautiful lost swimmer, the ennuyee, the onanist, the female
    that loves unrequited, the moneymaker,
The actor and actress . . those through with their parts and those
    waiting to commence,
The affectionate boy, the husband and wife, the voter, the nominee
    that is chosen and the nominee that has failed,
The great already known, and the great anytime after to day,
The stammerer, the sick, the perfectformed, the homely,
The criminal that stood in the box, the judge that sat and sentenced
    him, the fluent lawyers, the jury, the audience,
The laugher and weeper, the dancer, the midnight widow, the red squaw,
The consumptive, the erysipalite,* the idiot, he that is wronged,
The antipodes, and every one between this and them in the dark,
I swear they are averaged now.... one is no better than the other,
The night and sleep have likened them and restored them.

I swear they are all beautiful,
Every one that sleeps is beautiful.... every thing in the dim night is
    beautiful,
The wildest and bloodiest is over and all is peace.

Peace is always beautiful,
The myth of heaven indicates peace and night.

The myth of heaven indicates the soul;
The soul is always beautiful.... it appears more or it appears
    less.... it comes or lags behind,
It comes from its embowered garden and looks pleasantly on itself
    and encloses the world;
Perfect and clean the genitals previously jetting, and perfect and
    clean the womb cohering,
The head wellgrown and proportioned and plumb, and the bowels
    and joints proportioned and plumb.

The soul is always beautiful,
The universe is duly in order.... every thing is in its place,
What is arrived is in its place, and what waits is in its place;
The twisted skull waits.... the watery or rotten blood waits,
The child of the glutton or venerealee waits long, and the child of
    the drunkard waits long, and the drunkard himself waits long,
The sleepers that lived and died wait.... the far advanced are to go
    on in their turns, and the far behind are to go on in their turns,
The diverse shall be no less diverse, but they shall flow and unite....
    they unite now.

The sleepers are very beautiful as they lie unclothed,
They flow hand in hand over the whole earth from east to west as
    they lie unclothed;
The Asiatic and African are hand in hand.... the European and
    American are hand in hand,
Learned and unlearned are hand in hand .. and male and female are
    hand in hand;
The bare arm of the girl crosses the bare breast of her lover.... they
    press close without lust.... his lips press her neck,
The father holds his grown or ungrown son in his arms with
    measureless love.... and the son holds the father in his arms
    with measureless love,
The white hair of the mother shines on the white wrist of the
    daughter,
The breath of the boy goes with the breath of the man.... friend is
    inarmed by friend,
The scholar kisses the teacher and the teacher kisses the scholar....
    the wronged is made right,

The call of the slave is one with the master's call . . and the master
    salutes the slave,
The felon steps forth from the prison . . . . the insane becomes
    sane . . . . the suffering of sick persons is relieved,
The sweatings and fevers stop . . the throat that was unsound is
    sound . . the lungs of the consumptive are resumed . . the poor
    distressed head is free,
The joints of the rheumatic move as smoothly as ever, and smoother
    than ever,
Stiflings and passages open . . . . the paralysed become supple,
The swelled and convulsed and congested awake to themselves in
    condition,
They pass the invigoration of the night and the chemistry of the
    night and awake.

I too pass from the night;
I stay awhile away O night, but I return to you again and love you;
Why should I be afraid to trust myself to you?
I am not afraid . . . . I have been well brought forward by you;
I love the rich running day, but I do not desert her in whom I lay so
    long:
I know not how I came of you, and I know not where I go with
    you . . . . but I know I came well and shall go well.

I will stop only a time with the night . . . . and rise betimes.

I will duly pass the day O my mother and duly return to you;
Not you will yield forth the dawn again more surely than you will
    yield forth me again,
Not the womb yields the babe in its time more surely than I shall be
    yielded from you in my time.

*Leaves of Grass**

THE bodies of men and women engirth me, and I engirth them,
They will not let me off nor I them till I go with them and respond
    to them and love them.

Was it dreamed whether those who corrupted their own live bodies
    could conceal themselves?

And whether those who defiled the living were as bad as they who
　　defiled the dead?

The expression of the body of man or woman balks account,
The male is perfect and that of the female is perfect.

The expression of a wellmade man appears not only in his face,
It is in his limbs and joints also.... it is curiously in the joints of his
　　hips and wrists,
It is in his walk . . the carriage of his neck . . the flex of his waist and
　　knees.... dress does not hide him,
The strong sweet supple quality he has strikes through the cotton
　　and flannel;
To see him pass conveys as much as the best poem . . perhaps more,
You linger to see his back and the back of his neck and shoulderside.

The sprawl and fulness of babes.... the bosoms and heads of
　　women.... the folds of their dress.... their style as we pass in
　　the street.... the contour of their shape downwards;
The swimmer naked in the swimmingbath . . seen as he swims
　　through the salt transparent greenshine, or lies on his back and
　　rolls silently with the heave of the water;
Framers bare-armed framing a house . . hoisting the beams in their
　　places . . or using the mallet and mortising-chisel,
The bending forward and backward of rowers in rowboats.... the
　　horseman in his saddle;
Girls and mothers and housekeepers in all their exquisite offices,
The group of laborers seated at noontime with their open
　　dinnerkettles, and their wives waiting,
The female soothing a child.... the farmer's daughter in the garden
　　or cowyard,
The woodman rapidly swinging his axe in the woods.... the young
　　fellow hoeing corn.... the sleighdriver guiding his six horses
　　through the crowd,
The wrestle of wrestlers . . two apprentice-boys, quite grown, lusty,
　　goodnatured, nativeborn, out on the vacant lot at sundown after
　　work,
The coats vests and caps thrown down . . the embrace of love and
　　resistance,

The upperhold and underhold—the hair rumpled over and blinding
    the eyes;

The march of firemen in their own costumes—the play of the
    masculine muscle through cleansetting trowsers and
    waistbands,

The slow return from the fire .... the pause when the bell strikes
    suddenly again—the listening on the alert,

The natural perfect and varied attitudes .... the bent head, the
    curved neck, the counting:

Suchlike I love .... I loosen myself and pass freely .... and am at the
    mother's breast with the little child,

And swim with the swimmer, and wrestle with wrestlers, and march
    in line with the firemen, and pause and listen and count.

I knew a man .... he was a common farmer .... he was the father of
    five sons ... and in them were the fathers of sons ... and in them
    were the fathers of sons.

This man was of wonderful vigor and calmness and beauty of
    person;

The shape of his head, the richness and breadth of his manners, the
    pale yellow and white of his hair and beard, the immeasurable
    meaning of his black eyes,

These I used to go and visit him to see .... He was wise also,

He was six feet tall .... he was over eighty years old .... his sons were
    massive clean bearded tanfaced and handsome,

They and his daughters loved him ... all who saw him loved
    him ... they did not love him by allowance ... they loved him
    with personal love;

He drank water only .... the blood showed like scarlet through the
    clear brown skin of his face;

He was a frequent gunner and fisher ... he sailed his boat
    himself ... he had a fine one presented to him by a shipjoiner ....
    he had fowling-pieces, presented to him by men that loved him;

When he went with his five sons and many grandsons to hunt
    or fish you would pick him out as the most beautiful and
    vigorous of the gang,

You would wish long and long to be with him .... you would wish to
    sit by him in the boat that you and he might touch each other.

I have perceived that to be with those I like is enough,
To stop in company with the rest at evening is enough,
To be surrounded by beautiful curious breathing laughing flesh is
    enough,
To pass among them . . to touch any one . . . . to rest my arm
    ever so lightly round his or her neck for a moment . . . . what is
    this then?
I do not ask any more delight . . . . I swim in it as in a sea.

There is something in staying close to men and women and looking
    on them and in the contact and odor of them that pleases the
    soul well,
All things please the soul, but these please the soul well.

This is the female form,
A divine nimbus exhales from it from head to foot,
It attracts with fierce undeniable attraction,
I am drawn by its breath as if I were no more than a helpless
    vapor . . . . all falls aside but myself and it,
Books, art, religion, time . . the visible and solid earth . . the
    atmosphere and the fringed clouds . . what was expected of
    heaven or feared of hell are now consumed,
Mad filaments, ungovernable shoots play out of it . . the response
    likewise ungovernable,
Hair, bosom, hips, bend of legs, negligent falling hands—all
    diffused . . . . mine too diffused,
Ebb stung by the flow, and flow stung by the ebb . . . . loveflesh
    swelling and deliciously aching,
Limitless limpid jets of love hot and enormous . . . . quivering jelly of
    love . . . white-blow and delirious juice,
Bridegroom-night of love working surely and softly into the
    prostrate dawn,
Undulating into the willing and yielding day,
Lost in the cleave of the clasping and sweetfleshed day.

This is the nucleus . . . after the child is born of woman the man is
    born of woman,
This is the bath of birth . . . this is the merge of small and large and
    the outlet again.

Be not ashamed women . . your privilege encloses the rest . . it is the
    exit of the rest,
You are the gates of the body and you are the gates of the soul.

The female contains all qualities and tempers them . . . . she is in her
    place . . . . she moves with perfect balance,
She is all things duly veiled . . . . she is both passive and active . . . . she is
    to conceive daughters as well as sons and sons as well as daughters.

As I see my soul reflected in nature . . . . as I see through a mist one
    with inexpressible completeness and beauty . . . . see the bent
    head and arms folded over the breast . . . . the female I see,
I see the bearer of the great fruit which is immortality . . . . the good
    thereof is not tasted by roues, and never can be.

The male is not less the soul, nor more . . . . he too is in his place,
He too is all qualities . . . . he is action and power . . . . the flush of the
    known universe is in him,
Scorn becomes him well and appetite and defiance become him well,
The fiercest largest passions . . bliss that is utmost and sorrow that is
    utmost become him well . . . . pride is for him,
The fullspread pride of man is calming and excellent to the soul;
Knowledge becomes him . . . . he likes it always . . . . he brings
    everything to the test of himself,
Whatever the survey . . whatever the sea and the sail, he strikes
    soundings at last only here,
Where else does he strike soundings except here?

The man's body is sacred and the woman's body is sacred . . . . it is
    no matter who,
Is it a slave? Is it one of the dullfaced immigrants just landed on the
    wharf?

Each belongs here or anywhere just as much as the welloff . . . . just as
    much as you,
Each has his or her place in the procession.

All is a procession,
The universe is a procession with measured and beautiful motion.

Do you know so much that you call the slave or the dullface ignorant?
Do you suppose you have a right to a good sight...and he or she has
    no right to a sight?
Do you think matter has cohered together from its diffused float,
    and the soil is on the surface and water runs and vegetation
    sprouts for you . . and not for him and her?

A slave at auction!
I help the auctioneer.... the sloven does not half know his business.

Gentlemen look on this curious creature,
Whatever the bids of the bidders they cannot be high enough for
    him,
For him the globe lay preparing quintillions of years without one
    animal or plant,
For him the revolving cycles truly and steadily rolled.

In that head the allbaffling brain,
In it and below it the making of the attributes of heroes.

Examine these limbs, red black or white.... they are very cunning in
    tendon and nerve;
They shall be stript that you may see them.

Exquisite senses, lifelit eyes, pluck, volition,
Flakes of breastmuscle, pliant backbone and neck, flesh not flabby,
    goodsized arms and legs,
And wonders within there yet.

Within there runs his blood.... the same old blood . . the same red
    running blood;
There swells and jets his heart.... There all passions and desires . .
    all reachings and aspirations:
Do you think they are not there because they are not expressed in
    parlors and lecture-rooms?

This is not only one man.... he is the father of those who shall be
    fathers in their turns,
In him the start of populous states and rich republics,

Of him countless immortal lives with countless embodiments and
    enjoyments.

How do you know who shall come from the offspring of his offspring
    through the centuries?
Who might you find you have come from yourself if you could trace
    back through the centuries?

A woman at auction,
She too is not only herself . . . . she is the teeming mother of mothers,
She is the bearer of them that shall grow and be mates to the
    mothers.

Her daughters or their daughters' daughters . . who knows who shall
    mate with them?
Who knows through the centuries what heroes may come from
    them?

In them and of them natal love . . . . in them the divine mystery . . . .
    the same old beautiful mystery.

Have you ever loved a woman?
Your mother . . . . is she living? . . . . Have you been much with her?
    and has she been much with you?
Do you not see that these are exactly the same to all in all nations
    and times all over the earth?

If life and the soul are sacred the human body is sacred;
And the glory and sweet of a man is the token of manhood
    untainted,
And in man or woman a clean strong firmfibred body is beautiful as
    the most beautiful face.

Have you seen the fool that corrupted his own live body? or the fool
    that corrupted her own live body?
For they do not conceal themselves, and cannot conceal themselves.

Who degrades or defiles the living human body is cursed,
Who degrades or defiles the body of the dead is not more cursed.

*Leaves of Grass**

SAUNTERING the pavement or riding the country byroad here then
    are faces,
Faces of friendship, precision, caution, suavity, ideality,
The spiritual prescient face, the always welcome common
    benevolent face,
The face of the singing of music, the grand faces of natural lawyers
    and judges broad at the backtop,
The faces of hunters and fishers, bulged at the brows . . . . the shaved
    blanched faces of orthodox citizens,
The pure extravagant yearning questioning artist's face,
The welcome ugly face of some beautiful soul . . . . the handsome
    detested or despised face,
The sacred faces of infants . . . . the illuminated face of the mother of
    many children,
The face of an amour . . . . the face of veneration,
The face as of a dream . . . . the face of an immobile rock,
The face withdrawn of its good and bad . . a castrated face,
A wild hawk . . his wings clipped by the clipper,
A stallion that yielded at last to the thongs and knife of the gelder.

Sauntering the pavement or crossing the ceaseless ferry, here then
    are faces;
I see them and complain not and am content with all.

Do you suppose I could be content with all if I thought them their
    own finale?

This now is too lamentable a face for a man;
Some abject louse asking leave to be . . cringing for it,
Some milknosed maggot blessing what lets it wrig* to its hole.

This face is a dog's snout sniffing for garbage;
Snakes nest in that mouth . . I hear the sibilant threat.

This face is a haze more chill than the arctic sea,
Its sleepy and wobbling icebergs crunch as they go.

This is a face of bitter herbs.... this an emetic.... they need no
  label,
And more of the drugshelf .. laudanum, caoutchouc,* or hog's lard.

This face is an epilepsy advertising and doing business.... its
  wordless tongue gives out the unearthly cry,
Its veins down the neck distend.... its eyes roll till they show
  nothing but their whites,
Its teeth grit .. the palms of the hands are cut by the turned-in nails,
The man falls struggling and foaming to the ground while he
  speculates well.

This face is bitten by vermin and worms,
And this is some murderer's knife with a halfpulled scabbard.

This face owes to the sexton his dismalest fee,
An unceasing deathbell tolls there.

Those are really men!.... the bosses and tufts of the great round
  globe!

Features of my equals, would you trick me with your creased and
  cadaverous march?
Well then you cannot trick me.

I see your rounded never-erased flow,
I see neath the rims of your haggard and mean disguises.

Splay and twist as you like.... poke with the tangling fores of fishes
  or rats,
You'll be unmuzzled.... you certainly will.

I saw the face of the most smeared and slobbering idiot they had at
  the asylum,
And I knew for my consolation what they knew not;
I knew of the agents that emptied and broke my brother,*
The same wait to clear the rubbish from the fallen tenement;
And I shall look again in a score or two of ages,

And I shall meet the real landlord perfect and unharmed, every inch
      as good as myself.

The Lord advances and yet advances:
Always the shadow in front.... always the reached hand bringing up
      the laggards.

Out of this face emerge banners and horses.... O superb!.... I see
      what is coming,
I see the high pioneercaps.... I see the staves of runners clearing
      the way,
I hear victorious drums.

This face is a lifeboat;
This is the face commanding and bearded.... it asks no odds of the
      rest;
This face is flavored fruit ready for eating;
This face of a healthy honest boy is the programme of all good.

These faces bear testimony slumbering or awake,
They show their descent from the Master himself.

Off the word I have spoken I except not one.... red white or black,
      all are deific,
In each house is the ovum.... it comes forth after a thousand years.

Spots or cracks at the windows do not disturb me,
Tall and sufficient stand behind and make signs to me;
I read the promise and patiently wait.

This is a fullgrown lily's face,
She speaks to the limber hip'd man near the garden pickets,
Come here, she blushingly cries.... Come nigh to me limber-hip'd
      man and give me your finger and thumb,
Stand at my side till I lean as high as I can upon you,
Fill me with albescent* honey.... bend down to me,
Rub to me with your chafing beard .. rub to my breast and
      shoulders.

The old face of the mother of many children:
Whist! I am fully content.

Lulled and late is the smoke of the Sabbath morning,
It hangs low over the rows of trees by the fences,
It hangs thin by the sassafras, the wildcherry and the catbrier under
    them.

I saw the rich ladies in full dress at the soiree,
I heard what the run of poets were saying so long,
Heard who sprang in crimson youth from the white froth and the
    water-blue.

Behold a woman!
She looks out from her quaker cap.... her face is clearer and more
    beautiful than the sky.

She sits in an armchair under the shaded porch of the farmhouse,
The sun just shines on her old white head.

Her ample gown is of creamhued linen,
Her grandsons raised the flax, and her granddaughters spun it with
    the distaff and the wheel.

The melodious character of the earth!
The finish beyond which philosophy cannot go and does not wish to go!
The justified mother of men!

———————————————

A* YOUNG man came to me with a message from his brother,
How should the young man know the whether and when of his
    brother?
Tell him to send me the signs.

And I stood before the young man face to face, and took his right
    hand in my left hand and his left hand in my right hand,

And I answered for his brother and for men .... and I answered for
 the poet, and sent these signs.

Him all wait for .... him all yield up to .... his word is decisive and
 final,
Him they accept .... in him lave .... in him perceive themselves as
 amid light,
Him they immerse, and he immerses them.

Beautiful women, the haughtiest nations, laws, the landscape, people
 and animals,
The profound earth and its attributes, and the unquiet ocean,
All enjoyments and properties, and money, and whatever money
 will buy,
The best farms..... others toiling and planting, and he unavoidably
 reaps,
The noblest and costliest cities .... others grading and building, and
 he domiciles there;
Nothing for any one but what is for him .... near and far are for
 him,
The ships in the offing .... the perpetual shows and marches on land
 are for him if they are for any body.

He puts things in their attitudes,
He puts today out of himself with plasticity and love,
He places his own city, times, reminiscences, parents, brothers and
 sisters, associations employment and politics, so that the rest
 never shame them afterward, nor assume to command them.

He is the answerer,
What can be answered he answers, and what cannot be answered he
 shows how it cannot be answered.

A man is a summons and challenge,
It is vain to skulk .... Do you hear that mocking and laughter? Do
 you hear the ironical echoes?

Books friendships philosophers priests action pleasure pride beat up
 and down seeking to give satisfaction;

He indicates the satisfaction, and indicates them that beat up and
    down also.

Whichever the sex . . . whatever the season or place he may go freshly
    and gently and safely by day or by night,
He has the passkey of hearts . . . . to him the response of the prying
    of hands on the knobs.

His welcome is universal . . . . the flow of beauty is not more welcome
    or universal than he is,
The person he favors by day or sleeps with at night is blessed.

Every existence has its idiom . . . . every thing has an idiom and
    tongue;
He resolves all tongues into his own, and bestows it upon men . .
    and any man translates . . and any man translates himself also:
One part does not counteract another part . . . . He is the joiner . . he
    sees how they join.

He says indifferently and alike, How are you friend? to the President
    at his levee,
And he says Good day my brother, to Cudge* that hoes in the
    sugarfield;
And both understand him and know that his speech is right.

He walks with perfect ease in the capitol,
He walks among the Congress . . . . and one representative says to
    another, Here is our equal appearing and new.

Then the mechanics take him for a mechanic,
And the soldiers suppose him to be a captain . . . . and the sailors that
    he has followed the sea,
And the authors take him for an author . . . . and the artists for an
    artist,
And the laborers perceive he could labor with them and love them;
No matter what the work is, that he is one to follow it or has
    followed it,
No matter what the nation, that he might find his brothers and
    sisters there.

The English believe he comes of their English stock,
A Jew to the Jew he seems.... a Russ to the Russ.... usual and
    near .. removed from none.

Whoever he looks at in the traveler's coffeehouse claims him,
The Italian or Frenchman is sure, and the German is sure, and the
    Spaniard is sure.... and the island Cuban is sure.

The engineer, the deckhand on the great lakes or on the Mississippi
    or St Lawrence or Sacramento or Hudson or Delaware claims
    him.

The gentleman of perfect blood acknowledges his perfect blood,
The insulter, the prostitute, the angry person, the beggar, see
    themselves in the ways of him.... he strangely transmutes
    them,
They are not vile any more.... they hardly know themselves, they
    are so grown.

You think it would be good to be the writer of melodious verses,
Well it would be good to be the writer of melodious verses;
But what are verses beyond the flowing character you could
    have?.... or beyond beautiful manners and behaviour?
Or beyond one manly or affectionate deed of an apprenticeboy? .. or
    old woman? .. or man that has been in prison or is likely to be in
    prison?

SUDDENLY* out of its stale and drowsy lair, the lair of slaves,
Like lightning Europe le'pt forth.... half startled at itself,
Its feet upon the ashes and the rags.... Its hands tight to the
    throats of kings.

O hope and faith! O aching close of lives! O many a sickened
    heart!
Turn back unto this day, and make yourselves afresh.

And you, paid to defile the People.... you liars mark:
Not for numberless agonies, murders, lusts,
For court thieving in its manifold mean forms,
Worming from his simplicity the poor man's wages;
For many a promise sworn by royal lips, And broken, and laughed at
    in the breaking,
Then in their power not for all these did the blows strike of personal
    revenge . . or the heads of the nobles fall;
The People scorned the ferocity of kings.

But the sweetness of mercy brewed bitter destruction, and the
    frightened rulers come back:
Each comes in state with his train.... hangman, priest and tax-
    gatherer.... soldier, lawyer, jailer and sycophant.

Yet behind all, lo, a Shape,
Vague as the night, draped interminably, head front and form in
    scarlet folds,
Whose face and eyes none may see,
Out of its robes only this.... the red robes, lifted by the arm,
One finger pointed high over the top, like the head of a snake
    appears.

Meanwhile corpses lie in new-made graves.... bloody corpses of
    young men:
The rope of the gibbet hangs heavily.... the bullets of princes are
    flying.... the creatures of power laugh aloud,
And all these things bear fruits.... and they are good.

Those corpses of young men,
Those martyrs that hang from the gibbets...those hearts pierced by
    the gray lead,
Cold and motionless as they seem . . live elsewhere with
    unslaughter'd vitality.

They live in other young men, O kings,
They live in brothers, again ready to defy you:
They were purified by death.... They were taught and exalted.

Not a grave of the murdered for freedom but grows seed for
     freedom.... in its turn to bear seed,
Which the winds carry afar and re-sow, and the rains and the snows
     nourish.

Not a disembodied spirit can the weapons of tyrants let loose,
But it stalks invisibly over the earth .. whispering counseling
     cautioning.

Liberty let others despair of you.... I never despair of you.

Is the house shut? Is the master away?
Nevertheless be ready.... be not weary of watching,
He will soon return.... his messengers come anon.

———————————

CLEAR the way there Jonathan!*
Way for the President's marshal! Way for the government cannon!
Way for the federal foot and dragoons.... and the phantoms
     afterward.

I rose this morning early to get betimes in Boston town;
Here's a good place at the corner.... I must stand and see the show.

I love to look on the stars and stripes.... I hope the fifes will play
     Yankee Doodle.

How bright shine the foremost with cutlasses,
Every man holds his revolver.... marching stiff through Boston
     town

A fog follows.... antiques of the same come limping,
Some appear wooden-legged and some appear bandaged and
     bloodless.

Why this is a show! It has called the dead out of the earth,
The old graveyards of the hills have hurried to see;

Uncountable phantoms gather by flank and rear of it,
Cocked hats of mothy mould and crutches made of mist,
Arms in slings and old men leaning on young men's shoulders.

What troubles you, Yankee phantoms? What is all this chattering of
    bare gums?
Does the ague convulse your limbs? Do you mistake your crutches
    for firelocks, and level them?

If you blind your eyes with tears you will not see the President's
    marshal,
If you groan such groans you might balk the government cannon.

For shame old maniacs! .... Bring down those tossed arms, and let
    your white hair be;
Here gape your smart grandsons .... their wives gaze at them from
    the windows,
See how well-dressed .... see how orderly they conduct
    themselves.

Worse and worse .... Can't you stand it? Are you retreating?
Is this hour with the living too dead for you?

Retreat then! Pell-mell! .... Back to the hills, old limpers!
I do not think you belong here anyhow.

But there is one thing that belongs here .... Shall I tell you what it
    is, gentlemen of Boston?

I will whisper it to the Mayor .... he shall send a committee to
    England,
They shall get a grant from the Parliament, and go with a cart to the
    royal vault,
Dig out King George's coffin .... unwrap him quick from the
    graveclothes .... box up his bones for a journey:
Find a swift Yankee clipper .... here is freight for you blackbellied
    clipper,
Up with your anchor! shake out your sails! .... steer straight toward
    Boston bay.

Now call the President's marshal again, and bring out the
    government cannon,
And fetch home the roarers from Congress, and make another
    procession and guard it with foot and dragoons.

Here is a centrepiece for them:
Look! all orderly citizens.... look from the windows women.

The committee open the box and set up the regal ribs and glue those
    that will not stay,
And clap the skull on top of the ribs, and clap a crown on top of the
    skull.

You have got your revenge old buster!.... The crown is come to its
    own and more than its own.

Stick your hands in your pockets Jonathan.... you are a made man
    from this day,
You are mighty cute*.... and here is one of your bargains.

THERE* was a child went forth every day,
And the first object he looked upon and received with wonder or
    pity or love or dread, that object he became,
And that object became part of him for the day or a certain
    part of the day.... or for many years or stretching cycles
    of years.

The early lilacs became part of this child,
And grass, and white and red morningglories, and white and red
    clover, and the song of the phœbe-bird,
And the March-born lambs, and the sow's pink-faint litter, and the
    mare's foal, and the cow's calf, and the noisy brood of the
    barnyard or by the mire of the pondside . . and the fish
    suspending themselves so curiously below there . . and the
    beautiful curious liquid . . and the water-plants with their
    graceful flat heads . . all became part of him.

And the field-sprouts of April and May became part of him....
    wintergrain sprouts, and those of the light-yellow corn, and of
    the esculent roots of the garden,
And the appletrees covered with blossoms, and the fruit
    afterward.... and woodberries .. and the commonest weeds by
    the road;
And the old drunkard staggering home from the outhouse of the
    tavern whence he had lately risen,
And the schoolmistress that passed on her way to the school .. and
    the friendly boys that passed .. and the quarrelsome boys .. and
    the tidy and freshcheeked girls .. and the barefoot negro boy
    and girl,
And all the changes of city and country wherever he went.

His own parents .. he that had propelled the fatherstuff at night,
    and fathered him .. and she that conceived him in her womb
    and birthed him.... they gave this child more of themselves
    than that,
They gave him afterward every day.... they and of them became
    part of him.

The mother at home quietly placing the dishes on the suppertable,
The mother with mild words.... clean her cap and gown....
    a wholesome odor falling off her person and clothes as she
    walks by:
The father, strong, selfsufficient, manly, mean, angered, unjust,
The blow, the quick loud word, the tight bargain, the crafty lure,
The family usages, the language, the company, the furniture.... the
    yearning and swelling heart,
Affection that will not be gainsayed.... The sense of what is real....
    the thought if after all it should prove unreal,
The doubts of daytime and the doubts of nighttime...the curious
    whether and how,
Whether that which appears so is so.... Or is it all flashes and
    specks?
Men and women crowding fast in the streets .. if they are not flashes
    and specks what are they?
The streets themselves, and the facades of houses.... the goods in
    the windows,

Vehicles . . teams . . the tiered wharves, and the huge crossing at the
     ferries;
The village on the highland seen from afar at sunset . . . . the river
     between,
Shadows . . aureola and mist . . light falling on roofs and gables of
     white or brown, three miles off,
The schooner near by sleepily dropping down the tide . . the little
     boat slacktowed astern,
The hurrying tumbling waves and quickbroken crests and
     slapping;
The strata of colored clouds . . . . the long bar of maroontint away
     solitary by itself . . . . the spread of purity it lies motionless in,
The horizon's edge, the flying seacrow, the fragrance of saltmarsh
     and shoremud;
These became part of that child who went forth every day, and who
     now goes and will always go forth every day,
And these become of him or her that peruses them now.

WHO* learns my lesson complete?
Boss and journeyman and apprentice? . . . . churchman and atheist?
The stupid and the wise thinker . . . . parents and offspring . . . .
     merchant and clerk and porter and customer . . . . editor, author,
     artist and schoolboy?

Draw nigh and commence,
It is no lesson . . . . it lets down the bars to a good lesson,
And that to another . . . . and every one to another still.

The great laws take and effuse without argument,
I am of the same style, for I am their friend,
I love them quits and quits . . . . I do not halt and make salaams.

I lie abstracted and hear beautiful tales of things and the reasons of
     things,
They are so beautiful I nudge myself to listen.

I cannot say to any person what I hear .... I cannot say it to
myself .... it is very wonderful.

It is no little matter, this round and delicious globe, moving so
exactly in its orbit forever and ever, without one jolt or the
untruth of a single second;
I do not think it was made in six days, nor in ten thousand years, nor
ten decillions of years,
Nor planned and built one thing after another, as an architect plans
and builds a house.

I do not think seventy years is the time of a man or woman,
Nor that seventy millions of years is the time of a man or woman,
Nor that years will ever stop the existence of me or any one else.

Is it wonderful that I should be immortal? as every one is
immortal,
I know it is wonderful .... but my eyesight is equally wonderful ....
and how I was conceived in my mother's womb is equally
wonderful,
And how I was not palpable once but am now .... and was born on
the last day of May 1819 .... and passed from a babe in the
creeping trance of three summers and three winters to articulate
and walk .... are all equally wonderful.

And that I grew six feet high .... and that I have become a man
thirty-six years old in 1855 .... and that I am here anyhow—are
all equally wonderful;
And that my soul embraces you this hour, and we affect each other
without ever seeing each other, and never perhaps to see each
other, is every bit as wonderful:
And that I can think such thoughts as these is just as wonderful,
And that I can remind you, and you think them and know them to
be true is just as wonderful,
And that the moon spins round the earth and on with the earth is
equally wonderful,
And that they balance themselves with the sun and stars is equally
wonderful.

Come I should like to hear you tell me what there is in yourself that
    is not just as wonderful,
And I should like to hear the name of anything between Sunday
    morning and Saturday night that is not just as wonderful.

GREAT* are the myths.... I too delight in them,
Great are Adam and Eve.... I too look back and accept them;
Great the risen and fallen nations, and their poets, women, sages,
    inventors, rulers, warriors and priests.

Great is liberty! Great is equality! I am their follower,
Helmsmen of nations, choose your craft.... where you sail I sail,
Yours is the muscle of life or death.... yours is the perfect
    science.... in you I have absolute faith.

Great is today, and beautiful,
It is good to live in this age.... there never was any better.

Great are the plunges and throes and triumphs and falls of
    democracy,
Great the reformers with their lapses and screams,
Great the daring and venture of sailors on new explorations.

Great are yourself and myself,
We are just as good and bad as the oldest and youngest or any,
What the best and worst did we could do,
What they felt . . do not we feel it in ourselves?
What they wished . . do we not wish the same?

Great is youth, and equally great is old age.... great are the day and
    night;
Great is wealth and great is poverty.... great is expression and great
    is silence.

Youth large lusty and loving.... youth full of grace and force and
    fascination,

Do you know that old age may come after you with equal grace and
   force and fascination?

Day fullblown and splendid .... day of the immense sun, and action
   and ambition and laughter,
The night follows close, with millions of suns, and sleep and
   restoring darkness.

Wealth with the flush hand and fine clothes and hospitality:
But then the soul's wealth—which is candor and knowledge and
   pride and enfolding love:
Who goes for men and women showing poverty richer than wealth?

Expression of speech .. in what is written or said forget not that
   silence is also expressive,
That anguish as hot as the hottest and contempt as cold as the
   coldest may be without words,
That the true adoration is likewise without words and without
   kneeling.

Great is the greatest nation .. the nation of clusters of equal
   nations.

Great is the earth, and the way it became what it is,
Do you imagine it is stopped at this? .... and the increase
   abandoned?
Understand then that it goes as far onward from this as this is from
   the times when it lay in covering waters and gases.

Great is the quality of truth in man,
The quality of truth in man supports itself through all changes,
It is inevitably in the man .... He and it are in love, and never leave
   each other.

The truth in man is no dictum .... it is vital as eyesight,
If there be any soul there is truth .... if there be man or woman
   there is truth .... If there be physical or moral there is truth,
If there be equilibrium or volition there is truth .... if there be
   things at all upon the earth there is truth.

O truth of the earth! O truth of things! I am determined to press the
  whole way toward you,
Sound your voice! I scale mountains or dive in the sea after you.

Great is language.... it is the mightiest of the sciences,
It is the fulness and color and form and diversity of the earth....
  and of men and women.... and of all qualities and processes;
It is greater than wealth.... it is greater than buildings or ships or
  religions or paintings or music.

Great is the English speech.... What speech is so great as the
  English?
Great is the English brood.... What brood has so vast a destiny as
  the English?
It is the mother of the brood that must rule the earth with the new
  rule,
The new rule shall rule as the soul rules, and as the love and justice
  and equality that are in the soul rule.

Great is the law.... Great are the old few landmarks of the law....
  they are the same in all times and shall not be disturbed.

Great are marriage, commerce, newspapers, books, freetrade, railroads,
  steamers, international mails and telegraphs and exchanges.

Great is Justice;
Justice is not settled by legislators and laws.... it is in the soul,
It cannot be varied by statutes any more than love or pride or the
  attraction of gravity can,
It is immutable .. it does not depend on majorities.... majorities or
  what not come at last before the same passionless and exact
  tribunal.

For justice are the grand natural lawyers and perfect judges.... it is
  in their souls,
It is well assorted.... they have not studied for nothing.... the great
  includes the less,
They rule on the highest grounds.... they oversee all eras and states
  and administrations,

The perfect judge fears nothing .... he could go front to front
    before God,
Before the perfect judge all shall stand back .... life and death shall
    stand back .... heaven and hell shall stand back.

Great is goodness;
I do not know what it is any more than I know what health is .... but
    I know it is great.

Great is wickedness .... I find I often admire it just as much as
    I admire goodness:
Do you call that a paradox? It certainly is a paradox.

The eternal equilibrium of things is great, and the eternal overthrow
    of things is great,
And there is another paradox.

Great is life . . and real and mystical . . wherever and whoever,
Great is death .... Sure as life holds all parts together, death holds
    all parts together;
Sure as the stars return again after they merge in the light, death is
    great as life.

FROM LEAVES OF GRASS (1856)

2—*Poem of Women**

UNFOLDED only out of the folds of the
    woman, man comes unfolded, and is always
    to come unfolded,
Unfolded only out of the superbest woman of the
    earth is to come the superbest man of the
    earth,
Unfolded out of the friendliest woman is to come
    the friendliest man,
Unfolded only out of the perfect body of a
    woman, can a man be formed of perfect body,
Unfolded only out of the inimitable poem of
    the woman can come the poems of man—
    only thence have my poems come,
Unfolded out of the strong and arrogant woman
    I love, only thence can appear the strong
    and arrogant man I love,
Unfolded by brawny embraces from the well-
    muscled woman I love, only thence come the
    brawny embraces of the man,
Unfolded out of the folds of the woman's brain,
    come all the folds of the man's brain, duly
    obedient,
Unfolded out of the justice of the woman, all jus-
    tice is unfolded,
Unfolded out of the sympathy of the woman is all
    sympathy;
A man is a great thing upon the earth, and
    through eternity—but every jot of the great-
    ness of man is unfolded out of woman,
First the man is shaped in the woman, he can
    then be shaped in himself.

3—*Poem of Salutation**

O TAKE my hand, Walt Whitman!
Such gliding wonders! Such sights and
     sounds!
Such joined unended links, each hooked to the
     next!
Each answering all, each sharing the earth
     with all.

What widens within you, Walt Whitman?
What waves and soils exuding?
What climes? what persons and lands are
     here?
Who are the infants? some playing, some slum-
     bering?
Who are the girls? Who are the married
     women?
Who are the three old men going slowly with
     their arms about each others' necks?
What rivers are these? What forests and fruits
     are these?
What are the mountains called that rise so high
     in the mists?
What myriads of dwellings are they, filled with
     dwellers?

Within me latitude widens, longitude lengthens,
Asia, Africa, Europe, are to the east—America is
     provided for in the west,
Banding the bulge of the earth winds the hot
     equator,
Curiously north and south turn the axis-ends;
Within me is the longest day, the sun wheels in
     slanting rings, it does not set for months,
Stretched in due time within me the midnight sun
     just rises above the horizon, and sinks again;
Within me zones, seas, cataracts, plains, volca-
     noes, groups,

Oceanica, Australasia, Polynesia, and the great
    West Indian islands.

What do you hear, Walt Whitman?

I hear the workman singing, and the farmer's wife
    singing,
I hear in the distance the sounds of children, and
    of animals early in the day,
I hear the inimitable music of the voices of
    mothers,
I hear the persuasions of lovers,
I hear quick rifle-cracks from the riflemen of East
    Tennessee and Kentucky, hunting on hills,
I hear emulous shouts of Australians, pursuing the
    wild horse,
I hear the Spanish dance with castanets, in
    the chestnut shade, to the rebeck and
    guitar,
I hear continual echoes from the Thames,
I hear fierce French liberty songs,
I hear of the Italian boat-sculler the musical reci-
    tative of old poems,
I hear the Virginia plantation chorus of negroes,
    of a harvest night, in the glare of pine
    knots,
I hear the strong baritone of the 'long-shore-men
    of Manahatta—I hear the stevedores unlad-
    ing the cargoes, and singing,
I hear the screams of the water-fowl of solitary
    northwest lakes,
I hear the rustling pattering of locusts, as they
    strike the grain and grass with the showers
    of their terrible clouds,
I hear the Coptic refrain toward sun-down pen-
    sively falling on the breast of the black ven-
    erable vast mother, the Nile,
I hear the bugles of raft-tenders on the streams
    of Canada,
I hear the chirp of the Mexican muleteer, and
    the bells of the mule,

I hear the Arab muezzin, calling from the top of
    the mosque,
I hear Christian priests at the altars of their
    churches—I hear the responsive base and
    soprano,
I hear the wail of utter despair of the white-
    haired Irish grand-parents, when they learn
    the death of their grand-son,
I hear the cry of the Cossack, and the sailor's
    voice, putting to sea at Okotsk,
I hear the wheeze of the slave-coffle,* as the
    slaves march on, as the husky gangs pass on
    by twos and threes, fastened together with
    wrist-chains and ankle-chains,
I hear the entreaties of women tied up for punish-
    ment, I hear the sibilant whisk of thongs
    through the air,
I hear the appeal of the greatest orator, he that
    turns states by the tip of his tongue,
I hear the Hebrew reading his records and
    psalms,
I hear the rhythmic myths of the Greeks, and
    the strong legends of the Romans,
I hear the tale of the divine life and bloody death
    of the beautiful god, the Christ,
I hear the Hindoo teaching his favorite pupil the
    loves, wars, adages, transmitted safely to this
    day from poets who wrote three thousand
    years ago.

What do you see, Walt Whitman?

Who are they you salute, and that one after
    another salute you?

I see a great round wonder rolling through the
    air,
I see diminute farms, hamlets, ruins, grave-yards,
    jails, factories, palaces, hovels, huts of barba-
    rians, tents of nomads, upon the surface,

I see the shaded part on one side where the
sleepers are sleeping, and the sun-lit part on
the other side,
I see the curious silent change of the light and
shade,
I see distant lands, as real and near to the
inhabitants of them as my land is to me.

I see plenteous waters,
I see mountain peaks—I see the sierras of
Andes and Alleghanies, I see where they
range,
I see plainly the Himmalehs, Chian Shahs, Al-
tays, Gauts,
I see the Rocky Mountains, and the Peak of
Winds,
I see the Styrian Alps and the Karnac Alps,
I see the Pyrenees, Balks, Carpathians, and to
the north the Dofrafields, and off at sea
Mount Hecla,
I see Vesuvius and Etna—I see the Anahuacs,
I see the Mountains of the Moon, and the Snow
Mountains, and the Red Mountains of Mada-
gascar,
I see the Vermont hills, and the long string of
Cordilleras;
I see the vast deserts of Western America,
I see the Libyan, Arabian, and Asiatic deserts;
I see huge dreadful Arctic and Antarctic icebergs,
I see the superior oceans and the inferior ones—
the Atlantic and Pacific, the sea of Mexico,
the Brazilian sea, and the sea of Peru,
The Japan waters, those of Hindostan, the China
Sea, and the Gulf of Guinea,
The spread of the Baltic, Caspian, Bothnia, the
British shores, and the Bay of Biscay,
The clear-sunned Mediterranean, and from one to
another of its islands,
The inland fresh-tasted seas of North America,
The White Sea, and the sea around Greenland.

I behold the mariners of the world,
Some are in storms, some in the night, with
    the watch on the look-out, some drifting
    helplessly, some with contagious diseases.

I behold the steam-ships of the world,
Some double the Cape of Storms, some Cape
    Verde, others Cape Guardafui, Bon, or Baja-
    dore,
Others Dondra Head, others pass the Straits of
    Sunda, others Cape Lopatka, others Beh-
    ring's Straits,
Others Cape Horn, others the Gulf of Mexico, or
    along Cuba or Hayti, others Hudson's Bay or
    Baffin's Bay,
Others pass the Straits of Dover, others enter the
    Wash, others the Firth of Solway, others
    round Cape Clear, others the Land's End,
Others traverse the Zuyder Zee or the Scheld,
Others add to the exits and entrances at Sandy
    Hook,
Others to the comers and goers at Gibraltar or the
    Dardanelles,
Others sternly push their way through the north-
    ern winter-packs,
Others descend or ascend the Obi or the Lena,
Others the Niger or the Congo, others the Hoang-
    ho and Amoor, others the Indus, the Buram-
    pooter and Cambodia,
Others wait at the wharves of Manahatta,
    steamed up, ready to start,
Wait swift and swarthy in the ports of Australia,
Wait at Liverpool, Glasgow, Dublin, Marseilles,
    Lisbon, Naples, Hamburgh, Bremen, Bor-
    deaux, the Hague, Copenhagen,
Wait at Valparaiso, Rio Janeiro, Panama,
Wait at their moorings at Boston, Philadelphia,
    Baltimore, Charleston, New Orleans, Galves-
    ton, San Francisco.

I see the tracks of the rail-roads of the earth,
I see them welding state to state, county to
    county, city to city, through North America,
I see them in Great Britain, I see them in Eu-
    rope,
I see them in Asia and in Africa.

I see the electric telegraphs of the earth,
I see the filaments of the news of the wars,
    deaths, losses, gains, passions, of my race.

I see the long thick river-stripes of the earth,
I see where the Mississippi flows, I see where
    the Columbia flows,
I see the St. Lawrence and the falls of Niagara,
I see the Amazon and the Paraguay,
I see where the Seine flows, and where the
    Loire, the Rhone, and the Guadalquivir
    flow,
I see the windings of the Volga, the Dnieper,
    the Oder,
I see the Tuscan going down the Arno, and the
    Venetian along the Po,
I see the Greek seaman sailing out of Egina bay.

I see the site of the great old empire of Assyria,
    and that of Persia, and that of India,
I see the falling of the Ganges over the high rim
    of Saukara.

I see the place of the idea of the Deity incarnated
    by avatars* in human forms,
I see the spots of the successions of priests on the
    earth, oracles, sacrificers, brahmins, sabians
    lamas, monks, muftis, exhorters,
I see where druids walked the groves of Mona, I
    see the misletoe and vervain,*
I see the temples of the deaths of the bodies of
    gods, I see the old signifiers,

I see Christ once more eating the bread of his last
    supper in the midst of youths and old persons,
I see where the strong divine young man, the Her-
    cules, toiled faithfully and long, and then died,
I see the place of the innocent rich life and hap-
    less fate of the beautiful nocturnal son, the
    full-limbed Bacchus,
I see Kneph, blooming, dressed in blue, with the
    crown of feathers on his head,
I see Hermes, unsuspected, dying, well-beloved,
    saying to the people, Do not weep for me,
    this is not my true country, I have lived
    banished from my true country, I now go
    back there, I return to the celestial sphere
    where every one goes in his turn.

I see the battle-fields of the earth—grass grows
    upon them, and blossoms and corn,
I see the tracks of ancient and modern expedi-
    tions.
I see the nameless masonries, venerable messages
    of the unknown events, heroes, records of the
    earth.

I see the places of the sagas,
I see pine-trees and fir-trees torn by northern
    blasts,
I see granite boulders and cliffs, I see green mea-
    dows and lakes,
I see the burial-cairns of Scandinavian warriors,
I see them raised high with stones, by the marge
    of restless oceans, that the dead men's spirits,
    when they wearied of their quiet graves,
    might rise up through the mounds, and gaze
    on the tossing billows, and be refreshed by
    storms, immensity, liberty, action.

I see the steppes of Asia,
I see the tumuli of Mongolia, I see the tents of
    Kalmucks and Baskirs,

I see the nomadic tribes with herds of oxen and
    cows,
I see the table-lands notched with ravines, I see
    the jungles and deserts,
I see the camel, the wild steed, the bustard, the
    fat-tailed sheep, the antelope, and the bur-
    rowing wolf.

I see the high-lands of Abyssinia,
I see flocks of goats feeding, I see the fig-tree,
    tamarind, date,
I see fields of teff-wheat, I see the places of
    verdure and gold.

I see the Brazilian vaquero,
I see the Bolivian ascending Mount Sorata,
I see the Guacho crossing the plains, I see the
    incomparable rider of horses with his lasso
    on his arm,
I see over the pampas the pursuit of wild cattle
    for their hides.

I see the little and large sea-dots, some inhabited,
    some uninhabited;
I see two boats with nets, lying off the shore of
    Paumanok,* quite still,
I see ten fishermen waiting—they discover now
    a thick school of mossbonkers, they drop
    the joined seine-ends in the water,
The boats separate, they diverge and row off,
    each on its rounding course to the beach,
    enclosing the mossbonkers,
The net is drawn in by a windlass by those
    who stop ashore,
Some of the fishermen lounge in the boats,
    others stand negligently ankle-deep in the
    water, poised on strong legs,
The boats are partly drawn up, the water slaps
    against them,

On the sand, in heaps and winrows,* well out from
    the water, lie the green-backed spotted moss-
    bonkers.

I see the despondent red man in the west,
    lingering about the banks of Moingo, and
    about Lake Pepin,
He has beheld the quail and honey-bee, and
    sadly prepared to depart.

I see the regions of snow and ice,
I see the sharp-eyed Samoiede and the Finn,
I see the seal-seeker in his boat, poising his
    lance,
I see the Siberian on his slight-built sledge, drawn
    by dogs,
I see the porpoise-hunters, I see the whale-crews
    of the South Pacific and the North Atlantic,
I see the cliffs, glaciers, torrents, valleys, of Switz-
    erland—I mark the long winters and the
    isolation.

I see the cities of the earth, and make myself a
    part of them,
I am a real Londoner, Parisian, Viennese,
I am a habitan of St. Petersburgh, Berlin, Con-
    stantinople,
I am of Adelaide, Sidney, Melbourne,
I am of Manchester, Bristol, Edinburgh, Limerick,
I am of Madrid, Cadiz, Barcelona, Oporto, Lyons,
    Brussels, Berne, Frankfort, Stuttgart, Turin,
    Florence,
I belong in Moscow, Cracow, Warsaw—or north-
    ward in Christiana or Stockholm—or in
    some street in Iceland,
I descend upon all those cities, and rise from them
    again.

I see vapors exhaling from unexplored coun-
    tries,

I see the savage types, the bow and arrow, the
    poisoned splint, the fetish and the obi.

I see African and Asiatic towns,
I see Algiers, Tripoli, Derne, Mogadore, Timbuc-
    too, Monrovia,
I see the swarms of Pekin, Canton, Benares,
    Delhi, Calcutta,
I see the Kruman in his hut, and the Dahoman
    and Ashantee-man in their huts,
I see the Turk smoking opium in Aleppo,
I see the picturesque crowds at the fairs of Khiva,
    and those of Herat,
I see Teheran, I see Muscat and Medina, and the
    intervening sands—I see the caravans toil-
    ing onward;
I see Egypt and the Egyptians, I see the pyramids
    and obelisks,
I look on chiselled histories, songs, philosophies,
    cut in slabs of sand-stone or granite blocks,
I see at Memphis mummy-pits, containing mum-
    mies, embalmed, swathed in linen cloth, lying
    there many centuries,
I look on the fall'n Theban, the large-ball'd eyes,
    the side-drooping neck, the hands folded
    across the breast.

I see the menials of the earth, laboring,
I see the prisoners in the prisons,
I see the defective human bodies of the earth,
I see the blind, the deaf and dumb, idiots, hunch-
    backs, lunatics,
I see the pirates, thieves, betrayers, murderers,
    slave-makers of the earth,
I see the helpless infants, and the helpless old
    men and women.

I see male and female everywhere,
I see the serene brotherhood of philosophs,

I see the constructiveness of my race,
I see the results of the perseverance and industry
    of my race,
I see ranks, colors, barbarisms, civilizations—I
    go among them, I mix indiscriminately,
And I salute all the inhabitants of the earth.

You, inevitable where you are!
You daughter or son of England!
You free man of Australia! you of Tasmania! you
    of Papua! you free woman of the same!
You of the mighty Slavic tribes and empires! you
    Russ in Russia!
You dim-descended, black, divine-souled African,
    large, fine-headed, nobly-formed, superbly
    destined, on equal terms with me!
You Norwegian! Swede! Dane! Icelander! you
    Prussian!
You Spaniard of Spain! you Portuguese!
You Frenchwoman and Frenchman of France!
You Belge! you liberty-lover of the Netherlands!
You sturdy Austrian! you Lombard! Hun! Bohe-
    mian! farmer of Styria!
You neighbor of the Danube!
You working-man of the Rhine, the Elbe, or the
    Weser! you working-woman too!
You Sardinian! you Bavarian! you Swabian!
    Saxon! Wallachian! Bulgarian!
You citizen of Prague! you Roman! Napolitan!
    Greek!
You lithe matador in the arena at Seville!
You mountaineer living lawlessly on the Taurus
    or Caucasus!
You Bokh horse-herd watching your mares and
    stallions feeding!
You beautiful-bodied Persian, at full speed in the
    saddle, shooting arrows to the mark!
You Chinaman and Chinawoman of China! you
    Tartar of Tartary!

You women of the earth, subordinated at your
    tasks!
You Jew journeying in your old age through every
    risk to stand once on Syrian ground!
You other Jews waiting in all lands for your
    Messiah!
You thoughtful Armenian pondering by some
    stream of the Euphrates! you peering amid
    the ruins of Nineveh! you ascending Mount
    Ararat!
You foot-worn pilgrim welcoming the far-away
    sparkle of the minarets of Mecca!
You sheiks along the stretch from Suez to Babel-
    mandel, ruling your families and tribes!
You olive-grower tending your fruit on fields off
    Nazareth, Damascus, or Lake Tiberias!
You Thibet trader on the wide inland, or bargain-
    ing in the shops of Lassa!
You Japanese man or woman! you liver in
    Madagascar, Ceylon, Sumatra, Borneo!
All you continentals of Asia, Africa, Europe,
    Australia, indifferent of place!
All you on the numberless islands of the archi-
    pelagoes of the sea!
And you of centuries hence, when you listen to me!
And you everywhere whom I specify not, but in-
    clude just the same!
I salute you for myself and for America.

Each of us inevitable,
Each of us limitless—each of us with his or her
    right upon the earth,
Each of us allowed the eternal purport of the earth,
Each of us here as divinely as any is here.

You Hottentot with clicking palate!
You woolly-haired hordes! you white or black
    owners of slaves!
You owned persons dropping sweat-drops or
    blood-drops!

You felons, deformed persons, idiots!
You human forms with the fathomless ever-
    impressive countenances of brutes!
You poor koboo* whom the meanest of the rest
    look down upon, for all your glimmering
    language and spirituality!
You low expiring aborigines of the hills of Utah,
    Oregon, California!
You dwarfed Kamskatkan, Greenlander, Lapp!
You Austral negro, naked, red, sooty, with pro-
    trusive lip, grovelling, seeking your food!
You Caffre, Berber, Soudanese!
You haggard, uncouth, untutored Bedowee!
You plague-swarms in Madras, Nankin, Kaubul,
    Cairo!
You bather bathing in the Ganges!
You benighted roamer of Amazonia! you Pat-
    agonian! you Fegee-man!
You peon of Mexico! you Russian serf! you
    quadroon of Carolina, Texas, Tennessee!
I do not refuse you my hand, or prefer others
    before you,
I do not say one word against you.

My spirit has passed in compassion and deter-
    mination around the whole earth,
I have looked for brothers, sisters, lovers, and
    found them ready for me in all lands.

I think I have risen with you, you vapors, and
    moved away to distant continents, and fallen
    down there, for reasons,
I think I have blown with you, you winds,
I think, you waters, I have fingered every shore
    with you,
I think I have run through what any river or strait
    of the globe has run through,
I think I have taken my stand on the bases of
    peninsulas, and on imbedded rocks.

What cities the light or warmth penetrates, I
    penetrate those cities myself,
All islands to which birds wing their way, I
    wing my way myself,
I find my home wherever there are any homes of
    men.

5—Broad-Axe Poem*

BROAD-AXE, shapely, naked, wan!
Head from the mother's bowels drawn!
Wooded flesh and metal bone! limb only one and
    lip only one!
Gray-blue leaf by red-heat grown! helve* produced
    from a little seed sown!
Resting, the grass amid and upon,
To be leaned, and to lean on.

Strong shapes, and attributes of strong shapes,
    masculine trades, sights and sounds,
Long varied train of an emblem, dabs of music,
Fingers of the organist skipping staccato over the
    keys of the great organ.

Welcome are all earth's lands, each for its kind,
Welcome are lands of pine and oak,
Welcome are lands of the lemon and fig,
Welcome are lands of gold,
Welcome are lands of wheat and maize—welcome
    those of the grape,
Welcome are lands of sugar and rice,
Welcome the cotton-lands—welcome those of the
    white potato and sweet potato,
Welcome are mountains, flats, sands, forests, prai-
    ries,
Welcome the rich borders of rivers, table-lands,
    openings,
Welcome the measureless grazing lands—wel-
    come the teeming soil of orchards, flax,
    honey, hemp,

Welcome just as much the other more hard-faced
     lands,
Lands rich as lands of gold, or wheat and fruit
     lands,
Lands of mines, lands of the manly and rugged ores,
Lands of coal, copper, lead, tin, zinc,
Lands of iron! lands of the make of the axe!

The log at the wood-pile, the axe supported by it,
The sylvan hut, the vine over the doorway, the
     space cleared for a garden,
The irregular tapping of rain down on the leaves,
     after the storm is lulled,
The wailing and moaning at intervals, the thought
     of the sea,
The thought of ships struck in the storm, and put
     on their beam-ends, and the cutting away of
     masts;
The sentiment of the huge timbers of old-fashioned
     houses and barns;
The remembered print or narrative, the voyage at
     a venture of men, families, goods,
The disembarcation, the founding of a new city,
The voyage of those who sought a New England
     and found it,
The Year 1 of These States, the weapons that year
     began with, scythe, pitch-fork, club, horse-
     pistol,
The settlements of the Arkansas, Colorado, Ottawa,
     Willamette,
The slow progress, the scant fare, the axe, rifle,
     saddle-bags;
The beauty of all adventurous and daring per-
     sons,
The beauty of wood-boys and wood-men, with
     their clear untrimmed faces,
The beauty of independence, departure, actions
     that rely on themselves,
The American contempt for statutes and cere-
     monies, the boundless impatience of restraint,

The loose drift of character, the inkling through
    random types, the solidification;
The butcher in the slaughter-house, the hands
    aboard schooners and sloops, the rafts-man,
    the pioneer,
Lumber-men in their winter camp, day-break in the
    woods, stripes of snow on the limbs of trees,
    the occasional snapping,
The glad clear sound of one's own voice, the
    merry song, the natural life of the woods, the
    strong day's work,
The blazing fire at night, the sweet taste of supper,
    the talk, the bed of hemlock boughs, and the
    bear-skin;
The house-builder at work in cities or anywhere,
The preparatory jointing, squaring, sawing, mor-
    tising,
The hoist-up of beams, the push of them in their
    places, laying them regular,
Setting the studs by their tenons in the mortises,
    according as they were prepared,
The blows of mallets and hammers, the attitudes
    of the men, their curved limbs,
Bending, standing, astride the beams, driving in
    pins, holding on by posts and braces,
The hooked arm over the plate, the other arm
    wielding the axe,
The floor-men forcing the planks close, to be
    nailed,
Their postures bringing their weapons downward
    on the bearers,
The echoes resounding through the vacant building;
The huge store-house carried up in the city, well
    under way,
The six framing-men, two in the middle and two
    at each end, carefully bearing on their
    shoulders a heavy stick for a cross-beam,
The crowded line of masons with trowels in their
    right hands rapidly laying the long side-wall,
    two hundred feet from front to rear,

The flexible rise and fall of backs, the continual
    click of the trowels and bricks,

The bricks, one after another, each laid so work-
    man-like in its place, and set with a knock of
    the trowel-handle,

The piles of materials, the mortar on the mortar-
    boards, and the steady replenishing by the
    hod-men;*

Spar-makers in the spar-yard, the swarming row
    of well-grown apprentices,

The swing of their axes on the square-hewed
    log, shaping it toward the shape of a
    mast,

The brisk short crackle of the steel driven slant-
    ingly into the pine,

The butter-colored chips flying off in great flakes
    and slivers,

The limber motion of brawny young arms and hips
    in easy costumes;

The constructor of wharves, bridges, piers, bulk-
    heads, floats, stays against the sea;

The city fire-man—the fire that suddenly bursts
    forth in the close-packed square,

The arriving engines, the hoarse shouts, the
    nimble stepping and daring,

The strong command through the fire-trumpets,
    the forming in line, the echoed rise and fall
    of the arms forcing the water,

The slender, spasmic blue-white jets—the bring-
    ing to bear of the hooks and ladders, and
    their execution,

The crash and cut away of connecting wood-work,
    or through floors, if the fire smoulders under
    them,

The crowd with their lit faces, watching—the
    glare and dense shadows;

The forger at his forge-furnace, and the user of
    iron after him,

The maker of the axe large and small, and the
    welder and temperer,

The chooser breathing his breath on the cold
    steel and trying the edge with his thumb,
The one who clean-shapes the handle and sets it
    firmly in the socket,
The shadowy processions of the portraits of the
    past users also,
The primal patient mechanics, the architects and
    engineers,
The far-off Assyrian edifice and Mizra edifice,
The Roman lictors preceding the consuls,
The antique European warrior with his axe in
    combat,
The uplifted arm, the clatter of blows on the
    helmeted head,
The death-howl, the limpsey tumbling, the
    rush of friend and foe thither,
The siege of revolted lieges determined for lib-
    erty,
The summons to surrender, the battering at castle
    gates, the truce and parley,
The sack of an old city in its time,
The bursting in of mercenaries and bigots tumult-
    uously and disorderly,
Roar, flames, blood, drunkenness, madness,
Goods freely rifled from houses and temples,
    screams of women in the gripe of brigands,
Craft and thievery of camp-followers, men running,
    old persons despairing,
The hell of war, the cruelties of creeds,
The list of all executive deeds and words, just or
    unjust,
The power of personality, just or unjust.

Muscle and pluck forever!
What invigorates life, invigorates death,
And the dead advance as much as the living
    advance,
And the future is no more uncertain than the
    present,

And the roughness of the earth and of man en-
　　closes as much as the delicatesse of the earth
　　and of man,
And nothing endures but personal qualities.

What do you think endures?
Do you think the greatest city endures?
Or a teeming manufacturing state? or a prepared
　　constitution? or the best built steam-ships?
Or hotels of granite and iron? or any chef-
　　d'oeuvres of engineering, forts, armaments?

Away! These are not to be cherished for them-
　　selves,
They fill their hour, the dancers dance, the musi-
　　cians play for them,
The show passes, all does well enough of course,
All does very well till one flash of defiance.

The greatest city is that which has the greatest
　　man or woman,
If it be a few ragged huts, it is still the greatest
　　city in the whole world.

The place where the greatest city stands is not
　　the place of stretched wharves, docks, manu-
　　factures, deposites of produce,
Nor the place of ceaseless salutes of new-comers,
　　or the anchor-lifters of the departing,
Nor the place of the tallest and costliest build-
　　ings, or shops selling goods from the rest of
　　the earth,
Nor the place of the best libraries and schools,
　　nor the place where money is plentiest,
Nor the place of the most numerous population.

Where the city stands with the brawniest breed
　　of orators and bards,
Where the city stands that is beloved by these,
　　and loves them in return, and understands
　　them,

Where these may be seen going every day in the
    streets, with their arms familiar to the shoul-
    ders of their friends,
Where no monuments exist to heroes but in the
    common words and deeds,
Where thrift is in its place, and prudence is in its
    place,
Where behavior is the finest of the fine arts,
Where the men and women think lightly of the
    laws,
Where the slave ceases and the master of slaves
    ceases,
Where the populace rise at once against the auda-
    city of elected persons,
Where fierce men and women pour forth as the
    sea to the whistle of death pours its sweeping
    and unript waves,
Where outside authority enters always after the
    precedence of inside authority,
Where the citizen is always the head and ideal,
    and President, Mayor, Governor, and what
    not, are agents for pay,
Where children are taught from the jump that
    they are to be laws to themselves, and to
    depend on themselves,
Where equanimity is illustrated in affairs,
Where speculations on the soul are encouraged,
Where women walk in public processions in the
    streets the same as the men,
Where they enter the public assembly and take
    places the same as the men, and are appealed
    to by the orators the same as the men,
Where the city of the faithfulest friends stands,
Where the city of the cleanliness of the sexes
    stands,
Where the city of the healthiest fathers stands,
Where the city of the best-bodied mothers stands,
There the greatest city stands.

How beggarly appear poems, arguments, orations,
    before an electric deed!
How the floridness of the materials of cities
    shrivels before a man's or woman's look!

All waits, or goes by default, till a strong being
    appears;
A strong being is the proof of the race, and of the
    ability of the universe,
When he or she appears, materials are over-
    awed,
The dispute on the soul stops,
The old customs and phrases are confronted,
    turned back, or laid away.

What is your money-making now? What can it
    do now?
What is your respectability now?
What are your theology, tuition, society, traditions,
    statute-books now?
Where are your jibes of being now?
Where are your cavils about the soul now?

Was that your best? Were those your vast and
    solid?
Riches, opinions, politics, institutions, to part obe-
    diently from the path of one man or woman!
The centuries, and all authority, to be trod under
    the foot-soles of one man or woman!

—A sterile landscape covers the ore—there is as
    good as the best, for all the forbidding
    appearance,
There is the mine, there are the miners,
The forge-furnace is there, the melt is accom-
    plished, the hammers-men are at hand with
    their tongs and hammers,
What always served and always serves, is at hand.

Than this nothing has better served—it has served
    all,

Served the fluent-tongued and subtle-sensed
    Greek, and long ere the Greek,
Served in building the buildings that last longer
    than any,
Served the Hebrew, the Persian, the most ancient
    Hindostanee,
Served the mound-raiser on the Mississippi,
    served those whose relics remain in Central
    America,
Served Albic temples in woods or on plains, with
    unhewn pillars, and the druids, and the
    bloody body laid in the hollow of the great
    stone,
Served the artificial clefts, vast, high, silent, on
    the snow-covered hills of Scandinavia,
Served those who, time out of mind, made on the
    granite walls rough sketches of the sun,
    moon, stars, ships, ocean-waves,
Served the paths of the irruptions of the Goths,
    served the pastoral tribes and nomads,
Served the incalculably distant Celt, served the
    hardy pirates of the Baltic,
Served before any of those, the venerable and
    harmless men of Ethiopia,
Served the making of helms for the galleys
    of pleasure, and the making of those for
    war,
Served all great works on land, and all great
    works on the sea,
For the medieval ages, and before the medieval
    ages,
Served not the living only, then as now, but
    served the dead.

I see the European headsman,
He stands masked, clothed in red, with huge legs,
    and strong naked arms,
And leans on a ponderous axe.

Whom have you slaughtered lately, European
    headsman?
Whose is that blood upon you, so wet and
    sticky?

I see the clear sun-sets of the martyrs,
I see from the scaffolds the descending
    ghosts,
Ghosts of dead princes, uncrowned ladies, im-
    peached ministers, rejected kings,
Rivals, traitors, poisoners, disgraced chieftains,
    and the rest.

I see those who in any land have died for the
    good cause,
The seed is spare, nevertheless the crop shall
    never run out,
Mind you, O foreign kings, O priests, the crop
    shall never run out.

I see the blood washed entirely away from the
    axe,
Both blade and helve are clean,
They spirt no more the blood of European nobles,
    —they clasp no more the necks of queens.

I see the headsman withdraw and become use-
    less,
I see the scaffold untrodden and mouldy, I see no
    longer any axe upon it,
I see the mighty and friendly emblem of the power
    of my own race, the newest largest race.

America! I do not vaunt my love for you,
I have what I have.

The axe leaps!
The solid forest gives fluid utterances,
They tumble forth, they rise and form,
Hut, tent, landing, survey,
Flail, plough, pick, crowbar, spade,

Shingle, rail, prop, wainscot, jamb, lath, panel,
 gable,
Citadel, ceiling, saloon, academy, organ, exhibi-
 tion-house, library,
Cornice, trellis, pilaster, balcony, window, shutter,
 turret, porch,
Hoe, rake, pitch-fork, pencil, wagon, staff, saw,
 jackplane, mallet, wedge, rounce,
Chair, tub, hoop, table, wicket, vane, sash, floor,
Work-box, chest, stringed instrument, boat, frame,
 and what not,
Capitols of States, and capitol of the nation of
 States,
Long stately rows in avenues, hospitals for or-
 phans or for the poor or sick,
Manhattan steamboats and clippers, taking the
 measure of all seas.

The shapes arise!
Shapes of the using of axes anyhow, and the
 users, and all that neighbors them,
Cutters down of wood, and haulers of it to the
 Penobscot, or St. John's, or Kennebec,
Dwellers in cabins among the Californian moun-
 tains, or by the little lakes,
Dwellers south on the banks of the Gila or Rio
 Grande—friendly gatherings, the characters
 and fun,
Dwellers up north in Minnesota and by the
 Yellowstone river, dwellers on coasts and
 off coasts,
Seal-fishers, whalers, arctic seamen breaking pas-
 sages through the ice.

The shapes arise!
Shapes of factories, arsenals, foundries, markets,
Shapes of the two-threaded tracks of railroads,
Shapes of the sleepers of bridges, vast frame-
 works, girders, arches,

Shapes of the fleets of barges, tows, lake craft,
river craft.

The shapes arise!
Ship-yards and dry-docks along the Atlantic and
Pacific, and in many a bay and by-place,
The live-oak kelsons, the pine planks, the spars,
the hackmatuck-roots for knees,*
The ships themselves on their ways, the tiers of
scaffolds, the workmen busy outside and in-
side,
The tools lying around, the great augur and little
augur, the adze, bolt, line, square, gouge,
bead-plane.

The shapes arise!
The shape measured, sawed, jacked, joined,
stained,
The coffin-shape for the dead to lie within in his
shroud;
The shape got out in posts, in the bedstead posts,
in the posts of the bride's-bed,
The shape of the little trough, the shape of the
rockers beneath, the shape of the babe's
cradle,
The shape of the floor-planks, the floor-planks for
dancers' feet,
The shape of the planks of the family home, the
home of the friendly parents and children,
The shape of the roof of the home of the happy
young man and woman, the roof over the well-
married young man and woman,
The roof over the supper joyously cooked by the
chaste wife, and joyously eaten by the chaste
husband, content after his day's work.

The shapes arise!
The shape of the prisoner's place in the court-
room, and of him or her seated in the place,

The shape of the pill-box, the disgraceful oint-
　　ment-box, the nauseous application, and him
　　or her applying it,
The shape of the liquor-bar leaned against by the
　　young rum-drinker and the old rum-drinker,
The shape of the shamed and angry stairs, trod
　　by sneaking footsteps,
The shape of the sly settee, and the adulterous
　　unwholesome couple,
The shape of the gambling board with its devilish
　　winnings and losings,
The shape of the slats of the bed of a corrupted
　　body, the bed of the corruption of gluttony or
　　alcoholic drinks,
The shape of the step-ladder for the convicted
　　and sentenced murderer, the murderer with
　　haggard face and pinioned arms,
The sheriff at hand with his deputies, the silent
　　and white-lipped crowd, the sickening dan-
　　gling of the rope.

The shapes arise!
Shapes of doors giving so many exits and
　　entrances,
The door passing the dissevered friend, flushed,
　　and in haste,
The door that admits good news and bad news,
The door whence the son left home, confident and
　　puffed up,
The door he entered from a long and scandalous
　　absence, diseased, broken down, without in-
　　nocence, without means.

Their shapes arise, the shapes of full-sized men!
Men taciturn yet loving, used to the open air, and
　　the manners of the open air,
Saying their ardor in native forms, saying the old
　　response,
Take what I have then, (saying fain,) take the pay
　　you approached for,

Take the white tears of my blood, if that is what
you are after.

Her shape arises!
She, less guarded than ever, yet more guarded
than ever,
The gross and soiled she moves among do not
make her gross and soiled,
She knows the thoughts as she passes, nothing is
concealed from her,
She is none the less considerate or friendly there-
fore,
She is the best-beloved, it is without exception,
she has no reason to fear, and she does not
fear,
Oaths, quarrels, hiccuped songs, smutty expres-
sions, are idle to her as she passes,
She is silent, she is possessed of herself, they do
not offend her,
She receives them as the laws of nature receive
them, she is strong,
She too is a law of nature, there is no law greater
than she is.

His shape arises!
Arrogant, masculine, naive, rowdyish,
Laugher, weeper, worker, idler, citizen, country-
man,
Saunterer of woods, stander upon hills, summer
swimmer in rivers or by the sea,
Of pure American breed, of reckless health, his
body perfect, free from taint from top to toe,
free forever from headache and dyspepsia,
clean-breathed,
Ample-limbed, a good feeder, weight a hundred
and eighty pounds, full-blooded, six feet high,
forty inches round the breast and back,
Countenance sun-burnt, bearded, calm, unrefined,
Reminder of animals, meeter of savage and gen-
tleman on equal terms,

Attitudes lithe and erect, costume free, neck open,
  of slow movement on foot,
Passer of his right arm round the shoulders of his
  friends, companion of the street,
Persuader always of people to give him their
  sweetest touches, and never their meanest,
A Manhattanese bred, fond of Brooklyn, fond of
  Broadway, fond of the life of the wharves
  and the great ferries,
Enterer everywhere, welcomed everywhere, eas-
  ily understood after all,
Never offering others, always offering himself,
  corroborating his phrenology,
Voluptuous, inhabitive, combative, conscientious,
  alimentive, intuitive, of copious friendship,
  sublimity, firmness, self-esteem, comparison,
  individuality, form, locality, eventuality,
Avowing by life, manners, works, to contribute
  illustrations of results of The States,
Teacher of the unquenchable creed, namely,
  egotism,
Inviter of others continually henceforth to try
  their strength against his.

The shapes arise!
Shapes of America, shapes of centuries,
Shapes of those that do not joke with life, but are
  in earnest with life,
Shapes ever projecting other shapes,
Shapes of a hundred Free States, begetting
  another hundred north and south,
Shapes of the turbulent manly cities,
Shapes of the untamed breed of young men and
  natural persons,
Shapes of women fit for These States,
Shapes of the composition of all the varieties of
  the earth,
Shapes of the friends and home-givers of the
  whole earth,

Shapes bracing the whole earth, and braced with
    the whole earth.

9—Poem of Wonder at The Resurrection of The Wheat*

SOMETHING startles me where I thought I
    was safest,
I withdraw from the still woods I loved,
I will not go now on the pastures to walk,
I will not strip my clothes from my body to meet
    my lover the sea,
I will not touch my flesh to the earth, as to other
    flesh, to renew me.

How can the ground not sicken of men?
How can you be alive, you growths of spring?
How can you furnish health, you blood of herbs,
    roots, orchards, grain?
Are they not continually putting distempered
    corpses in the earth?
Is not every continent worked over and over with
    sour dead?
Where have you disposed of those carcasses of
    the drunkards and gluttons of so many gen-
    erations?
Where have you drawn off all the foul liquid and
    meat?
I do not see any of it upon you today—or per-
    haps I am deceived,
I will run a furrow with my plough—I will press
    my spade through the sod, and turn it up
    underneath,
I am sure I shall expose some of the foul meat.

Behold!
This is the compost of billions of premature
    corpses,

Perhaps every mite has once formed part of a
    sick person,
Yet Behold!
The grass covers the prairies,
The bean bursts noiselessly through the mould in
    the garden,
The delicate spear of the onion pierces upward,
The apple-buds cluster together on the apple-
    branches,
The resurrection of the wheat appears with pale
    visage out of its graves,
The tinge awakes over the willow-tree and the
    mulberry-tree,
The he-birds carol mornings and evenings, while
    the she-birds sit on their nests,
The young of poultry break through the hatched
    eggs,
The new-born of animals appear, the calf is
    dropt from the cow, the colt from the mare,
Out of its little hill faithfully rise the potato's
    dark green leaves,
Out of its hill rises the yellow maize-stalk;
The summer growth is innocent and disdainful
    above all those strata of sour dead.

What chemistry!
That the winds are really not infectious!
That this is no cheat, this transparent green-wash
    of the sea, which is so amorous after me!
That it is safe to allow it to lick my naked
    body all over with its tongues!
That it will not endanger me with the fevers that
    have deposited themselves in it!
That all is clean, forever and forever!
That the cool drink from the well tastes so good!
That blackberries are so flavorous and juicy!
That the fruits of the apple-orchard, and of the
    orange-orchard—that melons, grapes, peaches,
    plums, will none of them poison me!

That when I recline on the grass I do not catch
    any disease!
Though probably every spear of grass rises out
    of what was once a catching disease.

Now I am terrified at the earth! it is that calm
    and patient,
It grows such sweet things out of such corrup-
    tions,
It turns harmless and stainless on its axis, with
    such endless successions of diseased corpses,
It distils such exquisite winds out of such infused
    fetor,
It renews with such unwitting looks, its prodigal,
    annual, sumptuous crops,
It gives such divine materials to men, and accepts
    such leavings from them at last.

*11—Sun-Down Poem**

FLOOD-TIDE of the river, flow on! I watch
    you, face to face,
Clouds of the west! sun half an hour high! I see
    you also face to face.

Crowds of men and women attired in the usual
    costumes, how curious you are to me!
On the ferry-boats the hundreds and hundreds
    that cross are more curious to me than you
    suppose,
And you that shall cross from shore to shore
    years hence, are more to me, and more in my
    meditations, than you might suppose.

The impalpable sustenance of me from all things
    at all hours of the day,
The simple, compact, well-joined scheme—my-
    self disintegrated, every one disintegrated,
    yet part of the scheme,

The similitudes of the past and those of the
    future,
The glories strung like beads on my smallest
    sights and hearings—on the walk in the
    street, and the passage over the river,
The current rushing so swiftly, and swimming
    with me far away,
The others that are to follow me, the ties between
    me and them,
The certainty of others—the life, love, sight,
    hearing of others.

Others will enter the gates of the ferry, and cross
    from shore to shore,
Others will watch the run of the flood-tide,
Others will see the shipping of Manhattan north
    and west, and the heights of Brooklyn to the
    south and east,
Others will see the islands large and small,
Fifty years hence others will see them as they
    cross, the sun half an hour high,
A hundred years hence, or ever so many hundred
    years hence, others will see them,
Will enjoy the sun-set, the pouring in of the flood-
    tide, the falling back to the sea of the ebb-
    tide.

It avails not, neither time or place—distance
    avails not,
I am with you, you men and women of a genera-
    tion, or ever so many generations hence,
I project myself, also I return—I am with you,
    and know how it is.

Just as you feel when you look on the river and
    sky, so I felt,
Just as any of you is one of a living crowd, I was
    one of a crowd,

Just as you are refreshed by the gladness
  of the river, and the bright flow, I was
  refreshed,
Just as you stand and lean on the rail, yet hurry
  with the swift current, I stood, yet was hur-
  ried,
Just as you look on the numberless masts of ships,
  and the thick-stemmed pipes of steamboats, I
  looked.

I too many and many a time crossed the river,
  the sun half an hour high,
I watched the December sea-gulls, I saw them
  high in the air floating with motionless
  wings oscillating their bodies,
I saw how the glistening yellow lit up parts of
  their bodies, and left the rest in strong
  shadow,
I saw the slow-wheeling circles and the gradual
  edging toward the south.

I too saw the reflection of the summer-sky in the
  water,
Had my eyes dazzled by the shimmering track of
  beams,
Looked at the fine centrifugal spokes of light
  round the shape of my head in the sun-lit
  water,
Looked on the haze on the hills southward and
  southwestward,
Looked on the vapor as it flew in fleeces tinged
  with violet,
Looked toward the lower bay to notice the arriv-
  ing ships,
Saw their approach, saw aboard those that were
  near me,
Saw the white sails of schooners and sloops, saw
  the ships at anchor,
The sailors at work in the rigging or out astride
  the spars,

The round masts, the swinging motion of the
    hulls, the slender serpentine pennants,
The large and small steamers in motion, the pi-
    lots in their pilot-houses,
The white wake left by the passage, the quick
    tremulous whirl of the wheels,
The flags of all nations, the falling of them at
    sun-set,
The scallop-edged waves in the twilight, the
    ladled cups, the frolicsome crests and glisten-
    ing,
The stretch afar growing dimmer and dimmer, the
    gray walls of the granite store-houses by the
    docks,
On the river the shadowy group, the big steam-
    tug closely flanked on each side by the
    barges—the hay-boat, the belated lighter,
On the neighboring shore the fires from the foun-
    dry chimneys burning high and glaringly into
    the night,
Casting their flicker of black, contrasted with wild
    red and yellow light, over the tops of houses,
    and down into the clefts of streets.

These and all else were to me the same as they
    are to you,
I project myself a moment to tell you—also I
    return.

I loved well those cities,
I loved well the stately and rapid river,
The men and women I saw were all near to me,
Others the same—others who look back on me,
    because I looked forward to them,
The time will come, though I stop here today and
    tonight.

What is it, then, between us? What is the
    count of the scores or hundreds of years
    between us?

Whatever it is, it avails not—distance avails not,
and place avails not.

I too lived,
I too walked the streets of Manhattan Island, and
bathed in the waters around it;
I too felt the curious abrupt questionings stir with-
in me,
In the day, among crowds of people, sometimes
they came upon me,
In my walks home late at night, or as I lay in my
bed, they came upon me.

I too had been struck from the float forever held
in solution,
I too had received identity by my body,
That I was, I knew was of my body, and what I
should be, I knew I should be of my body.

It is not upon you alone the dark patches fall,
The dark threw patches down upon me also,
The best I had done seemed to me blank and sus-
picious,
My great thoughts, as I supposed them, were they
not in reality meagre? Would not people
laugh at me?

It is not you alone who know what it is to be
evil,
I am he who knew what it was to be evil,
I too knitted the old knot of contrariety,
Blabbed, blushed, resented, lied, stole, grudged,
Had guile, anger, lust, hot wishes I dared not
speak,
Was wayward, vain, greedy, shallow, sly, a solitary
committer, a coward, a malignant person,
The wolf, the snake, the hog, not wanting in me,
The cheating look, the frivolous word, the adul-
terous wish, not wanting,

Refusals, hates, postponements, meanness, lazi-
ness, none of these wanting.

But I was a Manhattanese, free, friendly, and
proud!
I was called by my nighest name by clear loud
voices of young men as they saw me ap-
proaching or passing,
Felt their arms on my neck as I stood, or the neg-
ligent leaning of their flesh against me as I sat,
Saw many I loved in the street, or ferry-boat, or
public assembly, yet never told them a word,
Lived the same life with the rest, the same old
laughing, gnawing, sleeping,
Played the part that still looks back on the actor
or actress,
The same old role, the role that is what we make
it, as great as we like, or as small as we
like, or both great and small.

Closer yet I approach you,
What thought you have of me, I had as much of
you—I laid in my stores in advance,
I considered long and seriously of you before you
were born.

Who was to know what should come home to me?
Who knows but I am enjoying this?
Who knows but I am as good as looking at you
now, for all you cannot see me?

It is not you alone, nor I alone,
Not a few races, not a few generations, not a few
centuries,
It is that each came, or comes, or shall come,
from its due emission, without fail, either
now, or then, or henceforth.

Every thing indicates—the smallest does, and
the largest does,

A necessary film envelops all, and envelops the
    soul for a proper time.

Now I am curious what sight can ever be more
    stately and admirable to me than my mast-
    hemm'd Manhatta, my river and sun-set, and
    my scallop-edged waves of flood-tide, the
    sea-gulls oscillating their bodies, the hay-boat
    in the twilight, and the belated lighter,
Curious what gods can exceed these that clasp
    me by the hand, and with voices I love call
    me promptly and loudly by my nighest name
    as I approach,
Curious what is more subtle than this which ties
    me to the woman or man that looks in my
    face,
Which fuses me into you now, and pours my
    meaning into you.

We understand, then, do we not?
What I promised without mentioning it, have
    you not accepted?
What the study could not teach—what the
    preaching could not accomplish is accom-
    plished, is it not?
What the push of reading could not start is
    started by me personally, is it not?

Flow on, river! Flow with the flood-tide, and
    ebb with the ebb-tide!
Frolic on, crested and scallop-edged waves!
Gorgeous clouds of the sun-set, drench with your
    splendor me, or the men and women genera-
    tions after me!
Cross from shore to shore, countless crowds of
    passengers!
Stand up, tall masts of Manahatta!—stand up,
    beautiful hills of Brooklyn!
Bully for you! you proud, friendly, free Manhat-
    tanese!

Throb, baffled and curious brain! throw out ques-
   tions and answers!
Suspend here and everywhere, eternal float of
   solution!
Blab, blush, lie, steal, you or I or any one after
   us!
Gaze, loving and thirsting eyes, in the house or
   street or public assembly!
Sound out, voices of young men! loudly and mu-
   sically call me by my nighest name!
Live, old life! play the part that looks back on the
   actor or actress!
Play the old role, the role that is great or small,
   according as one makes it!
Consider, you who peruse me, whether I may
   not in unknown ways be looking upon you!
Be firm, rail over the river, to support those who
   lean idly, yet haste with the hasting cur-
   rent!
Fly on, sea-birds! fly sideways, or wheel in large
   circles high in the air!
Receive the summer-sky, you water! faithfully
   hold it till all downcast eyes have time to
   take it from you!
Diverge, fine spokes of light, from the shape of
   my head, or any one's head, in the sun-lit
   water!
Come on, ships, from the lower bay! pass up
   or down, white-sailed schooners, sloops,
   lighters!
Flaunt away, flags of all nations! be duly lowered
   at sun-set!
Burn high your fires, foundry chimneys! cast
   black shadows at night-fall! cast red and
   yellow light over the tops of the houses!
Appearances, now or henceforth, indicate what
   you are!
You necessary film, continue to envelop the
   soul!

About my body for me, and your body for you, be
　　hung our divinest aromas!
Thrive, cities! Bring your freight, bring your
　　shows, ample and sufficient rivers!
Expand, being than which none else is perhaps
　　more spiritual!
Keep your places, objects than which none else is
　　more lasting!

We descend upon you and all things, we arrest
　　you all,
We realize the soul only by you, you faithful solids
　　and fluids,
Through you color, form, location, sublimity,
　　ideality,
Through you every proof, comparison, and all the
　　suggestions and determinations of ourselves.

You have waited, you always wait, you dumb
　　beautiful ministers! you novices!
We receive you with free sense at last, and are
　　insatiate henceforward,
Not you any more shall be able to foil us, or with-
　　hold yourselves from us,
We use you, and do not cast you aside—we
　　plant you permanently within us,
We fathom you not—we love you—there is
　　perfection in you also,
You furnish your parts toward eternity,
Great or small, you furnish your parts toward the
　　soul.

12—*Poem of The Road**

AFOOT and light-hearted I take to the open
　　road!
Healthy, free, the world before me!
The long brown path before me, leading wherever
　　I choose!

Henceforth I ask not good-fortune, I am good-
fortune,
Henceforth I whimper no more, postpone no more,
need nothing,
Strong and content, I travel the open road.

The earth—that is sufficient,
I do not want the constellations any nearer,
I know they are very well where they are,
I know they suffice for those who belong to them.

Still here I carry my old delicious burdens,
I carry them, men and women—I carry them
with me wherever I go,
I swear it is impossible for me to get rid of them,
I am filled with them, and I will fill them in
return.

You road I travel and look around! I believe you
are not all that is here!
I believe that something unseen is also here.

Here is the profound lesson of reception, neither
preference or denial,
The black with his woolly head, the felon, the
diseased, the illiterate person, are not de-
nied,
The birth, the hasting after the physician, the
beggar's tramp, the drunkard's stagger, the
laughing party of mechanics,
The escaped youth, the rich person's carriage, the
fop, the eloping couple,
The early market-man, the hearse, the moving of
furniture into the town, the return back from
the town,
They pass, I also pass, any thing passes, none can
be interdicted,
None but are accepted, none but are dear to me.

You air that serves me with breath to speak!
You objects that call from diffusion my meanings
    and give them shape!
You light that wraps me and all things in delicate
    equable showers!
You animals moving serenely over the earth!
You birds that wing yourselves through the air!
    you insects!
You sprouting growths from the farmers' fields!
    you stalks and weeds by the fences!
You paths worn in the irregular hollows by the
    road-sides!
I think you are latent with curious existences—
    you are so dear to me.

You flagged walks of the cities! you strong curbs
    at the edges!
You ferries! you planks and posts of wharves!
    you timber-lined sides! you distant ships!
You rows of houses! you window-pierced facades!
    you roofs!
You porches and entrances! you copings and iron
    guards!
You windows whose transparent shells might
    expose so much!
You doors and ascending steps! you arches!
You gray stones of interminable pavements! you
    trodden crossings!
From all that has been near you I believe you
    have imparted to yourselves, and now would
    impart the same secretly to me,
From the living and the dead I think you have
    peopled your impassive surfaces, and the
    spirits thereof would be evident and ami-
    cable with me.

The earth expanding right hand and left hand,
The picture alive, every part in its best light,
The music falling in where it is wanted, and
    stopping where it is not wanted,

The cheerful voice of the public road—the gay
    fresh sentiment of the road.

O highway I travel! O public road! do you say
    to me, Do not leave me?
Do you say, Venture not? If you leave me, you
    are lost?
Do you say, I am already prepared—I am well-
    beaten and undenied—Adhere to me?

O public road! I say back, I am not afraid to
    leave you—yet I love you,
You express me better than I can express myself,
You shall be more to me than my poem.

I think heroic deeds were all conceived in the
    open air,
I think I could stop here myself, and do miracles,
I think whatever I meet on the road I shall like,
    and whatever beholds me shall like me,
I think whoever I see must be happy.

From this hour, freedom!
From this hour, I ordain myself loosed of limits
    and imaginary lines!
Going where I list—my own master, total and
    absolute,
Listening to others, and considering well what
    they say,
Pausing, searching, receiving, contemplating,
Gently but with undeniable will divesting myself
    of the holds that would hold me.

I inhale great draughts of air,
The east and the west are mine, and the north
    and the south are mine.

I am larger than I thought!
I did not know I held so much goodness!

All seems beautiful to me,
I can repeat over to men and women, You have
    done such good to me, I would do the same
    to you.

I will recruit for myself and you as I go,
I will scatter myself among men and women as
    I go,
I will toss the new gladness and roughness among
    them;
Whoever denies me, it shall not trouble me,
Whoever accepts me, he or she shall be blessed,
    and shall bless me.

Now if a thousand perfect men were to appear,
    it would not amaze me,
Now if a thousand beautiful forms of women ap-
    peared, it would not astonish me.

Now I see the secret of the making of the best
    persons,
It is to grow in the open air, and to eat and
    sleep with the earth.

Here is space—here a great personal deed has
    room,
A great deed seizes upon the hearts of the whole
    race of men,
Its effusion of strength and will overwhelms law,
    and mocks all authority and all argument
    against it.

Here is the test of wisdom,
Wisdom is not finally tested in schools,
Wisdom cannot be passed from one having it, to
    another not having it,
Wisdom is of the soul, is not susceptible of proof,
    is its own proof,
Applies to all stages and objects and qualities, and
    is content,

Is the certainty of the reality and immortality of
    things, and the excellence of things,
Something there is in the float of the sight of
    things that provokes it out of the soul.

Now I re-examine philosophies and religions,
They may prove well in lecture-rooms, yet not
    prove at all under the spacious clouds, and
    along the landscape and flowing currents.

Here is realization,
Here is a man tallied—he realizes here what he
    has in him,
The animals, the past, the future, light, space,
    majesty, love, if they are vacant of you, you
    are vacant of them.

Only the kernel of every object nourishes;
Where is he who tears off the husks for you and
    me?
Where is he that undoes stratagems and envelopes
    for you and me?

Here is adhesiveness*—it is not previously
    fashioned, it is apropos;
Do you know what it is as you pass to be loved
    by strangers?
Do you know the talk of those turning eye-balls?

Here is the efflux of the soul,
The efflux of the soul comes through beautiful
    gates of laws, provoking questions,
These yearnings, why are they? these thoughts
    in the darkness, why are they?
Why are there men and women that while they
    are nigh me the sun-light expands my blood?
Why when they leave me do my pennants of joy
    sink flat and lank?

Why are there trees I never walk under but large
    and melodious thoughts descend upon me?
(I think they hang there winter and summer on
    those trees, and always drop fruit as I pass;)
What is it I interchange so suddenly with stran-
    gers?
What with some driver as I ride on the seat by
    his side?
What with some fisherman, drawing his seine by
    the shore, as I walk by and pause?
What gives me to be free to a woman's or man's
    good-will? What gives them to be free to
    mine?

The efflux of the soul is happiness—here is
    happiness,
I think it pervades the air, waiting at all times,
Now it flows into us—we are rightly charged.

Here rises the fluid and attaching character;
The fluid and attaching character is the freshness
    and sweetness of man and woman,
The herbs of the morning sprout no fresher and
    sweeter every day out of the roots of them-
    selves, than it sprouts fresh and sweet contin-
    ually out of itself.

Toward the fluid and attaching character exudes
    the sweat of the love of young and old,
From it falls distilled the charm that mocks beauty
    and attainments,
Toward it heaves the shuddering longing ache of
    contact.

Allons!* Whoever you are, come travel with
    me!
Traveling with me, you find what never tires.

The earth never tires!
The earth is rude, silent, incomprehensible at

first—nature is rude and incomprehensible
    at first,
Be not discouraged—keep on—there are divine
    things, well enveloped,
I swear to you there are divine things more beau-
    tiful than words can tell!

Allons! We must not stop here!
However sweet these laid-up stores, however
    convenient this dwelling, we cannot remain
    here!
However sheltered this port, however calm these
    waters, we must not anchor here!
However welcome the hospitality that surrounds
    us, we are permitted to receive it but a little
    while.

Allons! the inducements shall be great to you,
We will sail pathless and wild seas,
We will go where winds blow, waves dash,
    and the Yankee clipper speeds by under full
    sail.

Allons! With power, liberty, the earth, the
    elements!
Health, defiance, gaiety, self-esteem, curiosity!

Allons! From all formulas!
From your formulas, O bat-eyed and materialistic
    priests!

The stale cadaver blocks up the passage—the
    burial waits no longer.

Allons! Yet take warning!
He traveling with me needs the best blood, thews,*
    endurance,
None may come to the trial till he or she bring
    courage and health.

Come not here if you have already spent the best
    of yourself!
Only those may come who come in sweet and
    determined bodies,
No diseased person—no rum-drinker or venereal
    taint is permitted here,
I and mine do not convince by arguments,
    similes, rhymes,
We convince by our presence.

Listen! I will be honest with you,
I do not offer the old smooth prizes, but offer
    rough new prizes,
These are the days that must happen to you:
You shall not heap up what is called riches,
You shall scatter with lavish hand all that you
    earn or achieve,
You but arrive at the city to which you were
    destined—you hardly settle yourself to satis-
    faction, before you are called by an irresistible
    call to depart,
You shall be treated to the ironical smiles and
    mockings of those who remain behind you,
What beckonings of love you receive, you shall
    only answer with passionate kisses of parting,
You shall not allow the hold of those who spread
    their reached hands toward you.

Allons! After the great companions! and to be-
    long to them!
They too are on the road! they are the swift and
    majestic men! they are the greatest women!

Over that which hindered them, over that which
    retarded, passing impediments large or small,
Committers of crimes, committers of many beauti-
    ful virtues,
Enjoyers of calms of seas, and storms of seas,
Sailors of many a ship, walkers of many a mile of
    land,

Habitues of many different countries, habitues of
    far-distant dwellings,
Trusters of men and women, observers of cities,
    solitary toilers,
Pausers and contemplaters of tufts, blossoms, shells
    of the shore,
Dancers at wedding-dances, kissers of brides,
    tender helpers of children, bearers of children,
Soldiers of revolts, standers by gaping graves,
    lowerers down of coffins,
Journeyers over consecutive seasons, over the
    years—the curious years, each emerging
    from that which preceded it,
Journeyers as with companions, namely, their own
    diverse phases,
Forth-steppers from the latent unrealized baby-
    days,
Journeyers gaily with their own youth—journey-
    ers with their bearded and well-grained
    manhood,
Journeyers with their womanhood, ample, unsur-
    passed, content,
Journeyers with their sublime old age of manhood
    or womanhood,
Old age, calm, expanded, broad with the haughty
    breadth of the universe,
Old age, flowing free with the delicious near-by
    freedom of death.

Allons! to that which is endless as it was
    beginningless!
To undergo much, tramps of days, rests of nights!
To merge all in the travel they tend to, and the
    days and nights they tend to!
Again to merge them in the start of superior
    journeys!
To see nothing anywhere but what you may reach
    it and pass it!
To conceive no time, however distant, but what
    you may reach it and pass it!

To look up or down no road but it stretches and
　　　waits for you! however long, but it stretches
　　　and waits for you!
To see no being, not God's or any, but you also
　　　go thither!
To see no possession but you may possess it!
　　　enjoying all without labor or purchase—
　　　abstracting the feast, yet not abstracting one
　　　particle of it;
To take the best of the farmer's farm and the rich
　　　man's elegant villa, and the chaste blessings
　　　of the well-married couple, and the fruits of
　　　orchards and flowers of gardens!
To take to your use out of the compact cities as
　　　you pass through!
To carry buildings and streets with you afterward
　　　wherever you go!
To gather the minds of men out of their brains as
　　　you encounter them! to gather the love out
　　　of their hearts!
To take your own lovers on the road with
　　　you, for all that you leave them behind
　　　you!
To know the universe itself as a road—as many
　　　roads—as roads for traveling souls!

The soul travels,
The body does not travel as much as the soul,
The body has just as great a work as the soul,
　　　and parts away at last for the journeys of the
　　　soul.

All parts away for the progress of souls,
All religion, all solid things, arts, governments—
　　　all that was or is apparent upon this globe or
　　　any globe, falls into niches and corners before
　　　the processions of souls along the grand roads
　　　of the universe,

Of the progress of the souls of men and women
    along the grand roads of the universe, all
    other progress is the needed emblem and
    sustenance.

Forever alive, forever forward,
Stately, solemn, sad, withdrawn, baffled, mad,
    turbulent, feeble, dissatisfied,
Desperate, proud, fond, sick, accepted by men,
    rejected by men,
They go! they go! I know that they go, but I
    know not where they go,
But I know that they go toward the best—
    toward something great.

Allons! Whoever you are! come forth!
You must not stay in your house, though you built
    it, or though it has been built for you.

Allons! out of the dark confinement!
It is useless to protest—I know all, and expose it.

Behold through you as bad as the rest!
Through the laughter, dancing, dining, supping, of
    people,
Inside of dresses and ornaments, inside of those
    washed and trimmed faces,
Behold a secret silent loathing and despair!

No husband, no wife, no friend, no lover, so
    trusted as to hear the confession,
Another self, a duplicate of every one, skulking and
    hiding it goes, open and above-board it goes,
Formless and wordless through the streets of the
    cities, polite and bland in the parlors,
In the cars of rail-roads, in steam-boats, in the
    public assembly,

Home to the houses of men and women, among
    their families, at the table, in the bed-room,
    everywhere,
Smartly attired, countenance smiling, form upright,
    death under the breast-bones, hell under the
    skull-bones,
Under the broad-cloth and gloves, under the
    ribbons and artificial flowers,
Keeping fair with the customs, speaking not a
    syllable of itself,
Speaking of anything else, but never of itself.

Allons! through struggles and wars!
The goal that was named cannot be counter-
    manded.

Have the past struggles succeeded?
What has succeeded? Yourself? Your nation?
    Nature?
Now understand me well—it is provided in the
    essence of things, that from any fruition of
    success, no matter what, shall come forth
    something to make a greater struggle neces-
    sary.

My call is the call of battle—I nourish active
    rebellion,
He going with me must go well armed,
He going with me goes often with spare diet,
    poverty, angry enemies, contentions.

Allons! the road is before us!
It is safe—I have tried it—my own feet have
    tried it well.

Allons! be not detained!
Let the paper remain on the desk unwritten, and
    the book on the shelf unopened!

Let the tools remain in the work-shop! let the
    money remain unearned!
Let the school stand! mind not the cry of the
    teacher!
Let the preacher preach in his pulpit! let the
    lawyer plead in the court, and the judge
    expound the law!

Mon enfant! I give you my hand!
I give you my love, more precious than money,
I give you myself, before preaching or law;
Will you give me yourself? Will you come
    travel with me?
Shall we stick by each other as long as we live?

*13—Poem of Procreation**

A WOMAN waits for me—she contains all,
    nothing is lacking,
Yet all were lacking, if sex were lacking, or if
    the moisture of the right man were lacking.

Sex contains all,
Bodies, souls, meanings, proofs, purities, delica-
    cies, results, promulgations,
Songs, commands, health, pride, the maternal
    mystery, the semitic milk,
All hopes, benefactions, bestowals,
All the passions, loves, beauties, delights of the
    earth,
All the governments, judges, gods, followed per-
    sons of the earth,
These are contained in sex, as parts of itself
    and justifications of itself

Without shame the man I like knows and avows
    the deliciousness of his sex,

Without shame the woman I like knows and
    avows hers.

O I will fetch bully breeds of children yet!
They cannot be fetched, I say, on less terms than
    mine,
Electric growth from the male, and rich ripe fibre
    from the female, are the terms.

I will dismiss myself from impassive women,
I will go stay with her who waits for me, and
    with those women that are warm-blooded and
    sufficient for me,
I see that they understand me, and do not deny
    me,
I see that they are worthy of me—so I will be
    the robust husband of those women!
They are not one jot less than I am,
They are tanned in the face by shining suns and
    blowing winds,
Their flesh has the old divine suppleness and
    strength,
They know how to swim, row, ride, wrestle,
    shoot, run, strike, retreat, advance, resist,
    defend themselves,
They are ultimate in their own right—they are
    calm, clear, well-possessed of themselves.

I draw you close to me, you women!
I cannot let you go, I would do you good,
I am for you, and you are for me, not only for our
    own sake, but for others' sakes,
Enveloped in you sleep greater heroes and bards,
They refuse to awake at the touch of any man but
    me.

It is I, you women—I make my way,
I am stern, acrid, large, undissuadable—but I
    love you,

I do not hurt you any more than is necessary for
    you,
I pour the stuff to start sons and daughters fit for
    These States—I press with slow rude muscle,
I brace myself effectually—I listen to no en-
    treaties,
I dare not withdraw till I deposite what has so
    long accumulated within me.

Through you I drain the pent-up rivers of myself,
In you I wrap a thousand onward years,
On you I graft the grafts of the best-beloved of
    me and of America,
The drops I distil upon you are drops of fierce
    and athletic girls, and of new artists, musi-
    cians, singers,
The babes I beget upon you are to beget babes in
    their turn,
I shall demand perfect men and women out of my
    love-spendings,
I shall expect them to interpenetrate with others,
    as I and you interpenetrate now,
I shall count on the fruits of the gushing showers
    of them, as I count on the fruits of the gush-
    ing showers I give now,
I shall look for loving crops from the birth, life,
    death, immortality I plant so lovingly now.

*15—Clef Poem**

THIS night I am happy,
As I watch the stars shining, I think a
    thought of the clef* of the universes, and
    of the future.

What can the future bring me more than I have?
Do you suppose I wish to enjoy life in other
    spheres?

I say distinctly I comprehend no better sphere
    than this earth,
I comprehend no better life than the life of my
    body.

I do not know what follows the death of my body,
But I know well that whatever it is, it is best for
    me,
And I know well that what is really Me shall live
    just as much as before.

I am not uneasy but I shall have good housing to
    myself,
But this is my first—how can I like the rest any
    better?
Here I grew up—the studs and rafters are grown
    parts of me.

I am not uneasy but I am to be beloved by young
    and old men, and to love them the same,
I suppose the pink nipples of the breasts of women
    with whom I shall sleep will taste the same
    to my lips,
But this is the nipple of a breast of my mother,
    always near and always divine to me, her
    true child and son.

I suppose I am to be eligible to visit the stars, in
    my time,
I suppose I shall have myriads of new experiences
    —and that the experience of this earth will
    prove only one out of myriads;
But I believe my body and my soul already
    indicate those experiences,
And I believe I shall find nothing in the stars
    more majestic and beautiful than I have
    already found on the earth,
And I believe I have this night a clue through
    the universes,

And I believe I have this night thought a thought
    of the clef of eternity.

A vast similitude interlocks all,
All spheres, grown, ungrown, small, large, suns,
    moons, planets, comets, asteroids,
All the substances of the same, and all that is
    spiritual upon the same,
All distances of place, however wide,
All distances of time—all inanimate forms,
All souls—all living bodies, though they be in
    different worlds,
All gaseous, watery, vegetable, mineral processes,
    the fishes, the brutes,
All men and women—me also,
All nations, colors, barbarisms, civilizations, lan-
    guages,
All identities that have existed or may exist on
    this globe or any globe,
All lives and deaths—all of past, present, future,
This vast similitude spans them, and always has
    spanned, and shall forever span them.

21—Liberty Poem for Asia, Africa, Europe, America, Australia, Cuba, and the Archipelagoes of the Sea*

COURAGE! my brother or my sister!
Keep on! Liberty is to be subserved, what-
    ever occurs;
That is nothing, that is quelled by one or two fail-
    ures, or any number of failures,
Or by the indifference or ingratitude of the
    people,
Or the show of the tushes of power—soldiers,
    cannon, penal statutes.

What we believe in waits latent forever through
    Asia, Africa, Europe, America, Australia,
    Cuba, and all the islands and archipelagoes
    of the sea;
What we believe in invites no one, promises
    nothing, sits in calmness and light, is positive
    and composed, knows no discouragement,
Waits patiently its time—a year—a century—
    a hundred centuries.

The battle rages with many a loud alarm and
    frequent advance and retreat,
The infidel triumphs—or supposes he triumphs,
The prison, scaffold, garrote, hand-cuffs, iron neck-
    lace and anklet, lead-balls, do their work,
The named and unnamed heroes pass to other
    spheres,
The great speakers and writers are exiled—they
    lie sick in distant lands,
The cause is asleep—the strong throats are
    choked with their own blood,
The young men drop their eye-lashes toward the
    ground when they meet,
But for all this, liberty has not gone out of the
    place, nor the infidel entered into pos-
    session.

When liberty goes out of a place, it is not the
    first to go, nor the second or third to go,
It waits for all the rest to go—it is the last.

When there are no more memories of the lovers
    of the whole of the nations of the world,
The lovers' names scouted in the public gatherings
    by the lips of the orators,
Boys not christened after them, but christened
    after traitors and murderers instead,
Laws for slaves sweet to the taste of people—
    the slave-hunt acknowledged,

You or I walking abroad upon the earth, elated
    at the sight of slaves, no matter who they
    are,
And when all life and all the souls of men and
    women are discharged from any part of the
    earth,
Then shall the instinct of liberty be discharged
    from that part of the earth,
Then shall the infidel and the tyrant come into
    possession.

28—Bunch Poem*

THE friend I am happy with,
The arm of my friend hanging idly over my
    shoulder,
The hill-side whitened with blossoms of the
    mountain ash,
The same, late in autumn—the gorgeous hues of
    red, yellow, drab, purple, and light and dark
    green,
The rich coverlid of the grass—animals and
    birds—the private untrimmed bank—the
    primitive apples—the pebble-stones,
Beautiful dripping fragments—the negligent list
    of one after another, as I happen to call them
    to me, or think of them,
The real poems, (what we call poems being merely
    pictures,)
The poems of the privacy of the night, and of
    men like me,
This poem, drooping shy and unseen, that I al-
    ways carry, and that all men carry,
(Know, once for all, avowed on purpose, wherever
    are men like me, are our lusty, lurking, mas
    culine poems,)
Love-thoughts, love-juice, love-odor, love-yielding,
    love-climbers, and the climbing sap,

Arms and hands of love—lips of love—phallic
   thumb of love—breasts of love—bellies,
   pressed and glued together with love,
Earth of chaste love—life that is only life after
   love,
The body of my love—the body of the woman I
   love—the body of the man—the body of the
   earth,
Soft forenoon airs that blow from the south-west,
The hairy wild-bee that murmurs and hankers up
   and down—that gripes the full-grown lady-
   flower, curves upon her with amorous firm
   legs, takes his will of her, and holds himself
   tremulous and tight upon her till he is satis-
   fied,
The wet of woods through the early hours,
Two sleepers at night lying close together as they
   sleep, one with an arm slanting down across
   and below the waist of the other,
The smell of apples, aromas from crushed sage-
   plant, mint, birch-bark,
The boy's longings, the glow and pressure as he
   confides to me what he was dreaming,
The dead leaf whirling its spiral whirl, and falling
   still and content to the ground,
The no-formed stings that sights, people, objects,
   sting me with,
The hubbed sting of myself, stinging me as much
   as it ever can any one,
The sensitive, orbic, underlapped brothers, that
   only privileged feelers may be intimate where
   they are,
The curious roamer, the hand, roaming all over
   the body—the bashful withdrawing of flesh
   where the fingers soothingly pause and edge
   themselves,
The limpid liquid within the young man,
The vexed corrosion, so pensive and so painful,
The torment—the irritable tide that will not be
   at rest,

The like of the same I feel—the like of the same
    in others,
The young woman that flushes and flushes, and
    the young man that flushes and flushes,
The young man that wakes, deep at night, the hot
    hand seeking to repress what would master
    him—the strange half-welcome pangs, vis-
    ions, sweats—the pulse pounding through
    palms and trembling encirling fingers—the
    young man all colored, red, ashamed, angry;
The souse upon me of my lover the sea, as I lie
    willing and naked,
The merriment of the twin-babes that crawl over
    the grass in the sun, the mother never turn-
    ing her vigilant eyes from them,
The walnut-trunk, the walnut-husks, and the ripen-
    ing or ripened long-round walnuts,
The continence of vegetables, birds, animals,
The consequent meanness of me should I skulk
    or find myself indecent, while birds and
    animals never once skulk or find themselves
    indecent,
The great chastity of paternity, to match the great
    chastity of maternity,
The oath of procreation I have sworn,
The greed that eats in me day and night with
    hungry gnaw, till I saturate what shall pro-
    duce boys to fill my place when I am through,
The wholesome relief, repose, content,
And this bunch plucked at random from myself,
It has done its work—I toss it carelessly to fall
    where it may.

31—Poem of The Sayers of The
Words of The Earth*

EARTH, round, rolling, compact—suns, moons,
    animals—all these are words,

Watery, vegetable, sauroid advances—beings,
    premonitions, lispings of the future—these
    are vast words.

Were you thinking that those were the words—
    those upright lines? those curves, angles,
    dots?
No, those are not the words—the substantial
    words are in the ground and sea,
They are in the air—they are in you.

Were you thinking that those were the words—
    those delicious sounds out of your friends'
    mouths?
No, the real words are more delicious than they.

Human bodies are words, myriads of words,
In the best poems re-appears the body, man's or
    woman's, well-shaped, natural, gay,
Every part able, active, receptive, without shame
    or the need of shame

Air, soil, water, fire, these are words,
I myself am a word with them—my qualities
    interpenetrate with theirs—my name is noth-
    ing to them,
Though it were told in the three thousand lan-
    guages, what would air, soil, water, fire,
    know of my name?

A healthy presence, a friendly or commanding
    gesture, are words, sayings, meanings,
The charms that go with the mere looks of some
    men and women are sayings and meanings
    also.

The workmanship of souls is by the inaudible
    words of the earth,
The great masters, the sayers, know the earth's
    words, and use them more than the audible
    words.

Syllables are not the earth's words,
Beauty, reality, manhood, time, life—the realities
of such as these are the earth's words.

Amelioration is one of the earth's words,
The earth neither lags nor hastens,
It has all attributes, growths, effects, latent in it-
self from the jump,
It is not half beautiful only—defects and excres-
cences show just as much as perfections
show.

The earth does not withhold, it is generous
enough,
The truths of the earth continually wait, they are
not so concealed either,
They are calm, subtle, untransmissible by print,
They are imbued through all things, conveying
themselves willingly,
Conveying a sentiment and invitation of the earth
—I utter and utter,
I speak not, yet if you hear me not, of what avail
am I to you?
To bear—to better—lacking these, of what
avail am I?

Accouche! Accouchez!*
Will you rot your own fruit in yourself there?
Will you squat and stifle there?

The earth does not argue,
Is not pathetic, has no arrangements,
Does not scream, haste, persuade, threaten,
promise,
Makes no discriminations, has no conceivable
failures,
Closes nothing, refuses nothing, shuts none out,
Of all the powers, objects, states, it notifies, shuts
none out.

The earth does not exhibit itself nor refuse to
    exhibit itself—possesses still underneath,
Underneath the ostensible sounds, the august
    chorus of heroes, the wail of slaves,
Persuasions of lovers, curses, gasps of the dying,
    laughter of young people, accents of bar-
    gainers,
Underneath these possessing the words that never
    fail.

To her children the words of the eloquent dumb
    great mother never fail,
The true words do not fail, for motion does not
    fail, and reflection does not fail,
Also the day and night do not fail, and the voyage
    we pursue does not fail.

Of the interminable sisters,*
Of the ceaseless cotillions* of sisters,
Of the centripetal and centrifugal sisters, the elder
    and younger sisters,
The beautiful sister* we know dances on with the
    rest.

With her ample back toward every beholder,
With the fascinations of youth and the equal fas-
    cinations of age,
Sits she whom I too love like the rest, sits undis-
    turbed,
Holding up in her hand what has the character
    of a mirror, her eyes glancing back from
    it,
Glancing thence as she sits, inviting none, denying
    none,
Holding a mirror day and night tirelessly before
    her own face.

Seen at hand, or seen at a distance,
Duly the twenty-four appear in public every day,

Duly approach and pass with their companions, or
    a companion,
Looking from no countenances of their own, but
    from the countenances of those who are with
    them,
From the countenances of children or women, or
    the manly countenance,
From the open countenances of animals, from in-
    animate things,
From the landscape or waters, or from the exqui-
    site apparition of the sky,
From our own countenances, mine and yours,
    faithfully returning them,
Every day in public appearing without fail, but
    never twice with the same companions.

Embracing man, embracing all, proceed the three
    hundred and sixty-five resistlessly round the
    sun,
Embracing all, soothing, supporting, follow close
    three hundred and sixty-five offsets of the
    first, sure and necessary as they.

Tumbling on steadily, nothing dreading,
Sunshine, storm, cold, heat, forever withstanding,
    passing, carrying,
The soul's realization and determination still in-
    heriting,
The liquid vacuum around and ahead still entering
    and dividing,
No balk retarding, no anchor anchoring, on no
    rock striking,
Swift, glad, content, unbereaved, nothing losing,
Of all able and ready at any time to give strict
    account,
The divine ship sails the divine sea.

Whoever you are! motion and reflection are espe-
    cially for you,
The divine ship sails the divine sea for you.

Whoever you are! you are he or she for whom
　　the earth is solid and liquid,
You are he or she for whom the sun and moon
　　hang in the sky,
For none more than you are the present and the
　　past,
For none more than you is immortality.

Each man to himself, and each woman to herself,
　　is the word of the past and present, and the
　　word of immortality,
Not one can acquire for another—not one!
Not one can grow for another—not one!

The song is to the singer, and comes back most to
　　him,
The teaching is to the teacher, and comes back
　　most to him,
The murder is to the murderer, and comes back
　　most to him,
The theft is to the thief, and comes back most to
　　him,
The love is to the lover, and comes back most to
　　him,
The gift is to the giver, and comes back most to
　　him—it cannot fail,
The oration is to the orator, and the acting is to
　　the actor and actress, not to the audience,
And no man understands any greatness or good-
　　ness but his own, or the indication of his
　　own.

I swear the earth shall surely be complete to him
　　or her who shall be complete!
I swear the earth remains broken and jagged only
　　to him or her who remains broken and
　　jagged!

I swear there is no greatness or power that does
　　not emulate those of the earth!

I swear there can be no theory of any account,
    unless it corroborate the theory of the earth!
No politics, art, religion, behaviour, or what not, is
    of account, unless it compare with the ampli-
    tude of the earth,
Unless it face the exactness, vitality, impartiality,
    rectitude of the earth.

I swear I begin to see love with sweeter spasms
    than that which responds love!
It is that which contains itself, which never in-
    vites and never refuses.

I swear I begin to see little or nothing in audible
    words!
I swear I think all merges toward the presentation
    of the unspoken meanings of the earth!
Toward him who sings the songs of the body, and
    of the truths of the earth,
Toward him who makes the dictionaries of the
    words that print cannot touch.

I swear I see what is better than to tell the best,
It is always to leave the best untold.

When I undertake to tell the best, I find I can-
    not,
My tongue is ineffectual on its pivots,
My breath will not be obedient to its organs,
I become a dumb man.

The best of the earth cannot be told anyhow—all
    or any is best,
It is not what you anticipated, it is cheaper, easier,
    nearer,
Things are not dismissed from the places they
    held before,
The earth is just as positive and direct as it was
    before,

Facts, religions, improvements, politics, trades, are
    as real as before,
But the soul is also real, it too is positive and
    direct,
No reasoning, no proof has established it,
Undeniable growth has established it.

This is a poem for the sayers of the earth—
    these are hints of meanings,
These are they that echo the tones of souls, and
    the phrases of souls;
If they did not echo the phrases of souls, what
    were they then?
If they had not reference to you in especial, what
    were they then?

I swear I will never henceforth have to do with
    the faith that tells the best!
I will have to do with that faith only that leaves
    the best untold.

Say on, sayers of the earth!
Delve! mould! pile the substantial words of the
    earth!
Work on, age after age! nothing is to be lost,
It may have to wait long, but it will certainly come
    in use,
When the materials are all prepared, the archi-
    tects shall appear,
I swear to you the architects shall appear without
    fail! I announce them and lead them!
I swear to you they will understand you and justify
    you!
I swear to you the greatest among them shall be
    he who best knows you, and encloses all, and
    is faithful to all!
I swear to you, he and the rest shall not forget
    you! they shall perceive that you are not an
    iota less than they!
I swear to you, you shall be glorified in them!

FROM LEAVES OF GRASS
(1860–1861)

Proto–Leaf*

1 FREE, fresh, savage,
Fluent, luxuriant, self-content, fond of persons and
    places,
Fond of fish-shape Paumanok, where I was born,
Fond of the sea—lusty-begotten and various,
Boy of the Mannahatta,* the city of ships, my city,
Or raised inland, or of the south savannas,
Or full-breath'd on Californian air, or Texan or
    Cuban air,
Tallying, vocalizing all—resounding Niagara—
    resounding Missouri,
Or rude in my home in Kanuck woods,
Or wandering and hunting, my drink water, my diet
    meat,
Or withdrawn to muse and meditate in some deep
    recess,
Far from the clank of crowds, an interval passing,
    rapt and happy,
Stars, vapor, snow, the hills, rocks, the Fifth Month
    flowers, my amaze, my love,
Aware of the buffalo, the peace-herds, the bull,
    strong-breasted and hairy,
Aware of the mocking-bird of the wilds at day-
    break,
Solitary, singing in the west, I strike up for a new
    world.

2 Victory, union, faith, identity, time, the Soul, your-
    self, the present and future lands, the indisso-
    luble compacts, riches, mystery, eternal progress,
    the kosmos, and the modern reports.

3 This then is life,
Here is what has come to the surface after so many
    throes and convulsions.

4 How curious! How real!
   Underfoot the divine soil—Overhead the sun.

5 See, revolving,
   The globe—the ancestor-continents, away, grouped
       together,
   The present and future continents, north and south,
       with the isthmus between.

6 See, vast, trackless spaces,
   As in a dream, they change, they swiftly fill,
   Countless masses debouch upon them,
   They are now covered with the foremost people, arts,
       institutions known.

7 See projected, through time,
   For me, an audience interminable.

8 With firm and regular step they wend—they never
       stop,
   Successions of men, Americanos, a hundred millions,
   One generation playing its part and passing on,
   And another generation playing its part and passing
       on in its turn,
   With faces turned sideways or backward toward me
       to listen,
   With eyes retrospective toward me.

9 Americanos! Masters!
   Marches humanitarian! Foremost!
   Century marches! Libertad!* Masses!
   For you a programme of chants.

10 Chants of the prairies,
   Chants of the long-running Mississippi,
   Chants of Ohio, Indiana, Illinois, Wisconsin, Iowa,
       and Minnesota,
   Inland chants—chants of Kanzas,
   Chants away down to Mexico, and up north to
       Oregon—Kanadian chants,

Chants of teeming and turbulent cities—chants of
    mechanics,
Yankee chants—Pennsylvanian chants—chants of
    Kentucky and Tennessee,
Chants of dim-lit mines—chants of mountain-tops,
Chants of sailors—chants of the Eastern Sea and the
    Western Sea,
Chants of the Mannahatta, the place of my dearest
    love, the place surrounded by hurried and
    sparkling currents,
Health chants—joy chants—robust chants of young
    men,
Chants inclusive—wide reverberating chants,
Chants of the Many In One.

11 In the Year 80 of The States,
My tongue, every atom of my blood, formed from
    this soil, this air,
Born here of parents born here,
From parents the same, and their parents' parents
    the same,
I, now thirty-six years old, in perfect health,
    begin,
Hoping to cease not till death.

12 Creeds and schools in abeyance,
Retiring back a while, sufficed at what they are, but
    never forgotten,
With accumulations, now coming forward in front,
Arrived again, I harbor, for good or bad—I permit
    to speak,
Nature, without check, with original energy.

13 Take my leaves, America!
Make welcome for them everywhere, for they are
    your own offspring;
Surround them, East and West! for they would
    surround you,
And you precedents! connect lovingly with them, for
    they connect lovingly with you.

14 I conned old times,
   I sat studying at the feet of the great masters;
   Now, if eligible, O that the great masters might
       return and study me!

15 In the name of These States, shall I scorn the
       antique?
   Why These are the children of the antique, to
       justify it.

16 Dead poets, philosophs, priests,
   Martyrs, artists, inventors, governments long since,
   Language-shapers, on other shores,
   Nations once powerful, now reduced, withdrawn, or
       desolate,
   I dare not proceed till I respectfully credit what you
       have left, wafted hither,
   I have perused it—I own it is admirable,
   I think nothing can ever be greater—Nothing can
       ever deserve more than it deserves;
   I regard it all intently a long while,
   Then take my place for good with my own day and
       race here.

17 Here lands female and male,
   Here the heirship and heiress-ship of the world—
       Here the flame of materials,
   Here Spirituality, the translatress, the openly-avowed,
   The ever-tending, the finale of visible forms,
   The satisfier, after due long-waiting, now advancing,
   Yes, here comes the mistress, the Soul.

18 The SOUL!
   Forever and forever—Longer than soil is brown and
       solid—Longer than water ebbs and flows.

19 I will make the poems of materials, for I think they
       are to be the most spiritual poems,
   And I will make the poems of my body and of
       mortality,

For I think I shall then supply myself with the
poems of my Soul and of immortality.

20 I will make a song for These States, that no one
State may under any circumstances be subjected
to another State,
And I will make a song that there shall be comity by
day and by night between all The States, and
between any two of them,
And I will make a song of the organic bargains of
These States—And a shrill song of curses on
him who would dissever the Union;
And I will make a song for the ears of the President,
full of weapons with menacing points,
And behind the weapons countless dissatisfied faces.

21 I will acknowledge contemporary lands,
I will trail the whole geography of the globe, and
salute courteously every city large and small;
And employments! I will put in my poems, that
with you is heroism, upon land and sea—And I
will report all heroism from an American point
of view;
And sexual organs and acts! do you concentrate in
me—For I am determined to tell you with
courageous clear voice, to prove you illustrious.

22 I will sing the song of companionship,
I will show what alone must compact These,
I believe These are to found their own ideal of manly
love, indicating it in me;
I will therefore let flame from me the burning fires
that were threatening to consume me,
I will lift what has too long kept down those smoul-
dering fires,
I will give them complete abandonment,
I will write the evangel-poem of comrades* and
of love,

(For who but I should understand love, with all its
    sorrow and joy?
And who but I should be the poet of comrades?)

23 I am the credulous man of qualities, ages, races,
I advance from the people en-masse in their own
    spirit,
Here is what sings unrestricted faith.

24 Omnes!* Omnes!
Let others ignore what they may,
I make the poem of evil also—I commemorate that
    part also,
I am myself just as much evil as good—And I say
    there is in fact no evil,
Or if there is, I say it is just as important to you, to
    the earth, or to me, as anything else.

25 I too, following many, and followed by many, inau-
    gurate a Religion—I too go to the wars,
It may be I am destined to utter the loudest cries
    thereof, the conqueror's shouts,
They may rise from me yet, and soar above every
    thing.

26 Each is not for its own sake,
I say the whole earth, and all the stars in the sky, are
    for Religion's sake.

27 I say no man has ever been half devout enough,
None has ever adored or worship'd half enough,
None has begun to think how divine he himself is,
    and how certain the future is.

28 I specifically announce that the real and perma-
    nent grandeur of These States must be their
    Religion,
Otherwise there is no real and permanent grandeur.

29 What are you doing, young man?
  Are you so earnest—so given up to literature,
    science, art, amours?
  These ostensible realities, materials, points?
  Your ambition or business, whatever it may be?

30 It is well—Against such I say not a word—I am
    their poet also;
  But behold! such swiftly subside—burnt up for
    Religion's sake,
  For not all matter is fuel to heat, impalpable flame,
    the essential life of the earth,
  Any more than such are to Religion.

31 What do you seek, so pensive and silent?
  What do you need, comrade?
  Mon cher! do you think it is love?

32 Proceed, comrade,
  It is a painful thing to love a man or woman to
    excess—yet it satisfies—it is great,
  But there is something else very great—it makes the
    whole coincide,
  It, magnificent, beyond materials, with continuous
    hands, sweeps and provides for all.

33 O I see the following poems are indeed to drop in the
    earth the germs of a greater Religion.

34 My comrade!
  For you, to share with me, two greatnesses—And a
    third one, rising inclusive and more resplendent,
  The greatness of Love and Democracy—and the
    greatness of Religion.

35 Melange mine!
  Mysterious ocean where the streams empty,
  Prophetic spirit of materials shifting and flickering
    around me,

Wondrous interplay between the seen and unseen,
Living beings, identities, now doubtless near us, in
    the air, that we know not of,
Extasy everywhere touching and thrilling me,
Contact daily and hourly that will not release me,
These selecting—These, in hints, demanded of me.

36 Not he, adhesive, kissing me so long with his daily
    kiss,
Has winded and twisted around me that which holds
    me to him,
Any more than I am held to the heavens, to the
    spiritual world,
And to the identities of the Gods, my unknown
    lovers,
After what they have done to me, suggesting
    such themes.

37 O such themes! Equalities!
O amazement of things! O divine average!
O warblings under the sun—ushered, as now, or at
    noon, or setting!
O strain, musical, flowing through ages—now
    reaching hither,
I take to your reckless and composite chords—I
    add to them, and cheerfully pass them forward.

38 As I have walked in Alabama my morning walk,
I have seen where the she-bird, the mocking-bird, sat
    on her nest in the briers, hatching her brood.

39 I have seen the he-bird also,
I have paused to hear him, near at hand, inflating his
    throat, and joyfully singing.

40 And while I paused, it came to me that what he
    really sang for was not there only,
Nor for his mate nor himself only, nor all sent back
    by the echoes,

But subtle, clandestine, away beyond,
A charge transmitted, and gift occult, for those
    being born.

41 Democracy!
Near at hand to you a throat is now inflating itself
    and joyfully singing.

42 Ma femme!*
For the brood beyond us and of us,
For those who belong here, and those to come,
I, exultant, to be ready for them, will now shake out
    carols stronger and haughtier than have ever yet
    been heard upon the earth.

43 I will make the songs of passions, to give them
    their way,
And your songs, offenders—for I scan you with
    kindred eyes, and carry you with me the same
    as any.

44 I will make the true poem of riches,
Namely, to earn for the body and the mind, what
    adheres, and goes forward, and is not dropt by
    death.

45 I will effuse egotism, and show it underlying all—
    And I will be the bard of Personality;
And I will show of male and female that either is but
    the equal of the other,
And I will show that there is no imperfection in male
    or female, or in the earth, or in the present—
    and can be none in the future,
And I will show that whatever happens to anybody, it
    may be turned to beautiful results—And I will
    show that nothing can happen more beautiful
    than death;
And I will thread a thread through my poems that no
    one thing in the universe is inferior to another
    thing,

And that all the things of the universe are perfect
    miracles, each as profound as any.

46 I will not make poems with reference to parts,
    But I will make leaves, poems, poemets, songs, says,
        thoughts, with reference to ensemble;
    And I will not sing with reference to a day, but with
        reference to all days,
    And I will not make a poem, nor the least part of
        a poem, but has reference to the Soul,
    Because, having looked at the objects of the universe,
        I find there is no one, nor any particle of one,
        but has reference to the Soul.

47 Was somebody asking to see the Soul?
    See! your own shape and countenance—persons,
        substances, beasts, the trees, the running rivers,
        the rocks and sands.

48 All hold spiritual joys, and afterward loosen them,
    How can the real body ever die, and be buried?

49 Of your real body, and any man's or woman's real
        body, item for item, it will elude the hands of
        the corpse-cleaners, and pass to fitting spheres,
        carrying what has accrued to it from the moment
        of birth to the moment of death.

50 Not the types set up by the printer return their im-
        pression, the meaning, the main concern, any
        more than a man's substance and life, or a
        woman's substance and life, return in the body
        and the Soul, indifferently before death and
        after death.

51 Behold! the body includes and is the meaning, the
        main concern—and includes and is the Soul;
    Whoever you are! how superb and how divine is your
        body, or any part of it.

52 Whoever you are! to you endless announcements.

53 Daughter of the lands, did you wait for your poet?
   Did you wait for one with a flowing mouth and
        indicative hand?

54 Toward the male of The States, and toward the
        female of The States,
   Toward the President, the Congress, the diverse Gov-
        ernors, the new Judiciary,
   Live words—words to the lands.

55 O the lands!
   Lands scorning invaders! Interlinked, food-yielding
        lands!
   Land of coal and iron! Land of gold! Lands of
        cotton, sugar, rice!
   Odorous and sunny land! Floridian land!
   Land of the spinal river, the Mississippi! Land of
        the Alleghanies! Ohio's land!
   Land of wheat, beef, pork! Land of wool and hemp!
        Land of the potato, the apple, and the grape!
   Land of the pastoral plains, the grass-fields of the
        world! Land of those sweet-aired interminable
        plateaus! Land there of the herd, the garden,
        the healthy house of adobie! Land there of rapt
        thought, and of the realization of the stars!
        Land of simple, holy, untamed lives!
   Lands where the northwest Columbia winds, and
        where the southwest Colorado winds!
   Land of the Chesapeake! Land of the Delaware!
   Land of Ontario, Erie, Huron, Michigan!
   Land of the Old Thirteen! Massachusetts land!
        Land of Vermont and Connecticut!
   Land of many oceans! Land of sierras and peaks!
   Land of boatmen and sailors! Fishermen's land!
   Inextricable lands! the clutched together! the
        passionate lovers!
   The side by side! the elder and younger brothers!
        the bony-limbed!

The great women's land! the feminine! the ex-
    perienced sisters and the inexperienced sisters!
Far breath'd land! Arctic braced! Mexican breezed!
    the diverse! the compact!
The Pennsylvanian! the Virginian! the double
    Carolinian!
O all and each well-loved by me! my intrepid nations!
    O I cannot be discharged from you!
O Death! O for all that, I am yet of you, unseen,
    this hour, with irrepressible love,
Walking New England, a friend, a traveller,
Splashing my bare feet in the edge of the summer
    ripples, on Paumanok's sands,
Crossing the prairies—dwelling again in Chicago—
    dwelling in many towns,
Observing shows, births, improvements, structures,
    arts,
Listening to the orators and the oratresses in public
    halls,
Of and through The States, as during life—each
    man and woman my neighbor,
The Louisianian, the Georgian, as near to me, and I
    as near to him and her,
The Mississippian and Arkansian—the woman and
    man of Utah, Dakotah, Nebraska, yet with me
    —and I yet with any of them,
Yet upon the plains west of the spinal river—yet
    in my house of adobie,
Yet returning eastward—yet in the Sea-Side State,
    or in Maryland,
Yet a child of the North—yet Kanadian, cheerily
    braving the winter—the snow and ice welcome
    to me,
Yet a true son either of Maine, or of the Granite
    State, or of the Narragansett Bay State, or of
    the Empire State,
Yet sailing to other shores to annex the same—yet
    welcoming every new brother,

Hereby applying these leaves to the new ones, from
the hour they unite with the old ones,
Coming among the new ones myself, to be their
companion—coming personally to you now,
Enjoining you to acts, characters, spectacles, with
me.

56 With me, with firm holding—yet haste, haste on.

57 For your life, adhere to me,
Of all the men of the earth, I only can unloose you
and toughen you,
I may have to be persuaded many times before I
consent to give myself to you—but what of
that?
Must not Nature be persuaded many times?

58 No dainty dolce affettuoso* I;
Bearded, sunburnt, gray-necked, forbidding, I have
arrived,
To be wrestled with as I pass, for the solid prizes
of the universe,
For such I afford whoever can persevere to win them.

59 On my way a moment I pause,
Here for you! And here for America!
Still the Present I raise aloft—Still the Future of
The States I harbinge, glad and sublime,
And for the Past I pronounce what the air holds of
the red aborigines.

60 The red aborigines!
Leaving natural breaths, sounds of rain and winds,
calls as of birds and animals in the woods,
syllabled to us for names,
Okonee, Koosa, Ottawa, Monongahela, Sauk, Natchez,
Chattahoochee, Kaqueta, Oronoco.

Wabash, Miami, Saginaw, Chippewa, Oshkosh, Walla-
  Walla,
Leaving such to The States, they melt, they depart,
  charging the water and the land with names.

61 O expanding and swift! O henceforth,
Elements, breeds, adjustments, turbulent, quick, and
  audacious,
A world primal again—Vistas of glory, incessant
  and branching,
A new race, dominating previous ones, and grander
  far,
New politics—New literatures and religions—New
  inventions and arts.

62 These! These, my voice announcing—I will sleep
  no more, but arise;
You oceans that have been calm within me! how
  I feel you, fathomless, stirring, preparing
  unprecedented waves and storms.

63 See! steamers steaming through my poems!
See, in my poems immigrants continually coming
  and landing;
See, in arriere, the wigwam, the trail, the hunter's
  hut, the flat-boat, the maize-leaf, the claim, the
  rude fence, and the backwoods village;
See, on the one side the Western Sea, and on the
  other side the Eastern Sea, how they advance
  and retreat upon my poems, as upon their own
  shores;
See, pastures and forests in my poems See, animals,
  wild and tame—See, beyond the Kanzas, count-
  less herds of buffalo, feeding on short curly
  grass;
See, in my poems, old and new cities, solid, vast,
  inland, with paved streets, with iron and stone
  edifices, and ceaseless vehicles, and commerce;

See the populace, millions upon millions, handsome,
   tall, muscular, both sexes, clothed in easy and
   dignified clothes—teaching, commanding, mar-
   rying, generating, equally electing and elective;
See, the many-cylinder'd steam printing-press—See,
   the electric telegraph—See, the strong and
   quick locomotive, as it departs, panting, blowing
   the steam-whistle;
See, ploughmen, ploughing farms—See, miners,
   digging mines—See, the numberless factories;
See, mechanics, busy at their benches, with tools—
   See from among them, superior judges, philo-
   sophs, Presidents, emerge, dressed in working
   dresses;
See, lounging through the shops and fields of The
   States, me, well-beloved, close-held by day and
   night,
Hear the loud echo of my songs there! Read the
   hints come at last.

64　O my comrade!
   O you and me at last—and us two only;
   O power, liberty, eternity at last!
   O to be relieved of distinctions! to make as much
      of vices as virtues!
   O to level occupations and the sexes! O to bring
      all to common ground! O adhesiveness!
   O the pensive aching to be together—you know not
      why, and I know not why.

65　O a word to clear one's path ahead endlessly!
   O something extatic and undemonstrable! O music
      wild!
   O now I triumph—and you shall also;
   O hand in hand　O wholesome pleasure—O one
      more desirer and lover,
   O haste, firm holding—haste, haste on, with me.

FROM CHANTS DEMOCRATIC AND NATIVE AMERICAN

*14.**

1 POETS to come!
  Not to-day is to justify me, and Democracy, and
      what we are for,
  But you, a new brood, native, athletic, continental,
      greater than before known,
  You must justify me.

2 Indeed, if it were not for you, what would I be?
  What is the little I have done, except to arouse you?

3 I depend on being realized, long hence, where the
      broad fat prairies spread, and thence to Oregon
      and California inclusive,
  I expect that the Texan and the Arizonian, ages
      hence, will understand me,
  I expect that the future Carolinian and Georgian will
      understand me and love me,
  I expect that Kanadians, a hundred, and perhaps
      many hundred years from now, in winter, in the
      splendor of the snow and woods, or on the icy
      lakes, will take me with them, and permanently
      enjoy themselves with me.

4 Of to-day I know I am momentary, untouched—I
      am the bard of the future,
  I but write one or two indicative words for the future,
  I but advance a moment, only to wheel and hurry
      back in the darkness.

5 I am a man who, sauntering along, without fully
      stopping, turns a casual look upon you, and then
      averts his face,

Leaving it to you to prove and define it,
Expecting the main things from you.

*18.**

ME imperturbe,
Me standing at ease in Nature,
Master of all, or mistress of all—aplomb in the
    midst of irrational things,
Imbued as they—passive, receptive, silent as they,
Finding my occupation, poverty, notoriety, foibles,
    crimes, less important than I thought;
Me private, or public, or menial, or solitary—all
    these subordinate, (I am eternally equal with
    the best—I am not subordinate;)
Me toward the Mexican Sea, or in the Mannahatta,
    or the Tennessee, or far north, or inland,
A river-man, or a man of the woods, or of any farm-
    life of These States, or of the coast, or the lakes,
    or Kanada,
Me, wherever my life is to be lived, O to be self-bal-
    anced for contingencies!
O to confront night, storms, hunger, ridicule, acci-
    dents, rebuffs, as the trees and animals do.

*20.**

1 AMERICAN mouth-songs!
    Those of mechanics—each one singing his, as it
        should be, blithe and strong,
    The carpenter singing his, as he measures his plank
        or beam,
    The mason singing his, as he makes ready for work,
        or leaves off work,
    The boatman singing what belongs to him in his boat
        —the deck-hand singing on the steamboat deck,
    The shoemaker singing as he sits on his bench—the
        hatter singing as he stands,

The wood-cutter's song—the ploughboy's, on his way
  in the morning, or at the noon intermission, or at
  sundown;
The delicious singing of the mother—or of the
  young wife at work—or of the girl sewing or
  washing—Each singing what belongs to her,
  and to none else,
The day what belongs to the day—At night, the
  party of young fellows, robust, friendly, clean-
  blooded, singing with melodious voices, melo-
  dious thoughts.

2   Come! some of you! still be flooding The States
  with hundreds and thousands of mouth-songs,
  fit for The States only.

FROM LEAVES OF GRASS

*1.**

1   ELEMENTAL drifts!
  O I wish I could impress others as you and the waves
  have just been impressing me.

2   As I ebbed with an ebb of the ocean of life,
  As I wended the shores I know,
  As I walked where the sea-ripples wash you, Pau-
  manok,
  Where they rustle up, hoarse and sibilant,
  Where the fierce old mother endlessly cries for her
  castaways,
  I, musing, late in the autumn day, gazing off south-
  ward,
  Alone, held by the eternal self of me that threatens
  to get the better of me, and stifle me,
  Was seized by the spirit that trails in the lines
  underfoot,
  In the rim, the sediment, that stands for all the water
  and all the land of the globe.

3 Fascinated, my eyes, reverting from the south,
      dropped, to follow those slender winrows,*
  Chaff, straw, splinters of wood, weeds, and the sea-
      gluten,
  Scum, scales from shining rocks, leaves of salt-
      lettuce, left by the tide;
  Miles walking, the sound of breaking waves the other
      side of me,
  Paumanok, there and then, as I thought the old
      thought of likenesses,
  These you presented to me, you fish-shaped island,
  As I wended the shores I know,
  As I walked with that eternal self of me, seeking
      types.

4 As I wend the shores I know not,
  As I listen to the dirge, the voices of men and women
      wrecked,
  As I inhale the impalpable breezes that set in
      upon me,
  As the ocean so mysterious rolls toward me closer
      and closer,
  At once I find, the least thing that belongs to me, or
      that I see or touch, I know not;
  I, too, but signify, at the utmost, a little washed-up
      drift,
  A few sands and dead leaves to gather,
  Gather, and merge myself as part of the sands and
      drift.

5 O baffled, balked,
  Bent to the very earth, here preceding what follows,
  Oppressed with myself that I have dared to open my
      mouth,
  Aware now, that, amid all the blab whose echoes
      recoil upon me, I have not once had the least
      idea who or what I am,
  But that before all my insolent poems the real ME
      still stands untouched, untold, altogether un-
      reached,

Withdrawn far, mocking me with mock-congrat-
    ulatory signs and bows,
With peals of distant ironical laughter at every word
    I have written or shall write,
Striking me with insults till I fall helpless upon the
    sand.

6   O I perceive I have not understood anything—not a
        single object—and that no man ever can.

7   I perceive Nature here, in sight of the sea, is taking
        advantage of me, to dart upon me, and sting me,
    Because I was assuming so much,
    And because I have dared to open my mouth to sing
        at all.

8   You oceans both! You tangible land! Nature!
    Be not too rough with me—I submit—I close with
        you,
    These little shreds shall, indeed, stand for all.

9   You friable shore, with trails of debris!
    You fish-shaped island! I take what is underfoot;
    What is yours is mine, my father.

10 I too Paumanok,
    I too have bubbled up, floated the measureless float,
        and been washed on your shores;
    I too am but a trail of drift and debris,
    I too leave little wrecks upon you, you fish-shaped
        island.

11 I throw myself upon your breast, my father,
    I cling to you so that you cannot unloose me,
    I hold you so firm, till you answer me something.

12 Kiss me, my father,
    Touch me with your lips, as I touch those I love,
    Breathe to me, while I hold you close, the secret of
        the wondrous murmuring I envy,

For I fear I shall become crazed, if I cannot emulate
    it, and utter myself as well as it.

13 Sea-raff! Crook-tongued waves!
    O, I will yet sing, some day, what you have said
        to me.

14 Ebb, ocean of life, (the flow will return,)
    Cease not your moaning, you fierce old mother,
    Endlessly cry for your castaways—but fear not,
        deny not me,
    Rustle not up so hoarse and angry against my feet, as
        I touch you, or gather from you.

15 I mean tenderly by you,
    I gather for myself, and for this phantom, looking
        down where we lead, and following me and
        mine.

16 Me and mine!
    We, loose winrows, little corpses,
    Froth, snowy white, and bubbles,
    (See! from my dead lips the ooze exuding at last!
    See—the prismatic colors, glistening and rolling!)
    Tufts of straw, sands, fragments,
    Buoyed hither from many moods, one contradicting
        another,
    From the storm, the long calm, the darkness, the
        swell,
    Musing, pondering, a breath, a briny tear, a dab of
        liquid or soil,
    Up just as much out of fathomless workings fer-
        mented and thrown,
    A limp blossom or two, torn, just as much over waves
        floating, drifted at random,
    Just as much for us that sobbing dirge of Nature,
    Just as much, whence we come, that blare of the
        cloud-trumpets;

We, capricious, brought hither, we know not whence,
    spread out before You, up there, walking or
    sitting,
Whoever you are—we too lie in drifts at your feet.

*16.**

SEA-WATER, and all living below it,
Forests at the bottom of the sea—the branches and
    leaves,
Sea-lettuce, vast lichens, strange flowers and seeds—
    the thick tangle, the openings, and the pink turf,
Different colors, pale gray and green, purple, white,
    and gold—the play of light through the water,
Dumb swimmers there among the rocks—coral,
    gluten, grass, rushes—and the aliment of the
    swimmers,
Sluggish existences grazing there, suspended, or
    slowly crawling close to the bottom,
The sperm-whale at the surface, blowing air and
    spray, or disporting with his flukes,
The leaden-eyed shark, the walrus, the turtle, the
    hairy sea-leopard, and the sting-ray;
Passions there—wars, pursuits, tribes—sight in
    those ocean-depths—breathing that thick-breath-
    ing air, as so many do,
The change thence to the sight here, and to the subtle
    air breathed by beings like us, who walk this
    sphere;
The change onward from ours to that of beings who
    walk other spheres.

*17.**

I SIT and look out upon all the sorrows of the world,
    and upon all oppression and shame,
I hear secret convulsive sobs from young men, at
    anguish with themselves, remorseful after deeds
    done;

I see, in low life, the mother misused by her children,
    dying, neglected, gaunt, desperate,
I see the wife misused by her husband—I see the
    treacherous seducer of the young woman,
I mark the ranklings of jealousy and unrequited love,
    attempted to be hid—I see these sights on the
    earth,
I see the workings of battle, pestilence, tyranny—I
    see martyrs and prisoners,
I observe a famine at sea—I observe the sailors
    casting lots who shall be killed, to preserve the
    lives of the rest,
I observe the slights and degradations cast by arro-
    gant persons upon laborers, the poor, and upon
    negroes, and the like;
All these—All the meanness and agony without end,
    I sitting, look out upon,
See, hear, and am silent.

Poem of Joys*

1 O TO make a most jubilant poem!
O full of music! Full of manhood, womanhood,
    infancy!
O full of common employments! Full of grain and
    trees.

2 O for the voices of animals! O for the swiftness and
    balance of fishes!
O for the dropping of rain-drops in a poem!
O for the sunshine and motion of waves in a poem.

3 O to be on the sea! the wind, the wide waters
    around;
O to sail in a ship under full sail at sea.

4 O the joy of my spirit! It is uncaged! It darts like
    lightning!
It is not enough to have this globe, or a certain time
    —I will have thousands of globes, and all time.

5   O the engineer's joys!
    To go with a locomotive!
    To hear the hiss of steam—the merry shriek—the
        steam-whistle—the laughing locomotive!
    To push with resistless way, and speed off in the
        distance.

6   O the horseman's and horsewoman's joys!
    The saddle—the gallop—the pressure upon the seat
        —the cool gurgling by the ears and hair.

7   O the fireman's joys!
    I hear the alarm at dead of night,
    I hear bells—shouts!—I pass the crowd—I run!
    The sight of the flames maddens me with pleasure.

8   O the joy of the strong-brawned fighter, towering
        in the arena, in perfect condition, conscious of
        power, thirsting to meet his opponent.

9   O the joy of that vast elemental sympathy which only
        the human Soul is capable of generating and
        emitting in steady and limitless floods.

10 O the mother's joys!
    The watching—the endurance—the precious love—
        the anguish—the patiently yielded life.

11 O the joy of increase, growth, recuperation,
    The joy of soothing and pacifying—the joy of
        concord and harmony.

12 O to go back to the place where I was born!
    O to hear the birds sing once more!
    To ramble about the house and barn, and over the
        fields, once more,
    And through the orchard and along the old lanes
        once more.

13 O male and female!
  O the presence of women! (I swear, nothing is more
    exquisite to me than the presence of women;)
  O for the girl, my mate! O for happiness with my
    mate!
  O the young man as I pass! O I am sick after the
    friendship of him who, I fear, is indifferent
    to me.

14 O the streets of cities!
  The flitting faces—the expressions, eyes, feet, cos-
    tumes! O I cannot tell how welcome they are
    to me;
  O of men—of women toward me as I pass—The
    memory of only one look—the boy lingering
    and waiting.

15 O to have been brought up on bays, lagoons, creeks,
    or along the coast!
  O to continue and be employed there all my life!
  O the briny and damp smell—the shore—the salt
    weeds exposed at low water,
  The work of fishermen—the work of the eel-fisher
    and clam-fisher.

16 O it is I!
  I come with my clam-rake and spade! I come with
    my eel-spear;
  Is the tide out? I join the group of clam-diggers on
    the flats,
  I laugh and work with them—I joke at my work,
    like a mettlesome young man.

17 In winter I take my eel-basket and eel-spear and travel
    out on foot on the ice—I have a small axe to cut
    holes in the ice;
  Behold me, well-clothed, going gayly, or returning in
    the afternoon—my brood of tough boys accom-
    panying me,

My brood of grown and part-grown boys, who love
    to be with none else so well as they love to be
    with me,
By day to work with me, and by night to sleep with
    me.

18 Or, another time, in warm weather, out in a boat, to
    lift the lobster-pots, where they are sunk with
    heavy stones, (I know the buoys;)
O the sweetness of the Fifth Month morning upon the
    water, as I row, just before sunrise, toward the
    buoys;
I pull the wicker pots up slantingly—the dark green
    lobsters are desperate with their claws, as I take
    them out—I insert wooden pegs in the joints of
    their pincers,
I go to all the places, one after another, and then row
    back to the shore,
There, in a huge kettle of boiling water, the lobsters
    shall be boiled till their color becomes scarlet.

19 Or, another time, mackerel-taking,
Voracious, mad for the hook, near the surface, they
    seem to fill the water for miles;
Or, another time, fishing for rock-fish in Chesapeake
    Bay—I one of the brown-faced crew;
Or, another time, trailing for blue-fish off Paumanok,
    I stand with braced body,
My left foot is on the gunwale—my right arm throws
    the coils of slender rope,
In sight around me the quick veering and darting of
    fifty skiffs, my companions.

20 O boating on the rivers!
The voyage down the Niagara, (the St. Lawrence,)—
    the superb scenery—the steamers,
The ships sailing—the Thousand Islands—the occa-
    sional timber-raft, and the raftsmen with long-
    reaching sweep-oars,

The little huts on the rafts, and the stream of smoke
    when they cook supper at evening.

21 O something pernicious and dread!
Something far away from a puny and pious life!
Something unproved! Something in a trance!
Something escaped from the anchorage, and driving
    free.

22 O to work in mines, or forging iron!
Foundry casting—the foundry itself—the rude high
    roof—the ample and shadowed space,
The furnace—the hot liquid poured out and running.

23 O the joys of the soldier!
To feel the presence of a brave general! to feel his
    sympathy!
To behold his calmness! to be warmed in the rays of
    his smile!
To go to battle! to hear the bugles play, and the drums
    beat!
To hear the artillery! to see the glittering of the bay-
    onets and musket-barrels in the sun!
To see men fall and die and not complain!
To taste the savage taste of blood! to be so devilish!
To gloat so over the wounds and deaths of the enemy.

24 O the whaleman's joys! O I cruise my old cruise
    again!
I feel the ship's motion under me—I feel the Atlantic
    breezes fanning me,
I hear the cry again sent down from the mast-head,
    There she blows,
Again I spring up the rigging, to look with the rest—
    We see—we descend, wild with excitement,
I leap in the lowered boat—We row toward our prey,
    where he lies,
We approach, stealthy and silent—I see the moun-
    tainous mass, lethargic, basking,

I see the harpooner standing up—I see the weapon
    dart from his vigorous arm;
O swift, again, now, far out in the ocean, the wounded
    whale, settling, running to windward, tows me,
Again I see him rise to breathe—We row close
    again,
I see a lance driven through his side, pressed deep,
    turned in the wound,
Again we back off—I see him settle again—the life
    is leaving him fast,
As he rises, he spouts blood—I see him swim in cir-
    cles narrower and narrower, swiftly cutting the
    water—I see him die,
He gives one convulsive leap in the centre of the cir-
    cle, and then falls flat and still in the bloody
    foam.

25 O the old manhood of me, my joy!
    My children and grand-children—my white hair and
        beard,
    My largeness, calmness, majesty, out of the long
        stretch of my life.

26 O the ripened joy of womanhood!
    O perfect happiness at last!
    I am more than eighty years of age—my hair, too, is
        pure white—I am the most venerable mother;
    How clear is my mind! how all people draw nigh to
        me!
    What attractions are these, beyond any before? what
        bloom, more than the bloom of youth?
    What beauty is this that descends upon me, and rises
        out of me?

27 O the joy of my Soul leaning poised on itself—receiv-
    ing identity through materials, and loving them
    —observing characters, and absorbing them;

O my Soul, vibrated back to me, from them—from
    facts, sight, hearing, touch, my phrenology,
    reason, articulation, comparison, memory, and
    the like;
O the real life of my senses and flesh, transcending
    my senses and flesh;
O my body, done with materials—my sight, done
    with my material eyes;
O what is proved to me this day, beyond cavil, that it
    is not my material eyes which finally see,
Nor my material body which finally loves, walks,
    laughs, shouts, embraces, procreates.

28 O the farmer's joys!
Ohioan's, Illinoisian's, Wisconsinese', Kanadian's, Io-
    wan's, Kansian's, Missourian's, Oregonese' joys,
To rise at peep of day, and pass forth nimbly to work,
To plough land in the fall for winter-sown crops,
To plough land in the spring for maize,
To train orchards—to graft the trees—to gather
    apples in the fall.

29 O the pleasure with trees!
The orchard—the forest—the oak, cedar, pine,
    pekan-tree,
The honey-locust, black-walnut, cottonwood, and mag-
    nolia.

30 O Death!
O the beautiful touch of Death, soothing and benumb-
    ing a few moments, for reasons;
O that of myself, discharging my excrementitious
    body, to be burned, or rendered to powder, or
    buried,
My real body doubtless left to me for other spheres,
My voided body, nothing more to me, returning to the
    purifications, further offices, eternal uses of the
    earth.

31 O to bathe in the swimming-bath, or in a good place
along shore!
To splash the water! to walk ankle-deep; to race
naked along the shore.

32 O to realize space!
The plenteousness of all—that there are no bounds;
To emerge, and be of the sky—of the sun and moon,
and the flying clouds, as one with them.

33 O, while I live, to be the ruler of life—not a slave,
To meet life as a powerful conqueror,
No fumes—no ennui—no more complaints or scorn-
ful criticisms.

34 O me repellent and ugly!
O to these proud laws of the air, the water, and
the ground, proving my interior Soul impreg-
nable,
And nothing exterior shall ever take command of me.

35 O to attract by more than attraction!
How it is I know not—yet behold! the something
which obeys none of the rest,
It is offensive, never defensive—yet how magnetic
it draws.

36 O the joy of suffering!
To struggle against great odds! to meet enemies un-
daunted!
To be entirely alone with them! to find how much I
can stand!
To look strife, torture, prison, popular odium, death,
face to face!
To mount the scaffold! to advance to the muzzles of
guns with perfect nonchalance!
To be indeed a God!

37 O the gleesome saunter over fields and hill-sides!
  The leaves and flowers of the commonest weeds—the
      moist fresh stillness of the woods,
  The exquisite smell of the earth at day-break, and all
      through the forenoon.

38 O love-branches! love-root! love-apples!
  O chaste and electric torrents! O mad-sweet drops.

39 O the orator's joys!
  To inflate the chest—to roll the thunder of the voice
      out from the ribs and throat,
  To make the people rage, weep, hate, desire, with
      yourself,
  To lead America—to quell America with a great
      tongue.

40 O the joy of a manly self-hood!
  Personality—to be servile to none—to defer to none
      —not to any tyrant, known or unknown,
  To walk with erect carriage, a step springy and
      elastic,
  To look with calm gaze, or with a flashing eye,
  To speak with a full and sonorous voice, out of a
      broad chest,
  To confront with your personality all the other per-
      sonalities of the earth.

41 O to have my life henceforth my poem of joys!
  To dance, clap hands, exult, shout, skip, leap, roll on,
      float on,
  An athlete—full of rich words—full of joys.

A Word Out of the Sea*

OUT of the rocked cradle,
Out of the mocking-bird's throat, the musical shuttle,
Out of the boy's mother's womb, and from the nipples
    of her breasts,

Out of the Ninth Month midnight,
Over the sterile sands, and the fields beyond, where
    the child, leaving his bed, wandered alone, bare-
    headed, barefoot,
Down from the showered halo,
Up from the mystic play of shadows, twining and
    twisting as if they were alive,
Out from the patches of briers and blackberries,
From the memories of the bird that chanted to me,
From your memories, sad brother—from the fitful
    risings and fallings I heard,
From under that yellow half-moon, late-risen, and
    swollen as if with tears,
From those beginning notes of sickness and love,
    there in the transparent mist,
From the thousand responses of my heart, never to
    cease,
From the myriad thence-aroused words,
From the word stronger and more delicious than any,
From such, as now they start, the scene revisiting,
As a flock, twittering, rising, or overhead passing,
Borne hither—ere all eludes me, hurriedly,
A man—yet by these tears a little boy again,
Throwing myself on the sand, confronting the waves,
I, chanter of pains and joys, uniter of here and here-
    after,
Taking all hints to use them—but swiftly leaping
    beyond them,
A reminiscence sing.

REMINISCENCE

1 Once, Paumanok,*
When the snows had melted, and the Fifth Month
    grass was growing,
Up this sea-shore, in some briers,
Two guests from Alabama—two together,
And their nest, and four light-green eggs, spotted with
    brown,
And every day the he-bird, to and fro, near at hand,

And every day the she-bird, crouched on her nest,
    silent, with bright eyes,
And every day I, a curious boy, never too close, never
    disturbing them,
Cautiously peering, absorbing, translating.

2 *Shine! Shine!*
  Pour down your warmth, great Sun!
  While we bask—we two together.

3 *Two together!*
  Winds blow South, or winds blow North,
  Day come white, or night come black,
  Home, or rivers and mountains from home,
  Singing all time, minding no time,
  If we two but keep together.

4 Till of a sudden,
  May-be killed, unknown to her mate,
  One forenoon the she-bird crouched not on the nest,
  Nor returned that afternoon, nor the next,
  Nor ever appeared again.

5 And thenceforward, all summer, in the sound of the
    sea,
  And at night, under the full of the moon, in calmer
    weather,
  Over the hoarse surging of the sea,
  Or flitting from brier to brier by day,
  I saw, I heard at intervals, the remaining one, the
    he-bird,
  The solitary guest from Alabama.

6 *Blow! Blow!*
  Blow up sea-winds along Paumanok's shore;
  I wait and I wait, till you blow my mate to me.

7 Yes, when the stars glistened,
  All night long, on the prong of a moss-scallop'd stake,

Down, almost amid the slapping waves,
Sat the lone singer, wonderful, causing tears.

8 He called on his mate,
  He poured forth the meanings which I, of all men,
      know.

9 Yes, my brother, I know,
  The rest might not—but I have treasured every note,
  For once, and more than once, dimly, down to the
      beach gliding,
  Silent, avoiding the moonbeams, blending myself with
      the shadows,
  Recalling now the obscure shapes, the echoes, the
      sounds and sights after their sorts,
  The white arms out in the breakers tirelessly tossing,
  I, with bare feet, a child, the wind wafting my hair,
  Listened long and long.

10 Listened, to keep, to sing—now translating the
      notes,
   Following you, my brother.

11 *Soothe! Soothe!*
   Close on its wave soothes the wave behind,
   And again another behind, embracing and lapping,
       every one close,
   But my love soothes not me.

12 *Low hangs the moon—it rose late,*
   O it is lagging—O I think it is heavy with love.

13 *O madly the sea pushes upon the land,*
   With love—with love.

14 *O night!*
   O do I not see my love fluttering out there among the
       breakers?

What is that little black thing I see there in the
    white?

15 *Loud! Loud!*
Loud I call to you my love!
High and clear I shoot my voice over the waves,
Surely you must know who is here,
You must know who I am, my love.

16 *Low-hanging moon!*
What is that dusky spot in your brown yellow?
O it is the shape of my mate!
O moon, do not keep her from me any longer.

17 *Land! O land!*
Whichever way I turn, O I think you could give me
    my mate back again, if you would,
For I am almost sure I see her dimly whichever way
    I look.

18 *O rising stars!*
Perhaps the one I want so much will rise with some
    of you.

19 *O throat!*
Sound clearer through the atmosphere!
Pierce the woods, the earth,
Somewhere listening to catch you must be the one I
    want.

20 *Shake out, carols!*
Solitary here—the night's carols!
Carols of lonesome love! Death's carols!
Carols under that lagging, yellow, waning moon!
O, under that moon, where she droops almost down
    into the sea!
O reckless, despairing carols.

21 *But soft!*
Sink low—soft!
Soft! Let me just murmur,
And do you wait a moment, you husky-noised sea,
For somewhere I believe I heard my mate responding
  to me,
So faint—I must be still to listen,
But not altogether still, for then she might not come
  immediately to me.

22 *Hither, my love!*
Here I am! Here!
With this just-sustained note I announce myself to
  you,
This gentle call is for you, my love.

23 *Do not be decoyed elsewhere!*
That is the whistle of the wind—it is not my voice,
That is the fluttering of the spray,
Those are the shadows of leaves.

24 *O darkness! O in vain!*
O I am very sick and sorrowful.

25 *O brown halo in the sky, near the moon, drooping*
  upon the sea!
O troubled reflection in the sea!
O throat! O throbbing heart!
O all—and I singing uselessly all the night.

26 *Murmur! Murmur on!*
O murmurs—you yourselves make me continue to
  sing, I know not why.

27 *O past! O joy!*
In the air—in the woods—over fields,
Loved! Loved! Loved! Loved! Loved!
Loved—but no more with me,
We two together no more.

28 The aria sinking,
    All else continuing—the stars shining,
    The winds blowing—the notes of the wondrous bird
        echoing,
    With angry moans the fierce old mother yet, as ever,
        incessantly moaning,
    On the sands of Paumanok's shore gray and rustling,
    The yellow half-moon, enlarged, sagging down, droop-
        ing, the face of the sea almost touching,
    The boy extatic—with his bare feet the waves, with
        his hair the atmosphere dallying,
    The love in the heart pent, now loose, now at last
        tumultuously bursting,
    The aria's meaning, the ears, the Soul, swiftly depos-
        iting,
    The strange tears down the cheeks coursing,
    The colloquy there—the trio—each uttering,
    The undertone—the savage old mother, incessantly
        crying,
    To the boy's Soul's questions sullenly timing—some
        drowned secret hissing,
    To the outsetting bard of love.

29 Bird! (then said the boy's Soul,)
    Is it indeed toward your mate you sing? or is it
        mostly to me?
    For I that was a child, my tongue's use sleeping,
    Now that I have heard you,
    Now in a moment I know what I am for—I awake,
    And already a thousand singers—a thousand songs,
        clearer, louder, more sorrowful than yours,
    A thousand warbling echoes have started to life
        within me,
    Never to die.

30 O throes!
    O you demon, singing by yourself—projecting me,
    O solitary me, listening—never more shall I cease
        imitating, perpetuating you,

Never more shall I escape,
Never more shall the reverberations,
Never more the cries of unsatisfied love be absent
    from me,
Never again leave me to be the peaceful child I was
    before what there, in the night,
By the sea, under the yellow and sagging moon,
The dusky demon aroused—the fire, the sweet hell
    within,
The unknown want, the destiny of me.

31 O give me some clew!
O if I am to have so much, let me have more!
O a word! O what is my destination?
O I fear it is henceforth chaos!
O how joys, dreads, convolutions, human shapes, and
    all shapes, spring as from graves around me!
O phantoms! you cover all the land, and all the sea!
O I cannot see in the dimness whether you smile or
    frown upon me;
O vapor, a look, a word! O well-beloved!
O you dear women's and men's phantoms!

32 A word then, (for I will conquer it,)
The word final, superior to all,
Subtle, sent up—what is it?—I listen;
Are you whispering it, and have been all the time,
    you sea-waves?
Is that it from your liquid rims and wet sands?

33 Answering, the sea,
Delaying not, hurrying not,
Whispered me through the night, and very plainly
    before daybreak,
Lisped to me constantly the low and delicious word
    DEATH,
And again Death—ever Death, Death, Death,

Hissing melodious, neither like the bird, nor like my
    aroused child's heart,
But edging near, as privately for me, rustling at
    my feet,
And creeping thence steadily up to my ears,
Death, Death, Death, Death, Death.

34 Which I do not forget,
    But fuse the song of two together,
    That was sung to me in the moonlight on Paumanok's
        gray beach,
    With the thousand responsive songs, at random,
    My own songs, awaked from that hour,
    And with them the key, the word up from the waves,
    The word of the sweetest song, and all songs,
    That strong and delicious word which, creeping to
        my feet,
    The sea whispered me.

FROM ENFANS D'ADAM

*1.**

To the garden, the world, anew ascending,
Potent mates, daughters, sons, preluding,
The love, the life of their bodies, meaning and being,
Curious, here behold my resurrection, after slumber,
The revolving cycles, in their wide sweep, having
    brought me again,
Amorous, mature—all beautiful to me—all won-
    drous,
My limbs, and the quivering fire that ever plays
    through them, for reasons, most wondrous;
Existing, I peer and penetrate still,
Content with the present—content with the past,
By my side, or back of me, Eve following,
Or in front, and I following her just the same.

2.*

FROM that of myself, without which I were nothing,
From what I am determined to make illustrious, even
     if I stand sole among men,
From my own voice resonant—singing the phallus,
Singing the song of procreation,
Singing the need of superb children, and therein
     superb grown people,
Singing the muscular urge and the blending,
Singing the bedfellow's song, (O resistless yearning!
O for any and each, the body correlative attracting!
O for you, whoever you are, your correlative body!
     O it, more than all else, you delighting!)
From the pent up rivers of myself,
From the hungry gnaw that eats me night and day,
From native moments—from bashful pains—sing-
     ing them,
Singing something yet unfound, though I have dili-
     gently sought it, ten thousand years,
Singing the true song of the Soul, fitful, at random,
Singing what, to the Soul, entirely redeemed her, the
     faithful one, the prostitute, who detained me when
     I went to the city,
Singing the song of prostitutes;
Renascent with grossest Nature, or among animals,
Of that—of them, and what goes with them, my
     poems informing,
Of the smell of apples and lemons—of the pairing
     of birds,
Of the wet of woods—of the lapping of waves,
Of the mad pushes of waves upon the land—I them
     chanting,
The overture lightly sounding—the strain antici-
     pating,
The welcome nearness—the sight of the perfect
     body,
The swimmer swimming naked in the bath, or mo-
     tionless on his back lying and floating,

The female form approaching—I, pensive, love-flesh
tremulous, aching;

The slave's body for sale—I, sternly, with harsh
voice, auctioneering,

The divine list, for myself or you, or for any one,
making,

The face—the limbs—the index from head to foot,
and what it arouses,

The mystic deliria—the madness amorous—the utter
abandonment,

(Hark, close and still, what I now whisper to you,

I love you—O you entirely possess me,

O I wish that you and I escape from the rest, and go
utterly off—O free and lawless,

Two hawks in the air—two fishes swimming in the
sea not more lawless than we;)

The furious storm through me careering—I passion-
ately trembling,

The oath of the inseparableness of two together—of
the woman that loves me, and whom I love more
than my life—That oath swearing,

(O I willingly stake all, for you!

O let me be lost, if it must be so!

O you and I—what is it to us what the rest do or
think?

What is all else to us? only that we enjoy each other,
and exhaust each other, if it must be so;)

From the master—the pilot I yield the vessel to,

The general commanding me, commanding all—from
him permission taking,

From time the programme hastening, (I have loitered
too long, as it is;)

From sex—From the warp and from the woof,

(To talk to the perfect girl who understands me—the
girl of The States,

To waft to her these from my own lips—to effuse
them from my own body;)

From privacy—From frequent repinings alone,

From plenty of persons near, and yet the right person
not near,

From the soft sliding of hands over me, and thrusting
    of fingers through my hair and beard,
From the long-sustained kiss upon the mouth or
    bosom,
From the close pressure that makes me or any man
    drunk, fainting with excess,
From what the divine husband knows—from the
    work of fatherhood,
From exultation, victory, and relief—from the bed-
    fellow's embrace in the night,
From the act-poems of eyes, hands, hips, and bosoms,
From the cling of the trembling arm,
From the bending curve and the clinch,
From side by side, the pliant coverlid off throwing,
From the one so unwilling to have me leave—and
    me just as unwilling to leave,
(Yet a moment, O tender waiter, and I return,)
From the hour of shining stars and dropping dews,
From the night, a moment, I, emerging, flitting out,
Celebrate you, enfans prepared for,
And you, stalwart loins.

8.*

NATIVE moments! when you come upon me—Ah
    you are here now!
Give me now libidinous joys only!
Give me the drench of my passions! Give me life
    coarse and rank!
To-day, I go consort with nature's darlings—to-night
    too,
I am for those who believe in loose delights—I share
    the midnight orgies of young men,
I dance with the dancers, and drink with the drink-
    ers,
The echoes ring with our indecent calls,
I take for my love some prostitute*—I pick out some
    low person for my dearest friend,

He shall be lawless, rude, illiterate—he shall be one
 condemned by others for deeds done;
I will play a part no longer—Why should I exile
 myself from my companions?
O you shunned persons! I at least do not shun you,
I come forthwith in your midst—I will be your poet,
I will be more to you than to any of the rest.

9.*

ONCE I passed through a populous city, imprinting
 my brain, for future use, with its shows, architec-
 ture, customs, and traditions;
Yet now, of all that city, I remember only a woman
 I casually met there, who detained me for love
 of me,
Day by day and night by night we were together,—
 All else has long been forgotten by me,
I remember I say only that woman who passionately
 clung to me,
Again we wander—we love—we separate again,
Again she holds me by the hand—I must not go!
I see her close beside me, with silent lips, sad and
 tremulous.

10.*

INQUIRING, tireless, seeking that yet unfound,
I, a child, very old, over waves, toward the house of
 maternity, the land of migrations, look afar,
Look off the shores of my Western Sea—having
 arrived at last where I am—the circle almost
 circled;
For coming westward from Hindustan, from the vales
 of Kashmere,
From Asia—from the north—from the God, the
 sage, and the hero,

From the south—from the flowery peninsulas, and
    the spice islands,
Now I face the old home again—looking over to it,
    joyous, as after long travel, growth, and sleep;
But where is what I started for, so long ago?
And why is it yet unfound?

*14.**

I AM he that aches with love;
Does the earth gravitate? Does not all matter, ach-
    ing, attract all matter?
So the body of me to all I meet, or that I know.

*15.**

EARLY in the morning,
Walking forth from the bower, refreshed with sleep,
Behold me where I pass—hear my voice—approach,
Touch me—touch the palm of your hand to my
    body as I pass,
Be not afraid of my body.

CALAMUS*

*1.**

IN paths untrodden,
In the growth by margins of pond-waters,
Escaped from the life that exhibits itself,
From all the standards hitherto published—from
    the pleasures, profits, conformities,
Which too long I was offering to feed to my Soul;
Clear to me now, standards not yet published—
    clear to me that my Soul,
That the Soul of the man I speak for, feeds, rejoices
    only in comrades;

Here, by myself, away from the clank of the world,
Tallying and talked to here by tongues aromatic,
No longer abashed—for in this secluded spot I can
    respond as I would not dare elsewhere,
Strong upon me the life that does not exhibit itself,
    yet contains all the rest,
Resolved to sing no songs to-day but those of manly
    attachment,
Projecting them along that substantial life,
Bequeathing, hence, types of athletic love,
Afternoon, this delicious Ninth Month, in my forty-
    first year,
I proceed, for all who are, or have been, young
    men,
To tell the secret of my nights and days,
To celebrate the need of comrades.

2.*

SCENTED herbage of my breast,
Leaves from you I yield, I write, to be perused best
    afterwards,
Tomb-leaves, body-leaves, growing up above me, above
    death,
Perennial roots, tall leaves—O the winter shall not
    freeze you, delicate leaves,
Every year shall you bloom again—Out from where
    you retired, you shall emerge again;
O I do not know whether many, passing by, will dis-
    cover you, or inhale your faint odor—but I
    believe a few will;
O slender leaves! O blossoms of my blood! I permit
    you to tell, in your own way, of the heart that is
    under you,
O burning and throbbing—surely all will one day be
    accomplished;
O I do not know what you mean, there underneath
    yourselves—you are not happiness,

You are often more bitter than I can bear—you burn
    and sting me,
Yet you are very beautiful to me, you faint-tinged
    roots—you make me think of Death,
Death is beautiful from you—(what indeed is beau-
    tiful, except Death and Love?)
O I think it is not for life I am chanting here my
    chant of lovers—I think it must be for Death,
For how calm, how solemn it grows, to ascend to the
    atmosphere of lovers,
Death or life I am then indifferent—my Soul de-
    clines to prefer,
I am not sure but the high Soul of lovers welcomes
    death most;
Indeed, O Death, I think now these leaves mean pre-
    cisely the same as you mean;
Grow up taller, sweet leaves, that I may see! Grow
    up out of my breast!
Spring away from the concealed heart there!
Do not fold yourselves so in your pink-tinged roots,
    timid leaves!
Do not remain down there so ashamed, herbage of my
    breast!
Come, I am determined to unbare this broad breast of
    mine—I have long enough stifled and choked;
Emblematic and capricious blades, I leave you—now
    you serve me not,
Away! I will say what I have to say, by itself,
I will escape from the sham that was proposed to me,
I will sound myself and comrades only—I will never
    again utter a call, only their call,
I will raise, with it, immortal reverberations through
    The States,
I will give an example to lovers, to take permanent
    shape and will through The States;
Through me shall the words be said to make death
    exhilarating,
Give me your tone therefore, O Death, that I may
    accord with it,

Give me yourself—for I see that you belong to me
    now above all, and are folded together above all
    —you Love and Death are,
Nor will I allow you to balk me any more with what
    I was calling life,
For now it is conveyed to me that you are the pur-
    ports essential,
That you hide in these shifting forms of life, for
    reasons—and that they are mainly for you,
That you, beyond them, come forth, to remain, the
    real reality,
That behind the mask of materials you patiently
    wait, no matter how long,
That you will one day, perhaps, take control of all,
That you will perhaps dissipate this entire show of
    appearance,
That may be you are what it is all for—but it does
    not last so very long,
But you will last very long.

*3.**

1 WHOEVER you are holding me now in hand,
Without one thing all will be useless,
  I give you fair warning, before you attempt me
    further,
  I am not what you supposed, but far different.

2 Who is he that would become my follower?
Who would sign himself a candidate for my affec-
    tions? Are you he?

3 The way is suspicious—the result slow, uncertain,
    may-be destructive;
You would have to give up all else—I alone would
    expect to be your God, sole and exclusive,
Your novitiate would even then be long and ex-
    hausting,

The whole past theory of your life, and all conformity
    to the lives around you, would have to be aban-
    doned;
Therefore release me now, before troubling yourself
    any further—Let go your hand from my
    shoulders,
Put me down, and depart on your way.

4 Or else, only by stealth, in some wood, for trial,
Or back of a rock, in the open air,
    (For in any roofed room of a house I emerge not—
    nor in company,
And in libraries I lie as one dumb, a gawk, or unborn,
    or dead,)
But just possibly with you on a high hill—first
    watching lest any person, for miles around,
    approach unawares,
Or possibly with you sailing at sea, or on the beach of
    the sea, or some quiet island,
Here to put your lips upon mine I permit you,
With the comrade's long-dwelling kiss, or the new
    husband's kiss,
For I am the new husband, and I am the comrade.

5 Or, if you will, thrusting me beneath your clothing,
Where I may feel the throbs of your heart, or rest
    upon your hip,
Carry me when you go forth over land or sea;
For thus, merely touching you, is enough—is best,
And thus, touching you, would I silently sleep and be
    carried eternally.

6 But these leaves conning, you con at peril,
For these leaves, and me, you will not understand,
They will elude you at first, and still more after-
    ward—I will certainly elude you,
Even while you should think you had unquestionably
    caught me, behold!
Already you see I have escaped from you.

7 For it is not for what I have put into it that I have
      written this book,
  Nor is it by reading it you will acquire it,
  Nor do those know me best who admire me, and
      vauntingly praise me,
  Nor will the candidates for my love, (unless at most a
      very few,) prove victorious,
  Nor will my poems do good only—they will do just
      as much evil, perhaps more,
  For all is useless without that which you may guess
      at many times and not hit—that which I
      hinted at,
  Therefore release me, and depart on your way.

4.*

THESE I, singing in spring, collect for lovers,
(For who but I should understand lovers, and all their
      sorrow and joy?
And who but I should be the poet of comrades?)
Collecting, I traverse the garden, the world—but
      soon I pass the gates,
Now along the pond-side—now wading in a little,
      fearing not the wet,
Now by the post-and-rail fences, where the old stones
      thrown there, picked from the fields, have accu-
      mulated,
Wild-flowers and vines and weeds come up through
      the stones, and partly cover them—Beyond these
      I pass,
Far, far in the forest, before I think where I get,
Solitary, smelling the earthy smell, stopping now and
      then in the silence,
Alone I had thought—yet soon a silent troop gathers
      around me,
Some walk by my side, and some behind, and some
      embrace my arms or neck,
They, the spirits of friends, dead or alive—thicker
      they come, a great crowd, and I in the middle,

Collecting, dispensing, singing in spring, there I wan-
     der with them,
Plucking something for tokens—something for these,
     till I hit upon a name—tossing toward whoever
     is near me,
Here! lilac, with a branch of pine,
Here, out of my pocket, some moss which I pulled off
     a live-oak in Florida, as it hung trailing down,
Here, some pinks and laurel leaves, and a handful of
     sage,
And here what I now draw from the water, wading in
     the pond-side,
(O here I last saw him that tenderly loves me—and
     returns again, never to separate from me,
And this, O this shall henceforth be the token of
     comrades—this calamus-root shall,
Interchange it, youths, with each other! Let none
     render it back!)
And twigs of maple, and a bunch of wild orange, and
     chestnut,
And stems of currants, and plum-blows, and the
     aromatic cedar;
These I, compassed around by a thick cloud of
     spirits,
Wandering, point to, or touch as I pass, or throw them
     loosely from me,
Indicating to each one what he shall have—giving
     something to each,
But what I drew from the water by the pond-side, that
     I reserve,
I will give of it—but only to them that love, as I
     myself am capable of loving.

5.*

1 STATES!
   Were you looking to be held together by the lawyers?
   By an agreement on a paper? Or by arms?

2 Away!
  I arrive, bringing these, beyond all the forces of
      courts and arms,
  These! to hold you together as firmly as the earth
      itself is held together.

3 The old breath of life, ever new,
  Here! I pass it by contact to you, America.

4 O mother! have you done much for me?
  Behold, there shall from me be much done for you.

5 There shall from me be a new friendship—It shall
      be called after my name,
  It shall circulate through The States, indifferent of
      place,
  It shall twist and intertwist them through and around
      each other—Compact shall they be, showing
      new signs,
  Affection shall solve every one of the problems of
      freedom,
  Those who love each other shall be invincible,
  They shall finally make America completely victo-
      rious, in my name.

6 One from Massachusetts shall be comrade to a Mis-
      sourian,
  One from Maine or Vermont, and a Carolinian and
      an Oregonese, shall be friends triune, more pre-
      cious to each other than all the riches of the
      earth.

7 To Michigan shall be wafted perfume from Florida,
  To the Mannahatta from Cuba or Mexico,
  Not the perfume of flowers, but sweeter, and wafted
      beyond death.

8 No danger shall balk Columbia's lovers,
  If need be, a thousand shall sternly immolate them-
      selves for one,

The Kanuck shall be willing to lay down his life for
    the Kansian, and the Kansian for the Kanuck,
    on due need.

9 It shall be customary in all directions, in the houses
    and streets, to see manly affection,
  The departing brother or friend shall salute the re-
    maining brother or friend with a kiss.

10 There shall be innovations,
  There shall be countless linked hands—namely, the
    Northeasterner's, and the Northwesterner's, and
    the Southwesterner's, and those of the interior,
    and all their brood,
  These shall be masters of the world under a new
    power,
  They shall laugh to scorn the attacks of all the re-
    mainder of the world.

11 The most dauntless and rude shall touch face to face
    lightly,
  The dependence of Liberty shall be lovers,
  The continuance of Equality shall be comrades.

12 These shall tie and band stronger than hoops of iron,
  I, extatic, O partners! O lands! henceforth with the
    love of lovers tie you.

13 I will make the continent indissoluble,
  I will make the most splendid race the sun ever yet
    shone upon,
  I will make divine magnetic lands.

14 I will plant companionship thick as trees along all the
    rivers of America, and along the shores of the
    great lakes, and all over the prairies,
  I will make inseparable cities, with their arms about
    each other's necks.

15 For you these, from me, O Democracy, to serve you,
　　ma femme!*
For you! for you, I am trilling these songs.

6.*

NOT heaving from my ribbed breast only,
Not in sighs at night, in rage, dissatisfied with myself,
Not in those long-drawn, ill-suppressed sighs,
Not in many an oath and promise broken,
Not in my wilful and savage soul's volition,
Not in the subtle nourishment of the air,
Not in this beating and pounding at my temples and
　　wrists,
Not in the curious systole and diastole within, which
　　will one day cease,
Not in many a hungry wish, told to the skies only,
Not in cries, laughter, defiances, thrown from me
　　when alone, far in the wilds,
Not in husky pantings through clenched teeth,
Not in sounded and resounded words—chattering
　　words, echoes, dead words,
Not in the murmurs of my dreams while I sleep,
Nor the other murmurs of these incredible dreams of
　　every day,
Nor in the limbs and senses of my body, that take you
　　and dismiss you continually—Not there,
Not in any or all of them, O adhesiveness! O pulse
　　of my life!
Need I that you exist and show yourself, any more
　　than in these songs.

7.*

OF the terrible question of appearances,
Of the doubts, the uncertainties after all,
That may-be reliance and hope are but speculations
　　after all,

That may-be identity beyond the grave is a beautiful
　　fable only,
May-be the things I perceive—the animals, plants,
　　men, hills, shining and flowing waters,
The skies of day and night—colors, densities, forms
　　—May-be these are, (as doubtless they are,) only
　　apparitions, and the real something has yet to be
　　known,
(How often they dart out of themselves, as if to con-
　　found me and mock me!
How often I think neither I know, nor any man
　　knows, aught of them;)
May-be they only seem to me what they are, (as
　　doubtless they indeed but seem,) as from my
　　present point of view—And might prove, (as of
　　course they would,) naught of what they appear,
　　or naught any how, from entirely changed points
　　of view;
To me, these, and the like of these, are curiously
　　answered by my lovers, my dear friends;
When he whom I love travels with me, or sits a long
　　while holding me by the hand,
When the subtle air, the impalpable, the sense that
　　words and reason hold not, surround us and
　　pervade us,
Then I am charged with untold and untellable wis-
　　dom—I am silent—I require nothing further,
I cannot answer the question of appearances, or that
　　of identity beyond the grave,
But I walk or sit indifferent—I am satisfied,
He ahold of my hand has completely satisfied me.

8.*

LONG I thought that knowledge alone would suffice
　　me—O if I could but obtain knowledge!
Then my lands engrossed me—Lands of the prairies,
　　Ohio's land, the southern savannas, engrossed

me—For them I would live—I would be their
    orator;
Then I met the examples of old and new heroes—I
    heard of warriors, sailors, and all dauntless per-
    sons—And it seemed to me that I too had it
    in me to be as dauntless as any—and would
    be so;
And then, to enclose all, it came to me to strike up
    the songs of the New World—And then I be-
    lieved my life must be spent in singing;
But now take notice, land of the prairies, land of
    the south savannas, Ohio's land,
Take notice, you Kanuck woods—and you Lake
    Huron—and all that with you roll toward
    Niagara—and you Niagara also,
And you, Californian mountains—That you each
    and all find somebody else to be your singer of
    songs,
For I can be your singer of songs no longer—One
    who loves me is jealous of me, and withdraws me
    from all but love,
With the rest I dispense—I sever from what I
    thought would suffice me, for it does not—it is
    now empty and tasteless to me,
I heed knowledge, and the grandeur of The States,
    and the example of heroes, no more,
I am indifferent to my own songs—I will go with
    him I love,
It is to be enough for us that we are together—We
    never separate again.

9.*

HOURS continuing long, sore and heavy-hearted,
Hours of the dusk, when I withdraw to a lonesome
    and unfrequented spot, seating myself, leaning
    my face in my hands;

Hours sleepless, deep in the night, when I go forth,
    speeding swiftly the country roads, or through
    the city streets, or pacing miles and miles, sti-
    fling plaintive cries;

Hours discouraged, distracted—for the one I cannot
    content myself without, soon I saw him content
    himself without me;

Hours when I am forgotten, (O weeks and months are
    passing, but I believe I am never to forget!)

Sullen and suffering hours! (I am ashamed—but it
    is useless—I am what I am;)

Hours of my torment—I wonder if other men ever
    have the like, out of the like feelings?

Is there even one other like me—distracted—his
    friend, his lover, lost to him?

Is he too as I am now? Does he still rise in the morn-
    ing, dejected, thinking who is lost to him? and
    at night, awaking, think who is lost?

Does he too harbor his friendship silent and endless?
    harbor his anguish and passion?

Does some stray reminder, or the casual mention of a
    name, bring the fit back upon him, taciturn and
    deprest?

Does he see himself reflected in me? In these hours,
    does he see the face of his hours reflected?

10. *

You bards of ages hence! when you refer to me, mind
    not so much my poems,

Nor speak of me that I prophesied of The States, and
    led them the way of their glories;

But come, I will take you down underneath this
    impassive exterior—I will tell you what to say
    of me:

Publish my name and hang up my picture as that of
    the tenderest lover,

The friend, the lover's portrait, of whom his friend, his
    lover, was fondest,

Who was not proud of his songs, but of the measure-
    less ocean of love within him—and freely poured
    it forth,
Who often walked lonesome walks, thinking of his
    dear friends, his lovers,
Who pensive, away from one he loved, often lay sleep-
    less and dissatisfied at night,
Who knew too well the sick, sick dread lest the one
    he loved might secretly be indifferent to him,
Whose happiest days were far away, through fields, in
    woods, on hills, he and another, wandering hand
    in hand, they twain, apart from other men,
Who oft as he sauntered the streets, curved with his
    arm the shoulder of his friend—while the arm of
    his friend rested upon him also.

*11.**

WHEN I heard at the close of the day how my name
    had been received with plaudits in the capitol,
    still it was not a happy night for me that fol-
    lowed;
And else, when I caroused, or when my plans were
    accomplished, still I was not happy;
But the day when I rose at dawn from the bed of
    perfect health, refreshed, singing, inhaling the
    ripe breath of autumn,
When I saw the full moon in the west grow pale and
    disappear in the morning light,
When I wandered alone over the beach, and, undress-
    ing, bathed, laughing with the cool waters, and
    saw the sun rise,
And when I thought how my dear friend, my lover,
    was on his way coming, O then I was happy;
O then each breath tasted sweeter—and all that day
    my food nourished me more—And the beautiful
    day passed well,
And the next came with equal joy—And with the
    next, at evening, came my friend;

And that night, while all was still, I heard the waters
    roll slowly continually up the shores,
I heard the hissing rustle of the liquid and sands,
    as directed to me, whispering, to congratulate
    me,
For the one I love most lay sleeping by me under the
    same cover in the cool night,
In the stillness, in the autumn moonbeams, his face
    was inclined toward me,
And his arm lay lightly around my breast—And that
    night I was happy.

*12.**

ARE you the new person drawn toward me, and asking
    something significant from me?
To begin with, take warning—I am probably far
    different from what you suppose;
Do you suppose you will find in me your ideal?
Do you think it so easy to have me become your
    lover?
Do you think the friendship of me would be unalloyed
    satisfaction?
Do you suppose I am trusty and faithful?
Do you see no further than this façade—this smooth
    and tolerant manner of me?
Do you suppose yourself advancing on real ground
    toward a real heroic man?
Have you no thought, O dreamer, that it may be all
    maya, illusion? O the next step may precipitate
    you!
O let some past deceived one hiss in your ears, how
    many have prest on the same as you are pressing
    now,
How many have fondly supposed what you are sup-
    posing now—only to be disappointed.

*13.**

Calamus taste,
(For I must change the strain—these are not to be
    pensive leaves, but leaves of joy,)
Roots and leaves unlike any but themselves,
Scents brought to men and women from the wild
    woods, and from the pond-side,
Breast-sorrel and pinks of love—fingers that wind
    around tighter than vines,
Gushes from the throats of birds, hid in the foliage
    of trees, as the sun is risen,
Breezes of land and love—Breezes set from living
    shores out to you on the living sea—to you,
    O sailors!
Frost-mellowed berries, and Third Month twigs, of-
    fered fresh to young persons wandering out in
    the fields when the winter breaks up,
Love-buds, put before you and within you, whoever
    you are,
Buds to be unfolded on the old terms,
If you bring the warmth of the sun to them, they will
    open, and bring form, color, perfume, to you,
If you become the aliment and the wet, they will
    become flowers, fruits, tall branches and trees,
They are comprised in you just as much as in them-
    selves—perhaps more than in themselves,
They are not comprised in one season or succession,
    but many successions,
They have come slowly up out of the earth and me,
    and are to come slowly up out of you.

*14.**

Not heat flames up and consumes,
Not sea-waves hurry in and out,
Not the air, delicious and dry, the air of the ripe
    summer, bears lightly along white down-balls of

myriads of seeds, wafted, sailing gracefully, to
    drop where they may,
Not these—O none of these, more than the flames
    of me, consuming, burning for his love whom I
    love!
O none, more than I, hurrying in and out;
Does the tide hurry, seeking something, and never
    give up? O I the same;
O nor down-balls, nor perfumes, nor the high
    rain-emitting clouds, are borne through the open
    air,
Any more than my Soul is borne through the open
    air,
Wafted in all directions, O love, for friendship, for
    you.

*15.**

O DROPS of me! trickle, slow drops,
Candid, from me falling—drip, bleeding drops,
From wounds made to free you whence you were
    prisoned,
From my face—from my forehead and lips,
From my breast—from within where I was con-
    cealed—Press forth, red drops—confession
    drops,
Stain every page—stain every song I sing, every
    word I say, bloody drops,
Let them know your scarlet heat—let them glisten,
Saturate them with yourself, all ashamed and wet,
Glow upon all I have written or shall write, bleed-
    ing drops,
Let it all be seen in your light, blushing drops.

*16.**

1 WHO is now reading this?

2 May-be one is now reading this who knows some
    wrong-doing of my past life,

Or may-be a stranger is reading this who has secretly
    loved me,
Or may-be one who meets all my grand assumptions
    and egotisms with derision,
Or may-be one who is puzzled at me.

3 As if I were not puzzled at myself!
Or as if I never deride myself! (O conscience-struck!
    O self-convicted!)
Or as if I do not secretly love strangers! (O tenderly,
    a long time, and never avow it;)
Or as if I did not see, perfectly well, interior in
    myself, the stuff of wrong-doing,
Or as if it could cease transpiring from me until it
    must cease.

*17.** *

OF him I love day and night, I dreamed I heard he
    was dead,
And I dreamed I went where they had buried him I
    love—but he was not in that place,
And I dreamed I wandered, searching among burial-
    places, to find him,
And I found that every place was a burial-place,
The houses full of life were equally full of death,
    (This house is now,)
The streets, the shipping, the places of amusement,
    the Chicago, Boston, Philadelphia, the Manna-
    hatta, were as full of the dead as of the living,
And fuller, O vastly fuller, of the dead than of the
    living;
—And what I dreamed I will henceforth tell to every
    person and age,
And I stand henceforth bound to what I dreamed;
And now I am willing to disregard burial-places, and
    dispense with them,
And if the memorials of the dead were put up indif-
    ferently everywhere, even in the room where I
    eat or sleep, I should be satisfied,

And if the corpse of any one I love, or if my own
    corpse, be duly rendered to powder, and poured
    in the sea, I shall be satisfied,
Or if it be distributed to the winds, I shall be sat-
    isfied.

*18.**

CITY of my walks and joys!
City whom that I have lived and sung there will one
    day make you illustrious,
Not the pageants of you—not your shifting tab-
    leaux, your spectacles, repay me,
Not the interminable rows of your houses—nor the
    ships at the wharves,
Nor the processions in the streets, nor the bright win-
    dows, with goods in them,
Nor to converse with learned persons, or bear my
    share in the soiree or feast;
Not those—but, as I pass, O Manhattan! your fre-
    quent and swift flash of eyes offering me love,
Offering me the response of my own—these repay
    me,
Lovers, continual lovers, only repay me.

*19.**

1   MIND you the timid models of the rest, the
        majority?
    Long I minded them, but hence I will not—for I
        have adopted models for myself, and now offer
        them to The Lands.

2   Behold this swarthy and unrefined face—these gray
        eyes,
    This beard—the white wool, unclipt upon my neck,
    My brown hands, and the silent manner of me, with-
        out charm;

Yet comes one, a Manhattanese, and ever at parting,
    kisses me lightly on the lips with robust love,
And I, in the public room, or on the crossing of the
    street, or on the ship's deck, kiss him in return;
We observe that salute of American comrades, land
    and sea,
We are those two natural and nonchalant persons.

20.*

I saw in Louisiana a live-oak growing,
All alone stood it, and the moss hung down from the
    branches,
Without any companion it grew there, uttering joyous
    leaves of dark green,
And its look, rude, unbending, lusty, made me think
    of myself,
But I wondered how it could utter joyous leaves,
    standing alone there, without its friend, its
    lover near—for I knew I could not,
And I broke off a twig with a certain number of
    leaves upon it, and twined around it a little
    moss,
And brought it away—and I have placed it in sight
    in my room,
It is not needed to remind me as of my own dear
    friends,
(For I believe lately I think of little else than of
    them,)
Yet it remains to me a curious token—it makes me
    think of manly love;
For all that, and though the live-oak glistens there in
    Louisiana, solitary, in a wide flat space,
Uttering joyous leaves all its life, without a friend, a
    lover, near,
I know very well I could not.

21.*

MUSIC always round me, unceasing, unbeginning—
    yet long untaught I did not hear,
But now the chorus I hear, and am elated,
A tenor, strong, ascending, with power and health,
    with glad notes of day-break I hear,
A soprano, at intervals, sailing buoyantly over the
    tops of immense waves,
A transparent base, shuddering lusciously under and
    through the universe,
The triumphant tutti*—the funeral wailings, with
    sweet flutes and violins—All these I fill myself
    with;
I hear not the volumes of sound merely—I am
    moved by the exquisite meanings,
I listen to the different voices winding in and out,
    striving, contending with fiery vehemence to
    excel each other in emotion,
I do not think the performers know themselves—But
    now I think I begin to know them.

22.*

PASSING stranger! you do not know how longingly I
    look upon you,
You must be he I was seeking, or she I was seeking,
    (It comes to me, as of a dream,)
I have somewhere surely lived a life of joy with
    you,
All is recalled as we flit by each other, fluid, affec-
    tionate, chaste, matured,
You grew up with me, were a boy with me, or a girl
    with me,
I ate with you, and slept with you—your body has
    become not yours only, nor left my body mine
    only,

You give me the pleasure of your eyes, face, flesh, as
    we pass—you take of my beard, breast, hands,
    in return,
I am not to speak to you—I am to think of you
    when I sit alone, or wake at night alone,
I am to wait—I do not doubt I am to meet you
    again,
I am to see to it that I do not lose you.

23.*

THIS moment as I sit alone, yearning and thoughtful,
    it seems to me there are other men in other
    lands, yearning and thoughtful;
It seems to me I can look over and behold them,
    in Germany, Italy, France, Spain—Or far, far
    away, in China, or in Russia or India—talking
    other dialects;
And it seems to me if I could know those men better,
    I should become attached to them, as I do to men
    in my own lands,
It seems to me they are as wise, beautiful, benevolent,
    as any in my own lands;
O I know we should be brethren and lovers,
I know I should be happy with them.

24.*

I HEAR it is charged against me that I seek to destroy
    institutions;
But really I am neither for nor against institutions,
(What indeed have I in common with them?—Or
    what with the destruction of them?)
Only I will establish in the Mannahatta, and in every
    city of These States, inland and seaboard,
And in the fields and woods, and above every keel
    little or large, that dents the water,

Without edifices, or rules, or trustees, or any ar-
  gument,
The institution of the dear love of comrades.

25.*

THE prairie-grass dividing—its own odor breathing,
I demand of it the spiritual corresponding,
Demand the most copious and close companionship
  of men,
Demand the blades to rise of words, acts, beings,
Those of the open atmosphere, coarse, sunlit, fresh,
  nutritious,
Those that go their own gait, erect, stepping with
  freedom and command—leading, not following,
Those with a never-quell'd audacity—those with
  sweet and lusty flesh, clear of taint, choice and
  chary of its love-power,
Those that look carelessly in the faces of Presidents
  and Governors, as to say, *Who are you?*
Those of earth-born passion, simple, never constrained,
  never obedient,
Those of inland America.

26.*

WE two boys together clinging,
One the other never leaving,
Up and down the roads going—North and South
  excursions making,
Power enjoying—elbows stretching—fingers clutch-
  ing,
Armed and fearless—eating, drinking, sleeping, lov-
  ing,
No law less than ourselves owning—sailing, soldier-
  ing, thieving, threatening,
Misers, menials, priests alarming—air breathing,
  water drinking, on the turf or the sea-beach
  dancing,

With birds singing—With fishes swimming—With
    trees branching and leafing,
Cities wrenching, ease scorning, statutes mocking,
    feebleness chasing,
Fulfilling our foray.

27.*

O LOVE!
O dying—always dying!
O the burials of me, past and present!
O me, while I stride ahead, material, visible, imperi-
    ous as ever!
O me, what I was for years, now dead, (I lament not
    —I am content;),
O to disengage myself from those corpses of me,
    which I turn and look at, where I cast them!
To pass on, (O living! always living!) and leave the
    corpses behind!

28.*

WHEN I peruse the conquered fame of heroes, and the
    victories of mighty generals, I do not envy the
    generals,
Nor the President in his Presidency, nor the rich in
    his great house;
But when I read of the brotherhood of lovers, how it
    was with them,
How through life, through dangers, odium, un-
    changing, long and long,
Through youth, and through middle and old age, how
    unfaltering, how affectionate and faithful they
    were,
Then I am pensive—I hastily put down the book,
    and walk away, filled with the bitterest envy.

29.*

ONE flitting glimpse, caught through an interstice,
Of a crowd of workmen and drivers in a bar-room,
    around the stove, late of a winter night—And
    I unremarked, seated in a corner;
Of a youth who loves me, and whom I love, silently
    approaching, and seating himself near, that he
    may hold me by the hand;
A long while, amid the noises of coming and going
    —of drinking and oath and smutty jest,
There we two, content, happy in being together,
    speaking little, perhaps not a word.

30.*

A PROMISE and gift to California,
Also to the great Pastoral Plains, and for Oregon:
Sojourning east a while longer, soon I travel to you,
    to remain, to teach robust American love;
For I know very well that I and robust love belong
    among you, inland, and along the Western
    Sea,
For These States tend inland, and toward the Western
    Sea—and I will also.

31.*

1 WHAT ship, puzzled at sea, cons for the true reck-
    oning?
   Or, coming in, to avoid the bars, and follow the chan-
    nel, a perfect pilot needs?
   Here, sailor! Here, ship! take aboard the most per-
    fect pilot,
   Whom, in a little boat, putting off, and rowing, I,
    hailing you, offer.

2 What place is besieged, and vainly tries to raise the
    siege?

Lo! I send to that place a commander, swift, brave,
    immortal,
And with him horse and foot—and parks of artillery,
And artillerymen, the deadliest that ever fired gun.

32.*

WHAT think you I take my pen in hand to record?
The battle-ship, perfect-model'd, majestic, that I saw
    pass the offing to-day under full sail?
The splendors of the past day? Or the splendor of the
    night that envelops me?
Or the vaunted glory and growth of the great city
    spread around me?—No;
But I record of two simple men I saw to-day, on the
    pier, in the midst of the crowd, parting the part-
    ing of dear friends,
The one to remain hung on the other's neck, and pas-
    sionately kissed him,
While the one to depart, tightly prest the one to
    remain in his arms.

33.*

NO labor-saving machine,
Nor discovery have I made,
Nor will I be able to leave behind me any wealthy
    bequest to found a hospital or library,
Nor reminiscence of any deed of courage, for America,
Nor literary success, nor intellect—nor book for the
    book-shelf;
Only these carols, vibrating through the air, I leave,
For comrades and lovers.

34.*

I DREAMED in a dream, I saw a city invincible to the
    attacks of the whole of the rest of the earth,

I dreamed that was the new City of Friends,
Nothing was greater there than the quality of robust
    love—it led the rest,
It was seen every hour in the actions of the men of
    that city,
And in all their looks and words.

*35.**

To you of New England,
To the man of the Seaside State, and of Pennsylvania,
To the Kanadian of the north—to the Southerner I
    love,
These, with perfect trust, to depict you as myself—
    the germs are in all men;
I believe the main purport of These States is to found
    a superb friendship, exalté, previously unknown,
Because I perceive it waits, and has been always wait-
    ing, latent in all men.

*36.**

EARTH! my likeness!
Though you look so impassive, ample and spheric
    there,
I now suspect that is not all;
I now suspect there is something fierce in you, eligible
    to burst forth;
For an athlete is enamoured of me—and I of him,
But toward him there is something fierce and terrible
    in me, eligible to burst forth,
I dare not tell it in words—not even in these songs.

*37.**

A LEAF for hand in hand!
You natural persons old and young! You on the
    Eastern Sea, and you on the Western!

You on the Mississippi, and on all the branches and
　　bayous of the Mississippi!
You friendly boatmen and mechanics! You roughs!
You twain! And all processions moving along the
　　streets!
I wish to infuse myself among you till I see it com-
　　mon for you to walk hand in hand.

38. *

PRIMEVAL my love for the woman I love,
O bride! O wife! more resistless, more enduring
　　than I can tell, the thought of you!
Then separate, as disembodied, the purest born,
The ethereal, the last athletic reality, my consolation,
I ascend—I float in the regions of your love, O man,
O sharer of my roving life.

39. *

SOMETIMES with one I love, I fill myself with rage, for
　　fear I effuse unreturned love;
But now I think there is no unreturned love—the
　　pay is certain, one way or another,
Doubtless I could not have perceived the universe,
　　or written one of my poems, if I had not freely
　　given myself to comrades, to love.

40. *

THAT shadow, my likeness, that goes to and fro, seek-
　　ing a livelihood, chattering, chaffering,
How often I find myself standing and looking at it
　　where it flits,
How often I question and doubt whether that is really
　　me;
But in these, and among my lovers, and carolling my
　　songs,
O I never doubt whether that is really me.

41.*

1   AMONG the men and women, the multitude, I per-
        ceive one picking me out by secret and divine
        signs,
    Acknowledging none else—not parent, wife, hus-
        band, brother, child, any nearer than I am;
    Some are baffled—But that one is not—that one
        knows me.

2   Lover and perfect equal!
    I meant that you should discover me so, by my faint
        indirections,
    And I, when I meet you, mean to discover you by the
        like in you.

42.*

To the young man, many things to absorb, to engraft,
    to develop, I teach, to help him become élève* of
    mine,
But if blood like mine circle not in his veins,
If he be not silently selected by lovers, and do not
    silently select lovers,
Of what use is it that he seek to become élève of
    mine?

43.*

O YOU whom I often and silently come where you
    are, that I may be with you,
As I walk by your side, or sit near, or remain in the
    same room with you,
Little you know the subtle electric fire that for your
    sake is playing within me.

44.*

HERE my last words, and the most baffling,
Here the frailest leaves of me, and yet my strongest-
    lasting,
Here I shade down and hide my thoughts—I do not
    expose them,
And yet they expose me more than all my other
    poems.

45.*

1 FULL of life, sweet-blooded, compact, visible,
I, forty years old the Eighty-third Year of The States,
To one a century hence, or any number of centuries
    hence,
To you, yet unborn, these, seeking you.

2 When you read these, I, that was visible, am become
    invisible;
Now it is you, compact, visible, realizing my poems,
    seeking me,
Fancying how happy you were, if I could be with
    you, and become your lover;
Be it as if I were with you. Be not too certain but I
    am now with you.

FROM MESSENGER LEAVES

To Him That Was Crucified

MY spirit to yours, dear brother,
Do not mind because many, sounding your name, do
    not understand you,
I do not sound your name, but I understand you,
    (there are others also;)

I specify you with joy, O my comrade, to salute you,
and to salute those who are with you, before and
since—and those to come also,

That we all labor together, transmitting the same
charge and succession;

We few, equals, indifferent of lands, indifferent of
times,

We, enclosers of all continents, all castes—allowers
of all theologies,

Compassionaters, perceivers, rapport of men,

We walk silent among disputes and assertions, but
reject not the disputers, nor any thing that is
asserted,

We hear the bawling and din—we are reached at
by divisions, jealousies, recriminations on every
side,

They close peremptorily upon us, to surround us,
my comrade,

Yet we walk unheld, free, the whole earth over,
journeying up and down, till we make our in-
effaceable mark upon time and the diverse eras,

Till we saturate time and eras, that the men and
women of races, ages to come, may prove breth-
ren and lovers, as we are.

To One Shortly to Die

1 FROM all the rest I single out you, having a message
for you:

You are to die—Let others tell you what they
please, I cannot prevaricate,

I am exact and merciless, but I love you—There is
no escape for you.

2 Softly I lay my right hand upon you—you just
feel it,

I do not argue—I bend my head close, and half-
envelop it,

I sit quietly by—I remain faithful,
I am more than nurse, more than parent or neighbor,
I absolve you from all except yourself, spiritual,
    bodily—that is eternal,
(The corpse you will leave will be but excremen-
    titious.)

3 The sun bursts through in unlooked-for directions!
  Strong thoughts fill you, and confidence—you smile!
  You forget you are sick, as I forget you are sick,
  You do not see the medicines—you do not mind the
    weeping friends—I am with you,
  I exclude others from you—there is nothing to be
    commiserated,
  I do not commiserate—I congratulate you.

To a Common Prostitute

1 BE composed—be at ease with me—I am Walt
    Whitman, liberal and lusty as Nature,
  Not till the sun excludes you, do I exclude you,
  Not till the waters refuse to glisten for you, and the
    leaves to rustle for you, do my words refuse to
    glisten and rustle for you.

2 My girl, I appoint with you an appointment—and I
    charge you that you make preparation to be
    worthy to meet me,
  And I charge you that you be patient and perfect till
    I come.

3 Till then, I salute you with a significant look, that
    you do not forget me.

Walt Whitman's Caution*

To The States, or any one of them, or any city of
    The States, *Resist much, obey little,*

Once unquestioning obedience, once fully enslaved,
Once fully enslaved, no nation, state, city, of this
    earth, ever afterward resumes its liberty.

To You

STRANGER! if you, passing, meet me, and desire to
    speak to me, why should you not speak to me?
And why should I not speak to you?

Mannahatta

I WAS asking for something specific and perfect for
    my city, and behold! here is the aboriginal
    name!
Now I see what there is in a name, a word, liquid,
    sane, unruly, musical, self-sufficient,
I see that the word of my city, is that word up there,
Because I see that word nested in nests of water-bays,
    superb, with tall and wonderful spires,
Rich, hemmed thick all around with sailships and
    steamships—an island sixteen miles long, solid-
    founded,
Numberless crowded streets—high growths of iron,
    slender, strong, light, splendidly uprising toward
    clear skies;
Tides swift and ample, well-loved by me, toward sun-
    down,
The flowing sea currents, the little islands, the larger
    adjoining islands, the heights, the villas,
The countless masts, the white shore-steamers, the
    lighters, the ferry-boats, the black sea-steamers,
    well-model'd;
The down-town streets, the jobbers' houses of business
    —the houses of business of the ship-merchants,
    and money-brokers—the river-streets,

Immigrants arriving, fifteen or twenty thousand in a
    week,
The carts hauling goods—the manly race of drivers
    of horses—the brown-faced sailors,
The summer-air, the bright sun shining, and the sail-
    ing clouds aloft,
The winter snows, the sleigh-bells—the broken ice in
    the river, passing along, up or down, with the
    flood-tide or ebb-tide;
The mechanics of the city, the masters, well-formed,
    beautiful-faced, looking you straight in the eyes;
Trottoirs* thronged—vehicles—Broadway—the wo-
    men—the shops and shows,
The parades, processions, bugles playing, flags flying,
    drums beating;
A million people—manners free and superb—open
    voices—hospitality—the most courageous and
    friendly young men;
The free city! no slaves! no owners of slaves!
The beautiful city! the city of hurried and sparkling
    waters! the city of spires and masts!
The city nested in bays! my city!
The city of such women, I am mad to be with them!
    I will return after death to be with them!
The city of such young men, I swear I cannot live
    happy, without I often go talk, walk, eat, drink,
    sleep, with them!

A Hand-Mirror

HOLD it up sternly! See this it sends back! (Who is
    it? Is it you?)
Outside fair costume—within, ashes and filth,
No more a flashing eye—no more a sonorous voice
    or springy step,
Now some slave's eye, voice, hands, step,
A drunkard's breath, unwholesome eater's face, ve-
    nerealee's flesh,

Lungs rotting away piecemeal, stomach sour and
    cankerous,
Joints rheumatic, bowels clogged with abomination,
Blood circulating dark and poisonous streams,
Words babble, hearing and touch callous,
No brain, no heart left—no magnetism of sex;
Such, from one look in this looking-glass ere you go
    hence,
Such a result so soon—and from such a beginning!

*So long!**

1 To conclude—I announce what comes after me,
    The thought must be promulged, that all I know at
        any time suffices for that time only—not subse-
        quent time;
    I announce greater offspring, orators, days, and then
        depart.

2 I remember I said to myself at the winter-close, before
        my leaves sprang at all, that I would become a
        candid and unloosed summer-poet,
    I said I would raise my voice jocund and strong, with
        reference to consummations.

3 When America does what was promised,
    When each part is peopled with free people,
    When there is no city on earth to lead my city, the
        city of young men, the Mannahatta city—But
        when the Mannahatta leads all the cities of the
        earth,
    When there are plentiful athletic bards, inland and
        seaboard,
    When through These States walk a hundred millions
        of superb persons,
    When the rest part away for superb persons, and con-
        tribute to them,

When fathers, firm, unconstrained, open-eyed—When
    breeds of the most perfect mothers denote
    America,
Then to me ripeness and conclusion.

4 Yet not me, after all—let none be content with me,
I myself seek a man better than I am, or a woman
    better than I am,
I invite defiance, and to make myself superseded,
All I have done, I would cheerfully give to be trod
    under foot, if it might only be the soil of supe-
    rior poems.

5 I have established nothing for good,
I have but established these things, till things farther
    onward shall be prepared to be established,
And I am myself the preparer of things farther
    onward.

6 I have pressed through in my own right,
I have offered my style to every one—I have jour-
    neyed with confident step,
While my pleasure is yet at the full, I whisper
    So long,
And take the young woman's hand, and the young
    man's hand, for the last time.

7 Once more I enforce you to give play to yourself—
    and not depend on me, or on any one but
    yourself,
Once more I proclaim the whole of America for each
    individual, without exception.

8 As I have announced the true theory of the youth,
    manhood, womanhood, of The States, I adhere
    to it;
As I have announced myself on immortality, the body,
    procreation, hauteur, prudence,

As I joined the stern crowd that still confronts the
　　President with menacing weapons—I adhere
　　to all,
As I have announced each age for itself, this moment
　　I set the example.

9　I demand the choicest edifices to destroy them;
　Room! room! for new far-planning draughtsmen and
　　engineers!
　Clear that rubbish from the building-spots and the
　　paths!

10　*So long!*
　I announce natural persons to arise,
　I announce justice triumphant,
　I announce uncompromising liberty and equality,
　I announce the justification of candor, and the justi-
　　fication of pride.

11　I announce that the identity of These States is a
　　single identity only,
　I announce the Union more and more compact,
　I announce splendors and majesties to make all the
　　previous politics of the earth insignificant.

12　I announce adhesiveness—I say it shall be limitless,
　　unloosened,
　I say you shall yet find the friend you was look-
　　ing for.

13　*So long!*
　I announce a man or woman coming—perhaps you
　　are the one,
　I announce a great individual, fluid as Nature, chaste,
　　affectionate, compassionate, fully armed.

14　*So long!*
　I announce a life that shall be copious, vehement,
　　spiritual, bold,

And I announce an old age that shall lightly and
　　joyfully meet its translation.

15　O thicker and faster!
　　O crowding too close upon me!
　　I foresee too much—it means more than I thought,
　　It appears to me I am dying.

16　Now throat, sound your last!
　　Salute me—salute the future once more. Peal the
　　　　old cry once more.

17　Screaming electric, the atmosphere using,
　　At random glancing, each as I notice absorbing,
　　Swiftly on, but a little while alighting,
　　Curious enveloped messages delivering,
　　Sparkles hot, seed ethereal, down in the dirt dropping,
　　Myself unknowing, my commission obeying, to ques-
　　　　tion it never daring,
　　To ages, and ages yet, the growth of the seed leaving,
　　To troops out of me rising—they the tasks I have set
　　　　promulging,
　　To women certain whispers of myself bequeathing—
　　　　their affection me more clearly explaining,
　　To young men my problems offering—no dallier I—
　　　　I the muscle of their brains trying,
　　So I pass—a little time vocal, visible, contrary,
　　Afterward, a melodious echo, passionately bent for—
　　　　death making me undying,
　　The best of me then when no longer visible—for
　　　　toward that I have been incessantly preparing.

18　What is there more, that I lag and pause, and crouch
　　　　extended with unshut mouth?
　　Is there a single final farewell?

19　My songs cease—I abandon them,
　　From behind the screen where I hid, I advance per-
　　　　sonally.

20 This is no book,
   Who touches this, touches a man,
   (Is it night? Are we here alone?)
   It is I you hold, and who holds you,
   I spring from the pages into your arms—decease
       calls me forth.

21 O how your fingers drowse me!
   Your breath falls around me like dew—your pulse
       lulls the tympans of my ears,
   I feel immerged from head to foot,
   Delicious—enough.

22 Enough, O deed impromptu and secret!
   Enough, O gliding present! Enough, O summed-up
       past!

23 Dear friend, whoever you are, here, take this kiss,
   I give it especially to you—Do not forget me,
   I feel like one who has done his work—I progress on,
   The unknown sphere, more real than I dreamed,
       more direct, darts awakening rays about me—
       So long!
   Remember my words—I love you—I depart from
       materials,
   I am as one disembodied, triumphant, dead.

FROM DRUM-TAPS (1865)

Drum-Taps*

1 FIRST, O songs, for a prelude,
  Lightly strike on the stretch'd tympanum, pride and joy
      in my city,
  How she led the rest to arms—how she gave the cue,
  How at once with lithe limbs, unwaiting a moment, she
      sprang;
  (O superb! O Manhattan, my own, my peerless!
  O strongest you in the hour of danger, in crisis! O
      truer than steel!)
  How you sprang! how you threw off the costumes of
      peace with indifferent hand;
  How your soft opera-music changed, and the drum and
      fife were heard in their stead;
  How you led to the war, (that shall serve for our pre-
      lude songs of soldiers,)
  How Manhattan drum-taps led.

2 Forty years had I in my city seen soldiers parading;
  Forty years as a pageant—till unawares, the Lady of
      this teeming and turbulent city,
  Sleepless, amid her ships, her houses, her incalculable
      wealth,
  With her million children around her—suddenly,
  At dead of night, at news from the south,
  Incens'd, struck with clench'd hand the pavement.

3 A shock electric—the night sustain'd it;
  Till with ominous hum, our hive at day-break, pour'd
      out its myriads.

4 From the houses then, and the workshops, and
      through all the doorways,
  Leapt they tumultuous—and lo! Manhattan arming.

5 To the drum-taps prompt,
  The young men falling in and arming;

The mechanics arming, (the trowel, the jack-plane, the
    blacksmith's hammer, tost aside with precipi-
    tation;)
The lawyer leaving his office, and arming—the judge
    leaving the court;
The driver deserting his wagon in the street, jumping
    down, throwing the reins abruptly down on the
    horses' backs;
The salesman leaving the store—the boss, book-keeper,
    porter, all leaving;
Squads gathering everywhere by common consent, and
    arming;
The new recruits, even boys—the old men show them
    how to wear their accoutrements—they buckle
    the straps carefully;
Outdoors arming—indoors arming—the flash of the
    musket-barrels;
The white tents cluster in camps—the arm'd sentries
    around—the sunrise cannon, and again at sunset;
Arm'd regiments arrive every day, pass through the
    city, and embark from the wharves;
(How good they look, as they tramp down to the river,
    sweaty, with their guns on their shoulders!
How I love them! how I could hug them, with their
    brown faces, and their clothes and knapsacks cov-
    er'd with dust!)
The blood of the city up—arm'd! arm'd! the cry
    everywhere;
The flags flung out from the steeples of churches, and
    from all the public buildings and stores;
The tearful parting—the mother kisses her son—the
    son kisses his mother;
(Loth is the mother to part—yet not a word does she
    speak to detain him;)
The tumultuous escort—the ranks of policemen preceed-
    ing, clearing the way;
The unpent enthusiasm—the wild cheers of the crowd
    for their favorites;

The artillery—the silent cannons, bright as gold, drawn
    along, rumble lightly over the stones;
(Silent cannons—soon to cease your silence!
Soon, unlimber'd, to begin the red business;)
All the mutter of preparation—all the determin'd
    arming;
The hospital service—the lint, bandages, and medi-
    cines;
The women volunteering for nurses—the work begun
    for, in earnest—no mere parade now;
War! an arm'd race is advancing!—the welcome for
    battle—no turning away;
War! be it weeks, months, or years—an arm'd race is
    advancing to welcome it.

6 Mannahatta a-march!—and it's O to sing it well!
It's O for a manly life in the camp!

7 And the sturdy artillery!
The guns, bright as gold—the work for giants—to
    serve well the guns:
Unlimber them! no more, as the past forty years, for
    salutes for courtesies merely;
Put in something else now besides powder and wadding.

8 And you, Lady of Ships! you Mannahatta!
Old matron of the city! this proud, friendly, turbulent
    city!
Often in peace and wealth you were pensive, or covertly
    frown'd amid all your children;
But now you smile with joy, exulting old Mannahatta!

*Shut not your Doors to me proud Libraries**

SHUT not your doors to me, proud libraries,
For that which was lacking among you all, yet needed
    most, I bring;

A book I have made for your dear sake, O soldiers,
And for you, O soul of man, and you, love of comrades;
The words of my book nothing, the life of it every-
　　　thing;
A book separate, not link'd with the rest, nor felt by
　　　the intellect;
But you will feel every word, O Libertad! arm'd
　　　Libertad!
It shall pass by the intellect to swim the sea, the air,
With joy with you, O soul of man.

Cavalry Crossing a Ford

A LINE in long array, where they wind betwixt green
　　　islands;
They take a serpentine course—their arms flash in the
　　　sun—Hark to the musical clank;
Behold the silvery river—in it the splashing horses,
　　　loitering, stop to drink;
Behold the brown-faced men—each group, each person,
　　　a picture—the negligent rest on the saddles;
Some emerge on the opposite bank—others are just
　　　entering the ford;
The guidon flags flutter gaily in the wind.

Pioneers! O Pioneers!

1

　COME, my tan-faced children,
Follow well in order, get your weapons ready;
Have you your pistols? have you your sharp edged
　　　axes?
　　　　Pioneers! O pioneers!

2

　For we cannot tarry here,
We must march my darlings, we must bear the brunt of
　　　danger,

We, the youthful sinewy races, all the rest on us depend,
 Pioneers! O pioneers!

3

 O you youths, western youths,
So impatient, full of action, full of manly pride and
 friendship,
Plain I see you, western youths, see you tramping with
 the foremost,
  Pioneers! O pioneers!

4

 Have the elder races halted?
Do they droop and end their lesson, wearied, over there
 beyond the seas?
We take up the task eternal, and the burden, and the
 lesson,
  Pioneers! O pioneers!

5

 All the past we leave behind;
We debouch upon a newer, mightier world, varied
 world;
Fresh and strong the world we seize, world of labor and
 the march,
  Pioneers! O pioneers!

6

 We detachments steady throwing,
Down the edges, through the passes, up the mountains
 steep,
Conquering, holding, daring, venturing, as we go, the
 unknown ways,
  Pioneers! O pioneers!

7

 We primeval forests felling,
We the rivers stemming, vexing we, and piercing deep
 the mines within;

We the surface broad surveying, and the virgin soil up-
      heaving,
          Pioneers! O pioneers!

8

Colorado men are we,
From the peaks gigantic, from the great sierras and the
      high plateaus,
From the mine and from the gully, from the hunting
      trail we come,
          Pioneers! O pioneers!

9

From Nebraska, from Arkansas,
Central inland race are we, from Missouri, with the con-
      tinental blood intervein'd;
All the hands of comrades clasping, all the Southern, all
      the Northern,
          Pioneers! O pioneers!

10

O resistless, restless race!
O beloved race in all! O my breast aches with tender
      love for all!
O I mourn and yet exult—I am rapt with love for all,
          Pioneers! O pioneers!

11

Raise the mighty mother mistress,
Waving high the delicate mistress, over all the starry
      mistress, (bend your heads all,)
Raise the fang'd and warlike mistress, stern, impassive,
      weapon'd mistress,
          Pioneers! O pioneers!

12

See, my children, resolute children,
By those swarms upon our rear, we must never yield or
      falter,

Ages back in ghostly millions, frowning there behind us
    urging,
      Pioneers! O pioneers!

13

  On and on, the compact ranks,
With accessions ever waiting, with the places of the
    dead quickly fill'd,
Through the battle, through defeat, moving yet and
    never stopping,
      Pioneers! O pioneers!

14

  O to die advancing on!
Are there some of us to droop and die? has the hour
    come?
Then upon the march we fittest die, soon and sure the
    gap is fill'd,
      Pioneers! O pioneers!

15

  All the pulses of the world,
Falling in, they beat for us, with the western movement
    beat;
Holding single or together, steady moving, to the front,
    all for us,
      Pioneers! O pioneers!

16

  Life's involv'd and varied pageants,
All the forms and shows, all the workmen at their
    work,
All the seamen and the landsmen, all the masters with
    their slaves,
      Pioneers! O pioneers!

17

  All the hapless silent lovers,
All the prisoners in the prisons, all the righteous and
    the wicked,

All the joyous, all the sorrowing, all the living, all the
    dying,
        Pioneers! O pioneers!

18

I too with my soul and body,
We, a curious trio, picking, wandering on our way,
Through these shores, amid the shadows, with the
    apparitions pressing,
        Pioneers! O pioneers!

19

Lo! the darting bowling orb!
Lo! the brother orbs around! all the clustering suns and
    planets;
All the dazzling days, all the mystic nights with dreams,
        Pioneers! O pioneers!

20

These are of us, they are with us,
All for primal needed work, while the followers there in
    embryo wait behind,
We to-day's procession heading, we the route for travel
    clearing,
        Pioneers! O pioneers!

21

O you daughters of the west!
O you young and elder daughters! O you mothers and
    you wives!
Never must you be divided, in our ranks you move
    united,
        Pioneers! O pioneers!

22

Minstrels latent on the prairies!
(Shrouded bards of other lands! you may sleep—you
    have done your work;)

Soon I hear you coming warbling, soon you rise and
    tramp amid us,
        Pioneers! O pioneers!

23

 Not for delectations sweet;
Not the cushion and the slipper, not the peaceful and
    the studious;
Not the riches safe and palling, not for us the tame en-
    joyment,
        Pioneers! O pioneers!

24

 Do the feasters gluttonous feast?
Do the corpulent sleepers sleep? have they lock'd and
    bolted doors?
Still be ours the diet hard, and the blanket on the
    ground,
        Pioneers! O pioneers!

25

 Has the night descended?
Was the road of late so toilsome? did we stop discour-
    aged, nodding on our way?
Yet a passing hour I yield you, in your tracks to pause
    oblivious,
        Pioneers! O pioneers!

26

 Till with sound of trumpet,
Far, far off the day-break call—hark! how loud and
    clear I hear it wind;
Swift! to the head of the army!—swift! spring to
    your places,
        Pioneers! O pioneers!

*Quicksand years that whirl me
I know not whither**

QUICKSAND years that whirl me I know not whither,
Your schemes, politics, fail—lines give way—substan-
    ces mock and elude me;
Only the theme I sing, the great and strong-possess'd
    soul, eludes not;
One's-self, must never give way—that is the final sub-
    tance—that out of all is sure;
Out of politics, triumphs, battles, death—what at last
    finally remains?
When shows break up, what but One's-Self is sure?

*The Dresser**

1 An old man bending, I come, among new faces,
  Years looking backward, resuming, in answer to chil-
      dren,
  Come tell us old man, as from young men and maidens
      that love me;
  Years hence of these scenes, of these furious passions,
      these chances,
  Of unsurpass'd heroes, (was one side so brave? the
      other was equally brave;)
  Now be witness again—paint the mightiest armies of
      earth;
  Of those armies so rapid, so wondrous, what saw you to
      tell us?
  What stays with you latest and deepest? of curious
      panics,
  Of hard-fought engagements, or sieges tremendous,
      what deepest remains?

2 O maidens and young men I love, and that love me,
  What you ask of my days, those the strangest and sud-
      den your talking recals;

Soldier alert I arrive, after a long march, cover'd with
    sweat and dust;
In the nick of time I come, plunge in the fight, loudly
    shout in the rush of successful charge;
Enter the captur'd works.... yet lo! like a swift-
    running river, they fade;
Pass and are gone, they fade—I dwell not on soldiers'
    perils or soldiers' joys;
(Both I remember well—many the hardships, few the
    joys, yet I was content.)

3 But in silence, in dream's projections,
While the world of gain and appearance and mirth goes
    on,
So soon what is over forgotten, and waves wash the
    imprints off the sand,
In nature's reverie sad, with hinged knees returning, I
    enter the doors—(while for you up there,
Whoever you are, follow me without noise, and be of
    strong heart.)

4 Bearing the bandages, water and sponge,
Straight and swift to my wounded I go,
Where they lie on the ground, after the battle brought
    in;
Where their priceless blood reddens the grass, the
    ground;
Or to the rows of the hospital tent, or under the roof'd
    hospital;
To the long rows of cots, up and down, each side, I
    return;
To each and all, one after another, I draw near—not
    one do I miss;
An attendant follows, holding a tray—he carries a
    refuse pail,
Soon to be fill'd with clotted rags and blood, emptied,
    and fill'd again.

5 I onward go, I stop,
  With hinged knees and steady hand, to dress wounds;
  I am firm with each—the pangs are sharp, yet unavoid-
      able;
  One turns to me his appealing eyes—(poor boy! I
      never knew you,
  Yet I think I could not refuse this moment to die for
      you, if that would save you.)

6 On, on I go—(open, doors of time! open, hospital
      doors!)
  The crush'd head I dress, (poor crazed hand, tear not the
      bandage away;)
  The neck of the cavalry-man, with the bullet through
      and through, I examine;
  Hard the breathing rattles, quite glazed already the eye,
      yet life struggles hard;
  (Come, sweet death! be persuaded, O beautiful death!
  In mercy come quickly.)

7 From the stump of the arm, the amputated hand,
  I undo the clotted lint, remove the slough, wash off the
      matter and blood;
  Back on his pillow the soldier bends, with curv'd neck,
      and side-falling head;
  His eyes are closed, his face is pale, he dares not look on
      the bloody stump,
  And has not yet looked on it.

8 I dress a wound in the side, deep, deep;
  But a day or two more—for see, the frame all wasted
      and sinking,
  And the yellow-blue countenance see.

9 I dress the perforated shoulder, the foot with the bul-
      let wound,
  Cleanse the one with a gnawing and putrid gangrene, so
      sickening, so offensive,

While the attendant stands behind aside me, holding
    the tray and pail.

10 I am faithful, I do not give out;
    The fractur'd thigh, the knee, the wound in the abdo-
        men,
    These and more I dress with impassive hand—(yet
        deep in my breast a fire, a burning flame.)

11 Thus in silence, in dream's projections,
    Returning, resuming, I thread my way through the hos-
        pitals;
    The hurt and the wounded I pacify with soothing hand,
    I sit by the restless all the dark night—some are so
        young;
    Some suffer so much—I recall the experience sweet
        and sad;
    (Many a soldier's loving arms about this neck have
        cross'd and rested,
    Many a soldier's kiss dwells on these bearded lips.)

When I heard the learn'd Astronomer

WHEN I heard the learn'd astronomer;
When the proofs, the figures, were ranged in columns
    before me;
When I was shown the charts and the diagrams, to add,
    divide, and measure them;
When I, sitting, heard the astronomer, where he
    lectured with much applause in the lecture-room,
How soon, unaccountable, I became tired and sick;
Till rising and gliding out, I wander'd off by myself,
In the mystical moist night-air, and from time to time,
Look'd up in perfect silence at the stars.

Beat! Beat! Drums!

1

BEAT! beat! drums!—Blow! bugles! blow!
Through the windows—through doors—burst like a
    force of ruthless men,
Into the solemn church, and scatter the congregation;
Into the school where the scholar is studying:
Leave not the bridegroom quiet—no happiness must
    he have now with his bride;
Nor the peaceful farmer any peace, plowing his field or
    gathering his grain;
So fierce you whirr and pound, you drums—so shrill
    you bugles blow.

2

Beat! beat! drums!—Blow! bugles! blow!
Over the traffic of cities—over the rumble of wheels in
    the streets:
Are beds prepared for sleepers at night in the houses?
    No sleepers must sleep in those beds;
No bargainers' bargains by day—no brokers or specu-
    lators—Would they continue?
Would the talkers be talking? would the singer attempt
    to sing?
Would the lawyer rise in the court to state his case
    before the judge?
Then rattle quicker, heavier drums—you bugles wilder
    blow.

3

Beat! beat! drums!—Blow! bugles! blow!
Make no parley—stop for no expostulation;
Mind not the timid—mind not the weeper or prayer;
Mind not the old man beseeching the young man;
Let not the child's voice be heard, nor the mother's en-
    treaties;
Make even the trestles to shake the dead, where they lie
    awaiting the hearses,

So strong you thump, O terrible drums—so loud
    you bugles blow.

City of Ships

CITY of ships!
(O the black ships! O the fierce ships!
O the beautiful, sharp bow'd steam-ships and sail-ships!)
City of the world! (for all races are here;
All the lands of the earth make contributions here;)
City of the sea! city of hurried and glittering tides!
City whose gleeful tides continually rush or recede,
    whirling in and out, with eddies and foam!
City of wharves and stores! city of tall façades of mar-
    ble and iron!
Proud and passionate city! mettlesome, mad, extrava-
    gant city!
Spring up, O city! not for peace alone, but be indeed
    yourself, warlike!
Fear not! submit to no models but your own, O city!
Behold me! incarnate me, as I have incarnated you!
I have rejected nothing you offer'd me—whom you
    adopted, I have adopted;
Good or bad, I never question you—I love all—I do
    not condemn anything;
I chant and celebrate all that is yours—yet peace no
    more;
In peace I chanted peace, but now the drum of war is
    mine;
War, red war, is my song through your streets, O city!

Vigil strange I kept on the field one night

VIGIL strange I kept on the field one night,
When you, my son and my comrade, dropt at my side
    that day,

One look I but gave, which your dear eyes return'd,
    with a look I shall never forget;
One touch of your hand to mine, O boy, reach'd up as
    you lay on the ground;
Then onward I sped in the battle, the even-contested
    battle;
Till late in the night reliev'd, to the place at last again I
    made my way;
Found you in death so cold, dear comrade—found your
    body, son of responding kisses, (never again on
    earth responding;)
Bared your face in the starlight—curious the scene—
    cool blew the moderate night-wind;
Long there and then in vigil I stood, dimly around me
    the battle-field spreading;
Vigil wondrous and vigil sweet, there in the fragrant
    silent night;
But not a tear fell, not even a long-drawn sigh—Long,
    long I gazed;
Then on the earth partially reclining, sat by your side,
    leaning my chin in my hands;
Passing sweet hours, immortal and mystic hours with
    you, dearest comrade—Not a tear, not a word;
Vigil of silence, love and death—vigil for you, my son
    and my soldier,
As onward silently stars aloft, eastward new ones up-
    ward stole;
Vigil final for you, brave boy, (I could not save you,
    swift was your death,
I faithfully loved you and cared for you living—I think
    we shall surely meet again;)
Till at latest lingering of the night, indeed just as the
    dawn appear'd,
My comrade I wrapt in his blanket, envelop'd well his
    form,
Folded the blanket well, tucking it carefully over head,
    and carefully under feet;
And there and then, and bathed by the rising sun, my
    son in his grave, in his rude-dug grave I de-
    posited;

Ending my vigil strange with that—vigil of night and
    battle-field dim;
Vigil for boy of responding kisses, (never again on earth
    responding;)
Vigil for comrade swiftly slain—vigil I never forget,
    how as day brighten'd,
I rose from the chill ground, and folded my soldier well
    in his blanket,
And buried him where he fell.

A march in the ranks hard-prest, and the road unknown

A MARCH in the ranks hard-prest, and the road unknown;
A route through a heavy wood, with muffled steps in the
    darkness;
Our army foil'd with loss severe, and the sullen remnant
    retreating;
Till after midnight glimmer upon us, the lights of a
    dim-lighted building;
We come to an open space in the woods, and halt by the
    dim-lighted building;
'Tis a large old church, at the crossing roads—'tis now
    an impromptu hospital;
—Entering but for a minute, I see a sight beyond all
    the pictures and poems ever made:
Shadows of deepest, deepest black, just lit by moving
    candles and lamps,
And by one great pitchy torch, stationary, with wild red
    flame, and clouds of smoke;
By these, crowds, groups of forms, vaguely I see, on the
    floor, some in the pews laid down;
At my feet more distinctly, a soldier, a mere lad, in
    danger of bleeding to death, (he is shot in the ab-
    domen;)
I staunch the blood temporarily, (the youngster's face is
    white as a lily;)
Then before I depart I sweep my eyes o'er the scene,
    fain to absorb it all;

Faces, varieties, postures beyond description, most in
    obscurity, some of them dead;
Surgeons operating, attendants holding lights, the smell
    of ether, the odor of blood;
The crowd, O the crowd of the bloody forms of soldiers
    —the yard outside also fill'd;
Some on the bare ground, some on planks or stretchers,
    some in the death-spasm sweating;
An occasional scream or cry, the doctor's shouted orders
    or calls;
The glisten of the little steel instruments catching the
    glint of the torches;
These I resume as I chant—I see again the forms, I
    smell the odor;
Then hear outside the orders given, *Fall in, my men,*
    Fall in;
But first I bend to the dying lad—his eyes open—a
    half-smile gives he me;
Then the eyes close, calmly close, and I speed forth to
    the darkness,
Resuming, marching, as ever in darkness marching, on
    in the ranks,
The unknown road still marching.

Give me the splendid silent
Sun

I

GIVE me the splendid silent sun, with all his beams full-
    dazzling;
Give me juicy autumnal fruit, ripe and red from the
    orchard;
Give me a field where the unmow'd grass grows;
Give me an arbor, give me the trellis'd grape;
Give me fresh corn and wheat—give me serene-moving
    animals, teaching content;
Give me nights perfectly quiet, as on high plateaus west
    of the Mississippi, and I looking up at the stars;

Give me odorous at sunrise a garden of beautiful flowers,
    where I can walk undisturb'd;
Give me for marriage a sweet-breath'd woman, of whom
    I should never tire;
Give me a perfect child—give me, away, aside from the
    noise of the world, a rural domestic life;
Give me to warble spontaneous songs, reliev'd, recluse
    by myself, for my own ears only;
Give me solitude—give me Nature—give me again,
    O Nature, your primal sanities!
—These, demanding to have them, (tired with ceaseless
    excitement, and rack'd by the war-strife;)
These to procure, incessantly asking, rising in cries from
    my heart,
While yet incessantly asking, still I adhere to my city;
Day upon day, and year upon year, O city, walking
    your streets,
Where you hold me enchain'd a certain time, refusing
    to give me up;
Yet giving to make me glutted, enrich'd of soul—you
    give me forever faces;
(O I see what I sought to escape, confronting, reversing
    my cries;
I see my own soul trampling down what it ask'd for.)

2

Keep your splendid silent sun;
Keep your woods, O Nature, and the quiet places by
    the woods;
Keep your fields of clover and timothy, and your corn-
    fields and orchards;
Keep the blossoming buckwheat fields, where the Ninth-
    month bees hum;
Give me faces and streets! give me these phantoms in-
    cessant and endless along the trottoirs!
Give me interminable eyes! give me women! give me
    comrades and lovers by the thousand!
Let me see new ones every day! let me hold new ones
    by the hand every day!

Give me such shows! give me the streets of Manhattan!
Give me Broadway, with the soldiers marching—give
me the sound of the trumpets and drums!
(The soldiers in companies or regiments—some, starting
away, flush'd and reckless;
Some, their time up, returning, with thinn'd ranks—
young, yet very old, worn, marching, noticing
nothing;)
—Give me the shores and the wharves heavy-fringed
with the black ships!
O such for me! O an intense life! O full to repletion,
and varied!
The life of the theatre, bar-room, huge hotel, for me!
The saloon of the steamer! the crowded excursion for
me! the torch-light procession!
The dense brigade, bound for the war, with high piled
military wagons following;
People, endless, streaming, with strong voices, passions,
pageants;
Manhattan streets, with their powerful throbs, with the
beating drums, as now;
The endless and noisy chorus, the rustle and clank of
muskets, (even the sight of the wounded;)
Manhattan crowds with their turbulent musical chorus
—with varied chorus and light of the sparkling
eyes;
Manhattan faces and eyes forever for me.

Over the carnage rose prophetic
a voice

1 OVER the carnage rose prophetic a voice,
Be not dishearten'd—Affection shall solve the problems
of Freedom yet;
Those who love each other shall become invincible—
they shall yet make Columbia victorious.

2 Sons of the Mother of All! you shall yet be victo-
 rious!
 You shall yet laugh to scorn the attacks of all the re-
 mainder of the earth.

3 No danger shall balk Columbia's lovers;
 If need be, a thousand shall sternly immolate themselves
 for one.

4 One from Massachusetts shall be a Missourian's com-
 rade;
 From Maine and from hot Carolina, and another an Ore-
 gonese, shall be friends triune,
 More precious to each other than all the riches of the
 earth.

5 To Michigan, Florida perfumes shall tenderly come;
 Not the perfumes of flowers, but sweeter, and wafted
 beyond death.

6 It shall be customary in the houses and streets to see
 manly affection;
 The most dauntless and rude shall touch face to face
 lightly;
 The dependence of Liberty shall be lovers,
 The continuance of Equality shall be comrades.

7 These shall tie you and band you stronger than hoops
 of iron;
 I, extatic, O partners! O lands! with the love of lovers
 tie you.

8 Were you looking to be held together by the lawyers?
 Or by an agreement on a paper? or by arms?
 —Nay—nor the world, nor any living thing, will so
 cohere.

Year of Meteors
(1859–60)

YEAR of meteors! brooding year!
I would bind in words retrospective, some of your deeds
    and signs;
I would sing your contest for the 19th Presentiad;*
I would sing how an old man,* tall, with white hair,
    mounted the scaffold in Virginia;
(I was at hand—silent I stood, with teeth shut close—I
    watch'd;
I stood very near you, old man, when cool and indiffer-
    ent, but trembling with age and your unheal'd
    wounds, you mounted the scaffold;)
I would sing in my copious song your census returns of
    The States,
The tables of population and products—I would sing of
    your ships and their cargoes,
The proud black ships of Manhattan, arriving, some
    fill'd with immigrants, some from the isthmus
    with cargoes of gold;
Songs thereof would I sing—to all that hitherward
    comes would I welcome give;
And you would I sing, fair stripling! welcome to you
    from me, sweet boy of England!*
Remember you surging Manhattan's crowds, as you
    passed with your cortege of nobles?
There in the crowds stood I, and singled you out with
    attachment;
I know not why, but I loved you…(and so go forth
    little song,
Far over sea speed like an arrow, carrying my love all
    folded,
And find in his palace the youth I love, and drop these
    lines at his feet;)
—Nor forget I to sing of the wonder, the ship as she
    swam up my bay,
Well-shaped and stately the Great Eastern* swam up my
    bay, she was 600 feet long,

Her moving swiftly, surrounded by myriads of small
    craft, I forget not to sing;
Nor the comet that came unannounced, out of the north,
    flaring in heaven,
Nor the strange huge meteor procession, dazzling and
    clear, shooting over our heads,
(A moment, a moment long, it sail'd its balls of unearth-
    ly light over our heads,
Then departed, dropt in the night, and was gone;)
—Of such, and fitful as they, I sing—with gleams from
    them would I gleam and patch these chants;
Your chants, O year all mottled with evil and good!
    year of forebodings! year of the youth I love!
Year of comets and meteors transient and strange!—lo!
    even here, one equally transient and strange!
As I flit through you hastily, soon to fall and be gone,
    what is this book,
What am I myself but one of your meteors?

Year that trembled and reel'd beneath me

YEAR that trembled and reel'd beneath me!
Your summer wind was warm enough—yet the air I
    breathed froze me;
A thick gloom fell through the sunshine and darken'd
    me;
Must I change my triumphant songs? said I to myself;
Must I indeed learn to chant the cold dirges of the baf-
    fled?
And sullen hymns of defeat?

Look down fair moon

LOOK down, fair moon, and bathe this scene;
Pour softly down night's nimbus floods, on faces ghast-
    ly, swollen, purple;

On the dead, on their backs, with their arms toss'd wide,
Pour down your unstinted nimbus, sacred moon.

Out of the rolling ocean,
the crowd

1

OUT of the rolling ocean, the crowd, came a drop gently
    to me,
Whispering, *I love you, before long I die,*
I have travel'd a long way, merely to look on you, to touch you,
For I could not die till I once look'd on you,
For I fear'd I might afterward lose you.

2

(Now we have met, we have look'd, we are safe;
Return in peace to the ocean my love;
I too am part of that ocean, my love—we are not so
    much separated;
Behold the great rondure—the cohesion of all, how per-
    fect!
But as for me, for you, the irresistible sea is to separ-
    ate us,
As for an hour carrying us diverse—yet cannot carry
    us diverse for ever;
Be not impatient—a little space—know you, I salute
    the air, the ocean and the land,
Every day, at sundown, for your dear sake, my love.)

I saw old General at bay

I saw old General at bay;
(Old as he was, his grey eyes yet shone out in battle
    like stars;)
His small force was now completely hemmed in, in his
    works;

He call'd for volunteers to run the enemy's lines—a
    desperate emergency;
I saw a hundred and more step forth from the ranks—
    but two or three were selected;
I saw them receive their orders aside—they listen'd
    with care—the adjutant was very grave;
I saw them depart with cheerfulness, freely risking their
    lives.

Not youth pertains to me

NOT youth pertains to me,
Nor delicatesse—I cannot beguile the time with talk;
Awkward in the parlor, neither a dancer nor elegant;
In the learn'd coterie sitting constrain'd and still—for
    learning inures not to me;
Beauty, knowledge, fortune, inure not to me—yet
    there are two things inure to me;
I have nourish'd the wounded, and sooth'd many a
    dying soldier;
And at intervals I have strung together a few songs,
Fit for war, and the life of the camp.

FROM SEQUEL TO DRUM-TAPS
(1865–1866)

When Lilacs Last in the
Door-Yard Bloom'd

1

1 WHEN lilacs last in the door-yard bloom'd,
And the great star early droop'd in the western sky in the
   night,
I mourn'd...and yet shall mourn with ever-returning
   spring.

2 O ever-returning spring! trinity sure to me you bring;
Lilac blooming perennial, and drooping star in the west,
And thought of him I love.

2

3 O powerful, western, fallen star!
O shades of night! O moody, tearful night!
O great star disappear'd! O the blank murk that hides the
   star!
O cruel hands that hold me powerless! O helpless soul of
   me!
O harsh surrounding cloud that will not free my soul!

3

4 In the door-yard fronting an old farm-house, near the
   white-wash'd palings,
Stands the lilac bush, tall-growing, with heart-shaped leaves
   of rich green,
With many a pointed blossom, rising, delicate, with the
   perfume strong I love,
With every leaf a miracle......and from this bush in the
   door-yard,
With its delicate-color'd blossoms, and heart-shaped leaves
   of rich green,
A sprig, with its flower, I break.

4

5   In the swamp, in secluded recesses,
     A shy and hidden bird is warbling a song.

6   Solitary, the thrush,
     The hermit, withdrawn to himself, avoiding the settlements,
     Sings by himself a song.

7   Song of the bleeding throat!
     Death's outlet song of life—(for well, dear brother, I know,
     If thou wast not gifted to sing, thou would'st surely die.)

5

8   Over the breast of the spring, the land, amid cities,
     Amid lanes, and through old woods, (where lately the
         violets peep'd from the ground, spotting the gray
         debris;)
     Amid the grass in the fields each side of the lanes—passing
         the endless grass;
     Passing the yellow-spear'd wheat, every grain from its
         shroud in the dark-brown fields uprising;
     Passing the apple-tree blows of white and pink in the
         orchards;
     Carrying a corpse to where it shall rest in the grave,
     Night and day journeys a coffin.

6

9   Coffin that passes through lanes and streets,
     Through day and night, with the great cloud darkening the
         land,
     With the pomp of the inloop'd flags, with the cities draped
         in black,
     With the show of the States themselves, as of crape-veil'd
         women, standing,
     With processions long and winding, and the flambeaus* of
         the night,
     With the countless torches lit—with the silent sea of faces,
         and the unbared heads,

With the waiting depot, the arriving coffin, and the sombre
    faces,
With dirges through the night, with the thousand voices
    rising strong and solemn;
With all the mournful voices of the dirges, pour'd around
    the coffin,
The dim-lit churches and the shuddering organs—Where
    amid these you journey,
With the tolling, tolling bells' perpetual clang;
Here! coffin that slowly passes.
I give you my sprig of lilac.

7

10 (Nor for you, for one, alone;
Blossoms and branches green to coffins all I bring:
For fresh as the morning—thus would I chant a song for
    you, O sane and sacred death.

11 All over bouquets of roses,
O death! I cover you over with roses and early lilies;
But mostly and now the lilac that blooms the first,
Copious, I break, I break the sprigs from the bushes:
With loaded arms I come, pouring for you,
For you and the coffins all of you, O death.)

8

12 O western orb, sailing the heaven!
Now I know what you must have meant, as a month since
    we walk'd,
As we walk'd up and down in the dark blue so mystic,
As we walk'd in silence the transparent shadowy night,
As I saw you had something to tell, as you bent to me night
    after night,
As you droop'd from the sky low down, as if to my side,
    (while the other stars all look'd on;)
As we wander'd together the solemn night, (for something
    I know not what, kept me from sleep;)
As the night advanced, and I saw on the rim of the west,
    ere you went, how full you were of woe;

As I stood on the rising ground in the breeze, in the cool
    transparent night,
As I watch'd where you pass'd and was lost in the nether-
    ward black of the night,
As my soul, in its trouble, dissatisfied, sank, as where you,
    sad orb,
Concluded, dropt in the night, and was gone.

9

13 Sing on, there in the swamp!
    O singer bashful and tender! I hear your notes—I hear
        your call;
    I hear—I come presently—I understand you;
    But a moment I linger—for the lustrous star has detain'd
        me;
    The star, my comrade, departing, holds and detains me.

10

14 O how shall I warble myself for the dead one there I
        loved?
    And how shall I deck my song for the large sweet soul that
        has gone?
    And what shall my perfume be, for the grave of him I love?

15 Sea-winds, blown from east and west,
    Blown from the eastern sea, and blown from the western sea,
        till there on the prairies meeting:
    These, and with these, and the breath of my chant,
    I perfume the grave of him I love.

11

16 O what shall I hang on the chamber walls?
    And what shall the pictures be that I hang on the walls,
    To adorn the burial-house of him I love?

17 Pictures of growing spring, and farms, and homes,
    With the Fourth-month eve at sundown, and the gray-smoke
        lucid and bright,

With floods of the yellow gold of the gorgeous, indolent,
    sinking sun, burning, expanding the air;
With the fresh sweet herbage under foot, and the pale green
    leaves of the trees prolific;
In the distance the flowing glaze, the breast of the river,
    with a wind-dapple here and there;
With ranging hills on the banks, with many a line against
    the sky, and shadows;
And the city at hand, with dwellings so dense, and stacks
    of chimneys,
And all the scenes of life, and the workshops, and the
    workmen homeward returning.

12

18 Lo! body and soul! this land!
Mighty Manhattan, with spires, and the sparkling and hur-
    rying tides, and the ships;
The varied and ample land—the South and the North in
    the light—Ohio's shores, and flashing Missouri,
And ever the far-spreading prairies, cover'd with grass and
    corn.

19 Lo! the most excellent sun, so calm and haughty;
The violet and purple morn, with just-felt breezes;
The gentle, soft-born, measureless light;
The miracle, spreading, bathing all—the fulfill'd noon;
The coming eve, delicious—the welcome night, and the
    stars,
Over my cities shining all, enveloping man and land.

13

20 Sing on! sing on, you gray-brown bird!
Sing from the swamps, the recesses—pour your chant from
    the bushes;
Limitless out of the dusk, out of the cedars and pines.

21 Sing on, dearest brother—warble your reedy song;
Loud human song, with voice of uttermost woe.

22 O liquid, and free, and tender!
  O wild and loose to my soul! O wondrous singer!
  You only I hear......yet the star holds me, (but will soon
      depart;)
  Yet the lilac, with mastering odor, holds me.

14

23 Now while I sat in the day, and look'd forth,
  In the close of the day, with its light, and the fields of
      spring, and the farmer preparing his crops,
  In the large unconscious scenery of my land, with its lakes
      and forests,
  In the heavenly aerial beauty, (after the perturb'd winds,
      and the storms;)
  Under the arching heavens of the afternoon swift passing,
      and the voices of children and women,
  The many-moving sea-tides,—and I saw the ships how they
      sail'd,
  And the summer approaching with richness, and the fields
      all busy with labor,
  And the infinite separate houses, how they all went on, each
      with its meals and minutia of daily usages;
  And the streets, how their throbbings throbb'd, and the cities
      pent,—lo! then and there,
  Falling among them all, and upon them all, enveloping me
      with the rest,
  Appear'd the cloud, appear'd the long black trail;
  And I knew Death, its thought, and the sacred knowledge
      of death.

15

24 Then with the knowledge of death as walking one side of
      me,
  And the thought of death close-walking the other side of me,
  And I in the middle, as with companions, and as holding the
      hands of companions,
  I fled forth to the hiding receiving night, that talks not,
  Down to the shores of the water, the path by the swamp in
      the dimness,
  To the solemn shadowy cedars, and ghostly pines so still.

25 And the singer so shy to the rest receiv'd me;
    The gray-brown bird I know, receiv'd us comrades three;
    And he sang what seem'd the song of death, and a verse for
        him I love.

26 From deep secluded recesses,
    From the fragrant cedars, and the ghostly pines so still,
    Came the singing of the bird.

27 And the charm of the singing rapt me,
    As I held, as if by their hands, my comrades in the night;
    And the voice of my spirit tallied the song of the bird.

16

28 Come, lovely and soothing Death,
    Undulate round the world, serenely arriving, arriving,
    In the day, in the night, to all, to each,
    Sooner or later, delicate Death.

29 Prais'd be the fathomless universe,
    For life and joy, and for objects and knowledge curious;
    And for love, sweet love—But praise! O praise and praise,
    For the sure-enwinding arms of cool-enfolding Death.

30 Dark Mother, always gliding near, with soft feet,
    Have none chanted for thee a chant of fullest welcome?
    Then I chant it for thee—I glorify thee above all;
    I bring thee a song that when thou must indeed come, come
        unfalteringly.

31 Approach, encompassing Death—strong Deliveress!
    When it is so—when thou hast taken them, I joyously sing
        the dead,
    Lost in the loving, floating ocean of thee,
    Laved in the flood of thy bliss, O Death.

32 From me to thee glad serenades,
    Dances for thee I propose, saluting thee—adornments and
        feastings for thee;

And the sights of the open landscape, and the high-spread
    sky, are fitting,
And life and the fields, and the huge and thoughtful night.

33 The night, in silence, under many a star;
    The ocean shore, and the husky whispering wave, whose
        voice I know;
    And the soul turning to thee, O vast and well-veil'd Death,
    And the body gratefully nestling close to thee.

34 Over the tree-tops I float thee a song!
    Over the rising and sinking waves—over the myriad fields,
        and the prairies wide;
    Over the dense-pack'd cities all, and the teeming wharves
        and ways,
    I float this carol with joy, with joy to thee, O Death!

17

35 To the tally of my soul,
    Loud and strong kept up the gray-brown bird,
    With pure, deliberate notes, spreading, filling the night.

36 Loud in the pines and cedars dim,
    Clear in the freshness moist, and the swamp-perfume;
    And I with my comrades there in the night.

37 While my sight that was bound in my eyes unclosed,
    As to long panoramas of visions.

18

38 I saw the vision of armies;
    And I saw, as in noiseless dreams, hundreds of battle-flags;
    Borne through the smoke of the battles, and pierc'd with
        missiles, I saw them,
    And carried hither and yon through the smoke, and torn
        and bloody;
    And at last but a few shreds of the flags left on the staffs,
        (and all in silence,)
    And the staffs all splinter'd and broken.

39 I saw battle-corpses, myriads of them,
  And the white skeletons of young men—I saw them;
  I saw the debris and debris of all dead soldiers;
  But I saw they were not as was thought;
  They themselves were fully at rest—they suffer'd not;
  The living remain'd and suffer'd—the mother suffer'd,
  And the wife and the child, and the musing comrade suf-
    fer'd,
  And the armies that remain'd suffer'd.

19

40 Passing the visions, passing the night;
  Passing, unloosing the hold of my comrades' hands;
  Passing the song of the hermit bird, and the tallying song
    of my soul,
  Victorious song, death's outlet song, (yet varying, ever-
    altering song,
  As low and wailing, yet clear the notes, rising and falling,
    flooding the night,
  Sadly sinking and fainting, as warning and warning, and
    yet again bursting with joy,)
  Covering the earth, and filling the spread of the heaven,
  As that powerful psalm in the night I heard from recesses.

20

41 Must I leave thee, lilac with heart-shaped leaves?
  Must I leave thee there in the door-yard, blooming, return-
    ing with spring?

42 Must I pass from my song for thee;
  From my gaze on thee in the west, fronting the west, com-
    muning with thee,
  O comrade lustrous, with silver face in the night?

21

43 Yet each I keep, and all;
  The song, the wondrous chant of the gray-brown bird, I keep,
  And the tallying chant, the echo arous'd in my soul, I keep,

With the lustrous and drooping star, with the countenance
    full of woe;
With the lilac tall, and its blossoms of mastering odor;
Comrades mine, and I in the midst, and their memory ever
    I keep—for the dead I loved so well;
For the sweetest, wisest soul of all my days and lands...
    and this for his dear sake;
Lilac and star and bird, twined with the chant of my soul,
With the holders holding my hand, nearing the call of the
    bird,
There in the fragrant pines, and the cedars dusk and dim.

O Captain! my Captain!

1

O CAPTAIN! my captain! our fearful trip is done;
The ship has weather'd every rack, the prize we sought is
    won;
The port is near, the bells I hear, the people all exulting,
While follow eyes the steady keel, the vessel grim and daring:
    But O heart! heart! heart!
        Leave you not the little spot,
            Where on the deck my captain lies.
            Fallen cold and dead.

2

O captain! my captain! rise up and hear the bells;
Rise up—for you the flag is flung—for you the bugle trills;
For you bouquets and ribbon'd wreaths—for you the shores
    a-crowding;
For you they call, the swaying mass, their eager faces
    turning;
    O captain! dear father!
        This arm I push beneath you;
            It is some dream that on the deck,
                You've fallen cold and dead.

3

My captain does not answer, his lips are pale and still;
My father does not feel my arm, he has no pulse nor will:
But the ship, the ship is anchor'd safe, its voyage closed and
    done;
From fearful trip, the victor ship, comes in with object won:
    Exult, O shores, and ring, O bells!
       But I, with silent tread,
         Walk the spot my captain lies,
          Fallen cold and dead.

Chanting the Square Deific

1

CHANTING the square deific, out of the One advancing, out
    of the sides;
Out of the old and new—out of the square entirely divine,
Solid, four-sided, (all the sides needed)…from this side
    JEHOVAH am I,
Old Brahm I, and I Saturnius am;
Not Time affects me—I am Time, modern as any;
Unpersuadable, relentless, executing righteous judgments;
As the Earth, the Father, the brown old Kronos, with laws,
Aged beyond computation—yet ever new—ever with those
    mighty laws rolling,
Relentless, I forgive no man—whoever sins, dies—I will
    have that man's life;
Therefore let none expect mercy—Have the seasons, gravi-
    tation, the appointed days, mercy?—No more have I;
But as the seasons, and gravitation—and as all the appointed
    days, that forgive not,
I dispense from this side judgments inexorable, without the
    least remorse.

2

Consolator most mild, the promis'd one advancing,
With gentle hand extended, the mightier God am I,

Foretold by prophets and poets, in their most rapt proph-
　　ecies and poems;
From this side, lo! the Lord CHRIST gazes—lo! Hermes I—
　　lo! mine is Hercules' face;
All sorrow, labor, suffering, I, tallying it, absorb in myself;
Many times have I been rejected, taunted, put in prison,
　　and crucified—and many times shall be again;
All the world have I given up for my dear brothers' and
　　sisters' sake—for the soul's sake;
Wending my way through the homes of men, rich or
　　poor, with the kiss of affection;
For I am affection—I am the cheer-bringing God, with hope,
　　and all-enclosing Charity;
(Conqueror yet—for before me all the armies and soldiers
　　of the earth shall yet bow—and all the weapons of
　　war become impotent:)
With indulgent words, as to children—with fresh and sane
　　words, mine only;
Young and strong I pass, knowing well I am destin'd my-
　　self to an early death:
But my Charity has no death—my Wisdom dies not, neither
　　early nor late,
And my sweet Love, bequeath'd here and elsewhere, never
　　dies.

3

Aloof, dissatisfied, plotting revolt,
Comrade of criminals, brother of slaves,
Crafty, despised, a drudge, ignorant,
With sudra* face and worn brow—black, but in the depths
　　of my heart, proud as any;
Lifted, now and always, against whoever, scorning, assumes
　　to rule me;
Morose, full of guile, full of reminiscences, brooding, with
　　many wiles,
(Though it was thought I was baffled and dispell'd, and
　　my wiles done—but that will never be;)
Defiant, I, SATAN, still live—still utter words—in new lands
　　duly appearing, (and old ones also;)

Permanent here, from my side, warlike, equal with any,
    real as any,
Nor time, nor change, shall ever change me or my words.

4

Santa SPIRITA,* breather, life,
Beyond the light, lighter than light,
Beyond the flames of hell—joyous, leaping easily above hell;
Beyond Paradise—perfumed solely with mine own perfume;
Including all life on earth—touching, including God—
    including Saviour and Satan;
Ethereal, pervading all, (for without me, what were all?
    what were God?)
Essence of forms—life of the real identities, permanent,
    positive, (namely the unseen,)
Life of the great round world, the sun and stars, and of
    man—I, the general Soul,
Here the square finishing, the solid, I the most solid,
Breathe my breath also through these little songs.

As I lay with my head in your lap, Camerado

As I lay with my head in your lap, camerado,*
The confession I made I resume—what I said to you and
    the open air I resume:
I know I am restless, and make others so;
I know my words are weapons, full of danger, full of death;
(Indeed I am myself the real soldier;
It is not he, there, with his bayonet, and not the red-striped
    artilleryman;)
For I confront peace, security, and all the settled laws, to
    unsettle them;
I am more resolute because all have denied me, than I could
    ever have been had all accepted me;
I heed not, and have never heeded, either experience, cau-
    tions, majorities, nor ridicule;

And the threat of what is call'd hell is little or nothing to
　　me;
And the lure of what is call'd heaven is little or nothing
　　to me;
…Dear camerado! I confess I have urged you onward
　　with me, and still urge you, without the least idea
　　what is our destination,
Or whether we shall be victorious, or utterly quell'd and
　　defeated.

Reconciliation

WORD over all, beautiful as the sky!
Beautiful that war, and all its deeds of carnage, must in
　　time be utterly lost;
That the hands of the sisters Death and Night, incessantly
　　softly wash again, and ever again, this soil'd world:
…For my enemy is dead—a man divine as myself is dead;
I look where he lies, white-faced and still, in the coffin—I
　　draw near;
I bend down and touch lightly with my lips the white face
　　in the coffin.

FROM LEAVES OF GRASS (1867)

Inscription*

SMALL *is the theme of the following Chant, yet the
greatest—namely,* ONE'S-SELF—*that wondrous
thing, a simple, separate person. That, for the
use of the New World, I sing.*
*Man's physiology complete, from top to toe, I sing. Not
physiognomy alone, nor brain alone, is worthy for
the muse;—I say the Form complete is worthier
far. The female equally with the male, I sing.*
*Nor cease at the theme of One's-Self. I speak the word
of the modern, the word* EN-MASSE.
*My Days I sing, and the Lands—with interstice I knew
of hapless War.*
*O friend, whoe'er you are, at last arriving hither to com-
mence, I feel through every leaf the pressure of
your hand, which I return. And thus upon our
journey link'd together let us go.*

The Runner

ON a flat road runs the well-train'd runner;
He is lean and sinewy, with muscular legs;
He is thinly clothed—he leans forward as he runs,
With lightly closed fists, and arms partially rais'd.

2.*

TEARS! tears! tears!
In the night, in solitude, tears;
On the white shore dripping, dripping, suck'd in by
the sand;
Tears—not a star shining—all dark and desolate;
Moist tears from the eyes of a muffled head:
—O who is that ghost?—that form in the dark, with
tears?
What shapeless lump is that, bent, crouch'd there on
the sand?

Streaming tears—sobbing tears—throes, choked with
　　wild cries;
O storm, embodied, rising, careering, with swift steps
　　along the beach;
O wild and dismal night storm, with wind! O belch-
　　ing and desperate!
O shade, so sedate and decorous by day, with calm
　　countenance and regulated pace;
But away, at night, as you fly, none looking—O then
　　the unloosen'd ocean,
Of tears! tears! tears!

When I Read the Book

WHEN I read the book, the biography famous;
And is this, then, (said I,) what the author calls a
　　man's life?
And so will some one, when I am dead and gone,
　　write my life?
(As if any man really knew aught of my life;
As if you, O cunning Soul, did not keep your secret
　　well!)

The City Dead-House

BY the City Dead-House, by the gate,
As idly sauntering, wending my way from the clangor,
I curious pause—for lo! an outcast form, a poor dead
　　prostitute brought;
Her corpse they deposit unclaim'd, it lies on the
　　damp brick pavement;
The divine woman, her body—I see the Body—I look
　　on it alone,
That house once full of passion and beauty—all else I
　　notice not;
Nor stillness so cold, nor running water from faucet,
　　nor odors morbific impress me;

But the house alone—that wondrous house—that de-
licate fair house—that ruin!
That immortal house, more than all the rows of dwel-
lings ever built!
Or white-domed Capitol itself, with magestic figure sur-
mounted—or all the old high-spired cathedrals,
That little house alone, more than them all—poor,
desperate house!
Fair, fearful wreck! tenement of a Soul! itself a Soul!
Unclaim'd, avoided house! take one breath from my
tremulous lips;
Take one tear, dropt aside as I go, for thought of you,
Dead house of love! house of madness and sin, crum-
bled! crush'd!
House of life—erewhile talking and laughing—but
ah, poor house! dead, even then;
Months, years, an echoing, garnish'd house—but
dead, dead, dead.

FROM LEAVES OF GRASS
(1871–1872)

One's-Self I Sing*

1 ONE'S SELF I sing—a simple, separate Person;
  Yet utter the word Democratic, the word *En-masse*.

2 Of Physiology from top to toe I sing;
  Not physiognomy alone, nor brain alone, is worthy for
      the muse—I say the Form complete is worthier
      far;
  The Female equally with the male I sing.

3 Of Life immense in passion, pulse, and power,
  Cheerful—for freest action form'd, under the laws di-
      vine,
  The Modern Man I sing.

For Him I Sing

FOR him I sing,
I raise the Present on the Past,
(As some perennial tree, out of its roots, the present on
    the past:)
With time and space I him dilate—and fuse the im-
    mortal laws,
To make himself, by them, the law unto himself.

To Thee, Old Cause!

1 To thee, old Cause!*
  Thou peerless, passionate, good cause!
  Thou stern, remorseless, sweet Idea!
  Deathless throughout the ages, races, lands!
  After a strange, sad war—great war for thee,
  (I think all war through time was really fought, and
      ever will be really fought, for thee;)
  These chants for thee—the eternal march of thee.

2 Thou orb of many orbs!
   Thou seething principle! Thou well-kept, latent germ!
       Thou centre!
   Around the idea of thee the strange sad war revolv-
       ing,
   With all its angry and vehement play of causes,
   (With yet unknown results to come, for thrice a thou-
       sand years,)
   These recitatives for thee—my Book and the War are
       one,
   Merged in its spirit I and mine—as the contest hinged
       on thee,
   As a wheel on its axis turns, this Book, unwitting to
       itself,
   Around the Idea of thee.

The Base of all Metaphysics

1 AND now, gentlemen,
   A word I give to remain in your memories and minds,
   As base, and finale too, for all metaphysics.

2 (So, to the students, the old professor,
   At the close of his crowded course.)

3 Having studied the new and antique, the Greek and
       Germanic systems,
   Kant having studied and stated—Fichte and Schelling
       and Hegel,
   Stated the lore of Plato—and Socrates, greater than
       Plato,
   And greater than Socrates sought and stated—Christ
       divine having studied long,
   I see reminiscent to-day those Greek and Germanic
       systems,
   See the philosophies all—Christian churches and tenets
       see,

Yet underneath Socrates clearly see—and underneath
    Christ the divine I see,
The dear love of man for his comrade—the attraction
    of friend to friend,
Of the well-married husband and wife—of children and
    parents,
Of city for city, and land for land.

Ethiopia Saluting the Colors

(A REMINISCENCE OF 1864)

1

WHO are you, dusky woman, so ancient, hardly human,
With your woolly-white and turban'd head, and bare
    bony feet?
Why, rising by the roadside here, do you the colors
    greet?

2

('Tis while our army lines Carolina's sands and pines,
Forth from thy hovel door, thou, Ethiopia com'st to me,
As, under doughty Sherman, I march toward the sea.)

3

Me, master, years a hundred, since from my parents sun-
    der'd,
A little child, they caught me as the savage beast is caught;
Then hither me, across the sea, the cruel slaver brought.

4

No further does she say, but lingering all the day,
Her high-borne turban'd head she wags, and rolls her
    darkling eye,
And curtseys to the regiments, the guidons* moving by.

5

What is it, fateful woman—so blear, hardly human?
Why wag your head, with turban bound—yellow, red
    and green?
Are the things so strange and marvelous, you see or
    have seen?

FROM PASSAGE TO INDIA (1871)*

Passage to India

1 SINGING my days,
    Singing the great achievements of the present,
    Singing the strong light works of engineers,
    Our modern wonders, (the antique ponderous Seven*
        outvied,)
    In the Old World the east the Suez canal,
    The New by its mighty railroad spann'd,
    The seas inlaid with eloquent gentle wires,*
    I sound, to commence, the cry, with thee, O soul,
    The Past! the Past! the Past!

2 The Past! the dark unfathom'd retrospect!
    The teeming gulf! the sleepers and the shadows!
    The past! the infinite greatness of the past!
    For what is the present, after all, but a growth out of
        the past?
    (As a projectile, form'd, impell'd, passing a certain line,
        still keeps on,
    So the present, utterly form'd, impell'd by the past.)

3 Passage, O soul, to India!
    Eclaircise* the myths Asiatics—the primitive fables.

4 Not you alone, proud truths of the world!
    Nor you alone, ye facts of modern science!
    But myths and fables of eld, Asia's, Africa's fables!
    The far-darting beams of the spirit!—the unloos'd
        dreams!
    The deep diving bibles and legends;
    The daring plots of the poets—the elder religions;
    —O you temples fairer than lilies, pour'd over by the
        rising sun!
    O you fables, spurning the known, eluding the hold of

the known, mounting to heaven!
You lofty and dazzling towers, pinnacled, red as roses,
    burnish'd with gold!
Towers of fables immortal, fashion'd from mortal
    dreams!
You too I welcome, and fully, the same as the rest;
You too with joy I sing.

3

5 Passage to India!
Lo, soul, seest thou not God's purpose from the first?
The earth to be spann'd, connected by net-work,
The people to become brothers and sisters,
The races, neighbors, to marry and be given in mar-
    riage,
The oceans to be cross'd, the distant brought near,
The lands to be welded together.

6 (A worship new, I sing;
You captains, voyagers, explorers, yours!
You engineers! you architects, machinists, yours!
You, not for trade or transportation only,
But in God's name, and for thy sake, O soul.)

4

7 Passage to India!
Lo, soul, for thee, of tableaus twain,
I see, in one, the Suez canal initiated, open'd,
I see the procession of steamships, the Empress Euge-
    nie's leading the van;
I mark, from on deck, the strange landscape, the pure sky, the
    level sand in the distance;
I pass swiftly the picturesque groups, the workmen
    gather'd,
The gigantic dredging machines.

8 In one, again, different, (yet thine, all thine, O soul,
    the same,)
I see over my own continent the Pacific Railroad sur-
    mounting every barrier;

I see continual trains of cars winding along the Platte,
    carrying freight and passengers;
I hear the locomotives rushing and roaring, and the
    shrill steam-whistle,
I hear the echoes reverberate through the grandest
    scenery in the world;
I cross the Laramie plains—I note the rocks in gro-
    tesque shapes—the buttes;
I see the plentiful larkspur and wild onions—the bar-
    ren, colorless, sage-deserts,
I see in glimpses afar, or towering immediately above
    me the great mountains—I see the Wind River
    and the Wahsatch mountains;
I see the Monument mountain and the Eagle's Nest—
    I pass the Promontory—I ascend the Nevadas;
I scan the noble Elk mountain, and wind around its
    base;
I see the Humboldt range—I thread the valley and
    cross the river,
I see the clear waters of lake Tahoe—I see forests of
    majestic pines,
Or, crossing the great desert, the alkaline plains, I be-
    hold enchanting mirages of waters and meadows;
Marking through these, and after all, in duplicate slen-
    der lines,
Bridging the three or four thousand miles of land
    travel,
Tying the Eastern to the Western sea,
The road between Europe and Asia.

9 (Ah Genoese,* thy dream! thy dream!
Centuries after thou art laid in thy grave,
The shore thou foundest verifies thy dream!)

5

10 Passage to India!
Struggles of many a captain—tales of many a sailor
    dead!

Over my mood, stealing and spreading they come,
Like clouds and cloudlets in the unreach'd sky.

11 Along all history, down the slopes,
As a rivulet running, sinking now, and now again to
the surface rising,
A ceaseless thought, a varied train—Lo, soul! to thee,
thy sight, they rise,
The plans, the voyages again, the expeditions:
Again Vasco de Gama sails forth;
Again the knowledge gain'd, the mariner's compass,
Lands found, and nations born—thou born, America,
(a hemisphere unborn,)
For purpose vast, man's long probation fill'd,
Thou, rondure of the world, at last accomplish'd.

6

12 O, vast Rondure, swimming in space!
Cover'd all over with visible power and beauty!
Alternate light and day, and the teeming, spiritual
darkness;
Unspeakable, high processions of sun and moon, and
countless stars above;
Below, the manifold grass and waters, animals, moun-
tains, trees;
With inscrutable purpose—some hidden, prophetic
intention;
Now, first, it seems, my thought begins to span thee.

13 Down from the gardens of Asia, descending radiat-
ing,
Adam and Eve appear, then their myriad progeny after
them,
Wandering, yearning, curious—with restless explo-
rations,
With questionings, baffled, formless, feverish—with
never-happy hearts,
With that sad, incessant refrain, *Wherefore unsatisfied
Soul?* and *Whither, O mocking life?*

14 Ah, who shall soothe these feverish children?
Who justify these restless explorations?
Who speak the secret of impassive Earth?
Who bind it to us? What is this separate Nature, so
    unnatural?
What is this Earth, to our affections? (unloving earth,
    without a throb to answer ours;
Cold earth, the place of graves.)

15 Yet, soul, be sure the first intent remains—and shall
    be carried out;
(Perhaps even now the time has arrived.)

16 After the seas are all cross'd, (as they seem already
    cross'd,)
After the great captains and engineers have accomplish'd
    their work,
After the noble inventors—after the scientists, the
    chemist, the geologist, ethnologist,
Finally shall come the Poet, worthy that name;
The true son of God shall come, singing his songs.

17 Then not your deeds only, O voyagers, O scientists
    and inventors, shall be justified,
All these hearts, as of fretted children, shall be sooth'd,
All affection shall be fully responded to—the secret
    shall be told;
All these separations and gaps shall be taken up, and
    hook'd and link'd together;
The whole Earth—this cold, impassive, voiceless Earth,
    shall be completely justified;
Trinitas divine shall be gloriously accomplish'd and
    compacted by the true son of God, the poet,
(He shall indeed pass the straits and conquer the
    mountains,
He shall double the Cape of Good Hope to some pur-
    pose;)
Nature and Man shall be disjoin'd and diffused no more,
The true son of God shall absolutely fuse them.

7

18 Year at whose open'd, wide-flung door I sing!
Year of the purpose accomplish'd!
Year of the marriage of continents, climates
and oceans!
(No mere Doge of Venice now, wedding the Adriatic;)
I see, O year, in you, the vast terraqueous globe, given,
and giving all,
Europe to Asia, Africa join'd, and they to the New
World;
The lands, geographies, dancing before you, holding a
festival garland,
As brides and bridegrooms hand in hand.

8

19 Passage to India!
Cooling airs from Caucasus far, soothing cradle of man,
The river Euphrates flowing, the past lit up again.

20 Lo, soul, the retrospect, brought forward;
The old, most populous, wealthiest of earth's lands,
The streams of the Indus and the Ganges, and their
many affluents;
(I, my shores of America walking to-day, behold, resum-
ing all,)
The tale of Alexander, on his warlike marches, suddenly
dying,
On one side China, and on the other side Persia and
Arabia,
To the south the great seas, and the Bay of Bengal;
The flowing literatures, tremendous epics, religions,
castes,
Old occult Brahma, interminably far back—the tender
and junior Buddha,
Central and southern empires, and all their belongings,
possessors,
The wars of Tamerlane, the reign of Aurungzebe,
The traders, rulers, explorers, Moslems, Venetians,
Byzantium, the Arabs, Portuguese,

The first travelers, famous yet, Marco Polo, Batouta
    the Moor,
Doubts to be solv'd, the map incognita, blanks to be
    fill'd,
The foot of man unstay'd, the hands never at rest,
Thyself, O soul, that will not brook a challenge.

9

21   The mediaeval navigators rise before me,
    The world of 1492, with its awaken'd enterprise;
    Something swelling in humanity now like the sap of
       the earth in spring,
    The sunset splendor of chivalry declining.

22   And who art thou, sad shade?
    Gigantic, visionary, thyself a visionary,
    With majestic limbs, and pious, beaming eyes,
    Spreading around, with every look of thine, a golden
       world,
    Enhuing it with gorgeous hues.

23   As the chief histrion,
    Down to the footlights walks, in some great scena,
    Dominating the rest, I see the Admiral himself,*
    (History's type of courage, action, faith,)
    Behold him sail from Palos, leading his little fleet;
    His voyage behold—his return—his great fame,
    His misfortunes, calumniators—behold him a prisoner,
       chain'd,
    Behold his dejection, poverty, death.

24   (Curious, in time, I stand, noting the efforts of
       heroes;
    Is the deferment long? bitter the slander, poverty,
       death?
    Lies the seed unreck'd for centuries in the ground?
       Lo! to God's due occasion,
    Uprising in the night, it sprouts, blooms,
    And fills the earth with use and beauty.)

10

25 Passage indeed, O soul, to primal thought!
    Not lands and seas alone—thy own clear freshness,
    The young maturity of brood and bloom;
    To realms of budding bibles.

26 O soul, repressless, I with thee, and thou with me,
    Thy circumnavigation of the world begin;
    Of man, the voyage of his mind's return,
    To reason's early paradise,
    Back, back to wisdom's birth, to innocent intuitions,
    Again with fair Creation.

11

27 O we can wait no longer!
    We too take ship, O soul!
    Joyous, we too launch out on trackless seas!
    Fearless, for unknown shores, on waves of extasy to
        sail,
    Amid the wafting winds, (thou pressing me to thee, I
        thee to me, O soul,)
    Caroling free—singing our song of God,
    Chanting our chant of pleasant exploration.

28 With laugh, and many a kiss,
    (Let others deprecate—let others weep for sin, remorse,
        humiliation;)
    O soul, thou pleasest me—I thee.

29 Ah, more than any priest, O soul, we too believe in
        God,
    But with the mystery of God we dare not dally.

30 O soul, thou pleasest me—I thee;
    Sailing these seas, or on the hills, or waking in the
        night,
    Thoughts, silent thoughts, of Time, and Space, and
        Death, like waters flowing;

Bear me, indeed, as through the regions infinite,
Whose air I breathe, whose ripples hear—lave me all
    over;
Bathe me, O God, in thee—mounting to thee,
I and my soul to range in range of thee.

31 O Thou transcendent!
    Nameless—the fibre and the breath!
    Light of the light—shedding forth universes—thou
        centre of them,
    Thou mightier centre of the true, the good, the loving!
    Thou moral, spiritual fountain! affection's source! thou
        reservoir!
    (O pensive soul of me! O thirst unsatisfied! waitest not
        there?
    Waitest not haply for us, somewhere there, the Com-
        rade perfect?)
    Thou pulse! thou motive of the stars, suns, systems,
    That, circling, move in order, safe, harmonious,
    Athwart the shapeless vastnesses of space!
    How should I think—how breathe a single breath—
        how speak—if, out of myself,
    I could not launch, to those, superior universes?

32 Swiftly I shrivel at the thought of God,
    At Nature and its wonders, Time and Space and Death,
    But that I, turning, call to thee, O soul, thou actual Me,
    And lo! thou gently masterest the orbs,
    Thou matest Time, smilest content at Death,
    And fillest, swellest full, the vastnesses of Space.

33 Greater than stars or suns,
    Bounding, O soul, thou journeyest forth;
    —What love, than thine and ours could wider amplify?
    What aspirations, wishes, outvie thine and ours, O soul?
    What dreams of the ideal? what plans of purity, per-
        fection, strength?
    What cheerful willingness, for others' sake, to give up
        all?
    For others' sake to suffer all?

34 Reckoning ahead, O soul, when thou, the time
       achiev'd,
    (The seas all cross'd, weather'd the capes, the voyage
       done,)
    Surrounded, copest, frontest God, yieldest, the aim
       attain'd,
    As, fill'd with friendship, love complete, the Elder
       Brother found,
    The Younger melts in fondness in his arms.

                        12

35 Passage to more than India!
    Are thy wings plumed indeed for such far flights?
    O Soul, voyagest thou indeed on voyages like these?
    Disportest thou on waters such as those?
    Soundest below the Sanscrit and the Vedas?
    Then have thy bent unleash'd.

36 Passage to you, your shores, ye aged fierce enigmas!
    Passage to you, to mastership of you, ye strangling
       problems!
    You, strew'd with the wrecks of skeletons, that, living,
       never reach'd you.

                        13

37 Passage to more than India!
    O secret of the earth and sky!
    Of you, O waters of the sea! O winding creeks and
       rivers!
    Of you, O woods and fields! Of you, strong mountains
       of my land!
    Of you, O prairies! Of you, gray rocks!
    O morning red! O clouds! O rain and snows!
    O day and night, passage to you!

38 O sun and moon, and all you stars! Sirius and
       Jupiter!
    Passage to you!

39 Passage—immediate passage! the blood burns in my
       veins!
   Away, O soul! hoist instantly the anchor!
   Cut the hawsers—haul out—shake out every sail!
   Have we not stood here like trees in the ground long
       enough?
   Have we not grovell'd here long enough, eating and
       drinking like mere brutes?
   Have we not darken'd and dazed ourselves with books
       long enough?

40 Sail forth! steer for the deep waters only!
   Reckless, O soul, exploring, I with thee, and thou with
       me,
   For we are bound where mariner has not yet dared to
       go,
   And we will risk the ship, ourselves and all.

41 O my brave soul!
   O farther, farther sail!
   O daring joy, but safe! Are they not all the seas of
       God?
   O farther, farther, farther sail!

Proud Music of the Storm

I

1 PROUD music of the storm!
   Blast that careers so free, whistling across the prairies!
   Strong hum of forest tree-tops! Wind of the moun-
       tains!
   Personified dim shapes! you hidden orchestras!
   You serenades of phantoms, with instruments alert,
   Blending, with Nature's rhythmus, all the tongues of
       nations;
   You chords left as by vast composers! you choruses!
   You formless, free, religious dances! you from the
       Orient!
   You undertone of rivers, roar of pouring cataracts;

You sounds from distant guns, with galloping cavalry!
Echoes of camps, with all the different bugle-calls!
Trooping tumultuous, filling the midnight late, bending
    me powerless,
Entering my lonesome slumber-chamber—Why have
    you seiz'd me?

2

2 Come forward, O my Soul, and let the rest retire;
Listen—lose not—it is toward thee they tend;
Parting the midnight, entering my slumber-chamber,
For thee they sing and dance, O Soul.

3 A festival song!
The duet of the bridegroom and the bride—a marriage-
    march,
With lips of love, and hearts of lovers, fill'd to the brim
    with love;
The red-flush'd cheeks and perfumes—the cortege
    swarming, full of friendly faces, young and old,
To flutes' clear notes, and sounding harps' cantabile.*

3

4 Now loud approaching drums!
Victoria! see'st thou in powder-smoke the banners torn
    but flying? the rout of the baffled?
Hearest those shouts of a conquering army?

5 (Ah Soul, the sobs of women—the wounded groaning
    in agony,
The hiss and crackle of flames—the blacken'd ruins—
    the embers of cities,
The dirge and desolation of mankind.)

4

6 Now airs antique and mediaeval fill me!
I see and hear old harpers with their harps, at Welsh
    festivals:
I hear the minnesingers, singing their lays of love,

I hear the minstrels, gleemen, troubadours, of the feudal
   ages.

5

7 Now the great organ sounds,
   Tremulous—while underneath, (as the hid footholds of
      the earth,
   On which arising, rest, and leaping forth, depend,
   All shapes of beauty, grace and strength—all hues we
      know,
   Green blades of grass, and warbling birds—children
      that gambol and play—the clouds of heaven
      above,)
   The strong base stands, and its pulsations intermits not,
   Bathing, supporting, merging all the rest—maternity
      of all the rest,
   And with it every instrument in multitudes,
   The players playing—all the world's musicians,
   The solemn hymns and masses, rousing adoration,
   All passionate heart-chants, sorrowful appeals,
   The measureless sweet vocalists of ages,
   And for their solvent setting, Earth's own diapason,
   Of winds and woods and mighty ocean waves;
   A new composite orchestra—binder of years and climes
      —ten-fold renewer,
   As of the far-back days the poets tell—the Paradiso,
   The straying thence, the separation long, but now the
      wandering done,
   The journey done, the Journeyman come home,
   And Man and Art, with Nature fused again.

6

8 Tutti! for Earth and Heaven!
   The Almighty Leader now for me, for once, once has signal'd
      with his wand.

9 The manly strophe of the husbands of the world,
   And all the wives responding.

10 The tongues of violins,
    (I think, O tongues, ye tell this heart, that cannot tell
        itself;
    This brooding, yearning heart, that cannot tell itself.)

7

11 Ah, from a little child,
    Thou knowest, Soul, how to me all sounds became
        music,
    My mother's voice, in lullaby or hymn;
    (The voice—O tender voices—memory's loving voices!
    Last miracle of all—O dearest mother's, sister's, voices;)
    The rain, the growing corn, the breeze among the
        long-leav'd corn,
    The measur'd sea-surf, beating on the sand,
    The twittering bird, the hawk's sharp scream,
    The wild-fowl's notes at night, as flying low, migrating
        north or south,
    The psalm in the country church, or mid the clustering
        trees, the open air camp-meeting,
    The fiddler in the tavern—the glee, the long-strung
        sailor-song,
    The lowing cattle, bleating sheep—the crowing cock at
        dawn.

8

12 All songs of current lands come sounding 'round me,
    The German airs of friendship, wine and love,
    Irish ballads, merry jigs and dances—English warbles,
    Chansons of France, Scotch tunes—and o'er the rest,
    Italia's peerless compositions.

13 Across the stage, with pallor on her face, yet lurid
        passion,
    Stalks Norma,* brandishing the dagger in her hand.

14 I see poor crazed Lucia's eyes' unnatural gleam;*
    Her hair down her back falls loose and dishevell'd.

15 I see where Ernani,* walking the bridal garden,
     Amid the scent of night-roses, radiant, holding his
          bride by the hand,
     Hears the infernal call, the death-pledge of the horn.

16 To crossing swords, and gray hairs bared to heaven,
     The clear, electric base and baritone of the world,
     The trombone duo—Libertad forever!*

17 From Spanish chestnut trees' dense shade,
     By old and heavy convent walls, a wailing song,
     Song of lost love—the torch of youth and life quench'd
          in despair,
     Song of the dying swan—Fernando's heart is breaking.*

18 Awaking from her woes at last, retriev'd Amina
          sings,*
     Copious as stars, and glad as morning light, the tor-
          rents of her joy.

19 (The teeming lady comes!
     The lustrious orb—Venus contralto—the blooming
          mother,
     Sister of loftiest gods—Alboni's self I hear.)*

                              9

20 I hear those odes, symphonies, operas;
     I hear in the *William Tell*, the music of an arous'd and
          Angry people;
     I hear Meyerbeer's *Huguenots*, the *Prophet*, or *Robert*;
     Gounod's *Faust*, or Mozart's *Don Juan*.

                             10

21 I hear the dance-music of all nations,
     The waltz, (some delicious measure, lapsing, bathing me
          in bliss;)
     The bolero, to tinkling guitars and clattering castanets.

22 I see religious dances old and new,
   I hear the sound of the Hebrew lyre,
   I see the Crusaders marching bearing, the cross on
         high, to the martial clang of cymbals;
   I hear dervishes monotonously chanting, interspers'd
         with frantic shouts, as they spin around, turning
         always towards Mecca;
   I see the rapt religious dances of the Persians and the
         Arabs;
   Again, at Eleusis, home of Ceres, I see the modern
         Greeks dancing,
   I hear them clapping their hands, as they bend their
         bodies,
   I hear the metrical shuffling of their feet.

23 I see again the wild old Corybantian dance, the per-
         formers wounding each other;
   I see the Roman youth, to the shrill sound of flageolets,
         throwing and catching their weapons,
   As they fall on their knees, and rise again.

24 I hear from the Mussulman mosque the muezzin
         calling,
   I see the worshippers within, (nor form, nor sermon,
         argument, nor word,
   But silent, strange, devout—rais'd, glowing heads—
         ecstatic faces.)

I I

25 I hear the Egyptian harp of many strings,
   The primitive chants of the Nile boatmen;
   The sacred imperial hymns of China,
   To the delicate sounds of the king,* (the stricken wood
         and stone,)
   Or to Hindu flutes, and the fretting twang of the vina,
   A band of bayaderes.

12

26 Now Asia, Africa leave me—Europe, seizing, inflates
       me,
    To organs huge, and bands, I hear as from vast con-
       courses of voices,
    Luther's strong hymn, *Eine feste Burg ist unser Gott;*
    Rossini's *Stabat Mater dolorosa;*
    Or, floating in some high cathedral dim with gorgeous
       color'd windows,
    The passionate *Agnus Dei* or *Gloria in Excelsis.*

13

27 Composers! mighty maestros!
    And you, sweet singers of old lands—Soprani! Tenori!
       Bassi!
    To you a new bard, carolling free in the west,
    Obeisant, sends his love.

28 (Such led to thee, O Soul!
    All senses, shows and objects, lead to thee,
    But now, it seems to me, sound leads o'er all the
       rest.)

14

29 I hear the annual singing of the children in St. Paul's
       Cathedral;
    Or, under the high roof of some colossal hall, the sym-
       phonies, oratorios of Beethoven, Handel, or
       Haydn;
    The *Creation,** in billows of godhood laves me.

30 Give me to hold all sounds, (I, madly struggling,
       cry,)
    Fill me with all the voices of the universe,
    Endow me with their throbbings—Nature's also,
    The tempests, waters, winds—operas and chants—
       marches and dances,
    Utter—pour in—for I would take them all.

15

31 Then I woke softly,
 And pausing, questioning awhile the music of my
  dream,
 And questioning all those reminiscences—the tempest
  in its fury,
 And all the songs of sopranos and tenors,
 And those rapt oriental dances, of religious fervor,
 And the sweet varied instruments, and the diapason of
  organs,
 And all the artless plaints of love, and grief and
  death,
 I said to my silent, curious Soul, out of the bed of the
  slumber-chamber,
 Come, for I have found the clew I sought so long,
 Let us go forth refresh'd amid the day,
 Cheerfully tallying life, walking the world, the real,
 Nourish'd henceforth by our celestial dream.

32 And I said, moreover,
 Haply what thou hast heard, O Soul, was not the sound
  of winds,
 Nor dream of raging storm, nor sea-hawk's flapping
  wings, nor harsh scream,
 Nor vocalism of sun-bright Italy,
 Nor German organ majestic—nor vast concourse of
  voices—nor layers of harmonies;
 Nor strophes of husbands and wives—nor sound of
  marching soldiers,
 Nor flutes, nor harps, nor the bugle-calls of camps;
 But, to a new rhythmus fitted for thee,
 Poems, bridging the way from Life to Death, vaguely
  wafted in night air, uncaught, unwritten,
 Which, let us go forth in the bold day, and write.

Whispers of Heavenly Death

1 WHISPERS of heavenly death, murmur'd I hear,
  Labial gossip of night—sibilant chorals;
  Footsteps gently ascending—mystical breezes, wafted
      soft and low;
  Ripples of unseen rivers—tides of a current, flowing,
      forever flowing,
  (Or is it the plashing of tears? the measureless waters
      of human tears?)

2 I see, just see skyward, great cloud-masses;
  Mournfully, slowly they roll, silently swelling and mix-
      ing;
  With, at times, a half-dimm'd, sadden'd, far-off star,
  Appearing and disappearing.

3 (Some parturition, rather—some solemn, immortal
      birth:
  On the frontiers, to eyes impenetrable,
  Some Soul is passing over.)

A Noiseless, Patient Spider

1 A NOISELESS patient spider,
  I mark'd, where, on a little promontory it stood
      isolated;
  Mark'd how, to explore the vacant, vast surrounding,
  It launch'd forth filament, filament, filament, out of
      itself,
  Ever unreeling them—ever tirelessly speeding them.

2 And you, O my Soul, where you stand,
  Surrounded, surrounded, in measureless oceans of
      space,
  Ceaselessly musing, venturing, throwing,—seeking the
      spheres, to connect them;

Till the bridge you will need, be form'd—till the ductile
    anchor hold,
Till the gossamer thread you fling, catch somewhere,
    O my Soul.

Sparkles from the Wheel

1

WHERE the city's ceaseless crowd moves on, the live-
    long day,
Withdrawn, I join a group of children watching—I
    pause aside with them.

By the curb, toward the edge of the flagging,
A knife-grinder works at his wheel, sharpening a great
    knife;
Bending over, he carefully holds it to the stone—by
    foot and knee,
With measur'd tread, he turns rapidly—As he presses
    with light but firm hand,
Forth issue, then, in copious golden jets,
Sparkles from the wheel.

2

The scene, and all its belongings—how they seize and
    affect me!
The sad, sharp-chinn'd old man, with worn clothes, and
    broad shoulder-band of leather;
Myself, effusing and fluid—a phantom curiously float-
    ing—now here absorb'd and arrested;
The group, (an unminded point, set in a vast surround-
    ing,)
The attentive, quiet children—the loud, proud, restive
    base of the streets;
The low, hoarse purr of the whirling stone—the light-
    press'd blade,

Diffusing, dropping, sideways-darting, in tiny showers
    of gold,
Sparkles from the wheel.

Gods

1

THOUGHT of the Infinite—the All!
Be thou my God.

2

Lover Divine, and Perfect Comrade!
Waiting, content, invisible yet, but certain,
Be thou my God.

3

Thou—thou, the Ideal Man!
Fair, able, beautiful, content, and loving,
Complete in Body, and dilate in Spirit,
Be thou my God.

4

O Death—(for Life has served its turn;)
Opener and usher to the heavenly mansion!
Be thou my God.

5

Aught, aught, of mightiest, best, I see, conceive, or
    know,
(To break the stagnant tie—thee, thee to free, O Soul.)
Be thou my God.

6

Or thee, Old Cause, whene'er advancing;
All great Ideas, the races' aspirations,
All that exalts, releases thee, my Soul!
All heroisms, deeds of rapt enthusiasts,
Be ye my Gods!

7

Or Time and Space!
Or shape of Earth, divine and wondrous,
Or shape in I myself—or some fair shape, I, viewing,
    worship,
Or lustrous orb of Sun, or star by night:
Be ye my Gods.

FROM AS A STRONG BIRD ON
PINIONS FREE (1872)

One Song, America, before I go*

ONE song, America, before I go,
I'd sing, o'er all the rest, with trumpet sound,
For thee—the Future.

I'd sow a seed for thee of endless Nationality;
I'd fashion thy Ensemble, including Body and
    Soul;
I'd show, away ahead, thy real Union, and how it
    may be accomplish'd.

(The paths to the House I seek to make,
But leave to those to come, the House itself.)

Belief I sing—and Preparation;
As Life and Nature are not great with reference to
    the Present only,
But greater still from what is yet to come,
Out of that formula for Thee I sing.

Souvenirs of Democracy*

THE business man, the acquirer vast,
After assiduous years, surveying results, preparing
    for departure,
Devises houses and lands to his children—bequeaths
    stocks, goods—funds for a school or hos-
    pital,
Leaves money to certain companions to buy tokens,
    souvenirs of gems and gold;
Parceling out with care—And then, to prevent all
    cavil,
His name to his testament formally signs.

But I, my life surveying,
With nothing to show, to devise, from its idle
    years,
Nor houses, nor lands—nor tokens of gems or gold
    for my friends,
Only these Souvenirs of Democracy—In them—in
    all my songs—behind me leaving,
To You, whoever you are, (bathing, leavening this
    leaf especially with my breath—pressing on it
    a moment with my own hands;
—Here! feel how the pulse beats in my wrists!—
    how my heart's-blood is swelling, contracting!)
I will You, in all, Myself, with promise to never
    desert you,
To which I sign my name,

Walt Whitman

As a Strong Bird on Pinions Free*

I

As a strong bird on pinions free,
Joyous, the amplest spaces heavenward cleaving,
Such be the thought I'd think to-day of thee, America;
Such be the recitative I'd bring to-day for thee.[1]

The conceits of the poets of other lands I bring thee
    not,
Nor the compliments that have served their turn so
    long,
Nor rhyme—nor the classics—nor perfume of foreign
    court or indoor library;
But an odor I'd bring to-day as from forests of

[1] Commencement Poem, Dartmouth College, N.H., June 26. 1872, on invitation United Literary Societies.

pine in the north, in Maine—or breath of an Illi-
nois prairie,
With open airs of Virginia, or Georgia or Tennessee
—or from Texas uplands or Florida's glades;
With presentment of Yellowstone's scenes or Yo-
semite;
And murmuring under, pervading all, I'd bring the
rustling sea-sound,
That endlessly sounds from the two great seas of the
world.

And for thy subtler sense, subtler refrains, O Union!
Preludes of intellect tallying these and thee—mind-
formulas fitted for thee—real and sane, and large
as these and thee;
Thou, mounting higher, diving deeper than we knew
—thou transcendental Union!
By thee Fact to be justified—blended with Thought;
Thought of Man justified—blended with God:
Through thy Idea—lo! the immortal Reality!
Through thy Reality—lo! the immortal idea!

2

Brain of the New World! what a task is thine!
To formulate the Modern..:..Out of the peerless
grandeur of the modern.
Out of Thyself—comprising Science—to recast
Poems, Churches, Art.
(Recast—may-be discard them, end them. May-be
their work is done—who knows?)
By vision, hand, conception, on the background of
the mighty past, the dead,
To limn, with absolute faith, the mighty living pre-
sent.

And yet, thou living, present brain! heir of the dead,
the Old World brain!
Thou that lay folded, like an unborn babe, within its
folds so long!

Thou carefully prepared by it so long!—haply thou
    but unfoldest it—only maturest it;
It to eventuate in thee—the essence of the by-gone
    time contain'd in thee;
Its poems, churches, arts, unwitting to themselves,
    destined with reference to thee,
The fruit of all the Old, ripening to-day in thee.

3

Sail—sail thy best, ship of Democracy!
Of value is thy freight—'tis not the Present only,
The Past is also stored in thee!
Thou holdest not the venture of thyself alone—not of
    thy western continent alone;
Earth's *résumé* entire floats on thy keel, O ship!—is
    steadied by thy spars;
With thee Time voyages in trust—the antecedent
    nations sink or swim with thee;
With all their ancient struggles, martyrs, heroes,
    epics, wars, thou bear'st the other continents;
Theirs, theirs as much as thine, the destination-
    port triumphant;
—Steer, steer with good strong hand and wary eye, O
    helmsman—thou carryest great companions,
Venerable, priestly Asia sails this day with thee,
And royal, feudal Europe sails with thee.

4

Beautiful World of new, superber Birth, that rises to
    my eyes,
Like a limitless golden cloud, filling the western sky;
Emblem of general Maternity, lifted above all;
Sacred shape of the bearer of daughters and sons;
Out of thy teeming womb, thy giant babes in cease-
    less procession issuing,
Acceding from such gestation, taking and giving con-
    tinual strength and life;
World of the Real! world of the twain in one!

World of the Soul—born by the world of the real
    alone—led to identity, body, by it alone;
Yet in beginning only—incalculable masses of compo-
    site, precious materials,
By history's cycles forwarded—by every nation, lan-
    guage, hither sent,
Ready, collected here—a freer, vast, electric World, to
    be constructed here,
(The true New World—the world of orbic Science,
    Morals, Literatures to come,)
Thou Wonder World, yet undefined, unform'd—
    neither do I define thee;
How can I pierce the impenetrable blank of the
    future?
I feel thy ominous greatness, evil as well as good;
I watch thee, advancing, absorbing the present,
    transcending the past.
I see thy light lighting and thy shadow shadowing,
    as if the entire globe;
But I do not undertake to define thee—hardly to com-
    prehend thee;
I but thee name—thee prophesy—as now!
I merely thee ejaculate!

Thee in thy future;
Thee in thy only permanent life, career—thy own
    unloosen'd mind—thy soaring spirit;
Thee as another equally needed sun, America—ra-
    diant, ablaze, swift-moving, fructifying all;
Thee! risen in thy potent cheerfulness and joy—thy
    endless, great hilarity!
(Scattering for good the cloud that hung so long—
    that weigh'd so long upon the mind of man,
The doubt, suspicion, dread of gradual, certain deca-
    dence of man;)
Thee in they larger, saner breeds of Female, Male—
    thee in thy athletes, moral spiritual, South,
    North, West, East,

(To thy immortal breasts, Mother of All, thy every
    daughter, son, endear'd alike, forever equal;)
Thee in thy own musicians, singers, artists, unborn
    yet, but certain;
Thee in thy moral wealth and civilization (until
    which thy proudest material wealth and civiliza-
    tion must remain in vain;)
Thee in thy all-supplying, all-enclosing Worship—
    thee in no single bible, saviour, merely,
Thy saviours countless, latent within thyself—thy
    bibles incessant, within thyself, equal to any,
    divine as any;
Thee in an education grown of thee—in teachers,
    studies, students, born of thee;
Thee in thy democratic fêtes, en masse—thy high
    original festivals, operas, lecturers, preachers;
Thee in thy ultimata (the preparations only now
    completed—the edifice on sure foundations
    tied),
Thee in thy pinnacles, intellect, thought—thy top-
    most rational joys—thy love and god-like aspira-
    tion,
In thy resplendent coming literati—thy full-lung'd
    orators—thy sacerdotal bards—cosmic savans,
These! these in thee, (certain to come), today I pro-
    phesy.

5

Land tolerating all—accepting all—not for the good
    alone—all good for thee;
Land in the realms of God to be a realm unto thy-
    self;
Under the rule of God to be a rule unto thyself.

(Lo! where arise three peerless stars,
To be thy natal stars, my country—Ensemble—Evo-
    lution—Freedom,
Set in the sky of Law.)

Land of unprecedented faith—God's faith!
Thy soil, thy very subsoil, all upheav'd;
The general inner earth, so long, so sedulously draped
    over, now and hence for it is boldly laid
    bare,
Open'd by thee to heaven's light, for benefit or bale.

Not for success alone;
Not to fair-sail unintermitted always;
The storm shall dash thy face—the murk of war, and
    worse than war, shall cover thee all over;
(Wert capable of war, its tags and trials? Be capa-
    ble of peace, its trials;
For the tug and mortal straits of nations come at last
    in peace—not war);
In many a smiling mask death shall approach, be-
    guiling thee—thou in disease shalt swelter;
The livid cancer spread its hideous claws, clinging
    upon thy breasts, seeking to strike thee deep
    within;
Consumption of the worst—moral consumption—
    shall rouge thy face with hectic:*
But thou shalt face thy fortunes, thy diseases, and
    surmount them all,
Whatever they are to-day, and whatever through time
    they may be,
They each and all shall lift, and pass away, and cease
    from thee;
While thou, Time's spirals rounding—out of thyself,
    thyself still extricating, fusing,
Equable, natural, mystical Union thou—(the mortal
    with immortal blent),
Shalt soar toward the fulfilment of the future—the
    spirit of the body and the mind,
The Soul—its destinies.

The Soul, its destinies—the real real,
(Purport of all these apparitions of the real;)
In thee, America, the Soul, its destinies;
Thou globe of globes! thou wonder nebulous!
By many a throe of heat and cold convuls'd—(by
    these thyself solidifying;)
Thou mental, moral orb! thou New, indeed new,
    Spiritual World!
The Present holds thee not—for such vast growth as
    thine—for such unparallel'd flight as thine,
The Future only holds thee, and can hold thee.

The Mystic Trumpeter

1

HARK! some wild trumpeter—some strange musician,
Hovering unseen in air, vibrates capricious tunes to-
    night.

I hear thee, trumpeter—listening, alert, I catch thy
    notes,
Now pouring, whirling like a tempest around me,
Now low, subdued—now in the distance lost.

2

Come nearer, bodiless one—haply, in thee resounds
Some dead composer—haply thy pensive life
Was fill'd with aspirations high—unform'd ideals,
Waves, oceans musical, chaotically surging,
That now, ecstatic ghost, close to me bending, thy
    cornet echoing, pealing,
Gives out to no one's ears but mine—but freely gives
    to mine,
That I may thee translate.

3

Blow, trumpeter, free and clear—I follow thee,
While at the liquid prelude, glad, serene,

The fretting world, the streets, the noisy hours of
    the day, withdraw;
A holy calm descends, like dew, upon me,
I walk, in cool refreshing night, the walks of Para-
    dise,
I scent the grass, the moist air, and the roses;
Thy song expands my numb'd, imbonded spirit—thou
    freest, launchest me,
Floating and basking upon Heaven's lake.

4

Blow again, trumpeter! and for my sensuous eyes,
Bring the old pageants—show the feudal world.

What charm thy music works!—that makest pass be-
    fore me,
Ladies and cavaliers long dead—barons are in their
    castle halls—the troubadours are singing;
Arm'd knights go forth to redress wrongs—some in
    quest of the Holy Graal:
I see the tournament—I see the contestants, encased
    in heavy armor, seated on stately, champing
    horses;
I hear the shouts—the sound of blows and smiting
    steel:
I see the Crusaders' tumultuous armies—Hark! how
    the cymbals clang!
Lo! where the monks walk in advance, bearing the
    cross on high!

5

Blow again, trumpeter! and for thy theme,
Take now the enclosing theme of all—the solvent and
    the setting;
Love, that is pulse of all—the sustenance and the
    pang;
The heart of man and woman all for love;
No other theme but love—knitting, enclosing, all-dif-
    fusing love.

Leaves of Grass

O, how the immortal phantoms crowd around me!
I see the vast alembic ever working—I see and know
 the flames that heat the world;
The glow, the blush, the beating hearts of lovers,
So blissful happy some—and some so silent, dark, and
 nigh to death:
Love, that is all the earth to lovers—Love, that mocks
 time and space,
Love, that is day and night—Love, that is sun and
 moon and stars;
Love, that is crimson, sumptuous, sick with perfume;
No other words, but words of love—no other thought
 but Love.

6

Blow again, trumpeter—conjure war's wild alarums.

Swift to thy spell, a shuddering hum like distant
 thunder rolls;
Lo! where the arm'd men hasten—Lo! mid the
 clouds of dust, the glint of bayonets;
I see the grime-faced cannoniers—I mark the rosy
 flash amid the smoke—I hear the cracking of the
 guns:
—Nor war alone—thy fearful music-song, wild player,
 brings every sight of fear,
The deeds of ruthless brigands—rapine, murder—I
 hear the cries for help!
I see ships foundering at sea—I behold on deck, and
 below deck, the terrible tableaux!

7

O trumpeter! methinks I am myself the instrument
 thou playest!
Thou melt'st my heart, my brain—thou movest, draw-
 est, changest them, at will:
And now thy sullen notes send darkness through me;

Thou takest away all cheering light—all hope:
I see the enslaved, the overthrown, the hurt, the op-
  prest of the whole earth;
I feel the measureless shame and humiliation of my
  race—it becomes all mine;
Mine too the revenges of humanity—the wrongs of
  ages—baffled feuds and hatreds;
Utter defeat upon me weighs—all lost! the foe vic-
  torious!
(Yet 'mid the ruins Pride colossal stands, unshaken to
  the last!
Endurance, resolution, to the last.)

8

Now, trumpeter, for thy close,
Vouchsafe a higher strain than any yet;
Sing to my soul—renew its languishing faith and
  hope;
Rouse up my slow belief—give me some vision of the
  future;
Give me, for once, its prophecy and joy.

O glad, exulting, culminating song!
A vigor more than earth's is in thy notes!
Marches of victory—man disenthrall'd—the con-
  queror at last!
Hymns to the universal God, from univeral Man—
  all joy!
A reborn race appears, a perfect World, all joy!
Women and Men, in wisdom, innocence and health—
  all joy!
Riotous, laughing bacchanals, filled with joy!
War, sorrow, suffering gone—The rank earth purged
  —nothing but joy left!
The ocean fill'd with joy—the atmosphere all joy!
Joy! Joy! in freedom, worship, love! Joy in the
  ecstasy of life!
Enough to merely be! Enough to breathe!
Joy! Joy! all over Joy!

FROM TWO RIVULETS (1876)

Eidólons*

I MET a seer,
Passing the hues and objects of the world,
The fields of art and learning, pleasure, sense,
    To glean Eidólons.

    Put in thy chants said he,
No more the puzzling hour nor day—nor segments, parts, put in,
Put first before the rest, as light for all, and entrance-song of all,
    That of Eidólons.

    Ever the dim beginning,
Ever the growth, the rounding of the circle;
Ever the summit, and the merge at last (to surely start again),
    Eidólons! Eidólons!

    Ever the mutable!
Ever materials, changing, crumbling, re-cohering,
Ever the ateliers, the factories divine,
    Issuing Eidólons.

    Lo! I or you!
Or woman, man, or state, known or unknown;
We seeming solid wealth, strength, beauty build,
    But really build Eidólons.

    The ostent evanescent;
The substance of an artist's mood, or savan's studies long,
Or warrior's, martyr's, hero's toils,
    To fashion his Eidólon.

    Of every human life,
(The units gather'd, posted—not a thought, emotion, deed, left out),
The whole, or large or small, summ'd, added up,
    In its Eidólon.

The old, old urge;
Based on the ancient pinnacles, lo, newer, higher pinnacles;
From Science and the Modern still impell'd,
        The old, old urge, Eidólons.

The present, now and here,
America's busy, teeming, intricate whirl,
Of aggregate and segregate, for only thence releasing,
        To-day's Eidólons.

These, with the past,
Of vanish'd lands—of all the reigns of kings across the sea,
Old conquerors, old campaigns, old sailors' voyages,
        Joining Eidólons.

Densities, growth, façades,
Strata of mountains, soils, rocks, giant trees,
Far-born, far-dying, living long, to leave,
        Eidólons everlasting.

Exaltè, rapt, ecstatic,
The visible but their womb of birth,
Of orbic tendencies to shape, and shape, and shape,
        The mighty Earth-Eidólon.

All space, all time,
(The stars, the terrible perturbations of the suns,
Swelling, collapsing, ending—serving their longer, shorter use),
        Fill'd with Eidólons only.

The noiseless myriads!
The infinite oceans where the rivers empty!
The separate, countless, free identities, like eyesight,
        The true realities, Eidólons.

Not this the World,
Nor these the Universes—they the Universes,
Purport and end—ever the permanent life of life,
        Eidólons, Eidólons.

Beyond thy lectures, learn'd professor,
Beyond thy telescope or spectroscope, observer keen—beyond all
    mathematics,
Beyond the doctor's surgery, anatomy—beyond the chemist with
    his chemistry,
        The entities of entities, Eidólons.

        Unfix'd, yet fix'd,
Ever shall be—ever have been, and are,
Sweeping the present to the infinite future,
        Eidólons, Eidólons, Eidólons.

        The prophet and the bard,
Shall yet maintain themselves—in higher stages yet,
Shall mediate to the Modern, to Democracy, interpret yet to them,
        God, and Eidólons.

        And thee, My Soul,
Joys, ceaseless exercises, exaltations!
Thy yearning amply fed at last, prepared to meet,
        Thy mates, Eidólons.

        Thy Body permanent,
The Body lurking there within thy Body,
The only purport of the Form thou art—the real I myself,
        An image, an Eidólon.

        Thy very songs, not in thy songs;
No special strains to sing—none for itself;
But from the whole resulting, rising at last and floating,
        A round full-orb'd Eidólon.

Prayer of Columbus*

IT was near the close of his indomitable and pious life—on his last voyage
when nearly 70 years of age—that Columbus, to save his two remaining
ships from foundering in the Caribbean Sea in a terrible storm, had to run
them ashore on the Island of Jamaica—where, laid up for a long and miser-
able year—1503—he was taken very sick, had several relapses, his men

Leaves of Grass

revolted, and death seem'd daily imminent; though he was eventually res-
cued, and sent home to Spain to die, unrecognized, neglected and in
want......It is only ask'd, as preparation and atmosphere for the following
lines, that the bare authentic facts be recall'd and realized, and nothing con-
tributed by the fancy. See, the Antillean Island, with its florid skies and rich
foliage and scenery, the waves beating the solitary sands, and the hulls of the
ships in the distance. See, the figure of the great Admiral, walking the beach,
as a stage, in this sublimest tragedy—for what tragedy, what poem, so
piteous and majestic as the real scene?—and hear him uttering—as his
mystical and religious soul surely utter'd, the ideas following—perhaps, in
their equivalents, the very words.

A BATTER'D, wreck'd old man,
Thrown on this savage shore, far, far from home,
Pent by the sea, and dark rebellious brows, twelve dreary
    months,
Sore, stiff with many toils, sicken'd, and nigh to death,
I take my way along the island's edge,
Venting a heavy heart.

I am too full of woe!
Haply, I may not live another day;
I cannot rest, O God—I can not eat or drink or sleep,
Till I put forth myself, my prayer, once more to Thee,
Breathe, bathe myself once more in Thee—commune with
    Thee,
Report myself once more to Thee.

Thou knowest my years entire, my life,
(My long and crowded life of active work—not adoration
    merely;)
Thou knowest the prayers and vigils of my youth;
Thou knowest my manhood's solemn and visionary medita-
    tions,
Thou knowest how before I commenced, I devoted all to
    come to Thee;
Thou knowest I have in age ratified all those vows, and
    strictly kept them;
Thou knowest I have not once lost nor faith nor ecstasy in
    Thee;

(In shackles, prison'd, in disgrace, repining not.
Accepting all from Thee—as duly come from Thee.)

All my emprises have been fill'd with Thee,
My speculations, plans, begun and carried on in thoughts of
    Thee,
Sailing the deep, or journeying the land for Thee;
Intentions, purports, aspirations mine—leaving results to
    Thee.

O I am sure they really came from Thee!
The urge, the ardor, the unconquerable will,
The potent, felt, interior command, stronger than words,
A message from the Heavens, whispering to me even in
    sleep,
These sped me on.

By me, and these, the work so far accomplish'd, (for what
    has been, has been;)
By me, Earth's elder, cloy'd and stifled lands, uncloy'd, un-
    loos'd,
By me the hemispheres rounded and tied—the unknown to
    the known.

The end I know not—it is all in Thee;
Or small, or great, I know not—haply, what broad fields,
    what lands,
Haply, the brutish, measureless human undergrowth I know,
Transplanted there, may rise to stature, knowledge worthy
    Thee,
Haply the swords I know may there indeed be turn'd to
    reaping-tools;
Haply the lifeless cross I know—Europe's dead cross—may
    bud and blossom there.

One effort more—my altar this bleak sand:
That Thou, O God, my life hast lighted,
With ray of light, steady, ineffable, vouchsafed of Thee,
(Light rare, untellable—lighting the very light!

Beyond all signs, descriptions, languages!)
For that, O God—be it my latest word—here on my knees,
Old, poor, and paralyzed—I thank Thee.

My terminus near,
The clouds already closing in upon me,
The voyage balk'd—the course disputed, lost,
I yield my ships to Thee.

Steersman unseen! henceforth the helms are Thine;
Take Thou command—(what to my petty skill Thy naviga-
  tion?)

My hands, my limbs grow nerveless;
My brain feels rack'd, bewilder'd,
Let the old timbers part—I will not part!
I will cling fast to Thee, O God, though the waves buffet
  me;
Thee, Thee, at least, I know.

Is it the prophet's thought I speak, or am I raving?
What do I know of life? what of myself?
I know not even my own work, past or present;
Dim, ever-shifting guesses of it spread before me,
Of newer, better worlds, their mighty parturition,
Mocking, perplexing me.

And these things I see suddenly—what mean they?
As if some miracle, some hand divine unseal'd my eyes,
Shadowy, vast shapes, smile through the air and sky,
And on the distant waves sail countless ships,
And anthems in new tongues I hear saluting me.

To a Locomotive in Winter

THEE for my recitative!
Thee in the driving storm, even as now—the snow—the
  winter-day declining;
Thee in thy panoply, thy measured dual throbbing, and thy
  beat convulsive;

Thy black cylindric body, golden brass, and silvery steel;
Thy ponderous side-bars, parallel and connecting rods,
    gyrating, shuttling at thy sides;
Thy metrical, now swelling pant and roar—now tapering in
    the distance;
Thy great protruding head-light fix'd in front;
Thy long, pale, floating vapor-pennants, tinged with delicate
    purple;
The dense and murky clouds out-belching from thy smoke-
    stack;
Thy knitted frame—thy springs and valves—the tremulous
    twinkle of thy wheels;
Thy train of cars behind, obedient, merrily-following,
Through gale or calm, now swift, now slack, yet steadily
    careering:
Type of the modern! emblem of motion and power! pulse
    of the continent!
For once, come serve the Muse, and merge in verse, even
    as here I see thee,
With storm, and buffeting gusts of wind, and falling snow;
By day, thy warning, ringing bell to sound its notes,
By night, thy silent signal lamps to swing.

Fierce-throated beauty!
Roll through my chant, with all thy lawless music! thy
    swinging lamps at night;
Thy piercing, madly-whistled laughter! thy echoes, rumb-
    ling like an earthquake, rousing all!
Law of thyself complete, thine own track firmly holding;
(No sweetness debonair of tearful harp or glib piano thine,)
Thy trills of shrieks by rocks and hills return'd,
Launch'd o'er the prairies wide—across the lakes,
To the free skies, unpent, and glad, and strong.

The Ox Tamer

IN a faraway northern county, in the placid, pastoral region,
Lives my farmer friend, the theme of my recitative, a
    famous Tamer of Oxen:

There they bring him the three-year-olds and the four-year-
    olds, to break them;
He will take the wildest steer in the world, and break him
    and tame him;
He will go, fearless, without any whip, where the young
    bullock chafes up and down the yard;
The bullock's head tosses restless high in the air, with
    raging eyes;
Yet, see you! how soon his rage subsides—how soon this
    Tamer tames him:
See you! on the farms hereabout, a hundred oxen, young
    and old—and he is the man who has tamed them;
They all know him—all are affectionate to him;
See you! some are such beautiful animals—so lofty looking!
Some are buffcolor'd—some mottled—one has a white line
    running along his back—some are brindled,
Some have wide flaring horns (a good sign)—See you! the
    bright hides;
See, the two with stars on their foreheads—See, the round
    bodies and broad backs;
See, how straight and square they stand on their legs—See,
    what fine sagacious eyes;
See, how they watch their Tamer—they wish him near them
    —how they turn to look after him!
What yearning expression! how uneasy they are when he
    moves away from them:
—Now I marvel what it can be he appears to them, (books,
    politics, poems, depart—all else departs;)
I confess I envy only his fascination—my silent, illiterate
    friend,
Whom a hundred oxen love, there in his life on farms,
In the northern county far, in the placid pastoral region.

FROM LEAVES OF GRASS
(1881–1882)

The Dalliance of the Eagles

SKIRTING the river road, (my forenoon walk, my rest,)
Skyward in air a sudden muffled sound, the dalliance of the eagles,
The rushing amorous contact high in space together,
The clinching interlocking claws, a living, fierce, gyrating wheel,
Four beating wings, two beaks, a swirling mass tight grappling,
In tumbling turning clustering loops, straight downward falling,
Till o'er the river pois'd, the twain yet one, a moment's lull,
A motionless still balance in the air, then parting, talons loosing,
Upward again on slow-firm pinions slanting, their separate diverse
    flight,
She hers, he his, pursuing.

Spirit That Form'd This Scene

WRITTEN IN PLATTE CAÑON, COLORADO

SPIRIT that form'd this scene,
These tumbled rock-piles grim and red,
These reckless heaven-ambitious peaks,
These gorges, turbulent-clear streams, this naked freshness,
These formless wild arrays, for reasons of their own,
I know thee, savage spirit—we have communed together,
Mine too such wild arrays, for reasons of their own;
Was't charged against my chants they had forgotten art?
To fuse within themselves its rules precise and delicatesse?
The lyrist's measur'd beat, the wrought-out temple's grace—
    column and polish'd arch forgot?
But thou that revelest here—spirit that form'd this scene,
They have remember'd thee.

A Clear Midnight

THIS is thy hour O Soul, thy free flight into the wordless,
Away from books, away from art, the day erased, the lesson done,
Thee fully forth emerging, silent, gazing, pondering the themes
    thou lovest best,
Night, sleep, death and the stars.

FROM NOVEMBER BOUGHS
(1888)

Mannahatta

MY city's fit and noble name resumed,
Choice aboriginal name, with marvellous beauty, meaning,
*A rocky founded island—shores where ever gayly dash the coming,
    going, hurrying sea waves.*

A Font of Type

THIS latent mine—these unlaunch'd voices—passionate powers,
Wrath, argument, or praise, or comic leer, or prayer devout,
(Not nonpareil, brevier, bourgeois, long primer* merely,)
These ocean waves arousable to fury and to death,
Or sooth'd to ease and sheeny sun and sleep,
Within the pallid slivers slumbering.

As I Sit Writing Here

AS I sit writing here, sick and grown old,
Not my least burden is that dulness of the years, querilities,
Ungracious glooms, aches, lethargy, constipation, whimpering
    ennui,
May filter in my daily songs.

My Canary Bird

DID we count great, O soul, to penetrate the themes of mighty
    books,
Absorbing deep and full from thoughts, plays, speculations?
But now from thee to me, caged bird, to feel thy joyous warble,
Filling the air, the lonesome room, the long forenoon,
Is it not just as great, O soul?

Queries to My Seventieth Year

APPROACHING, nearing, curious,
Thou dim, uncertain spectre—bringest thou life or death?
Strength, weakness, blindness, more paralysis and heavier?
Or placid skies and sun? Wilt stir the waters yet?
Or haply cut me short for good? Or leave me here as now,
Dull, parrot-like and old, with crack'd voice harping, screeching?

America

CENTRE of equal daughters, equal sons,
All, all alike endear'd, grown, ungrown, young or old,
Strong, ample, fair, enduring, capable, rich,
Perennial with the Earth, with Freedom, Law and Love,
A grand, sane, towering, seated Mother,
Chair'd in the adamant of Time.

Memories

HOW sweet the silent backward tracings!
The wanderings as in dreams—the meditation of old times re-
    sumed—their loves, joys, persons, voyages.

Halcyon Days

NOT from successful love alone,
Nor wealth, nor honor'd middle age, nor victories of politics or
    war;
But as life wanes, and all the turbulent passions calm,
As gorgeous, vapory, silent hues cover the evening sky,
As softness, fulness, rest, suffuse the frame, like freshier, balmier
    air,
As the days take on a mellower light, and the apple at last hangs
    really finish'd and indolent-ripe on the tree,
Then for the teeming quietest, happiest days of all!
The brooding and blissful halcyon days!

Broadway

WHAT hurrying human tides, or day or night!
What passions, winnings, losses, ardors, swim thy waters!
What whirls of evil, bliss and sorrow, stem thee!
What curious questioning glances—glints of love!
Leer, envy, scorn, contempt, hope, aspiration!
Thou portal—thou arena—thou of the myriad long-drawn lines
    and groups!
(Could but thy flagstones, curbs, façades, tell their inimitable
    tales;
Thy windows rich, and huge hotels—thy side-walks wide;)
Thou of the endless sliding, mincing, shuffling feet!
Thou, like the parti-colored* world itself—like infinite, teeming,
    mocking life!
Thou visor'd, vast, unspeakable show and lesson!

To Get the Final Lilt of Songs

To get the final lilt of songs,
To penetrate the inmost lore of poets—to know the mighty ones,
Job, Homer, Eschylus, Dante, Shakspere, Tennyson, Emerson;
To diagnose the shifting-delicate tints of love and pride and
    doubt—to truly understand,
To encompass these, the last keen faculty and entrance-price,
Old age, and what it brings from all its past experiences.

The Dead Tenor

As down the stage again,
With Spanish hat and plumes, and gait inimitable,
Back from the fading lessons of the past, I'd call, I'd tell and
    own,
How much from thee! the revelation of the singing voice from
    thee!
(So firm—so liquid-soft—again that tremulous, manly timbre!
The perfect singing voice—deepest of all to me the lesson—trial
    and test of all:)

How through those strains distill'd—how the rapt ears, the soul
    of me, absorbing
Fernando's heart, *Manrico's* passionate call, *Ernani's,* sweet
    Gennaro's,*
I fold thenceforth, or seek to fold, within my chants transmuting,
Freedom's and Love's and Faith's unloos'd cantabile,
(As perfume's, color's, sunlight's correlation:)
From these, for these, with these, a hurried line, dead tenor,
A wafted autumn leaf, dropt in the closing grave, the shovel'd
    earth,
To memory of thee.

Thanks in Old Age

THANKS in old age—thanks ere I go,
For health, the midday sun, the impalpable air—for life, mere
    life,
For precious ever-lingering memories, (of you my mother dear
    —you, father—you, brothers, sisters, friends,)
For all my days—not those of peace alone—the days of war the
    same,
For gentle words, caresses, gifts from foreign lands,
For shelter, wine and meat—for sweet appreciation,
(You distant, dim unknown—or young or old—countless, un-
    specified, readers belov'd,
We never met, and ne'er shall meet—and yet our souls embrace,
    long, close and long;)
For beings, groups, love, deeds, words, books—for colors, forms,
For all the brave strong men—devoted, hardy men—who've for-
    ward sprung in freedom's help, all years, all lands,
For braver, stronger, more devoted men—(a special laurel ere I
    go, to life's war's chosen ones,
The cannoneers of song and thought—the great artillerists—the
    foremost leaders, captains of the soul:)
As soldier from an ended war return'd—As traveler out of
    myriads, to the long procession retrospective,
Thanks—joyful thanks!—a soldier's, traveler's thanks.

Life and Death

THE two old, simple problems ever intertwined,
Close home, elusive, present, baffled, grappled.
By each successive age insoluble, pass'd on,
To ours to-day—and we pass on the same.

Twilight

THE soft voluptuous opiate shades,
The sun just gone, the eager light dispell'd—(I too will soon be
    gone, dispell'd,)
A haze—nirwana—rest and night—oblivion.

You Lingering Sparse Leaves of Me

YOU lingering sparse leaves of me on winter-nearing boughs,
And I some well-shorn tree of field or orchard-row;
You tokens diminute and lorn—(not now the flush of May, or
    July clover-bloom—no grain of August now;)
You pallid banner-staves—you pennants valueless—you over-
    stay'd of time,
Yet my soul-dearest leaves confirming all the rest,
The faithfulest—hardiest—last.

The Dismantled Ship

IN some unused lagoon, some nameless bay,
On sluggish, lonesome waters, anchor'd near the shore,
An old, dismasted, gray and batter'd ship, disabled, done,
After free voyages to all the seas of earth, haul'd up at last and
    hawser'd tight,
Lies rusting, mouldering.

After the Supper and Talk

AFTER the supper and talk—after the day is done,
As a friend from friends his final withdrawal prolonging,
Good-bye and Good-bye with emotional lips repeating,
(So hard for his hand to release those hands—no more will they
    meet,
No more for communion of sorrow and joy, of old and young,
A far-stretching journey awaits him, to return no more,)
Shunning, postponing severance—seeking to ward off the last
    word ever so little,
E'en at the exit-door turning—charges superfluous calling back—
    e'en as he descends the steps,
Something to eke out a minute additional—shadows of nightfall
    deepening,
Farewells, messages lessening—dimmer the forthgoer's visage
    and form,
Soon to be lost for aye in the darkness—loth, O so loth to de-
    part!
Garrulous to the very last.

FROM LEAVES OF GRASS
(1891–1892)

Good-Bye my Fancy

GOOD-BYE[1] my fancy—(I had a word to say,
But 'tis not quite the time—The best of any man's word or say,
Is when its proper place arrives—and for its meaning,
I keep mine till the last.)

On, on the Same, ye Jocund Twain!

ON, on the same, ye jocund twain!
My life and recitative, containing birth, youth, mid-age years,
Fitful as motley-tongues of flame, inseparably twined and merged
    in one—combining all,
My single soul—aims, confirmations, failures, joys—Nor single
    soul alone,
I chant my nation's crucial stage, (America's, haply humanity's)
    —the trial great, the victory great,
A strange *eclaircissement** of all the masses past, the eastern
    world, the ancient, medieval,
Here, here from wanderings, strayings, lessons, wars, defeats—
    here at the west a voice triumphant—justifying all,
A gladsome pealing cry—a song for once of utmost pride and
    satisfaction;
I chant from it the common bulk, the general average horde,
    (the best no sooner than the worst)—And now I chant old
    age,
(My verses, written first for forenoon life, and for the summer's,
    autumn's spread,
I pass to snow-white hairs the same, and give to pulses winter-
    cool'd the same;)

[1] Behind a Good-bye there lurks much of the salutation of another beginning—to me, Development, Continuity, Immortality, Transformation, are the chiefest life-meanings of Nature and Humanity, and are the *sine qua non* of all facts, and each fact.

    Why do folks dwell so fondly on the last words, advice, appearance, of the departing? Those last words are not samples of the best, which involve vitality at its full, and balance, and perfect control and scope. But they are valuable beyond measure to confirm and endorse the varied train, facts, theories and faith of the whole preceding life.

As here in careless trill, I and my recitatives, with faith and
    love,
Wafting to other work, to unknown songs, conditions,
On, on, ye jocund twain! continue on the same!

The Pallid Wreath

SOMEHOW I cannot let it go yet, funeral though it is,
Let it remain back there on its nail suspended,
With pink, blue, yellow, all blanch'd, and the white now gray
    and ashy,
One wither'd rose put years ago for thee, dear friend;
But I do not forget thee. Hast thou then faded?
Is the odor exhaled? Are the colors, vitalities, dead?
No, while memories subtly play—the past vivid as ever;
For but last night I woke, and in that spectral ring saw thee,
Thy smile, eyes, face, calm, silent, loving as ever:
So let the wreath hang still awhile within my eye-reach,
It is not yet dead to me, nor even pallid.

To the Sun-Set Breeze

AH, whispering, something again, unseen,
Where late this heated day thou enterest at my window, door,
Thou, laving, tempering all, cool-freshing, gently vitalizing
Me, old, alone, sick, weak-down, melted-worn with sweat;
Thou, nestling, folding close and firm yet soft, companion bet-
    ter than talk, book, art,
(Thou hast, O Nature! elements! utterance to my heart beyond
    the rest—and this is of them,)
So sweet thy primitive taste to breathe within—thy soothing
    fingers on my face and hands,
Thou, messenger-magical strange bringer to body and spirit of
    me,
(Distances balk'd—occult medicines penetrating me from head
    to foot,)
I feel the sky, the prairies vast—I feel the mighty northern
    lakes,

I feel the ocean and the forest—somehow I feel the globe itself
    swift-swimming in space;
Thou blown from lips so loved, now gone—haply from endless
    store, God-sent,
(For thou art spiritual, Godly, most of all known to my
    sense,)
Minister to speak to me, here and now, what word has never
    told, and cannot tell,
Art thou not universal concrete's distillation? Law's, all As-
    tronomy's last refinement?
Hast thou no soul? Can I not know, identify thee?

A Twilight Song

As I sit in twilight late alone by the flickering oak-flame,
Musing on long-pass'd war-scenes—of the countless buried un-
    known soldiers,
Of the vacant names, as unindented air's and sea's—the un-
    return'd,
The brief truce after battle, with grim burial-squads, and the
    deep-fill'd trenches
Of gather'd dead from all America, North, South, East, West,
    whence they came up,
From wooded Maine, New-England's farms, from fertile Penn-
    sylvania, Illinois, Ohio,
From the measureless West, Virginia, the South, the Carolinas,
    Texas,
(Even here in my room-shadows and half-lights in the noiseless
    flickering flames,
Again I see the stalwart ranks on-filing, rising—I hear the
    rhythmic tramp of the armies;)
You million unwrit names all, all—you dark bequest from all the
    war,
A special verse for you—a flash of duty long neglected—your
    mystic roll strangely gather'd here,
Each name recall'd by me from out the darkness and death's
    ashes,
Henceforth to be, deep, deep within my heart recording, for
    many a future year,

Your mystic roll entire of unknown names, or North or
    South,
Embalm'd with love in this twilight song.

L. of G.'s Purport

NOT to exclude or demarcate, or pick out evils from their formid-
    able masses (even to expose them,)
But add, fuse, complete, extend—and celebrate the immortal and
    the good.

Haughty this song, its words and scope,
To span vast realms of space and time,
Evolution—the cumulative—growths and generations.

Begun in ripen'd youth and steadily pursued,
Wandering, peering, dallying with all—war, peace, day and
    night absorbing,
Never even for one brief hour abandoning my task,
I end it here in sickness, poverty, and old age.

I sing of life, yet mind me well of death:
To-day shadowy Death dogs my steps, my seated shape, and
    has for years—
Draws sometimes close to me, as face to face.

Unseen Buds

UNSEEN buds, infinite, hidden well,
Under the snow and ice, under the darkness, in every square or
    cubic inch,
Germinal, exquisite, in delicate lace, microscopic, unborn,
Like babes in wombs, latent, folded, compact, sleeping;
Billions of billions, and trillions of trillions of them waiting,
(On earth and in the sea—the universe—the stars there in the
    heavens,)
Urging slowly, surely forward, forming endless,
And waiting ever more, forever more behind.

Good-Bye my Fancy!

GOOD-BYE my Fancy!
Farewell dear mate, dear love!
I'm going away, I know not where,
Or to what fortune, or whether I may ever see you again,
So Good-bye my Fancy.

Now for my last—let me look back a moment;
The slower fainter ticking of the clock is in me,
Exit, nightfall, and soon the heart-thud stopping.

Long have we lived, joy'd, caress'd together;
Delightful!—now separation—Good-bye my Fancy.

Yet let me not be too hasty,
Long indeed have we lived, slept, filter'd, become really blended
    into one;
Then if we die we die together, (yes, we'll remain one,)
If we go anywhere we'll go together to meet what happens,
May-be we'll be better off and blither, and learn something,
May-be it is yourself now really ushering me to the true songs,
    (who knows?)
May-be it is you the mortal knob really undoing, turning—so
    now finally,
Good-bye—and hail! my Fancy.

APPENDIX A

SELECTED PREFACES AND LETTERS

Preface to Leaves of Grass *(1855)*

AMERICA does not repel the past or what it has produced under its forms or amid other politics or the idea of castes or the old religions . . . . accepts the lesson with calmness . . . is not so impatient as has been supposed that the slough still sticks to opinions and manners and literature while the life which served its requirements has passed into the new life of the new forms . . . perceives that the corpse is slowly borne from the eating and sleeping rooms of the house . . . perceives that it waits a little while in the door . . . that it was fittest for its days . . . that its action has descended to the stalwart and wellshaped heir who approaches . . . and that he shall be fittest for his days.

The Americans of all nations at any time upon the earth have probably the fullest poetical nature. The United States themselves are essentially the greatest poem. In the history of the earth hitherto the largest and most stirring appear tame and orderly to their ampler largeness and stir. Here at last is something in the doings of man that corresponds with the broadcast doings of the day and night. Here is not merely a nation but a teeming nation of nations. Here is action untied from strings necessarily blind to particulars and details magnificently moving in vast masses. Here is the hospitality which forever indicates heroes . . . . Here are the roughs and beards and space and ruggedness and nonchalance that the soul loves. Here the performance disdaining the trivial unapproached in the tremendous audacity of its crowds and groupings and the push of its perspective spreads with crampless and flowing breadth and showers its prolific and splendid extravagance. One sees it must indeed own the riches of the summer and winter, and need never be bankrupt while corn grows from the ground or the orchards drop apples or the bays contain fish or men beget children upon women.

Other states indicate themselves in their deputies . . . . but the genius of the United States is not best or most in its executives or legislatures, nor in its ambassadors or authors or colleges or churches or parlors, nor even in its newspapers or inventors . . . but always most in the common people. Their manners speech dress friendships—the freshness and candor of their physiognomy—the picturesque looseness of their carriage . . . their deathless attachment to freedom—their aversion to anything indecorous or soft or mean—the practical acknowledgment of the citizens of one state by the citizens of all other states—the fierceness of their roused resentment—their curiosity and welcome of novelty—their self-esteem and wonderful sympathy—their susceptibility to a slight—the air they have of persons who never knew how it felt to stand in the presence of superiors—the fluency of their speech—their delight in music, the sure symptom of manly tenderness and native elegance of soul . . . their good temper and openhandedness—the terrible significance of their elections—the President's taking off his hat to them not they to him—these too are unrhymed poetry. It awaits the gigantic and generous treatment worthy of it.

The largeness of nature or the nation were monstrous without a corresponding largeness and generosity of the spirit of the citizen. Not nature nor swarming states nor streets and steamships nor prosperous business nor farms nor capital nor learning may suffice for the ideal of man . . . nor suffice the poet. No reminiscences may suffice either. A live nation can always cut a deep mark and can have the best authority the cheapest . . . namely from its own soul. This is the sum of the profitable uses of individuals or states and of present action and grandeur and of the subjects of poets.—As if it were necessary to trot back generation after generation to the eastern records! As if the beauty and sacredness of the demonstrable must fall behind that of the mythical! As if men do not make their mark out of any times! As if the opening of the western continent by discovery and what has transpired since in North and South America were less than the small theatre of the antique or the aimless sleepwalking of the middle ages! The pride of the United States leaves the wealth and finesse of the cities and all returns of commerce and agriculture and all the magnitude of geography or shows of exterior victory to enjoy the breed of fullsized men or one fullsized man unconquerable and simple.

The American poets are to enclose old and new for America is the race of races. Of them a bard is to be commensurate with a people. To him the other continents arrive as contributions . . . he gives them reception for their sake and his own sake. His spirit responds to his country's spirit . . . . he incarnates its geography and natural life and rivers and lakes. Mississippi with annual freshets and changing chutes, Missouri and Columbia and Ohio and Saint Lawrence with the falls and beautiful masculine Hudson, do not embouchure* where they spend themselves more than they embouchure into him. The blue breadth over the inland sea of Virginia and Maryland and the sea off Massachusetts and Maine and over Manhattan bay and over Champlain and Erie and over Ontario and Huron and Michigan and Superior, and over the Texan and Mexican and Floridian and Cuban seas and over the seas off California and Oregon, is not tallied by the blue breadth of the waters below more than the breadth of above and below is tallied by him. When the long Atlantic coast stretches longer and the Pacific coast stretches longer he easily stretches with them north or south. He spans between them also from east to west and reflects what is between them. On him rise solid growths that offset the growths of pine and cedar and hemlock and liveoak and locust and chestnut and cypress and hickory and limetree and cottonwood and tuliptree and cactus and wildvine and tamarind and persimmon . . . . and tangles as tangled as any canebrake or swamp . . . . and forests coated with transparent ice and icicles hanging from the boughs and crackling in the wind . . . . and sides and peaks of mountains . . . . and pasturage sweet and free as savannah or upland or prairie . . . . with flights and songs and screams that answer those of the wildpigeon and highhold and orchard-oriole and coot and surf-duck and redshouldered-hawk and fish-hawk and white-ibis and indian-hen and cat-owl and water-pheasant and qua-bird and pied-sheldrake and blackbird and mockingbird and buzzard and condor and night-heron and eagle. To him the hereditary countenance descends both mother's and father's. To him enter the essences of the real things and past and present events—of the enormous diversity of temperature and agriculture and mines—the tribes of red aborigines—the weatherbeaten vessels entering new ports or making landings on rocky coasts—the first settlements north or south—the rapid stature and muscle—the haughty defiance of '76, and the war and peace and formation of the constitution . . . . the union always surrounded by blatherers and always calm and impregnable—the perpetual coming of immigrants—the wharf hem'd cities and superior marine—the unsurveyed interior—the loghouses and clearings and wild animals and hunters and trappers . . . . the free commerce—the fisheries and whaling and gold-digging—the endless gestation of new states—the convening of Congress every December, the members duly coming up from all climates and the uttermost parts . . . . the noble character of the young mechanics and of all free American workmen and workwomen . . . . the general ardor and friendliness and enterprise—the perfect equality of the female with the male . . . . the large amativeness—the fluid movement of the population—the factories and mercantile life and laborsaving machinery—the Yankee swap—the New-York firemen and the target excursion—the southern plantation life—the character of the northeast and of the northwest and southwest—slavery and the tremulous spreading of hands to protect it, and the stern opposition to it which shall never cease till it ceases or the speaking of tongues and the moving of lips cease. For such the expression of the American poet is to be transcendant and new. It is to be indirect and not direct or descriptive or epic. Its quality goes through these to much more. Let the age and wars of other nations be chanted and their eras and characters be illustrated and that finish the verse. Not so the great psalm of the republic. Here the theme is creative and has vista. Here comes one among the wellbeloved stonecutters and plans with decision and science and sees the solid and beautiful forms of the future where there are now no solid forms.

Of all nations the United States with veins full of poetical stuff most need poets and will doubtless have the greatest and use them the greatest. Their Presidents shall not be their common referee so much as their poets shall. Of all mankind the great poet is the equable man. Not in him but off from him things are grotesque or eccentric or fail of their sanity. Nothing out of its place is good and nothing in its place is bad. He bestows on every object or quality its fit proportions neither more nor less. He is the arbiter of the diverse and he is the key. He is the equalizer of his age and land . . . . he supplies what wants supplying and checks what wants checking. If peace is the routine out of him speaks the spirit of peace, large, rich, thrifty, building vast and populous cities, encouraging agriculture and the arts and commerce—lighting the study of man, the soul, immortality—federal, state or municipal government, marriage, health, freetrade, intertravel by land and sea . . . . nothing too close, nothing too far off . . . the stars not too far off. In war he is the most deadly force of the war. Who recruits him recruits horse and foot . . . he fetches parks of artillery the best that engineer ever knew. If the time becomes slothful and heavy he knows how to arouse it . . . he can make every word he speaks draw blood. Whatever stagnates in the flat of custom or obedience or legislation he never stagnates. Obedience does not master him, he masters it. High up out of reach he stands turning a concentrated light . . . he turns the pivot with his finger . . . he baffles the swiftest runners as he stands and easily overtakes and envelops them. The time straying toward infidelity and confections and persiflage he withholds by his steady faith . . . he spreads out his dishes . . . he offers the sweet firmfibred meat that grows men and women. His brain is the ultimate brain. He is no arguer . . . he is judgment. He judges not as the judge judges but as the sun falling around a helpless thing. As he sees the farthest he has the most faith. His thoughts are the hymns of the praise of things. In the talk on the soul and eternity and God off of his equal plane he is silent. He sees eternity less like a play with a prologue and denouement . . . . he sees eternity in men and women . . . he does not see men and women as dreams or dots. Faith is the antiseptic of the soul . . . it pervades the common people and preserves them . . . they never give up believing and expecting and trusting. There is that indescribable freshness and unconsciousness about an illiterate person that humbles and mocks the power of the noblest expressive genius. The poet sees for a certainty how one not a great artist may be just as sacred and perfect as the greatest artist . . . . . . The power to destroy or remould is freely used by him but never the power of attack. What is past is past. If he does not expose superior models and prove himself by every step he takes he is not what is wanted. The presence of the greatest poet conquers . . . not parleying or struggling or any prepared attempts. Now he has passed that way see after him! there is not left any vestige of despair or misanthropy or cunning or exclusiveness or the ignominy of a nativity or color or delusion of hell or the necessity of hell . . . . . and no man thenceforward shall be degraded for ignorance or weakness or sin.

The greatest poet hardly knows pettiness or triviality. If he breathes into any thing that was before thought small it dilates with the grandeur and life of the universe. He is a seer . . . . he is individual . . . he is complete in himself . . . . the others are as good as he, only he sees it and they do not. He is not one of the chorus . . . . he does not stop for any regulation . . . he is the president of regulation. What the eyesight does to the rest he does to the rest. Who knows the curious mystery of the eyesight? The other senses corroborate themselves, but this is removed from any proof but its own and foreruns the identities of the spiritual world. A single glance of it mocks all the investigations of man and all the instruments and books of the earth and all reasoning. What is marvellous? what is unlikely? what is impossible or baseless or vague? after you have once just opened the space of a peachpit and given audience to far and near and to the sunset and had all things enter with electric swiftness softly and duly without confusion or jostling or jam.

The land and sea, the animals fishes and birds, the sky of heaven and the orbs, the forests mountains and rivers, are not small themes . . . but folks expect of the poet to indicate more than the beauty and dignity which always attach to dumb real objects . . . . they expect him to indicate the path between reality and their souls. Men and women perceive the beauty well enough . . probably as well as he. The passionate tenacity of hunters, woodmen, early risers, cultivators of gardens and orchards and fields, the love of healthy women for the manly form, seafaring persons, drivers of horses, the passion for light and the open air, all is an old varied sign of the unfailing perception of beauty and of a residence of the poetic in outdoor people. They can never be assisted by poets to perceive . . . some may but they never can. The poetic quality is not marshalled in rhyme or uniformity or abstract addresses to things nor in melancholy complaints or good precepts, but is the life of these and much else and is in the soul. The profit of rhyme is that it drops seeds of a sweeter and more luxuriant rhyme, and of uniformity that it conveys itself into its own roots in the ground out of sight. The rhyme and uniformity of perfect poems show the free growth of metrical laws and bud from them as unerringly and loosely as lilacs or roses on a bush, and take shapes as compact as the shapes of chestnuts and oranges and melons and pears, and shed the perfume impalpable to form. The fluency and ornaments of the finest poems or music or orations or recitations are not independent but dependent. All beauty comes from beautiful blood and a beautiful brain. If the greatnesses are in conjunction in a man or woman it is enough . . . . the fact will prevail through the universe . . . . but the gaggery and gilt of a million years will not prevail. Who troubles himself about his ornaments or fluency is lost. This is what you shall do: Love the earth and sun and the animals, despise riches, give alms to every one that asks, stand up for the stupid and crazy, devote your income and labor to others, hate tyrants, argue not concerning God, have patience and indulgence toward the people, take off your hat to nothing known or unknown or to any man or number of men, go freely with powerful uneducated persons and with the young and with the mothers of families, read these leaves in the open air every season of every year of your life, re examine all you have been told at school or church or in any book, dismiss whatever insults your own soul, and your very flesh shall be a great poem and have the richest fluency not only in its words but in the silent lines of its lips and face and between the lashes of your eyes and in every motion and joint of your body. . . . . The poet shall not spend his time in unneeded work. He shall know that the ground is always ready ploughed and manured . . . . others may not know it but he shall. He shall go directly to the creation. His trust shall master the trust of everything he touches . . . . and shall master all attachment.

The known universe has one complete lover and that is the greatest poet. He consumes an eternal passion and is indifferent which chance happens and which possible contingency of fortune or misfortune and persuades daily and hourly his delicious pay. What balks or breaks others is fuel for his burning progress to contact and amorous joy. Other proportions of the reception of pleasure dwindle to nothing to his proportions. All expected from heaven or from the highest he is rapport with in the sight of the daybreak or a scene of the winter woods or the presence of children playing or with his arm round the neck of a man or woman. His love above all love has leisure and expanse . . . . he leaves room ahead of himself. He is no irresolute or suspicious lover . . . he is sure . . . he scorns intervals. His experience and the showers and thrills are not for nothing. Nothing can jar him . . . . suffering and darkness cannot—death and fear cannot. To him complaint and jealousy and envy are corpses buried and rotten in the earth . . . . he saw them buried. The sea is not surer of the shore or the shore of the sea than he is of the fruition of his love and of all perfection and beauty.

The fruition of beauty is no chance of hit or miss . . . it is inevitable as life . . . . it is exact and plumb as gravitation. From the eyesight proceeds another eyesight and from the hearing proceeds another hearing and from the voice proceeds another voice eternally curious of the harmony of things with man. To these respond perfections not only in the committees that were supposed to stand for the rest but in the rest themselves just the same. These understand the law of perfection in masses and floods . . . that its finish is to each for itself and onward from itself . . . that it is profuse and impartial . . . that there is not a minute of the light or dark nor an acre of the earth or sea without it—nor any direction of the sky nor any trade or employment nor any turn of events. This is the reason that about the proper expression of beauty there is precision and balance . . . one part does not need to be thrust above another. The best singer is not the one who has the most lithe and powerful organ . . . the pleasure of poems is not in them that take the handsomest measure and similes and sound.

Without effort and without exposing in the least how it is done the greatest poet brings the spirit of any or all events and passions and scenes and persons some more and some less to bear on your individual character as you hear or read. To do this well is to compete with the laws that pursue and follow time. What is the purpose must surely be there and the clue of it must be there . . . . and the faintest indication is the indication of the best and then becomes the clearest indication. Past and present and future are not disjoined but joined. The greatest poet forms the consistence of what is to be from what has been and is. He drags the dead out of their coffins and stands them again on their feet . . . . he says to the past, Rise and walk before me that I may realize you. He learns the lesson . . . . he places himself where the future becomes present. The greatest poet does not only dazzle his rays over character and scenes and passions . . . he finally ascends and finishes all . . . he exhibits the pinnacles that no man can tell what they are for or what is beyond . . . . he glows a moment on the extremest verge. He is most wonderful in his last half-hidden smile or frown . . . by that flash of the moment of parting the one that sees it shall be encouraged or terrified afterward for many years. The greatest poet does not moralize or make applications of morals . . . he knows the soul. The soul has that measureless pride which consists in never acknowledging any lessons but its own. But it has sympathy as measureless as its pride and the one balances the other and neither can stretch too far while it stretches in company with the other. The inmost secrets of art sleep with the twain. The greatest poet has lain close betwixt both and they are vital in his style and thoughts.

The art of art, the glory of expression and the sunshine of the light of letters is simplicity. Nothing is better than simplicity . . . . nothing can make up for excess or for the lack of definiteness. To carry on the heave of impulse and pierce intellectual depths and give all subjects their articulations are powers neither common nor very uncommon. But to speak in literature with the perfect rectitude and insousiance of the movements of animals and the unimpeachableness of the sentiment of trees in the woods and grass by the roadside is the flawless triumph of art. If you have looked on him who has achieved it you have looked on one of the masters of the artists of all nations and times. You shall not contemplate the flight of the graygull over the bay or the mettlesome action of the blood horse or the tall leaning of sunflowers on their stalk or the appearance of the sun journeying through heaven or the appearance of the moon afterward with any more satisfaction than you shall contemplate him. The greatest poet has less a marked style and is more the channel of thoughts and things without increase or diminution, and is the free channel of himself. He swears to his art, I will not be meddlesome, I will not have in my writing any elegance or effect or originality to hang in the way between me and the rest like curtains. I will have nothing hang in the way, not the richest curtains. What I tell I tell for precisely what it is. Let who may exalt or startle or fascinate or sooth I will have purposes as health or heat or snow has and be as regardless of observation. What I experience or portray shall go from my composition without a shred of my composition. You shall stand by my side and look in the mirror with me.

The old red blood and stainless gentility of great poets will be proved by their unconstraint. A heroic person walks at his ease through and out of that custom or precedent or authority that suits him not. Of the traits of the brotherhood of writers savans musicians inventors and artists nothing is finer than silent defiance advancing from new free forms. In the need of poems philosophy politics mechanism science behaviour, the craft of art, an appropriate native grand-opera, shipcraft, or any craft, he is greatest forever and forever who contributes the greatest original practical example. The cleanest expression is that which finds no sphere worthy of itself and makes one.

The messages of great poets to each man and woman are, Come to us on equal terms, Only then can you understand us, We are no better than you, What we enclose you enclose, What we enjoy you may enjoy. Did you suppose there could be only one Supreme? We affirm there can be unnumbered Supremes, and that one does not countervail another any more than one eyesight countervails another . . and that men can be good or grand only of the consciousness of their supremacy within them. What do you think is the grandeur of storms and dismemberments and the deadliest battles and wrecks and the wildest fury of the elements and the power of the sea and the motion of nature and of the throes of human desires and dignity and hate and love? It is that something in the soul which says, Rage on, Whirl on, I tread master here and everywhere, Master of the spasms of the sky and of the shatter of the sea, Master of nature and passion and death, And of all terror and all pain.

The American bards shall be marked for generosity and affection and for encouraging competitors . . They shall be kosmos . . without monopoly or secresy . . glad to pass any thing to any one . . hungry for equals night and day. They shall not be careful of riches and privilege . . . . they shall be riches and privilege . . . . they shall perceive who the most affluent man is. The most affluent man is he that confronts all the shows he sees by equivalents out of the stronger wealth of himself. The American bard shall delineate no class of persons nor one or two out of the strata of interests nor love most nor truth most nor the soul most nor the body most . . . . and not be for the eastern states more than the western or the northern states more than the southern.

Exact science and its practical movements are no checks on the greatest poet but always his encouragement and support. The outset and remembrance are there . . there the arms that lifted him first and brace him best . . . . there he returns after all his goings and comings. The sailor and traveler . . the anatomist chemist astronomer geologist phrenologist spiritualist mathematician historian and lexicographer are not poets, but they are the lawgivers of poets and their construction underlies the structure of every perfect poem. No matter what rises or is uttered they sent the seed of the conception of it . . . of them and by them stand the visible proofs of souls . . . . . always of their fatherstuff must be begotten the sinewy races of bards. If there shall be love and content between the father and the son and if the greatness of the son is the exuding of the greatness of the father there shall be love between the poet and the man of demonstrable science. In the beauty of poems are the tuft and final applause of science.

Great is the faith of the flush of knowledge and of the investigation of the depths of qualities and things. Cleaving and circling here swells the soul of the poet yet is president of itself always. The depths are fathomless and therefore calm. The innocence and nakedness are resumed . . . they are neither modest nor immodest. The whole theory of the special and supernatural and all that was twined with it or educed out of it departs as a dream. What has ever happened . . . . what happens and whatever may or shall happen, the vital laws enclose all . . . . they are sufficient for any case and for all cases . . . none to be hurried or retarded . . . . any miracle of affairs or persons inadmissible in the vast clear scheme where every motion and every spear of grass and the frames and spirits of men and women and all that concerns them are unspeakably perfect miracles all referring to all and each distinct and in its place. It is also not consistent with the reality of the soul to admit that there is anything in the known universe more divine than men and women.

Men and women and the earth and all upon it are simply to be taken as they are, and the investigation of their past and present and future shall be unintermitted and shall be done with perfect candor. Upon this basis philosophy speculates ever looking toward the poet, ever regarding the eternal tendencies of all toward happiness never inconsistent with what is clear to the senses and to the soul. For the eternal tendencies of all toward happiness make the only point of sane philosophy. Whatever comprehends less than that . . . whatever is less than the laws of light and of astronomical motion . . . or less than the laws that follow the thief the liar the glutton and the drunkard through this life and doubtless afterward . . . . . . or less than vast stretches of time or the slow formation of density or the patient upheaving of strata—is of no account. Whatever would put God in a poem or system of philosophy as contending against some being or influence is also of no account. Sanity and ensemble characterise the great master . . . spoilt in one principle all is spoilt. The great master has nothing to do with miracles. He sees health for himself in being one of the mass . . . . he sees the hiatus in singular eminence. To the perfect shape comes common ground. To be under the general law is great for that is to correspond with it. The master knows that he is unspeakably great and that all are unspeakably great . . . . that nothing for instance is greater than to conceive children and bring them up well . . . that to be is just as great as to perceive or tell.

In the make of the great masters the idea of political liberty is indispensible. Liberty takes the adherence of heroes wherever men and women exist . . . . but never takes any adherence or welcome from the rest more than from poets. They are the voice and exposition of liberty. They out of ages are worthy the grand idea . . . . to them it is confided and they must sustain it. Nothing has precedence of it and nothing can warp or degrade it. The attitude of great poets is to cheer up slaves and horrify despots. The turn of their necks, the sound of their feet, the motions of their wrists, are full of hazard to the one and hope to the other. Come nigh them awhile and though they neither speak or advise you shall learn the faithful American lesson. Liberty is poorly served by men whose good intent is quelled from one failure or two failures or any number of failures, or from the casual indifference or ingratitude of the people, or from the sharp show of the tushes of power, or the bringing to bear soldiers and cannon or any penal statutes. Liberty relies upon itself, invites no one, promises nothing, sits in calmness and light, is positive and composed, and knows no discouragement. The battle rages with many a loud alarm and frequent advance and retreat . . . . the enemy triumphs . . . . the prison, the handcuffs, the iron necklace and anklet, the scaffold, garrote and leadballs do their work . . . . the cause is asleep . . . . the strong throats are choked with their own blood . . . . the young men drop their eyelashes toward the ground when they pass each other . . . . and is liberty gone out of that place? No never. When liberty goes it is not the first to go nor the second or third to go . . it waits for all the rest to go . . it is the last . . . When the memories of the old martyrs are faded utterly away . . . . when the large names of patriots are laughed at in the public halls from the lips of the orators . . . . when the boys are no more christened after the same but christened after tyrants and traitors instead . . . . when the laws of the free are grudgingly permitted and laws for informers and bloodmoney are sweet to the taste of the people . . . . when I and you walk abroad upon the earth stung with compassion at the sight of numberless brothers answering our equal friendship and calling no man master—and when we are elated with noble joy at the sight of slaves . . . . when the soul retires in the cool communion of the night and surveys its experience and has much extasy over the word and deed that put back a helpless innocent person into the gripe of the gripers or into any cruel inferiority . . . . when those in all parts of these states who could easier realize the true American character but do not yet—when the swarms of cringers, suckers, doughfaces, lice of politics, planners of sly involutions for their own preferment to city offices or state legislatures or the judiciary or congress or the presidency, obtain a response of love and natural deference from the people whether they get the offices or no . . . . when it is better to be a bound booby and rogue in office at a high salary than the poorest free mechanic or farmer with his hat unmoved from his head and firm eyes and a candid and generous heart . . . . and when servility by town or state or the federal government or any oppression on a large scale or small scale can be tried on without its own punishment following duly after in exact proportion against the smallest chance of escape . . . . or rather when all life and all the souls of men and women are discharged from any part of the earth—then only shall the instinct of liberty be discharged from that part of the earth.

As the attributes of the poets of the kosmos concentre in the real body and soul and in the pleasure of things they possess the superiority of genuineness over all fiction and romance. As they emit themselves facts are showered over with light . . . . the daylight is lit with more volatile light . . . . also the deep between the setting and rising sun goes deeper many fold. Each precise object or condition or combination or process exhibits a beauty . . . . the multiplication table its—old age its—the carpenter's trade its—the grand-opera its . . . . the hugehulled cleanshaped New-York clipper at sea under steam or full sail gleams with unmatched beauty . . . . the American circles and large harmonies of government gleam with theirs . . . . and the commonest definite intentions and actions with theirs. The poets of the kosmos advance through all interpositions and coverings and turmoils and stratagems to first principles. They are of use . . . . they dissolve poverty from its need and riches from its conceit. You large proprietor they say shall not realize or perceive more than any one else. The owner of the library is not he who holds a legal title to it having bought and paid for it. Any one and every one is owner of the library who can read the same through all the varieties of tongues and subjects and styles, and in whom they enter with ease and take residence and force toward paternity and maternity, and make supple and powerful and rich and large. . . . . These American states strong and healthy and accomplished shall receive no pleasure from violations of natural models and must not permit them. In paintings or mouldings or carvings in mineral or wood, or in the illustrations of books or newspapers, or in any comic or tragic prints, or in the patterns of woven stuffs or any thing to beautify rooms or furniture or costumes, or to put upon cornices or monuments or on the prows or sterns of ships, or to put anywhere before the human eye indoors or out, that which distorts honest shapes or which creates unearthly beings or places or contingencies is a nuisance and revolt. Of the human form especially it is so great it must never be made ridiculous. Of ornaments to a work nothing outre can be allowed . . but those ornaments can be allowed that conform to the perfect facts of the open air and that flow out of the nature of the work and come irrepressibly from it and are necessary to the completion of the work. Most works are most beautiful without ornament. . . Exaggerations will be revenged in human physiology. Clean and vigorous children are jetted and conceived only in those communities where the models of natural forms are public every day. . . . . Great genius and the people of these states must never be demeaned to romances. As soon as histories are properly told there is no more need of romances.

The great poets are also to be known by the absence in them of tricks and by the justification of perfect personal candor. Then folks echo a new cheap joy and a divine voice leaping from their brains: How beautiful is candor! All faults may be forgiven of him who has perfect candor. Henceforth let no man of us lie, for we have seen that openness wins the inner and outer world and that there is no single exception, and that never since our earth gathered itself in a mass have deceit or subterfuge or prevarication attracted its smallest particle or the faintest tinge of a shade—and that through the enveloping wealth and rank of a state or the whole republic of states a sneak or sly person shall be discovered and despised . . . . and that the soul has never been once fooled and never can be fooled . . . . and thrift without the loving nod of the soul is only a fœtid puff . . . . and there never grew up in any of the continents of the globe nor upon any planet or satellite or star, nor upon the asteroids, nor in any part of ethereal space, nor in the midst of density, nor under the fluid wet of the sea, nor in that condition which precedes the birth of babes, nor at any time during the changes of life, nor in that condition that follows what we term death, nor in any stretch of abeyance or action afterward of vitality, nor in any process of formation or reformation anywhere, a being whose instinct hated the truth.

Extreme caution or prudence, the soundest organic health, large hope and comparison and fondness for women and children, large alimentiveness and destructiveness and causality, with a perfect sense of the oneness of nature and the propriety of the same spirit applied to human affairs . . these are called up of the float of the brain of the world to be parts of the greatest poet from his birth out of his mother's womb and from her birth out of her mother's. Caution seldom goes far enough. It has been thought that the prudent citizen was the citizen who applied himself to solid gains and did well for himself and his family and completed a lawful life without debt or crime. The greatest poet sees and admits these economies as he sees the economies of food and sleep, but has higher notions of prudence than to think he gives much when he gives a few slight attentions at the latch of the gate. The premises of the prudence of life are not the hospitality of it or the ripeness and harvest of it. Beyond the independence of a little sum laid aside for burial-money, and of a few clapboards around and shingles overhead on a lot of American soil owned, and the easy dollars that supply the year's plain clothing and meals, the melancholy prudence of the abandonment of such a great being as a man is to the toss and pallor of years of moneymaking with all their scorching days and icy nights and all their stifling deceits and underhanded dodgings, or infinitessimals of parlors, or shameless stuffing while others starve . . and all the loss of the bloom and odor of the earth and of the flowers and atmosphere and of the sea and of the true taste of the women and men you pass or have to do with in youth or middle age, and the issuing sickness and desperate revolt at the close of a life without elevation or naivete, and the ghastly chatter of a death without serenity or majesty, is the great fraud upon modern civilization and forethought, blotching the surface and system which civilization undeniably drafts, and moistening with tears the immense features it spreads and spreads with such velocity before the reached kisses of the soul . . . Still the right explanation remains to be made about prudence. The prudence of the mere wealth and respectability of the most esteemed life appears too faint for the eye to observe at all when little and large alike drop quietly aside at the thought of the prudence suitable for immortality. What is wisdom that fills the thinness of a year or seventy or eighty years to wisdom spaced out by ages and coming back at a certain time with strong reinforcements and rich presents and the clear faces of wedding-guests as far as you can look in every direction running gaily toward you? Only the soul is of itself . . . . all else has reference to what ensues. All that a person does or thinks is of consequence. Not a move can a man or woman make that affects him or her in a day or a month or any part of the direct lifetime or the hour of death but the same affects him or her onward afterward through the indirect lifetime. The indirect is always as great and real as the direct. The spirit receives from the body just as much as it gives to the body. Not one name of word or deed . . not of venereal sores or discolorations . . not the privacy of the onanist . . not of the putrid veins of gluttons or rumdrinkers . . . not peculation or cunning or betrayal or murder . . no serpentine poison of those that seduce women . . not the foolish yielding of women . . not prostitution . . not of any depravity of young men . . not of the attainment of gain by discreditable means . . not any nastiness of appetite . . not any harshness of officers to men or judges to prisoners or fathers to sons or sons to fathers or of husbands to wives or bosses to their boys . . not of greedy looks or malignant wishes . . . nor any of the wiles practised by people upon themselves . . . ever is or ever can be stamped on the programme but it is duly realized and returned, and that returned in further performances . . . and they returned again. Nor can the push of charity or personal force ever be any thing else than the profoundest reason, whether it bring arguments to hand or no. No specification is necessary . . to add or subtract or divide is in vain. Little or big, learned or unlearned, white or black, legal or illegal, sick or well, from the first inspiration down the windpipe to the last expiration out of it, all that a male or female does that is vigorous and benevolent and clean is so much sure profit to him or her in the unshakable order of the universe and through the whole scope of it forever. If the savage or felon is wise it is well . . . . if the greatest poet or savan is wise it is simply the same . . if the President or chief justice is wise it is the same . . . if the young mechanic or farmer is wise it is no more or less . . if the prostitute is wise it is no more nor less. The interest will come round . . all will come round. All the best actions of war and peace . . . all help given to relatives and strangers and the poor and old and sorrowful and young children and widows and the sick, and to all shunned persons . . all furtherance of fugitives and of the escape of slaves . . all the self-denial that stood steady and aloof on wrecks and saw others take the seats of the boats . . . all offering of substance or life for the good old cause, or for a friend's sake or opinion's sake . . . all pains of enthusiasts scoffed at by their neighbors . . all the vast sweet love and precious suffering of mothers . . . all honest men baffled in strifes recorded or unrecorded . . . . all the grandeur and good of the few ancient nations whose fragments of annals we inherit . . and all the good of the hundreds of far mightier and more ancient nations unknown to us by name or date or location . . . . all that was ever manfully begun, whether it succeeded or no . . . . all that has at any time been well suggested out of the divine heart of man or by the divinity of his mouth or by the shaping of his great hands . . and all that is well thought or done this day on any part of the surface of the globe . . or on any of the wandering stars or fixed stars by those there as we are here . . or that is henceforth to be well thought or done by you whoever you are, or by any one—these singly and wholly inured at their time and inure now and will inure always to the identities from which they sprung or shall spring . . . Did you guess any of them lived only its moment? The world does not so exist . . no parts palpable or impalpable so exist . . . no result exists now without being from its long antecedent result, and that from its antecedent, and so backward without the farthest mentionable spot coming a bit nearer the beginning than any other spot. . . . . . Whatever satisfies the soul is truth. The prudence of the greatest poet answers at last the craving and glut of the soul, is not contemptuous of less ways of prudence if they conform to its ways, puts off nothing, permits no let-up for its own case or any case, has no particular sabbath or judgment-day, divides not the living from the dead or the righteous from the unrighteous, is satisfied with the present, matches every thought or act by its correlative, knows no possible forgiveness or deputed atonement . . knows that the young man who composedly periled his life and lost it has done exceeding well for himself, while the man who has not periled his life and retains it to old age in riches and ease has perhaps achieved nothing for himself worth mentioning . . and that only that person has no great prudence to learn who has learnt to prefer real longlived things, and favors body and soul the same, and perceives the indirect assuredly following the direct, and what evil or good he does leaping onward and waiting to meet him again—and who in his spirit in any emergency whatever neither hurries or avoids death.

The direct trial of him who would be the greatest poet is today. If he does not flood himself with the immediate age as with vast oceanic tides . . . . . and if he does not attract his own land body and soul to himself and hang on its neck with incomparable love and plunge his semitic muscle into its merits and demerits . . . and if he be not himself the age transfigured . . . . and if to him is not opened the eternity which gives similitude to all periods and locations and processes and animate and inanimate forms, and which is the bond of time, and rises up from its inconceivable vagueness and infiniteness in the swimming shape of today, and is held by the ductile anchors of life, and makes the present spot the passage from what was to what shall be, and commits itself to the representation of this wave of an hour and this one of the sixty beautiful children of the wave—let him merge in the general run and wait his developement. . . . . Still the final test of poems or any character or work remains. The prescient poet projects himself centuries ahead and judges performer or performance after the changes of time. Does it live through them? Does it still hold on untired? Will the same style and the direction of genius to similar points be satisfactory now? Has no new discovery in science or arrival at superior planes of thought and judgment and behaviour fixed him or his so that either can be looked down upon? Have the marches of tens and hundreds and thousands of years made willing detours to the right hand and the left hand for his sake? Is he beloved long and long after he is buried? Does the young man think often of him? and the young woman think often of him? and do the middleaged and the old think of him?

A great poem is for ages and ages in common and for all degrees and complexions and all departments and sects and for a woman as much as a man and a man as much as a woman. A great poem is no finish to a man or woman but rather a beginning. Has any one fancied he could sit at last under some due authority and rest satisfied with explanations and realize and be content and full? To no such terminus does the greatest poet bring . . . he brings neither cessation or sheltered fatness and ease. The touch of him tells in action. Whom he takes he takes with firm sure grasp into live regions previously unattained . . . . thenceforward is no rest . . . . they see the space and ineffable sheen that turn the old spots and lights into dead vacuums. The companion of him beholds the birth and progress of stars and learns one of the meanings. Now there shall be a man cohered out of tumult and chaos . . . . the elder encourages the younger and shows him how . . . they two shall launch off fearlessly together till the new world fits an orbit for itself and looks unabashed on the lesser orbits of the stars and sweeps through the ceaseless rings and shall never be quiet again.

There will soon be no more priests. Their work is done. They may wait awhile . . perhaps a generation or two . . dropping off by degrees. A superior breed shall take their place . . . . the gangs of kosmos and prophets en masse shall take their place. A new order shall arise and they shall be the priests of man, and every man shall be his own priest. The churches built under their umbrage shall be the churches of men and women. Through the divinity of themselves shall the kosmos and the new breed of poets be interpreters of men and women and of all events and things. They shall find their inspiration in real objects today, symptoms of the past and future . . . . They shall not deign to defend immortality or God or the perfection of things or liberty or the exquisite beauty and reality of the soul. They shall arise in America and be responded to from the remainder of the earth.

The English language befriends the grand American expression . . . . it is brawny enough and limber and full enough. On the tough stock of a race who through all change of circumstance was never without the idea of political liberty, which is the animus of all liberty, it has attracted the terms of daintier and gayer and subtler and more elegant tongues. It is the powerful language of resistance . . . it is the dialect of common sense. It is the speech of the proud and melancholy races and of all who aspire. It is the chosen tongue to express growth faith self-esteem freedom justice equality friendliness amplitude prudence decision and courage. It is the medium that shall well nigh express the inexpressible.

No great literature nor any like style of behaviour or oratory or social intercourse or household arrangements or public institutions or the treatment by bosses of employed people, nor executive detail or detail of the army or navy, nor spirit of legislation or courts or police or tuition or architecture or songs or amusements or the costumes of young men, can long elude the jealous and passionate instinct of American standards. Whether or no the sign appears from the mouths of the people, it throbs a live interrogation in every freeman's and freewoman's heart after that which passes by or this built to remain. Is it uniform with my country? Are its disposals without ignominious distinctions? Is it for the evergrowing communes of brothers and lovers, large, well-united, proud beyond the old models, generous beyond all models? Is it something grown fresh out of the fields or drawn from the sea for use to me today here? I know that what answers for me an American must answer for any individual or nation that serves for a part of my materials. Does this answer? or is it without reference to universal needs? or sprung of the needs of the less developed society of special ranks? or old needs of pleasure overlaid by modern science and forms? Does this acknowledge liberty with audible and absolute acknowledgement, and set slavery at nought for life and death? Will it help breed one goodshaped and wellhung man, and a woman to be his perfect and independent mate? Does it improve manners? Is it for the nursing of the young of the republic? Does it solve readily with the sweet milk of the nipples of the breasts of the mother of many children? Has it too the old ever-fresh forbearance and impartiality? Does it look with the same love on the last born and on those hardening toward stature, and on the errant, and on those who disdain all strength of assault outside of their own?

The poems distilled from other poems will probably pass away. The coward will surely pass away. The expectation of the vital and great can only be satisfied by the demeanor of the vital and great. The swarms of the polished deprecating and reflectors and the polite float off and leave no remembrance. America prepares with composure and goodwill for the visitors that have sent word. It is not intellect that is to be their warrant and welcome. The talented, the artist, the ingenious, the editor, the statesman, the erudite . . they are not unappreciated . . they fall in their place and do their work. The soul of the nation also does its work. No disguise can pass on it . . no disguise can conceal from it. It rejects none, it permits all. Only toward as good as itself and toward the like of itself will it advance half-way. An individual is as superb as a nation when he has the qualities which make a superb nation. The soul of the largest and wealthiest and proudest nation may well go half-way to meet that of its poets. The signs are effectual. There is no fear of mistake. If the one is true the other is true. The proof of a poet is that his country absorbs him as affectionately as he has absorbed it.

LETTER TO WALT WHITMAN

[APPENDED TO THE 1856 LEAVES]

CONCORD, MASSACHUSETTS, 21 *July*, 1855.

DEAR SIR—I am not blind to the worth of the wonderful gift of "LEAVES OF GRASS." I find it the most extraordinary piece of wit and wisdom that America has yet contributed. I am very happy in reading it, as great power makes us happy. It meets the demand I am always making of what seemed the sterile and stingy nature, as if too much handiwork, or too much lymph in the temperament, were making our western wits fat and mean.

I give you joy of your free and brave thought. I have great joy in it. I find incomparable things said incomparably well, as they must be. I find the courage of treatment which so delights us, and which large perception only can inspire.

I greet you at the beginning of a great career, which yet must have had a long foreground somewhere, for such a start. I rubbed my eyes a little, to see if this sunbeam were no illusion; but the solid sense of the book is a sober certainty. It has the best merits, namely, of fortifying and encouraging.

I did not know until I last night saw the book advertised in a newspaper that I could trust the name as real and available for a post-office. I wish to see my benefactor, and have felt much like striking my tasks and visiting New York to pay you my respects.

R. W. EMERSON.

LETTER TO RALPH WALDO EMERSON

BROOKLYN, *August*, 1856.

HERE are thirty-two Poems, which I send you, dear Friend and Master, not having found how I could satisfy myself with sending any usual acknowledgment of your letter. The first edition, on which you mailed me that till now unanswered letter, was twelve poems—I printed a thousand copies, and they readily sold; these thirty-two Poems I stereotype, to print several thousand copies of. I much enjoy making poems. Other work I have set for myself to do, to meet people and The States face to face, to confront them with an American rude tongue; but the work of my life is making poems. I keep on till I make a hundred, and then several hundred—perhaps a thousand. The way is clear to me. A few years, and the average annual call for my Poems is ten or twenty thousand copies—more, quite likely. Why should I hurry or compromise? In poems or in speeches I say the word or two that has got to be said, adhere to the body, step with the countless common footsteps, and remind every man and woman of something.

Master, I am a man who has perfect faith. Master, we have not come through centuries, caste, heroisms, fables, to halt in this land today. Or I think it is to collect a ten-fold impetus that any halt is made. As nature, inexorable, onward, resistless, impassive amid the threats and screams of disputants, so America. Let all defer. Let all attend respectfully the leisure of These States, their politics, poems, literature, manners, and their free-handed modes of training their own offspring. Their own comes, just matured, certain, numerous and capable enough, with egotistical tongues, with sinewed wrists, seizing openly what belongs to them. They resume Personality, too long left out of mind. Their shadows are projected in employments, in books, in the cities, in trade; their feet are on the flights of the steps of the Capitol; they dilate, a larger, brawnier, more candid, more democratic, lawless, positive native to The States, sweet-bodied, completer, dauntless, flowing, masterful, beard-faced, new race of men.

Swiftly, on limitless foundations, the United States too are founding a literature. It is all as well done, in my opinion, as could be practicable. Each element here is in condition. Every day I go among the people of Manhattan Island, Brooklyn, and other cities, and among the young men, to discover the spirit of them, and to refresh myself. These are to be attended to; I am myself more drawn here than to those authors, publishers, importations, reprints, and so forth. I pass coolly through those, understanding them perfectly well, and that they do the indispensable service, outside of men like me, which nothing else could do. In poems, the young men of The States shall be represented, for they out-rival the best of the rest of the earth.

The lists of ready-made literature which America inherits by the mighty inheritance of the English language—all the rich repertoire of traditions, poems, histories, metaphysics, plays, classics, translations, have made, and still continue, magnificent preparations for that other plainly signified literature, to be our own, to be electric, fresh, lusty, to express the full-sized body, male and female—to give the modern meanings of things, to grow up beautiful, lasting, commensurate with America, with all the passions of home, with the inimitable sympathies of having been boys and girls together, and of parents who were with our parents.

What else can happen The States, even in their own despite? That huge English flow, so sweet, so undeniable, has done incalculable good here, and is to be spoken of for its own sake with generous praise and with gratitude. Yet the price The States have had to lie under for the same has not been a small price. Payment prevails; a nation can never take the issues of the needs of other nations for nothing. America, grandest of lands in the theory of its politics, in popular reading, in hospitality, breadth, animal beauty, cities, ships, machines, money, credit, collapses quick as lightning at the repeated, admonishing, stern words, Where are any mental expressions from you, beyond what you have copied or stolen? Where the born throngs of poets, literats, orators, you promised? Will you but tag after other nations? They struggled long for their literature, painfully working their way, some with deficient languages, some with priest-craft, some in the endeavor just to live—yet achieved for their times, works, poems, perhaps the only solid consolation left to them through ages afterward of shame and decay. You are young, have the perfectest of dialects, a free press, a free government, the world forwarding its best to be with you. As justice has been strictly done to you, from this hour do strict justice to yourself. Strangle the singers who will not sing you loud and strong. Open the doors of The West. Call for new great masters to comprehend new arts, new perfections, new wants. Submit to the most robust bard till he remedy your barrenness. Then you will not need to adopt the heirs of others; you will have true heirs, begotten of yourself, blooded with your own blood.

With composure I see such propositions, seeing more and more every day of the answers that serve. Expressions do not yet serve, for sufficient reasons; but that is getting ready, beyond what the earth has hitherto known, to take home the expressions when they come, and to identify them with the populace of The States, which is the schooling cheaply procured by any outlay any number of years. Such schooling The States extract from the swarms of reprints, and from the current authors and editors. Such service and extract are done after enormous, reckless, free modes, characteristic of The States. Here are to be attained results never elsewhere thought possible; the modes are very grand too. The instincts of the American people are all perfect, and tend to make heroes. It is a rare thing in a man here to understand The States.

All current nourishments to literature serve. Of authors and editors I do not know how many there are in The States, but there are thousands, each one building his or her step to the stairs by which giants shall mount. Of the twenty-four modern mammoth two-double, three-double, and four-double cylinder presses now in the world, printing by steam, twenty-one of them are in These States. The twelve thousand large and small shops for dispensing books and newspapers—the same number of public libraries, any one of which has all the reading wanted to equip a man or woman for American reading—the three thousand different newspapers, the nutriment of the imperfect ones coming in just as usefully as any—the story papers, various, full of strong-flavored romances, widely circulated—the one-cent and two-cent journals—the political ones, no matter what side—the weeklies in the country—the sporting and pictorial papers—the monthly magazines, with plentiful imported feed—the sentimental novels, numberless copies of them—the low-priced flaring tales, adventures, biographies—all are prophetic; all waft rapidly on. I see that they swell wide, for reasons. I am not troubled at the movement of them, but greatly pleased. I see plying shuttles, the active ephemeral myriads of books also, faithfully weaving the garments of a generation of men, and a generation of women, they do not perceive or know. What a progress popular reading and writing has made in fifty years! What a progress fifty years hence! The time is at hand when inherent literature will be a main part of These States, as general and real as steam-power, iron, corn, beef, fish. First-rate American persons are to be supplied. Our perennial materials for fresh thoughts, histories, poems, music, orations, religions, recitations, amusements, will then not be disregarded, any more than our perennial fields, mines, rivers, seas. Certain things are established, and are immovable; in those things millions of years stand justified. The mothers and fathers of whom modern centuries have come, have not existed for nothing; they too had brains and hearts. Of course all literature, in all nations and years, will share marked attributes in common, as we all, of all ages, share the common human attributes. America is to be kept coarse and broad. What is to be done is to withdraw from precedents, and be directed to men and women—also to The States in their federalness; for the union of the parts of the body is not more necessary to their life than the union of These States is to their life.

A profound person can easily know more of the people than they know of themselves. Always waiting untold in the souls of the armies of common people, is stuff better than anything that can possibly appear in the leadership of the same. That gives final verdicts. In every department of These States, he who travels with a coterie, or with selected persons, or with imitators, or with infidels, or with the owners of slaves, or with that which is ashamed of the body of a man, or with that which is ashamed of the body of a woman, or with any thing less than the bravest and the openest, travels straight for the slopes of dissolution. The genius of all foreign literature is clipped and cut small, compared to our genius, and is essentially insulting to our usages, and to the organic compacts of These States. Old forms, old poems, majestic and proper in their own lands here in this land are exiles; the air here is very strong. Much that stands well and has a little enough place provided for it in the small scales of European kingdoms, empires, and the like, here stands haggard, dwarfed, ludicrous, or has no place little enough provided for it. Authorities, poems, models, laws, names, imported into America, are useful to America today to destroy them, and so move disencumbered to great works, great days.

Just so long, in our country or any country, as no revolutionists advance, and are backed by the people, sweeping off the swarms of routine representatives, officers in power, book-makers, teachers, ecclesiastics, politicians, just so long, I perceive, do they who are in power fairly represent that country, and remain of use, probably of very great use. To supersede them, when it is the pleasure of These States, full provision is made; and I say the time has arrived to use it with a strong hand. Here also the souls of the armies have not only overtaken the souls of the officer, but passed on, and left the souls of the officers behind out of sight many weeks' journey; and the souls of the armies now go en-masse without officers. Here also formulas, glosses, blanks, minutiæ, are choking the throats of the spokesmen to death. Those things most listened for, certainly those are the things least said. There is not a single History of the World. There is not one of America, or of the organic compacts of These States, or of Washington, or of Jefferson, nor of Language, nor any Dictionary of the English Language. There is no great author; every one has demeaned himself to some etiquette or some impotence. There is no manhood or life-power in poems; there are shoats and geldings more like. Or literature will be dressed up, a fine gentleman, distasteful to our instincts, foreign to our soil. Its neck bends right and left wherever it goes. Its costumes and jewelry prove how little it knows Nature. Its flesh is soft; it shows less and less of the indefinable hard something that is Nature. Where is any thing but the shaved Nature of synods and schools? Where is a savage and luxuriant man? Where is an overseer? In lives, in poems, in codes of law, in Congress, in tuitions, theatres, conversations, argumentations, not a single head lifts itself clean out, with proof that it is their master, and has subordinated them to itself, and is ready to try their superiors. None believes in These States, boldly illustrating them in himself. Not a man faces round at the rest with terrible negative voice, refusing all terms to be bought off from his own eye-sight, or from the soul that he is, or from friendship, or from the body that he is, or from the soil and sea. To creeds, literature, art, the army, the navy, the executive, life is hardly proposed, but the sick and dying are proposed to cure the sick and dying. The churches are one vast lie; the people do not believe them, and they do not believe themselves; the priests are continually telling what they know well enough is not so, and keeping back what they know is so. The spectacle is a pitiful one. I think there can never be again upon the festive earth more bad-disordered persons deliberately taking seats, as of late in These States, at the heads of the public tables—such corpses' eyes for judges—such a rascal and thief in the Presidency.

Up to the present, as helps best, the people, like a lot of large boys, have no determined tastes, are quite unaware of the grandeur of themselves, and of their destiny, and of their immense strides—accept with voracity whatever is presented them in novels, histories, newspapers, poems, schools, lectures, every thing. Pretty soon, through these and other means, their development makes the fibre that is capable of itself, and will assume determined tastes. The young men will be clear what they want, and will have it. They will follow none except him whose spirit leads them in the like spirit with themselves. Any such man will be welcome as the flowers of May. Others will be put out without ceremony. How much is there anyhow, to the young men of These States, in a parcel of helpless dandies, who can neither fight, work, shoot, ride, run, command—some of them devout, some quite insane, some castrated—all second-hand, or third, fourth, or fifth hand—waited upon by waiters, putting not this land first, but always other lands first, talking of art, doing the most ridiculous things for fear of being called ridiculous, smirking and skipping along, continually taking off their hats—no one behaving, dressing, writing, talking, loving, out of any natural and manly tastes of his own, but each one looking cautiously to see how the rest behave, dress, write, talk, love—pressing the noses of dead books upon themselves and upon their country—favoring no poets, philosophs, literats here, but dog-like danglers at the heels of the poets, philosophs, literats, of enemies' lands—favoring mental expressions, models of gentlemen and ladies, social habitudes in These States, to grow up in sneaking defiance of the popular substratums of The States? Of course they and the likes of them can never justify the strong poems of America. Of course no feed of theirs is to stop and be made welcome to muscle the bodies, male and female, for Manhattan Island, Brooklyn, Boston, Worcester, Hartford, Portland, Montreal, Detroit, Buffalo, Cleaveland, Milwaukee, St. Louis, Indianapolis, Chicago, Cincinnati, Iowa City, Philadelphia, Baltimore, Releigh, Savannah, Charleston, Mobile, New Orleans, Galveston, Brownsville, San Francisco, Havana, and a thousand equal cities, present and to come. Of course what they and the likes of them have been used for, draws toward its close, after which they will all be discharged, and not one of them will ever be heard of any more.

America, having duly conceived, bears out of herself offspring of her own to do the workmanship wanted. To freedom, to strength, to poems, to personal greatness, it is never permitted to rest, not a generation or part of a generation. To be ripe beyond further increase is to prepare to die. The architects of These States laid their foundations, and passed to further spheres. What they laid is a work done; as much more remains. Now are needed other architects, whose duty is not less difficult, but perhaps more difficult. Each age forever needs architects. America is not finished, perhaps never will be; now America is a divine true sketch. There are Thirty-Two States sketched—the population thirty millions. In a few years there will be Fifty States. Again in a few years there will be A Hundred States, the population hundreds of millions, the freshest and freest of men. Of course such men stand to nothing less than the freshest and freest expression.

Poets here, literats here, are to rest on organic different bases from other countries; not a class set apart, circling only in the circle of themselves, modest and pretty, desperately scratching for rhymes, pallid with white paper, shut off, aware of the old pictures and traditions of the race, but unaware of the actual race around them—not breeding in and in among each other till they all have the scrofula. Lands of ensemble, bards of ensemble! Walking freely out from the old traditions, as our politics has walked out, American poets and literats recognize nothing behind them superior to what is present with them—recognize with joy the sturdy living forms of the men and women of These States, the divinity of sex, the perfect eligibility of the female with the male, all The States, liberty and equality, real articles, the different trades, mechanics, the young fellows of Manhattan Island, customs, instincts, slang, Wisconsin, Georgia, the noble Southern heart, the hot blood, the spirit that will be nothing less than master, the filibuster spirit, the Western man, native-born perceptions, the eye for forms, the perfect models of made things, the wild smack of freedom, California, money, electric-telegraphs, free-trade, iron and the iron mines—recognize without demur those splendid resistless black poems, the steam-ships of the sea-board states, and those other resistless splendid poems, the locomotives, followed through the interior states by trains of rail-road cars.

A word remains to be said, as of one ever present, not yet permitted to be acknowledged, discarded or made dumb by literature, and the results apparent. To the lack of an avowed, empowered, unabashed development of sex, (the only salvation for the same,) and to the fact of speakers and writers fraudulently assuming as always dead what every one knows to be always alive, is attributable the remarkable non-personality and indistinctness of modern productions in books, art, talk; also that in the scanned lives of men and women most of them appear to have been for some time past of the neuter gender; and also the stinging fact that in orthodox society today, if the dresses were changed, the men might easily pass for women and the women for men.

Infidelism usurps most with fœtid polite face; among the rest infidelism about sex. By silence or obedience the pens of savans, poets, historians, biographers, and the rest, have long connived at the filthy law, and books enslaved to it, that what makes the manhood of a man, that sex, womanhood, maternity, desires, lusty animations, organs, acts, are unmentionable and to be ashamed of, to be driven to skulk out of literature with whatever belongs to them. This filthy law has to be repealed—it stands in the way of great reforms. Of women just as much as men, it is the interest that there should not be infidelism about sex, but perfect faith. Women in These States approach the day of that organic equality with men, without which, I see, men cannot have organic equality among themselves. This empty dish, gallantry, will then be filled with something. This tepid wash, this diluted deferential love, as in songs, fictions, and so forth, is enough to make a man vomit; as to manly friendship, everywhere observed in The States, there is not the first breath of it to be observed in print. I say that the body of a man or woman, the main matter, is so far quite unexpressed in poems; but that the body is to be expressed, and sex is. Of bards for These States, if it come to a question, it is whether they shall celebrate in poems the eternal decency of the amativeness of Nature, the motherhood of all, or whether they shall be the bards of the fashionable delusion of the inherent nastiness of sex, and of the feeble and querulous modesty of deprivation. This is important in poems, because the whole of the other expressions of a nation are but flanges out of its great poems. To me, henceforth, that theory of any thing, no matter what, stagnates in its vitals, cowardly and rotten, while it cannot publicly accept, and publicly name, with specific words, the things on which all existence, all souls, all realization, all decency, all health, all that is worth being here for, all of woman and of man, all beauty, all purity, all sweetness, all friendship, all strength, all life, all immortality depend. The courageous soul, for a year or two to come, may be proved by faith in sex, and by disdaining concessions.

To poets and literats—to every woman and man, today or any day, the conditions of the present, needs, dangers, prejudices, and the like, are the perfect conditions on which we are here, and the conditions for wording the future with undissuadable words. These States, receivers of the stamina of past ages and lands, initiate the outlines of repayment a thousand fold. They fetch the American great masters, waited for by old worlds and new, who accept evil as well as good, ignorance as well as erudition, black as soon as white, foreign-born materials as well as home-born, reject none, force discrepancies into range, surround the whole, concentrate them on present periods and places, show the application to each and any one's body and soul, and show the true use of precedents. Always America will be agitated and turbulent. This day it is taking shape, not to be less so, but to be more so, stormily, capriciously, on native principles, with such vast proportions of parts! As for me, I love screaming, wrestling, boiling-hot days.

Of course, we shall have a national character, an identity. As it ought to be, and as soon as it ought to be, it will be. That, with much else, takes care of itself, is a result, and the cause of greater results. With Ohio, Illinois, Missouri, Oregon—with the states around the Mexican sea—with cheerfully welcomed immigrants from Europe, Asia, Africa—with Connecticut, Vermont, New Hampshire, Rhode Island—with all varied interests, facts, beliefs, parties, genesis—there is being fused a determined character, fit for the broadest use for the freewomen and freemen of The States, accomplished and to be accomplished, without any exception whatever—each indeed free, each idiomatic, as becomes live states and men, but each adhering to one enclosing general form of politics, manners, talk, personal style, as the plenteous varieties of the race adhere to one physical form. Such character is the brain and spine to all, including literature, including poems. Such character, strong, limber, just, open-mouthed, American-blooded, full of pride, full of ease, of passionate friendliness, is to stand compact upon that vast basis of the supremacy of Individuality—that new moral American continent without which, I see, the physical continent remained incomplete, may-be a carcass, a bloat—that newer America, answering face to face with The States, with ever-satisfying and ever-unsurveyable seas and shores.

Those shores you found. I say you have led The States there—have led Me there. I say that none has ever done, or ever can do, a greater deed for The States, than your deed. Others may line out the lines, build cities, work mines, break up farms; it is yours to have been the original true Captain who put to sea, intuitive, positive, rendering the first report, to be told less by any report, and more by the mariners of a thousand bays, in each tack of their arriving and departing, many years after you.

Receive, dear Master, these statements and assurances through me, for all the young men, and for an earnest that we know none before you, but the best following you; and that we demand to take your name into our keeping, and that we understand what you have indicated, and find the same indicated in ourselves, and that we will stick to it and enlarge upon it through These States.

WALT WHITMAN.

Preface to 'As a Strong Bird on Pinions Free' *(1872)*

THE impetus and ideas urging me, for some years past, to an utterance, or attempt at utterance, of New World songs, and an epic of Democracy, having already had their published expression, as well as I can expect to give it, in LEAVES OF GRASS, the present and any future pieces from me are really but the surplusage forming after that Volume, or the wake eddying behind it. I fulfilled in that an imperious conviction, and the commands of my nature as total and irresistible as those which make the sea flow, or the globe revolve. But of this Supplementary Volume, I confess I am not so certain. Having from early manhood abandoned the business pursuits and applications usual in my time and country, and obediently yielded myself up ever since to the impetus mentioned, and to the work of expressing those ideas, it may be that mere habit has got dominion of me, when there is no real need of saying any thing further. . . . But what is life but an experiment? and mortality but an exercise? with reference to results beyond. And so shall my poems be. If incomplete here, and superfluous there, *n'importe*—the earnest trial and persistent exploration shall at least be mine, and other success failing, shall be success enough. I have been more anxious, anyhow, to suggest the songs of vital endeavor and manly evolution, and furnish something for races of outdoor athletes, than to make perfect rhymes, or reign in the parlors. I ventured from the beginning, my own way, taking chances—and would keep on venturing.

I will therefore not conceal from any persons, known or unknown to me, who take an interest in the matter, that I have the ambition of devoting yet a few years to poetic composition. . . . The mighty present age! To absorb and express in poetry, any thing of it—of its world—America—cities and States—the years, the events of our Nineteenth Century—the rapidity of movement—the violent contrasts, fluctuations of light and shade, of hope and fear—the entire revolution made by science in the poetic method—these great new underlying facts and new ideas rushing and spreading everywhere;—Truly a mighty age! As if in some colossal drama, acted again like those of old, under the open sun, the Nations of our time, and all the characteristics of Civilization, seem hurrying, stalking across, flitting from wing to wing, gathering, closing up, toward some long-prepared, most tremendous denouement. Not to conclude the infinite scenas of the race's life and toil and happiness and sorrow, but haply that the boards be cleared from oldest, worst incumbrances, accumulations, and Man resume the eternal play anew, and under happier, freer auspices. . . . To me, the United States are important because, in this colossal drama, they are unquestionably designated for the leading parts, for many a century to come. In them History and Humanity seem to seek to culminate. Our broad areas are even now the busy theatre of plots, passions, interests, and suspended problems, compared to which the intrigues of the past of Europe, the wars of dynasties, the scope of kings and kingdoms, and even the development of peoples, as hitherto, exhibit scales of measurement comparatively narrow and trivial. And on these areas of ours, as on a stage, sooner or later, something like an *eclaircissement* of all the past civilization of Europe and Asia is probably to be evolved.

The leading parts. . . . Not to be acted, emulated here, by us again, that role till now foremost in History—Not to become a conqueror nation, or to achieve the glory of mere military, or diplomatic, or commercial superiority—but to become the grand Producing Land of nobler Men and Women—of copious races, cheerful, healthy, tolerant, free—To become the most friendly Nation, (the United States indeed)—the modern composite nation, formed from all, with room for all, welcoming all immigrants—accepting the work of our own interior development, as the work fitly filling ages and ages to come;—the leading Nation of peace, but neither ignorant nor incapable of being the leading Nation of war;—not the Man's Nation only, but the Woman's Nation—a land of splendid mothers, daughters, sisters, wives.

Our America to-day I consider in many respects as but indeed a vast seething mass of *materials*, ampler, better, (worse also,) than previously known—eligible to be used to carry towards its crowning stage, and build for good, the great Ideal Nationality of the future, the Nation of the Body and the Soul,[1]—no limit here to land, help, opportunities, mines, products, demands, supplies, &c.;—with (I think) our political organization, National, State, and Municipal, permanently established, as far ahead as we can calculate—but, so far, no social, literary, religious, or esthetic organizations, consistent with our politics, or becoming to us—which organizations can only come, in time, through native schools or teachers of great Democratic Ideas, Religion—through Science, which now, like a new sunrise, ascending, begins to illuminate all—and through our own begotten Poets and Literatuses. . . . (The moral of a late well-written book on Civilization seems to be that the only real foundation walls and bases—and also *sine qua*

[1] The problems of the achievements of this crowning stage through future first-class National Singers, Orators, Artists, and others—of creating in literature an *imaginative* New World, the correspondent and counterpart of the current Scientific and Political New Worlds—and the perhaps distant, but still delightful prospect, (for our children, if not in our own day,) of delivering America, and, indeed, all Christian lands everywhere, from the thin moribund, and watery, but appallingly extensive nuisance of conventional poetry—by putting something really alive and substantial in its place—I have undertaken to grapple with, and argue, in DEMOCRATIC VISTAS.

non afterward—of true and full Civilization, is the eligibility and certainty of boundless products for feeding, clothing, sheltering every body— perennial fountains of physical and domestic comfort, with intercommun- ication, and with civil and ecclesiastical freedom;—and that then the esthetic and mental business will take care of itself. . . . Well, the United States have established this basis, and upon scales of extent, variety, vitality, and continuity, rivaling those of Nature; and have now to proceed to build an Edifice upon it. I say this Edifice is only to be fitly built by new Literatures, especially the poetic. I say a modern Image-Making creation is indispensable to fuse and express the modern Political and Scientific creations—and then the Trinity will be complete.)

When I commenced, years ago, elaborating the plan of my poems, and continued turning over that plan, and shifting it in my mind through many years, (from the age of twenty-eight to thirty-five,) experimenting much, and writing and abandoning much, one deep purpose underlay the others, and has underlain it and its execution ever since—and that has been the Religious purpose. Amid many changes, and a formulation taking far different shape from what I at first supposed, this basic purpose has never been departed from in the composition of my verses. Not of course to exhibit itself in the old ways, as in writing hymns or psalms with an eye to the church-pew, or to express conventional pietism, or the sickly yearnings of devotees, but in new ways, and aiming at the widest sub-bases and inclusions of Humanity, and tallying the fresh air of sea and land. I will see, (said I to myself,) whether there is not, for my purposes as poet, a Religion, and a sound Religious germenancy in the average Human Race, at least in their modern development in the United States, and in the hardy common fibre and native yearnings and elements, deeper and larger, and affording more profitable returns, than all mere sects or churches—as boundless, joyous, and vital as Nature itself—A germenancy that has too long been unencouraged, unsung, almost unknown. . . . With Science, the Old Theology of the East, long in its dotage, begins evidently to die and disappear. But (to my mind) Science—and may be such will prove its principal service—as evidently prepares the way for One indescribably grander—Time's young but perfect offspring—the New Theology—heir of the West—lusty and loving, and wondrous beautiful. For America, and for to-day, just the same as any day, the supreme and final Science is the Science of God—what we call science being only its minister—as Democracy is or shall be also. And a poet of America (I said) must fill himself with such thoughts, and chant his best out of them. . . . . . And as those were the convictions and aims, for good or bad, of LEAVES OF GRASS, they are no less the intention of this Volume. As there can be, in my opinion, no sane and complete Personality—nor any grand and electric

Nationality, without the stock element of Religion imbuing all the other elements, (like heat in chemistry, invisible itself, but the life of all visible life,) so there can be no Poetry worthy the name without that element behind all. . . . . . The time has certainly come to begin to discharge the idea of Religion, in the United States, from mere ecclesiasticism, and from Sundays and churches and church-going, and assign it to that general position, chiefest, most indispensable, most exhilarating, to which the others are to be adjusted, inside of all human character, and education, and affairs. The people, especially the young men and women of America, must begin to learn that Religion, (like Poetry,) is something far, far different from what they supposed. It is, indeed, too important to the power and perpetuity of the New World to be consigned any longer to the churches, old or new, Catholic or Protestant—Saint this, or Saint that. . . . It must be consigned henceforth to Democracy *en masse*, and to Literature. It must enter into the Poems of the Nation. It must make the Nation.

The Four Years' War is over—and in the peaceful, strong, exciting, fresh occasions of To-day, and of the Future, that strange, sad war is hurrying even now to be forgotten. The camp, the drill, the lines of sentries, the prisons, the hospitals,—(ah! the hospitals!)—all have passed away—all seem now like a dream. A new race, a young and lusty generation, already sweeps in with oceanic currents, obliterating the war, and all its scars, its mounded graves, and all its reminiscences of hatred, conflict, death. So let it be obliterated. I say the life of the present and the future makes undeniable demands upon us each and all, South, North, East, West. . . . To help put the United States (even if only in imagination) hand in hand, in one unbroken circle in a chant—To rouse them to the unprecedented grandeur of the part they are to play, and are even now playing—to the thought of their great Future, and the attitude conformed to it—especially their great Esthetic, Moral, Scientific Future, (of which their vulgar material and political present is but as the preparatory tuning of instruments by an orchestra,)—these, as hitherto, are still, for me, among my hopes, ambitions.

LEAVES OF GRASS, already published, is, in its intentions, the song of a great composite *Democratic Individual*, male or female. And following on and amplifying the same purpose, I suppose I have in my mind to run through the chants of this Volume, (if ever completed,) the thread-voice, more or less audible, of an aggregated, inseparable, unprecedented, vast, composite, electric *Democratic Nationality*.

Purposing, then, to still fill out, from time to time through years to come, the following Volume, (unless prevented,) I conclude this Preface to the first instalment of it, pencilled in the open air, on my fifty-third birth-day, by wafting to you, dear Reader, whoever you are, (from amid the fresh scent of the grass, the pleasant coolness of the forenoon breeze, the lights and shades of tree-boughs silently dappling and playing around me, and the notes of the cat-bird for undertone and accompaniment,) my true good-will and love.

Washington, D. C., May 31, 1872.   W. W.

Appendix A

Preface to Two Rivulets *(1876)*

AT the eleventh hour, under grave illness, I gather up the pieces of Prose and Poetry left over since publishing, a while since, my first and main Volume, LEAVES OF GRASS—pieces, here, some new, some old—nearly all of them (sombre as many are, making this almost Death's book) composed in by-gone atmospheres of perfect health—and, preceded by the freshest collection, the little TWO RIVULETS, and by this rambling Prefatory gossip,[2] now send them out, embodied in the present Melange, partly as my contribution and outpouring to celebrate, in some sort, the feature of the time, the first Centennial of our New World Nationality—and then as chyle and nutriment to that moral, Indissoluble Union, equally representing All, and the mother of many coming Centennials.

And e'en for flush and proof of our America—for reminder, just as much, or more, in moods of towering pride and joy, I keep my special chants of Death and Immortality[3] to stamp the coloring-finish of all,

---

[2] This Preface is not only for the present collection, but, in a sort, for all my writings, both Volumes.

[3] PASSAGE TO INDIA.—As in some ancient legend-play, to close the plot and the hero's career, there is a farewell gathering on ship's deck and on shore, a loosing of hawsers and ties, a spreading of sails to the wind—a starting out on unknown seas, to fetch up no one knows whither—to return no more—And the curtain falls, and there is the end of it—So I have reserv'd that Poem, with its cluster, to finish and explain much that, without them, would not be explain'd, and to take leave, and escape for good, from all that has preceded them. (Then probably *Passage to India*, and its cluster, are but freer vent and fuller expression to what, from the first, and so on throughout, more or less lurks in my writings, underneath every page, every line, every where.)

I am not sure but the last inclosing sublimation of Race or Poem is, What it thinks of Death. . . . . . . After the rest has been comprehended and said, even the grandest—After those contributions to mightiest Nationality, or to sweetest Song, or to the best Personalism,* male or female, have been glean'd from the rich and varied themes of tangible life, and have been fully accepted and sung, and the pervading fact of visible existence, with the duty it devolves, is rounded and apparently completed, it still remains to be really completed by suffusing through the whole and several, that other pervading invisible fact, so large a part, (is it not the largest part?) of life here, combining the rest, and furnishing, for Person or State, the only permanent and unitary meaning to all, even the meanest life, consistently with the dignity of the Universe, in Time. . . . . . As, from the eligibility to this thought, and the cheerful conquest of this fact, flash forth the first distinctive proofs of the Soul, so to me, (extending it only a little further,) the ultimate Democratic purports, the ethereal and spiritual ones, are to concentrate here, and as fixed stars, radiate hence. For, in my opinion, it is no less than this idea of Immortality, above all other ideas, that is to enter into, and vivify, and give crowning religious stamp, to Democracy in the New World.

It was originally my intention, after chanting in LEAVES OF GRASS the songs of the Body and Existence, to then compose a further, equally needed Volume, based on those

present and past. For terminus and temperer to all, they were originally written; and that shall be their office at the last.

convictions of perpetuity and conservation which, enveloping all precedents, make the unseen Soul govern absolutely at last. I meant, while in a sort continuing the theme of my first chants, to shift the slides, and exhibit the problem and paradox of the same ardent and fully appointed Personality entering the sphere of the resistless gravitation of Spiritual Law, and with cheerful face estimating Death, not at all as the cessation, but as somehow what I feel it must be, the entrance upon by far the greatest part of existence, and something that life is at least as much for, as it is for itself.

But the full construction of such a work (even if I lay the foundation, or give impetus to it) is beyond my powers, and must remain for some bard in the future. The physical and the sensuous, in themselves or in their immediate continuations, retain holds upon me which I think are never entirely releas'd; and those holds I have not only not denied, but hardly wish'd to weaken.

Meanwhile, not entirely to give the go-by to my original plan, and far more to avoid a mark'd hiatus in it, than to entirely fulfil it, I end my books with thoughts, or radiations from thoughts, on Death, Immortality, and a free entrance into the Spiritual world. In those thoughts, in a sort, I make the first steps or studies toward the mighty theme, from the point of view necessitated by my foregoing poems, and by Modern Science. In them I also seek to set the key-stone to my Democracy's enduring arch. I re-collate them now, for the press, (much the same, I transcribe my *Memoranda* following, of gloomy times out of the War, and Hospitals,) in order to partially occupy and offset days of strange sickness, and the heaviest affliction and bereavement of my life; and I fondly please myself with the notion of leaving that cluster to you, O unknown Reader of the future, as "something to remember me by," more especially than all else. Written in former days of perfect health, little did I think the pieces had the purport that now, under present circumstances, opens to me.

[As I write these lines, May 31, 1875, it is again early summer—again my birth-day—now my fifty-sixth. Amid the outside beauty and freshness, the sunlight and ver-dure of the delightful season, O how different the moral atmosphere amid which I now revise this Volume, from the jocund influences surrounding the growth and advent of LEAVES OF GRASS. I occupy myself, arranging these pages for publication, still envelopt in thoughts of the death two years since of my dear Mother, the most perfect and mag-netic character, the rarest combination of practical, moral and spiritual, and the least selfish, of all and any I have ever known—and by me O so much the most deeply loved. . . . . . . and also under the physical affliction of a tedious attack of paralysis, obstinately lingering and keeping its hold upon me, and quite suspending all bodily activity and comfort. . . . . . . I see now, much clearer than ever—perhaps these experi-ences were needed to show—how much my former poems, the bulk of them, are indeed the expression of health and strength, and sanest, joyfulest life.]

Under these influences, therefore, I still feel to keep *Passage to India* for last words even to this Centennial dithyramb. Not as, in antiquity, at highest festival of Egypt, the noi-some skeleton of Death was sent on exhibition to the revellers, for zest and shadow to the occasion's joy and light but as the perfect marble statue of the normal Greeks at Elis, suggesting death in the form of a beautiful and perfect young man, with closed eyes, leaning on an inverted torch—emblem of rest and aspiration after action—of crown and point which all lives and poems should steadily have reference to, namely, the justi-fied and noble termination of our identity, this grade of it, and outlet-preparation to another grade.

For some reason—not explainable or definite to my own mind, yet secretly pleasing and satisfactory to it—I have not hesitated to embody in, and run through the Volume, two altogether distinct veins, or strata—Politics for one, and for the other, the pensive thought of Immortality. Thus, too, the prose and poetic, the dual forms of the present book. . . . . . The pictures from the Hospitals during the War, in *Memoranda*,* I have also decided to include. Though they differ in character and composition from the rest of my pieces, yet I feel that they ought to go with them, and must do so. . . . . The present Volume, therefore, after its minor episodes, probably divides into these Two, at first sight far diverse, veins of topic and treatment. One will be found in the prose part of Two Rivulets, in *Democratic Vistas*, in the Preface to *As a Strong Bird*, and in the concluding Notes to *Memoranda* of the Hospitals. The other, wherein the all-engrossing thought and fact of Death is admitted (not for itself so much as a powerful factor in the adjustments of Life), in the realistic pictures of *Memoranda*, and the free speculations and ideal escapades of *Passage to India*.

Has not the time come, indeed, in the development of the New World, when its Politics should ascend into atmospheres and regions hitherto unknown—(far, far different from the miserable business that of late and current years passes under that name)—and take rank with Science, Philosophy and Art? . . . . Three points, in especial, have become very dear to me, and all through I seek to make them again and again, in many forms and repetitions, as will be seen: 1. That the true growth-characteristics of the Democracy of the New World are henceforth to radiate in superior Literary, Artistic and Religious Expressions, far more than in its Republican forms, universal suffrage, and frequent elections, (though these are unspeakably important). . . . . . 2. That the vital political mission of the United States is, to practically solve and settle the problem of two sets of rights—the fusion, thorough compatibility and junction of individual State prerogatives, with the indispensable necessity of centrality and Oneness—the national identity power—the sovereign Union, relentless, permanently comprising all, and over all, and in that never yielding an inch . . . . then 3d. Do we not, amid a general malaria of Fogs and Vapors, our day, unmistakably see two Pillars of Promise, with grandest, indestructible indications—One, that the morbid facts of American politics and society everywhere are but passing incidents and flanges of our unbounded impetus of growth—weeds, annuals, of the rank, rich soil—not central, enduring, perennial things? The Other, that all the hitherto experience of The States, their first Century, has been but preparation, adolescence—and that This Union is only now and henceforth, (*i.e.* since the Secession war,) to enter on its full Democratic career?

Of the whole, Poems and Prose, (not attending at all to chronological order, and with original dates and passing allusions in the heat and impression of the hour, left shuffled in, and undisturb'd,) the chants of LEAVES OF GRASS, my former Volume, yet serve as the indispensable deep soil, or basis, out of which, and out of which only, could come the roots and stems more definitely indicated by these later pages. (While that Volume radiates Physiology alone, the present One, though of the like origin in the main, more palpably doubtless shows the pathology which was pretty sure to come in time from the other.)

In that former and main volume, composed in the flush of my health and strength, from the age of 30 to 50 years, I dwelt on Birth and Life, clothing my ideas in pictures, days, transactions of my time, to give them positive place, identity—saturating them with that vehemence of pride and audacity of freedom necessary to loosen the mind of still-to-be-form'd America from the accumulated folds, the superstitions, and all the long, tenacious and stifling anti-democratic authorities of the Asiatic and European past—my enclosing purport being to express, above all artificial regulation and aid, the eternal Bodily Character of One's-Self.[4]

---

[4] LEAVES OF GRASS.—Namely, a Character, making most of common and normal elements, to the superstructure of which not only the precious accumulations of the learning and experiences of the Old World, and the settled social and municipal necessities and current requirements, so long a-building, shall still faithfully contribute, but which, at its foundations and carried up thence, and receiving its impetus from the Democratic spirit, and accepting its gauge, in all departments from the Democratic formulas, shall again directly be vitalized by the perennial influences of Nature at first hand, and the old heroic stamina of Nature, the strong air of prairie and mountain, the dash of the briny sea, the primary antiseptics—of the passions, in all their fullest heat and potency, of courage, rankness, amativeness, and of immense pride. . . . . . . Not to lose at all, therefore, the benefits of artificial progress and civilization, but to re-occupy for Western tenancy the oldest though ever-fresh fields, and reap from them the savage and sane nourishment indispensable to a hardy nation, and the absence of which, threatening to become worse and worse, is the most serious lack and defect to-day of our New World literature.

Not but what the brawn of LEAVES OF GRASS is, I think, thoroughly spiritualized everywhere, for final estimate, but, from the very subjects, the direct effect is a sense of the Life, as it should be, of flesh and blood, and physical urge, and animalism. . . . . . . While there are other themes, and plenty of abstract thoughts and poems in the Volume—While I have put in it (supplemented in the present Work by my prose *Memoranda*,) passing and rapid but actual glimpses of the great struggle between the Nation and the Slave-power, (1861–'65,) as the fierce and bloody panorama of that contest unroll'd itself—While the whole Book, indeed, revolves around that Four Years' War, which, as I was in the midst of it, becomes, in *Drum-Taps*, pivotal to the rest entire—follow'd by *Marches now the War is Over*—and here and there, before and afterward, not a few episodes and speculations—*that*—namely, to make a type-portrait for living, active, worldly, healthy Personality, objective as well as subjective, joyful and potent, and modern and free, distinctively for the use of the United States, male and female, through the long future—has been, I say,

The varieties and phases, (doubtless often paradoxical, contradictory,) of the two Volumes, of LEAVES, and of these RIVULETS, are ultimately to

my general object. (Probably, indeed, the whole of these varied songs, and all my writings, both Volumes, only ring changes in some sort, on the ejaculation, How vast, how eligible, how joyful, how real, is a Human Being, himself or herself.)

Though from no definite plan at the time, I see now that I have unconsciously sought, by indirections at least as much as directions, to express the whirls and rapid growth and intensity of the United States, the prevailing tendency and events of the Nineteenth Century, and largely the spirit of the whole current World, my time; for I feel that I have partaken of that spirit, as I have been deeply interested in all those events, the closing of longstretch'd eras and ages, and, illustrated in the history of the United States, the opening of larger ones. (The death of President Lincoln, for instance, fitly, historically closes, in the Civilization of Feudalism, many old influences—drops on them, suddenly, a vast, gloomy, as it were, separating curtain. The world's entire dramas afford none more indicative—none with folds more tragic, or more sombre or far spreading.)

Since I have been ill, (1873–74–75,) mostly without serious pain, and with plenty of time and frequent inclination to judge my poems, (never composed with eye on the book-market, nor for fame, nor for any pecuniary profit,) I have felt temporary depression more than once, for fear that in LEAVES OF GRASS the *moral* parts were not sufficiently pronounc'd. But in my clearest and calmest moods I have realized that as those LEAVES, all and several, surely prepare the way for, and necessitate Morals, and are adjusted to them, just the same as Nature does and is, they are what, consistently with my plan, they must and probably should be. . . . . . . (In a certain sense, while the Moral is the purport and last intelligence of all Nature, there is absolutely nothing of the moral in the works, or laws, or shows of Nature. Those only lead inevitably to it—begin and necessitate it.)

Then I meant LEAVES OF GRASS, as publish'd, to be the Poem of average Identity, (of *Yours*, whoever you are, now reading these lines). . . . . . For genius must realize that, precious as it may be, there is something far more precious, namely, simple Identity, One's-self. A man is not greatest as victor in war, nor inventor or explorer, nor even in science, or in his intellectual or artistic capacity, or exemplar in some vast benevolence. To the highest Democratic view, man is most acceptable in living well the average, practical life and lot which happens to him as ordinary farmer, sea-farer, mechanic, clerk, laborer, or driver—upon and from which position as a central basis or pedestal, while performing its labors, and his duties as citizen, son, husband, father and employ'd person, he preserves his physique, ascends, developing, radiating himself in other regions—and especially where and when, (greatest of all, and nobler than the proudest mere genius or magnate in any field,) he fully realizes the Conscience, the Spiritual, the divine faculty, cultivated well, exemplified in all his deeds and words, through life, uncompromising to the end— a flight loftier than any of Homer's or Shakspere's—broader than all poems and bibles—namely, Nature's own, and in the midst of it, Yourself, your own Identity, body and soul. (All serves, helps—but in the centre of all, absorbing all, giving, for your purpose, the only meaning and vitality to all, master or mistress of all, under the law, stands Yourself.). . . . . To sing the Song of that divine law of Identity, and of Yourself, consistently with the Divine Law of the Universal, is a main intention of those LEAVES.

Something more may be added—for, while I am about it, I would make a full confession. I also sent out LEAVES OF GRASS to arouse and set flowing in men's and women's hearts, young and old, (my present and future readers,) endless streams of living, pulsating love and friendship, directly from them to myself, now and ever. To this terrible, irrepressible yearning, (surely more or less down underneath in most human souls,)—this

be considered as One in structure, and as mutually explanatory of each other—as the multiplex results, like a tree, of series of successive growths, (yet from one central or seed-purport)—there having been five or six such cumulative issues, editions, commencing back in 1855 and thence progressing through twenty years down to date, (1875–76)—some things added or re-shaped from time to time, as they were found wanted, and other things represt. Of the former Book, more vehement, and perhaps pursuing a central idea with greater closeness—join'd with the present One, extremely varied in theme—I can only briefly reiterate here, that all my pieces, alternated through Both, are only of use and value, if any, as such an interpenetrating, composite, inseparable Unity.

Two of the pieces in this Volume were originally Public Recitations—the College Commencement Poem, *As a Strong Bird*—and then the *Song of the Exposition*, to identify these great Industrial gatherings, the majestic outgrowths of the Modern Spirit and Practice—and now fix'd upon, the grandest of them, for the Material event around which shall be concentrated and celebrated, (as far as any one event can combine them,) the associations and practical proofs of the Hundred Years' life of the Republic. The glory of Labor, and the bringing together not only representatives of all the trades and products, but, fraternally, of all the Workmen of all the Nations of the World, (for this is the Idea behind the Centennial at Philadelphia,)

never-satisfied appetite for sympathy, and this boundless offering of sympathy—this universal democratic comradeship—this old, eternal, yet ever-new interchange of adhesiveness, so fitly emblematic of America—I have given in that book, undisguisedly, declaredly, the openest expression . . . . Poetic literature has long been the formal and conventional tender of art and beauty merely, and of a narrow, constipated, special amativeness. I say, the subtlest, sweetest, surest tie between me and Him or Her, who, in the pages of *Calamus* and other pieces realizes me—though we never see each other, or though ages and ages hence—must, in this way, be personal affection. And those—be they few, or be they many—are at any rate *my readers*, in a sense that belongs not, and can never belong, to better, prouder poems.

Besides, important as they are in my purpose as emotional expressions for humanity, the special meaning of the *Calamus* cluster of LEAVES OF GRASS, (and more or less running through that book, and cropping out in *Drum-Taps,*) mainly resides in its Political significance. In my opinion it is by a fervent, accepted development of Comradeship, the beautiful and sane affection of man for man, latent in all the young fellows, North and South, East and West—it is by this, I say, and by what goes directly and indirectly along with it, that the United States of the future, (I cannot too often repeat,) are to be most effectually welded together, intercalated, anneal'd into a Living Union.

Then, for enclosing clue of all, it is imperatively and ever to be borne in mind that LEAVES OF GRASS entire is not to be construed as an intellectual or scholastic effort or Poem mainly, but more as a radical utterance out of the abysms of the Soul, the Emotions and the Physique—an utterance adjusted to, perhaps born of, Democracy and Modern Science, and in its very nature regardless of the old conventions, and, under the great Laws, following only its own impulses.

is, to me, so welcome and inspiring a theme, that I only wish I were a younger and a fresher man, to attempt the enduring Book, of poetic character, that ought to be written about it.

The arrangement in print of TWO RIVULETS—the indirectness of the name itself, (suggesting meanings, the start of other meanings, for the whole Volume)—are but parts of the Venture which my Poems entirely are. For really they have all been Experiments, under the urge of powerful, quite irresistible, perhaps wilful influences, (even escapades,) to see how such things will eventually turn out—and have been recited, as it were, by my Soul, to the special audience of Myself, far more than to the world's audience. Till now, by far the best part of the whole business is, that, these days, in leisure, in sickness and old age, my Spirit, by which they were written or permitted erewhile, does not go back on them, but still and in calmest hours, fully, deliberately allows them.

Estimating the American Union as so far and for some time to come, in its yet formative condition, I therefore bequeath Poems and Essays as nutriment and influences to help truly assimilate and harden, and especially to furnish something toward what The States most need of all, and which seems to me yet quite unsupplied in literature, namely, to show them, or begin to show them, Themselves distinctively, and what They are for. For though perhaps the main points of all ages and nations are points of resemblance, and, even while granting evolution, are substantially the same, there are some vital things in which this Republic, as to its individualities, and as a compacted Nation, is to specially stand forth, and culminate modern humanity. And these are the very things it least morally and mentally knows—(though, curiously enough, it is at the same time faithfully acting upon them.)

I count with such absolute certainty on the Great Future of The United States—different from, though founded on, the past—that I have always invoked that future, and surrounded myself with it, before or while singing my Songs. . . . (As ever, all tends to followings—America, too, is a prophecy. What, even of the best and most successful, would be justified by itself alone? by the present, or the material ostent alone? Of men or States, few realize how much they live in the future. That, rising like pinnacles, gives its main significance to all You and I are doing to-day. Without it, there were little meaning in lands or poems—little purport in human lives. . . . . . All ages, all Nations and States, have been such prophecies. But where any former ones with prophecy so broad, so clear, as our times, our lands—as those of the West?)

Without being a scientist, I have thoroughly adopted the conclusions of the great Savans and Experimentalists of our time, and of the last hundred years, and they have interiorly tinged the chyle of all my verse, for purposes beyond. Following the Modern Spirit, the real Poems of the Present, ever solidifying and expanding into the Future, must vocalize the vastness and splendor and reality with which Scientism has invested Man and the Universe, (all that is called Creation,) and must henceforth launch Humanity into new orbits, consonant with that vastness, splendor, and reality, (unknown to the old poems,) like new systems of orbs, balanced upon themselves, revolving in limitless space, more subtle than the stars. Poetry, so largely hitherto and even at present wedded to children's tales, and to mere amorousness, upholstery and superficial rhyme, will have to accept, and, while not denying the Past, nor the Themes of the past, will be revivified by this tremendous innovation, the Kosmic Spirit, which must henceforth, in my opinion, be the background and underlying impetus, more or less visible, of all first-class Songs.

Only, (for me, at any rate, in all my Prose and Poetry,) joyfully accepting Modern Science, and loyally following it without the slightest hesitation, there remains ever recognized still a higher flight, a higher fact, the Eternal Soul of Man, (of all Else too,) the Spiritual, the Religious—which it is to be the greatest office of Scientism, in my opinion, and of future Poetry also, to free from fables, crudities and superstitions, and launch forth in renew'd Faith and Scope a hundred fold. To me, the worlds of Religiousness, of the conception of the Divine, and of the Ideal, though mainly latent, are just as absolute in Humanity and the Universe as the world of Chemistry, or anything in the objective worlds.

To me,

> The Prophet and the Bard,
> Shall yet maintain themselves—in higher circles yet,
> Shall mediate to the Modern, to Democracy—interpret yet to them,
> God and Eidólons.

To me, the crown of Savantism is to be, that it surely opens the way for a more splendid Theology, and for ampler and diviner Songs. No year, nor even century, will settle this. There is a phase of the Real, lurking behind the Real, which it is all for. There is also in the Intellect of man, in time, far in prospective recesses, a judgment, a last appellate court, which will settle it.

In certain parts, in these flights, or attempting to depict or suggest them, I have not been afraid of the charge of obscurity, in either of my Two Volumes—because human thought, poetry or melody, must leave dim escapes and outlets—must possess a certain fluid, aerial character, akin to space itself, obscure to those of little or no imagination, but indispensable to the highest purposes. Poetic style, when address'd to the Soul, is less definite form, outline, sculpture, and becomes vista, music, half-tints, and even less than half-tints. True, it may be architecture; but again it may be the forest wild-wood, or the best effects thereof, at twilight, the waving oaks and cedars in the wind, and the impalpable odor.

Finally, as I have lived in fresh lands, inchoate, and in a revolutionary age, future-founding, I have felt to identify the points of that age, these lands, in my recitatives, altogether in my own way. Thus my form has strictly grown from my purports and facts, and is the analogy of them. . . . . . . Within my time the United States have emerg'd from nebulous vagueness and suspense, to full orbic, (though varied) decision—have done the deeds and achiev'd the triumphs of half a score of centuries—and are henceforth to enter upon their real history—the way being now, (i.e. since the result of the Secession War,) clear'd of death-threatening impedimenta, and the free areas around and ahead of us assured and certain, which were not so before—(the past century being but preparations, trial voyages and experiments of the Ship, before her starting out upon deep water.)

In estimating my Volumes, the world's current times and deeds, and their spirit, must be first profoundly estimated. Out of the Hundred Years just ending, (1776–1876,) with their genesis of inevitable wilful events, and new introductions, and many unprecedented things of war and peace, (to be realized better, perhaps only realized, at the remove of another Century hence)—Out of that stretch of time, and especially out of the immediately preceding Twenty-Five Years, (1850–75,) with all their rapid changes, innovations, and audacious movements—and bearing their own inevitable wilful birth-marks—my Poems too have found genesis.

W. W.

Preface to November Boughs *(1888)*

A BACKWARD GLANCE O'ER TRAVEL'D ROADS

PERHAPS the best of songs heard, or of any and all true love, or life's fairest episodes, or sailors', soldiers' trying scenes on land or sea, is the *résumé* of them, or any of them, long afterwards, looking at the actualities away back past, with all their practical excitations gone. How the soul loves to float amid such reminiscences!

So here I sit gossiping in the early candle-light of old age—I and my book—casting backward glances over our travel'd road. After completing, as it were, the journey—(a varied jaunt of years, with many halts and gaps of intervals—or some lengthen'd ship-voyage, wherein more than once the last hour had apparently arrived, and we seem'd certainly going down—yet reaching port in a sufficient way through all discomfitures at last)—After completing my poems, I am curious to review them in the light of their own (at the time unconscious, or mostly unconscious) intentions, with certain unfoldings of the thirty years they seek to embody. These lines, therefore, will probably blend the weft of first purposes and speculations, with the warp of that experience afterwards, always bringing strange developments.

Result of seven or eight stages and struggles extending through nearly thirty years, (as I nigh my three-score-and-ten I live largely on memory,) I look upon "Leaves of Grass," now finish'd to the end of its opportunities and powers, as my definitive *carte visite* to the coming generations of the New World,[5] if I may assume to say so. That I have not gain'd the acceptance of my own time, but have fallen back on fond dreams of the future—anticipations—("still lives the song, though Regnar dies")—That from a worldly and business point of view "Leaves of Grass" has been worse than a failure—that public criticism on the book and myself as author of it yet shows mark'd anger and contempt more than anything else—("I find a solid line of enemies to you everywhere,"—letter from W. S. K., Boston, May 28, 1884)—And that solely for publishing it I have been the object of two or three pretty serious special official buffetings—is all probably no more than I ought to have expected. I had my choice when I commenc'd. I bid neither for soft eulogies, big money returns, nor the approbation of existing schools and conventions. As fulfill'd, or partially fulfill'd, the best comfort of the whole business (after a small band of the dearest friends and upholders ever vouchsafed to man or cause—doubtless all the more faithful and uncompromising—this little phalanx!—for being so few) is

---

[5] When Champollion, on his death-bed, handed to the printer the revised proof of his "Egyptian Grammar," he said gayly, "Be careful of this—it is my *carte de visite* to posterity."

that, unstopp'd and unwarp'd by any influence outside the soul within me, I have had my say entirely my own way, and put it unerringly on record—the value thereof to be decided by time.

In calculating that decision, William O'Connor and Dr. Bucke* are far more peremptory than I am. Behind all else that can be said, I consider "Leaves of Grass" and its theory experimental—as, in the deepest sense, I consider our American republic itself to be, with its theory. (I think I have at least enough philosophy not to be too absolutely certain of any thing, or any results.) In the second place, the volume is a *sortie*—whether to prove triumphant, and conquer its field of aim and escape and construction, nothing less than a hundred years from now can fully answer. I consider the point that I have positively gain'd a hearing, to far more than make up for any and all other lacks and withholdings. Essentially, *that* was from the first, and has remain'd throughout, the main object. Now it seems to be achiev'd, I am certainly contented to waive any otherwise momentous drawbacks, as of little account. Candidly and dispassionately reviewing all my intentions, I feel that they were creditable—and I accept the result, whatever it may be.

After continued personal ambition and effort, as a young fellow, to enter with the rest into competition for the usual rewards, business, political, literary, &c.—to take part in the great *mêlée*, both for victory's prize itself and to do some good—After years of those aims and pursuits, I found myself remaining possess'd, at the age of thirty-one to thirty-three, with a special desire and conviction. Or rather, to be quite exact, a desire that had been flitting through my previous life, or hovering on the flanks, mostly indefinite hitherto, had steadily advanced to the front, defined itself, and finally dominated everything else. This was a feeling or ambition to articulate and faithfully express in literary or poetic form, and uncompromisingly, my own physical, emotional, moral, intellectual, and æsthetic Personality, in the midst of, and tallying, the momentous spirit and facts of its immediate days, and of current America—and to exploit that Personality, identified with place and date, in a far more candid and comprehensive sense than any hitherto poem or book.

Perhaps this is in brief, or suggests, all I have sought to do. Given the Nineteenth Century, with the United States, and what they furnish as area and points of view, "Leaves of Grass" is, or seeks to be, simply a faithful and doubtless self-will'd record. In the midst of all, it gives one man's—the author's—identity, ardors, observations, faiths, and thoughts, color'd hardly at all with any decided coloring from other faiths or other identities. Plenty of songs had been sung—beautiful, matchless songs—adjusted to other lands than these—another spirit and stage of evolution; but I would sing, and leave out or put in, quite solely with reference to America and to-day. Modern science and democracy seem'd to be throwing out their challenge to poetry to put them in its statements in contradistinction to the songs and myths of the past. As I see it now (perhaps too late,) I have unwittingly taken up that challenge and made an attempt at such statements—which I certainly would not assume to do now, knowing more clearly what it means.

For grounds for "Leaves of Grass," as a poem, I abandon'd the conventional themes, which do not appear in it: none of the stock ornamentation, or choice plots of love or war, or high, exceptional personages of Old-World song; nothing, as I may say, for beauty's sake—no legend, or myth, or romance, nor euphemism, nor rhyme. But the broadest average of humanity and its identities in the now ripening Nineteenth Century, and especially in each of their countless examples and practical occupations in the United States to-day.

One main contrast of the ideas behind every page of my verses, compared with establish'd poems, is their different relative attitude towards God, towards the objective universe, and still more (by reflection, confession, assumption, &c.) the quite changed attitude of the ego, the one chanting or talking, towards himself and towards his fellow-humanity. It is certainly time for America, above all, to begin this readjustment in the scope and basic point of view of verse; for everything else has changed. As I write, I see in an article on Wordsworth, in one of the current English magazines, the lines. "A few weeks ago an eminent French critic said that, owing to the special tendency to science and to its all-devouring force, poetry would cease to be read in fifty years." But I anticipate the very contrary. Only a firmer, vastly broader, new area begins to exist—nay, is already form'd—to which the poetic genius must emigrate. Whatever may have been the case in years gone by, the true use for the imaginative faculty of modern times is to give ultimate vivification to facts, to science, and to common lives, endowing them with the glows and glories and final illustriousness which belong to every real thing, and to real things only. Without that ultimate vivification—which the poet or other artist alone can give—reality would seem incomplete, and science, democracy, and life itself, finally in vain.

Few appreciate the moral revolutions, our age, which have been profounder far than the material or inventive or war-produced ones. The Nineteenth Century, now well towards its close (and ripening into fruit the seeds of the two preceding centuries[6])—the uprisings of national masses and shiftings of boundary-lines—the historical and other prominent facts of the United

---

[6] The ferment and germination even of the United States to-day, dating back to, and in my opinion mainly founded on, the Elizabethan age in English history, the age of Francis Bacon and Shakspere. Indeed, when we pursue it, what growth or advent is there

States—the war of attempted Secession—the stormy rush and haste of nebulous forces—never can future years witness more excitement and din of action—never completer change of army front along the whole line, the whole civilized world. For all these new and evolutionary facts, meanings, purposes, new poetic messages, new forms and expressions, are inevitable.

My Book and I—what a period we have presumed to span! those thirty years from 1850 to '80—and America in them! Proud, proud indeed may we be, if we have cull'd enough of that period in its own spirit to worthily waft a few live breaths of it to the future!

Let me not dare, here or anywhere, for my own purposes, or any purposes, to attempt the definition of Poetry, nor answer the question what it is. Like Religion, Love, Nature, while those terms are indispensable, and we all give a sufficiently accurate meaning to them, in my opinion no definition that has ever been made sufficiently encloses the name Poetry; nor can any rule or convention ever so absolutely obtain but some great exception may arise and disregard and overturn it.

Also it must be carefully remember'd that first-class literature does not shine by any luminosity of its own; nor do its poems. They grow of circumstances, and are evolutionary. The actual living light is always curiously from elsewhere—follows unaccountable sources, and is lunar and relative at the best. There are, I know, certain controling themes that seem endlessly appropriated to the poets—as war, in the past—in the Bible, religious rapture and adoration—always love, beauty, some fine plot, or pensive or other emotion. But, strange as it may sound at first, I will say there is something striking far deeper and towering far higher than those themes for the best elements of modern song.

Just as all the old imaginative works rest, after their kind, on long trains of presuppositions, often entirely unmention'd by themselves, yet supplying the most important bases of them, and without which they could have had no reason for being, so "Leaves of Grass," before a line was written, presupposed something different from any other, and, as it stands, is the result of such presupposition. I should say, indeed, it were useless to attempt reading the book without first carefully tallying that preparatory background and quality in the mind. Think of the United States to-day—the facts of these thirty-eight or forty empires solder'd in one—sixty or seventy millions of equals, with their lives, their passions, their future—these incalculable, modern, American, seething multitudes around us, of which we are inseparable parts! Think, in comparison, of the petty environage and limited area of the poets of past or present Europe, no matter how

---

that does not date back, back, until lost—perhaps its most tantalizing clues lost—in the receded horizons of the past?

great their genius. Think of the absence and ignorance, in all cases hitherto, of the multitudinousness, vitality, and the unprecedented stimulants of to-day and here. It almost seems as if a poetry with cosmic and dynamic features of magnitude and limitlessness suitable to the human soul, were never possible before. It is certain that a poetry of absolute faith and equality for the use of the democratic masses never was.

In estimating first-class song, a sufficient Nationality, or, on the other hand, what may be call'd the negative and lack of it, (as in Goethe's case, it sometimes seems to me,) is often, if not always, the first element. One needs only a little penetration to see, at more or less removes, the material facts of their country and radius, with the coloring of the moods of humanity at the time, and its gloomy or hopeful prospects, behind all poets and each poet, and forming their birth-marks. I know very well that my "Leaves" could not possibly have emerged or been fashion'd or completed, from any other era than the latter half of the Nineteenth Century, nor any other land than democratic America, and from the absolute triumph of the National Union arms.

And whether my friends claim it for me or not, I know well enough, too, that in respect to pictorial talent, dramatic situations, and especially in verbal melody and all the conventional technique of poetry, not only the divine works that to-day stand ahead in the world's reading, but dozens more, transcend (some of them immeasurably transcend) all I have done, or could do. But it seem'd to me, as the objects in Nature, the themes of æstheticism, and all special exploitations of the mind and soul, involve not only their own inherent quality, but the quality, just as inherent and important, of *their point of view*,[7] the time had come to reflect all themes and things, old and new, in the lights thrown on them by the advent of America and democracy—to chant those themes through the utterance of one, not only the grateful and reverent legatee of the past, but the born child of the New World—to illustrate all through the genesis and ensemble of to-day; and that such illustration and ensemble are the chief demands of America's prospective imaginative literature. Not to carry out, in the approved style, some choice plot of fortune or misfortune, or fancy, or fine thoughts, or incidents, or courtesies—all of which has been done overwhelmingly and well, probably never to be excell'd—but that while in such æsthetic presentation of objects, passions, plots, thoughts, &c., our lands and days do not want, and probably will never have, anything better than they already possess from the bequests of the past, it still remains to be said that there is even towards all those a subjective and contemporary

[7] According to Immanuel Kant, the last essential reality, giving shape and significance to all the rest.

point of view appropriate to ourselves alone, and to our new genius and environments, different from anything hitherto; and that such conception of current or gone-by life and art is for us the only means of their assimilation consistent with the Western world.

Indeed, and anyhow, to put it specifically, has not the time arrived when, (if it must be plainly said, for democratic America's sake, if for no other) there must imperatively come a readjustment of the whole theory and nature of Poetry? The question is important, and I may turn the argument over and repeat it: Does not the best thought of our day and Republic conceive of a birth and spirit of song superior to anything past or present? To the effectual and moral consolidation of our lands (already, as materially establish'd, the greatest factors in known history, and far, far greater through what they prelude and necessitate, and are to be in future)—to conform with and build on the concrete realities and theories of the universe furnish'd by science, and henceforth the only irrefragable basis for anything, verse included—to root both influences in the emotional and imaginative action of the modern time, and dominate all that precedes or opposes them—is not either a radical advance and step forward, or a new verteber of the best song indispensable?

The New World receives with joy the poems of the antique, with European feudalism's rich fund of epics, plays, ballads—seeks not in the least to deaden or displace those voices from our ear and area—holds them indeed as indispensable studies, influences, records, comparisons. But though the dawn-dazzle of the sun of literature is in those poems for us of to-day—though perhaps the best parts of current character in nations, social groups, or any man's or woman's individuality, Old World or New, are from them—and though if I were ask'd to name the most precious bequest to current American civilization from all the hitherto ages, I am not sure but I would name those old and less old songs ferried hither from east and west—some serious words and debits remain; some acrid considerations demand a hearing. Of the great poems receiv'd from abroad and from the ages, and to-day enveloping and penetrating America, is there one that is consistent with these United States, or essentially applicable to them as they are and are to be? Is there one whose underlying basis is not a denial and insult to democracy? What a comment it forms, anyhow, on this era of literary fulfilment, with the splendid day rise of science and resuscitation of history, that our chief religious and poetical works are not our own nor adapted to our light, but have been furnish'd by far-back ages out of their arriere and darkness, or, at most, twilight dimness! What is there in those works that so imperiously and scornfully dominates all our advanced civilization, and culture?

Even Shakspere, who so suffuses current letters and art (which indeed have in most degrees grown out of him,) belongs essentially to the buried past. Only he holds the proud distinction for certain important phases of that past, of being the loftiest of the singers life has yet given voice to. All, however, relate to and rest upon conditions, standards, politics, sociologies, ranges of belief, that have been quite eliminated from the Eastern hemisphere, and never existed at all in the Western. As authoritative types of song they belong in America just about as much as the persons and institutes they depict. True, it may be said, the emotional, moral, and æsthetic natures of humanity have not radically changed—that in these the old poems apply to our times and all times, irrespective of date; and that they are of incalculable value as pictures of the past. I willingly make those admissions, and to their fullest extent; then advance the points herewith as of serious, even paramount importance.

I have indeed put on record elsewhere my reverence and eulogy for those never-to-be-excell'd poetic bequests, and their indescribable preciousness as heirlooms for America. Another and separate point must now be candidly stated. If I had not stood before those poems with uncover'd head, fully aware of their colossal grandeur and beauty of form and spirit, I could not have written "Leaves of Grass." My verdict and conclusions as illustrated in its pages are arrived at through the temper and inculcation of the old works as much as through anything else—perhaps more than through anything else. As America fully and fairly construed is the legitimate result and evolutionary outcome of the past, so I would dare to claim for my verse. Without stopping to qualify the averment, the Old World has had the poems of myths, fictions, feudalism, conquest, caste, dynastic wars, and splendid exceptional characters and affairs, which have been great; but the New World needs the poems of realities and science and of the democratic average and basic equality, which shall be greater. In the centre of all, and object of all, stands the Human Being, towards whose heroic and spiritual evolution poems and everything directly or indirectly tend, Old World or New.

Continuing the subject, my friends have more than once suggested—or may be the garrulity of advancing age is possessing me—some further embryonic facts of "Leaves of Grass," and especially how I enter'd upon them. Dr. Bucke has, in his volume, already fully and fairly described the preparation of my poetic field, with the particular and general plowing, planting, seeding, and occupation of the ground, till everything was fertilized, rooted, and ready to start its own way for good or bad. Not till after all this, did I attempt any serious acquaintance with poetic literature. Along in my sixteenth year I had become possessor of a stout, well-cramm'd one thousand page octavo volume (I have it yet,) containing Walter Scott's poetry entire—an inexhaustible mine and treasury of poetic forage (especially the endless forests and jungles of notes)—has been so to me for fifty years, and remains so to this day.[8]

Later, at intervals, summers and falls, I used to go off, sometimes for a week at a stretch, down in the country, or to Long Island's seashores—there, in the presence of outdoor influences, I went over thoroughly the Old and New Testaments, and absorb'd (probably to better advantage for me than in any library or indoor room—it makes such difference *where* you read,) Shakspere, Ossian, the best translated versions I could get of Homer, Eschylus, Sophocles, the old German Nibelungen, the ancient Hindoo poems, and one or two other masterpieces, Dante's among them. As it happen'd, I read the latter mostly in an old wood. The Iliad (Buckley's prose version,) I read first thoroughly on the peninsula of Orient, northeast end of Long Island, in a shelter'd hollow of rocks and sand, with the sea on each side. (I have wonder'd since why I was not overwhelm'd by those mighty masters. Likely because I read them, as described, in the full presence of Nature, under the sun, with the far-spreading landscape and vistas, or the sea rolling in.)

Toward the last I had among much else look'd over Edgar Poe's poems—of which I was not an admirer, tho' I always saw that beyond their limited range of melody (like perpetual chimes of music bells, ringing from lower *b* flat up to *g*) they were melodious expressions, and perhaps never excell'd ones, of certain pronounc'd phases of human morbidity. (The Poetic area is very spacious—has room for all—has so many mansions!) But I was repaid in Poe's prose by the idea that (at any rate for our occasions, our day) there can be no such thing as a long poem. The same thought had been haunting my mind before, but Poe's argument, though short, work'd the sum out and proved it to me.

Another point had an early settlement, clearing the ground greatly. I saw, from the time my enterprise and questionings positively shaped themselves (how best can I express my own distinctive era and surroundings, America, Democracy?) that the trunk and centre whence the answer was to

---

[8] Sir Walter Scott's COMPLETE POEMS; especially including BORDER MINSTRELSY; then Sir Tristrem; Lay of the Last Minstrel; Ballads from the German; Marmion; Lady of the Lake; Vision of Don Roderick; Lord of the Isles; Rokeby; Bridal of Triermain; Field of Waterloo; Harold the Dauntless; all the Dramas; various Introductions, endless interesting Notes, and Essays on Poetry, Romance, &c.

Lockhart's 1833 (or '34) edition with Scott's latest and copious revisions and annotations. (All the poems were thoroughly read by me, but the ballads of the Border Minstrelsy over and over again.)

radiate, and to which all should return from straying however far a distance, must be an identical body and soul, a personality—which personality, after many considerations and ponderings I deliberately settled should be myself—indeed could not be any other. I also felt strongly (whether I have shown it or not) that to the true and full estimate of the Present both the Past and the Future are main considerations.

These, however, and much more might have gone on and come to naught (almost positively would have come to naught,) if a sudden, vast, terrible, direct and indirect stimulus for new and national declamatory expression had not been given to me. It is certain, I say, that, although I had made a start before, only from the occurrence of the Secession War, and what it show'd me as by flashes of lightning, with the emotional depths it sounded and arous'd (of course, I don't mean in my own heart only, I saw it just as plainly in others, in millions)—that only from the strong flare and provocation of that war's sights and scenes the final reasons-for-being of an autochthonic and passionate song definitely came forth.

I went down to the war fields in Virginia (end of 1862), lived thenceforward in camp—saw great battles and the days and nights afterward—partook of all the fluctuations, gloom, despair, hopes again arous'd, courage evoked—death readily risk'd—*the cause*, too—along and filling those agonistic and lurid following years, 1863-'64-'65—the real parturition years (more than 1776-'83) of this henceforth homogeneous Union. Without those three or four years and the experiences they gave, "Leaves of Grass" would not now be existing.

But I set out with the intention also of indicating or hinting some point-characteristics which I since see (though I did not then, at least not definitely) were bases and object-urgings toward those "Leaves" from the first. The word I myself put primarily for the description of them as they stand at last, is the word Suggestiveness. I round and finish little, if anything; and could not, consistently with my scheme. The reader will always have his or her part to do, just as much as I have had mine. I seek less to state or display any theme or thought, and more to bring you, reader, into the atmosphere of the theme or thought—there to pursue your own flight. Another impetus-word is Comradeship as for all lands, and in a more commanding and acknowledg'd sense than hitherto. Other word-signs would be Good Cheer, Content, and Hope.

The chief trait of any given poet is always the spirit he brings to the observation of Humanity and Nature—the mood out of which he contemplates his subjects. What kind of temper and what amount of faith report these things? Up to how recent a date is the song carried? What the equipment, and special raciness of the singer—what his tinge of coloring?

The last value of artistic expressers, past and present—Greek æsthetes, Shakspere—or in our own day Tennyson, Victor Hugo, Carlyle, Emerson—is certainly involv'd in such questions. I say the profoundest service that poems or any other writings can do for their reader is not merely to satisfy the intellect, or supply something polish'd and interesting, nor even to depict great passions, or persons or events, but to fill him with vigorous and clean manliness, religiousness, and give him *good heart* as a radical possession and habit. The educated world seems to have been growing more and more ennuyed for ages, leaving to our time the inheritance of it all. Fortunately there is the original inexhaustible fund of buoyancy, normally resident in the race, forever eligible to be appeal'd to and relied on.

As for native American individuality, though certain to come, and on a large scale, the distinctive and ideal type of Western character (as consistent with the operative political and even money-making features of United States' humanity in the Nineteenth Century as chosen knights, gentlemen and warriors were the ideals of the centuries of European feudalism) it has not yet appear'd. I have allow'd the stress of my poems from beginning to end to bear upon American individuality and assist it—not only because that is a great lesson in Nature, amid all her generalizing laws, but as counterpoise to the leveling tendencies of Democracy—and for other reasons. Defiant of ostensible literary and other conventions, I avowedly chant "the great pride of man in himself," and permit it to be more or less a *motif* of nearly all my verse. I think this pride indispensable to an American. I think it not inconsistent with obedience, humility, deference, and self-questioning.

Democracy has been so retarded and jeopardized by powerful personalities, that its first instincts are fain to clip, conform, bring in stragglers, and reduce everything to a dead level. While the ambitious thought of my song is to help the forming of a great aggregate Nation, it is, perhaps, altogether through the forming of myriads of fully develop'd and enclosing individuals. Welcome as are equality's and fraternity's doctrines and popular education, a certain liability accompanies them all, as we see. That primal and interior something in man, in his soul's abysms, coloring all, and, by exceptional fruitions, giving the last majesty to him—something continually touch'd upon and attain'd by the old poems and ballads of feudalism, and often the principal foundation of them—modern science and democracy appear to be endangering, perhaps eliminating. But that forms an appearance only; the reality is quite different. The new influences, upon the whole, are surely preparing the way for grander individualities than ever. To-day and here personal force is behind everything just the same. The times and depictions from the Iliad to Shakspere inclusive can happily never again be realized— but the elements of courageous and lofty manhood are unchanged.

Without yielding an inch the working-man and working-woman were to be in my pages from first to last. The ranges of heroism and loftiness with which Greek and feudal poets endow'd their god-like or lordly born characters—indeed prouder and better based and with fuller ranges than those—I was to endow the democratic averages of America. I was to show that we, here and to-day, are eligible to the grandest and the best—more eligible now than any times of old were. I will also want my utterances (I said to myself before beginning) to be in spirit the poems of the morning. (They have been founded and mainly written in the sunny forenoon and early midday of my life.) I will want them to be the poems of women entirely as much as men. I have wish'd to put the complete Union of the States in my songs without any preference or partiality whatever. Henceforth, if they live and are read, it must be just as much South as North—just as much along the Pacific as Atlantic—in the valley of the Mississippi, in Canada, up in Maine, down in Texas, and on the shores of Puget Sound.

From another point of view "Leaves of Grass" is avowedly the song of Sex and Amativeness, and even Animality—though meanings that do not usually go along with those words are behind all, and will duly emerge; and all are sought to be lifted into a different light and atmosphere. Of this feature, intentionally palpable in a few lines, I shall only say the espousing principle of those lines so gives breath of life to my whole scheme that the bulk of the pieces might as well have been left unwritten were those lines omitted. Difficult as it will be, it has become, in my opinion, imperative to achieve a shifted attitude from superior men and women towards the thought and fact of sexuality, as an element in character, personality, the emotions, and a theme in literature. I am not going to argue the question by itself; it does not stand by itself. The vitality of it is altogether in its relations, bearings, significance—like the clef of a symphony. At last analogy the lines I allude to, and the spirit in which they are spoken, permeate all "Leaves of Grass," and the work must stand or fall with them, as the human body and soul must remain as an entirety.

Universal as are certain facts and symptoms of communities or individuals all times, there is nothing so rare in modern conventions and poetry as their normal recognizance. Literature is always calling in the doctor for consultation and confession, and always giving evasions and swathing suppressions in place of that "heroic nudity"[9] on which only a genuine diagnosis of serious cases can be built. And in respect to editions of "Leaves of Grass" in time to come (if there should be such) I take occasion now to confirm those lines with the settled convictions and

[9] "Nineteenth Century," July, 1883.

deliberate renewals of thirty years, and to hereby prohibit, as far as word of mine can do so, any elision of them.

Then still a purpose enclosing all, and over and beneath all. Ever since what might be call'd thought, or the budding of thought, fairly began in my youthful mind, I had had a desire to attempt some worthy record of that entire faith and acceptance ("to justify the ways of God to man" is Milton's well-known and ambitious phrase) which is the foundation of moral America. I felt it all as positively then in my young days as I do now in my old ones; to formulate a poem whose every thought or fact should directly or indirectly be or connive at an implicit belief in the wisdom, health, mystery, beauty of every process, every concrete object, every human or other existence, not only consider'd from the point of view of all, but of each.

While I can not understand it or argue it out, I fully believe in a clue and purpose in Nature, entire and several; and that invisible spiritual results, just as real and definite as the visible, eventuate all concrete life and all materialism, through Time. My book ought to emanate buoyancy and gladness legitimately enough, for it was grown out of those elements, and has been the comfort of my life since it was originally commenced.

One main genesis-motive of the "Leaves" was my conviction (just as strong to-day as ever) that the crowning growth of the United States is to be spiritual and heroic. To help start and favor that growth—or even to call attention to it, or the need of it—is the beginning, middle and final purpose of the poems. (In fact, when really cipher'd out and summ'd to the last, plowing up in earnest the interminable average fallows of humanity—not "good government" merely, in the common sense—is the justification and main purpose of these United States.)

Isolated advantages in any rank or grace or fortune—the direct or indirect threads of all the poetry of the past—are in my opinion distasteful to the republican genius, and offer no foundation for its fitting verse. Establish'd poems, I know, have the very great advantage of chanting the already perform'd, so full of glories, reminiscences dear to the minds of men. But my volume is a candidate for the future. "All original art," says Taine, anyhow, "is self-regulated, and no original art can be regulated from without; it carries its own counterpoise, and does not receive it from elsewhere—lives on its own blood"—a solace to my frequent bruises and sulky vanity.

As the present is perhaps mainly an attempt at personal statement or illustration, I will allow myself as further help to extract the following anecdote from a book, "Annals of Old Painters," conn'd by me in youth. Rubens, the Flemish painter, in one of his wanderings through the galleries of old convents, came across a singular work. After looking at it thoughtfully for a good while, and listening to the criticisms of his suite of students, he said to the latter, in answer to their questions (as to what school the work implied or belong'd,) "I do not believe the artist, unknown and perhaps no longer living, who has given the world this legacy, ever belong'd to any school, or ever painted anything but this one picture, which is a personal affair—a piece out of a man's life."

"Leaves of Grass" indeed (I cannot too often reiterate) has mainly been the outcropping of my own emotional and other personal nature—an attempt, from first to last, to put *a Person*, a human being (myself, in the latter half of the Nineteenth Century, in America,) freely, fully and truly on record. I could not find any similar personal record in current literature that satisfied me. But it is not on "Leaves of Grass" distinctively as *literature*, or a specimen thereof, that I feel to dwell, or advance claims. No one will get at my verses who insists upon viewing them as a literary performance, or attempt at such performance, or as aiming mainly toward art or æstheticism.

I say no land or people or circumstances ever existed so needing a race of singers and poems differing from all others, and rigidly their own, as the land and people and circumstances of our United States need such singers and poems to-day, and for the future. Still further, as long as the States continue to absorb and be dominated by the poetry of the Old World, and remain unsupplied with autochthonous song, to express, vitalize and give color to and define their material and political success, and minister to them distinctively, so long will they stop short of first-class Nationality and remain defective.

In the free evening of my day I give to you, reader, the foregoing garrulous talk, thoughts, reminiscences,

> As idly drifting down the ebb,
> Such ripples, half-caught voices, echo from the shore.

Concluding with two items for the imaginative genius of the West, when it worthily rises—First, what Herder taught to the young Goethe, that really great poetry is always (like the Homeric or Biblical canticles) the result of a national spirit, and not the privilege of a polish'd and select few; Second, that the strongest and sweetest songs yet remain to be sung.

Song of Myself

1

I CELEBRATE myself, and sing myself,
And what I assume you shall assume,
For every atom belonging to me as good belongs to you.

I loafe and invite my soul,
I lean and loafe at my ease observing a spear of summer grass.

My tongue, every atom of my blood, form'd from this soil, this
    air,
Born here of parents born here from parents the same, and their
    parents the same,
I, now thirty-seven years old in perfect health begin,
Hoping to cease not till death.

Creeds and schools in abeyance,
Retiring back a while sufficed at what they are, but never forgotten,
I harbor for good or bad, I permit to speak at every hazard,
Nature without check with original energy.

2

Houses and rooms are full of perfumes, the shelves are crowded
    with perfumes,
I breathe the fragrance myself and know it and like it,
The distillation would intoxicate me also, but I shall not let it.

The atmosphere is not a perfume, it has no taste of the distillation,
    it is odorless,
It is for my mouth forever, I am in love with it,

I will go to the bank by the wood and become undisguised and
    naked,
I am mad for it to be in contact with me.

The smoke of my own breath,
Echoes, ripples, buzz'd whispers, love-root, silk-thread, crotch and
    vine,
My respiration and inspiration, the beating of my heart, the pass-
    ing of blood and air through my lungs,
The sniff of green leaves and dry leaves, and of the shore and
    dark-color'd sea-rocks, and of hay in the barn,
The sound of the belch'd words of my voice loos'd to the eddies
    of the wind,
A few light kisses, a few embraces, a reaching around of arms,
The play of shine and shade on the trees as the supple boughs
    wag,
The delight alone or in the rush of the streets, or along the fields
    and hill-sides,
The feeling of health, the full-noon trill, the song of me rising from
    bed and meeting the sun.

Have you reckon'd a thousand acres much? have you reckon'd
    the earth much?
Have you practis'd so long to learn to read?
Have you felt so proud to get at the meaning of poems?

Stop this day and night with me and you shall possess the origin
    of all poems,
You shall possess the good of the earth and sun, (there are millions
    of suns left,)
You shall no longer take things at second or third hand, nor look
    through the eyes of the dead, nor feed on the spectres in
    books,
You shall not look through my eyes either, nor take things from me,
You shall listen to all sides and filter them from your self.

3

I have heard what the talkers were talking, the talk of the begin-
    ning and the end,
But I do not talk of the beginning or the end.

There was never any more inception than there is now,
Nor any more youth or age than there is now,
And will never be any more perfection than there is now,
Nor any more heaven or hell than there is now.

Urge and urge and urge,
Always the procreant urge of the world.

Out of the dimness opposite equals advance, always substance and
    increase, always sex,
Always a knit of identity, always distinction, always a breed of life.

To elaborate is no avail, learn'd and unlearn'd feel that it is so.

Sure as the most certain sure, plumb in the uprights, well entretied,
    braced in the beams,
Stout as a horse, affectionate, haughty, electrical,
I and this mystery here we stand.

Clear and sweet is my soul, and clear and sweet is all that is not
    my soul.

Lack one lacks both, and the unseen is proved by the seen,
Till that becomes unseen and receives proof in its turn.

Showing the best and dividing it from the worst age vexes age,
Knowing the perfect fitness and equanimity of things, while they
    discuss I am silent, and go bathe and admire myself.

Welcome is every organ and attribute of me, and of any man
    hearty and clean,
Not an inch nor a particle of an inch is vile, and none shall be
    less familiar than the rest.

I am satisfied—I see, dance, laugh, sing;
As the hugging and loving bed-fellow sleeps at my side through
    the night, and withdraws at the peep of the day with
    stealthy tread,

Leaving me baskets cover'd with white towels swelling the house
    with their plenty,
Shall I postpone my acceptation and realization and scream at my
    eyes,
That they turn from gazing after and down the road,
And forthwith cipher and show me to a cent,
Exactly the value of one and exactly the value of two, and which
    is ahead?

4

Trippers and askers surround me,
People I meet, the effect upon me of my early life or the ward
    and city I live in, or the nation,
The latest dates, discoveries, inventions, societies, authors old and
    new,
My dinner, dress, associates, looks, compliments, dues,
The real or fancied indifference of some man or woman I love,
The sickness of one of my folks or of myself, or ill-doing or loss or
    lack of money, or depressions or exaltations,
Battles, the horrors of fratricidal war, the fever of doubtful news,
    the fitful events;
These come to me days and nights and go from me again,
But they are not the Me myself.

Apart from the pulling and hauling stands what I am,
Stands amused, complacent, compassionating, idle, unitary,
Looks down, is erect, or bends an arm on an impalpable certain
    rest,
Looking with side-curved head curious what will come next,
Both in and out of the game and watching and wondering at it.

Backward I see in my own days where I sweated through fog with
    linguists and contenders,
I have no mockings or arguments, I witness and wait.

5

I believe in you my soul, the other I am must not abase itself to you,
And you must not be abased to the other.

Loafe with me on the grass, loose the stop from your throat,
Not words, not music or rhyme I want, not custom or lecture, not
    even the best,
Only the lull I like, the hum of your valvèd voice.

I mind how once we lay such a transparent summer morning,
How you settled your head athwart my hips and gently turn'd over
    upon me,
And parted the shirt from my bosom-bone, and plunged your
    tongue to my bare-stript heart,
And reach'd till you felt my beard, and reach'd till you held my
    feet.

Swiftly arose and spread around me the peace and knowledge that
    pass all the argument of the earth,
And I know that the hand of God is the promise of my own,
And I know that the spirit of God is the brother of my own,
And that all the men ever born are also my brothers, and the
    women my sisters and lovers,
And that a kelson of the creation is love,
And limitless are leaves stiff or drooping in the fields,
And brown ants in the little wells beneath them,
And mossy scabs of the worm fence, heap'd stones, elder, mullein
    and poke-weed.

6

A child said *What is the grass?* fetching it to me with full hands;
How could I answer the child? I do not know what it is any
    more than he.

I guess it must be the flag of my disposition, out of hopeful green
    stuff woven.

Or I guess it is the handkerchief of the Lord,
A scented gift and remembrancer designedly dropt,
Bearing the owner's name someway in the corners, that we may
    see and remark, and say *Whose?*

Or I guess the grass is itself a child, the produced babe of the
    vegetation.

Or I guess it is a uniform hieroglyphic,
And it means, Sprouting alike in broad zones and narrow zones,
Growing among black folks as among white,
Kanuck, Tuckahoe, Congressman, Cuff, I give them the same,
    I receive them the same.

And now it seems to me the beautiful uncut hair of graves.

Tenderly will I use you curling grass,
It may be you transpire from the breasts of young men,
It may be if I had known them I would have loved them,
It may be you are from old people, or from offspring taken soon
    out of their mothers' laps,
And here you are the mothers' laps.

This grass is very dark to be from the white heads of old mothers,
Darker than the colorless beards of old men,
Dark to come from under the faint red roofs of mouths.

O I perceive after all so many uttering tongues,
And I perceive they do not come from the roofs of mouths for
    nothing.

I wish I could translate the hints about the dead young men and
    women,
And the hints about old men and mothers, and the offspring taken
    soon out of their laps.

What do you think has become of the young and old men?
And what do you think has become of the women and chil-
    dren?

They are alive and well somewhere,
The smallest sprout shows there is really no death,
And if ever there was it led forward life, and does not wait at the
    end to arrest it,
And ceas'd the moment life appear'd.

All goes onward and outward, nothing collapses,
And to die is different from what any one supposed, and luckier.

7

Has any one supposed it lucky to be born?
I hasten to inform him or her it is just as lucky to die, and I
    know it.

I pass death with the dying and birth with the new-wash'd babe,
    and am not contain'd between my hat and boots,
And peruse manifold objects, no two alike and every one good,
The earth good and the stars good, and their adjuncts all good.

I am not an earth nor an adjunct of an earth,
I am the mate and companion of people, all just as immortal and
    fathomless as myself,
(They do not know how immortal, but I know.)

Every kind for itself and its own, for me mine male and female,
For me those that have been boys and that love women,
For me the man that is proud and feels how it stings to be
    slighted,
For me the sweet-heart and the old maid, for me mothers and the
    mothers of mothers,
For me lips that have smiled, eyes that have shed tears,
For me children and the begetters of children.

Undrape! you are not guilty to me, nor stale nor discarded,
I see through the broadcloth and gingham whether or no,
And am around, tenacious, acquisitive, tireless, and cannot be
    shaken away.

8

The little one sleeps in its cradle,
I lift the gauze and look a long time, and silently brush away flies
    with my hand.

The youngster and the red-faced girl turn aside up the bushy hill,
I peeringly view them from the top.

The suicide sprawls on the bloody floor of the bedroom,
I witness the corpse with its dabbled hair, I note where the pistol
    has fallen.

The blab of the pave, tires of carts, sluff of boot-soles, talk of the
      promenaders,
The heavy omnibus, the driver with his interrogating thumb, the
      clank of the shod horses on the granite floor,
The snow-sleighs, clinking, shouted jokes, pelts of snow-balls,
The hurrahs for popular favorites, the fury of rous'd mobs,
The flap of the curtain'd litter, a sick man inside borne to the
      hospital,
The meeting of enemies, the sudden oath, the blows and fall,
The excited crowd, the policeman with his star quickly working
      his passage to the centre of the crowd,
The impassive stones that receive and return so many echoes,
What groans of over-fed or half-starv'd who fall sunstruck or in
      fits,
What exclamations of women taken suddenly who hurry home and
      give birth to babes,
What living and buried speech is always vibrating here, what howls
      restrain'd by decorum,
Arrests of criminals, slights, adulterous offers made, acceptances,
      rejections with convex lips,
I mind them or the show or resonance of them—I come and I
      depart.

9

The big doors of the country barn stand open and ready,
The dried grass of the harvest-time loads the slow-drawn wagon,
The clear light plays on the brown gray and green intertinged,
The armfuls are pack'd to the sagging mow.

I am there, I help, I came stretch'd atop of the load,
I felt its soft jolts, one leg reclined on the other,
I jump from the cross-beams and seize the clover and timothy,
And roll head over heels and tangle my hair full of wisps.

10

Alone far in the wilds and mountains I hunt,
Wandering amazed at my own lightness and glee,
In the late afternoon choosing a safe spot to pass the night,
Kindling a fire and broiling the fresh-kill'd game,

Falling asleep on the gather'd leaves with my dog and gun by my
    side.

The Yankee clipper is under her sky-sails, she cuts the sparkle and
    scud,
My eyes settle the land, I bend at her prow or shout joyously from
    the deck.

The boatmen and clam-diggers arose early and stopt for me,
I tuck'd my trowser-ends in my boots and went and had a good
    time;
You should have been with us that day round the chowder-kettle.

I saw the marriage of the trapper in the open air in the far west,
    the bride was a red girl,
Her father and his friends sat near cross-legged and dumbly
    smoking, they had moccasins to their feet and large thick
    blankets hanging from their shoulders,
On a bank lounged the trapper, he was drest mostly in skins, his
    luxuriant beard and curls protected his neck, he held his
    bride by the hand,
She had long eyelashes, her head was bare, her coarse straight
    locks descended upon her voluptuous limbs and reach'd to
    her feet.

The runaway slave came to my house and stopt outside,
I heard his motions crackling the twigs of the woodpile,
Through the swung half-door of the kitchen I saw him limpsy and
    weak,
And went where he sat on a log and led him in and assured him,
And brought water and fill'd a tub for his sweated body and bruis'd
    feet,
And gave him a room that enter'd from my own, and gave him
    some coarse clean clothes,
And remember perfectly well his revolving eyes and his awkwardness,
And remember putting plasters on the galls of his neck and ankles;
He staid with me a week before he was recuperated and pass'd
    north,
I had him sit next me at table, my fire-lock lean'd in the corner.

11

Twenty-eight young men bathe by the shore,
Twenty-eight young men and all so friendly;
Twenty-eight years of womanly life and all so lonesome.

She owns the fine house by the rise of the bank,
She hides handsome and richly drest aft the blinds of the window.

Which of the young men does she like the best?
Ah the homeliest of them is beautiful to her.

Where are you off to, lady? for I see you,
You splash in the water there, yet stay stock still in your room.

Dancing and laughing along the beach came the twenty-ninth bather,
The rest did not see her, but she saw them and loved them.

The beards of the young men glisten'd with wet, it ran from their
    long hair,
Little streams pass'd all over their bodies.

An unseen hand also pass'd over their bodies,
It descended tremblingly from their temples and ribs.

The young men float on their backs, their white bellies bulge to
    the sun, they do not ask who seizes fast to them,
They do not know who puffs and declines with pendant and bend-
    ing arch,
They do not think whom they souse with spray.

12

The butcher-boy puts off his killing-clothes, or sharpens his knife
    at the stall in the market,
I loiter enjoying his repartee and his shuffle and break-down.

Blacksmiths with grimed and hairy chests environ the anvil,
Each has his main-sledge, they are all out, there is a great heat in
    the fire.

From the cinder-strew'd threshold I follow their movements,
The lithe sheer of their waists plays even with their massive arms,
Overhand the hammers swing, overhand so slow, overhand so
    sure,
They do not hasten, each man hits in his place.

13

The negro holds firmly the reins of his four horses, the block swags
    underneath on its tied-over chain,
The negro that drives the long dray of the stone-yard, steady and
    tall he stands pois'd on one leg on the string-piece,
His blue shirt exposes his ample neck and breast and loosens over
    his hip-band,
His glance is calm and commanding, he tosses the slouch of his
    hat away from his forehead,
The sun falls on his crispy hair and mustache, falls on the black
    of his polish'd and perfect limbs.

I behold the picturesque giant and love him, and I do not stop
    there,
I go with the team also.

In me the caresser of life wherever moving, backward as well as
    forward sluing,*
To niches aside and junior bending, not a person or object miss-
    ing,
Absorbing all to myself and for this song.

Oxen that rattle the yoke and chain or halt in the leafy shade,
    what is that you express in your eyes?
It seems to me more than all the print I have read in my life.

My tread scares the wood-drake and wood-duck on my distant and
    day-long ramble,
They rise together, they slowly circle around.

I believe in those wing'd purposes,
And acknowledge red, yellow, white, playing within me,
And consider green and violet and the tufted crown intentional,

And do not call the tortoise unworthy because she is not something
   else,
And the jay in the woods never studied the gamut, yet trills pretty
   well to me,
And the look of the bay mare shames silliness out of me.

14

The wild gander leads his flock through the cool night,
Ya-honk he says, and sounds it down to me like an invitation,
The pert may suppose it meaningless, but I listening close,
Find its purpose and place up there toward the wintry sky.

The sharp-hoof'd moose of the north, the cat on the house-sill,
   the chickadee, the prairie-dog,
The litter of the grunting sow as they tug at her teats,
The brood of the turkey-hen and she with her half-spread wings,
I see in them and myself the same old law.

The press of my foot to the earth springs a hundred affections,
They scorn the best I can do to relate them.

I am enamour'd of growing out-doors,
Of men that live among cattle or taste of the ocean or woods,
Of the builders and steerers of ships and the wielders of axes and
   mauls, and the drivers of horses,
I can eat and sleep with them week in and week out.

What is commonest, cheapest, nearest, easiest, is Me,
Me going in for my chances, spending for vast returns,
Adorning myself to bestow myself on the first that will take me,
Not asking the sky to come down to my good will,
Scattering it freely forever.

15

The pure contralto sings in the organ loft,
The carpenter dresses his plank, the tongue of his foreplane whistles
   its wild ascending lisp,
The married and unmarried children ride home to their Thanks-
   giving dinner,
The pilot seizes the king-pin, he heaves down with a strong arm,

The mate stands braced in the whale-boat, lance and harpoon are
    ready,
The duck-shooter walks by silent and cautious stretches,
The deacons are ordain'd with cross'd hands at the altar,
The spinning-girl retreats and advances to the hum of the big
    wheel,
The farmer stops by the bars as he walks on a First-day loafe* and
    looks at the oats and rye,
The lunatic is carried at last to the asylum a confirm'd case,
(He will never sleep any more as he did in the cot in his mother's
    bed-room;)
The jour printer with gray head and gaunt jaws works at his case,
He turns his quid of tobacco while his eyes blurr with the manu-
    script;
The malform'd limbs are tied to the surgeon's table,
What is removed drops horribly in a pail;
The quadroon girl is sold at the auction-stand, the drunkard nods
    by the bar-room stove,
The machinist rolls up his sleeves, the policeman travels his beat,
    the gate-keeper marks who pass,
The young fellow drives the express-wagon, (I love him, though
    I do not know him;)
The half-breed straps on his light boots to compete in the race,
The western turkey-shooting draws old and young, some lean on
    their rifles, some sit on logs,
Out from the crowd steps the marksman, takes his position, levels
    his piece;
The groups of newly-come immigrants cover the wharf or levee,
As the woolly-pates hoe in the sugar-field, the overseer views them
    from his saddle,
The bugle calls in the ball-room, the gentlemen run for their part-
    ners, the dancers bow to each other,
The youth lies awake in the cedar-roof'd garret and harks to the
    musical rain,
The Wolverine sets traps on the creek that helps fill the Huron,
The squaw wrapt in her yellow-hemm'd cloth is offering moccasins
    and bead-bags for sale,
The connoisseur peers along the exhibition-gallery with half-shut
    eyes bent sideways,

As the deck-hands make fast the steamboat the plank is thrown for
    the shore-going passengers,
The young sister holds out the skein while the elder sister winds it
    off in a ball, and stops now and then for the knots,
The one-year wife is recovering and happy having a week ago
    borne her first child,
The clean-hair'd Yankee girl works with her sewing-machine or in
    the factory or mill,
The paving-man leans on his two-handed rammer, the reporter's
    lead flies swiftly over the note-book, the sign-painter is
    lettering with blue and gold,
The canal boy trots on the tow-path, the book-keeper counts at
    his desk, the shoemaker waxes his thread,
The conductor beats time for the band and all the performers
    follow him,
The child is baptized, the convert is making his first professions,
The regatta is spread on the bay, the race is begun, (how the
    white sails sparkle!)
The drover watching his drove sings out to them that would
    stray,
The pedler sweats with his pack on his back, (the purchaser hig-
    gling about the odd cent;)
The bride unrumples her white dress, the minute-hand of the clock
    moves slowly,
The opium-eater reclines with rigid head and just-open'd lips,
The prostitute draggles her shawl, her bonnet bobs on her tipsy
    and pimpled neck,
The crowd laugh at her blackguard oaths, the men jeer and wink
    to each other,
(Miserable! I do not laugh at your oaths nor jeer you;)
The President holding a cabinet council is surrounded by the great
    Secretaries,
On the piazza walk three matrons stately and friendly with twined
    arms,
The crew of the fish-smack pack repeated layers of halibut in the
    hold,
The Missourian crosses the plains toting his wares and his cattle,
As the fare-collector goes through the train he gives notice by the
    jingling of loose change,

The floor-men are laying the floor, the tinners are tinning the roof,
the masons are calling for mortar,

In single file each shouldering his hod pass onward the laborers;

Seasons pursuing each other the indescribable crowd is gather'd,
it is the fourth of Seventh-month, (what salutes of cannon
and small arms!)

Seasons pursuing each other the plougher ploughs, the mower
mows, and the winter-grain falls in the ground;

Off on the lakes the pike-fisher watches and waits by the hole in
the frozen surface,

The stumps stand thick round the clearing, the squatter strikes
deep with his axe,

Flatboatmen make fast towards dusk near the cotton-wood or
pecan-trees,

Coon-seekers go through the regions of the Red river or through
those drain'd by the Tennessee, or through those of the
Arkansas,

Torches shine in the dark that hangs on the Chattahooche or
Altamahaw,

Patriarchs sit at supper with sons and grandsons and great-grand-
sons around them,

In walls of adobie, in canvas tents, rest hunters and trappers after
their day's sport,

The city sleeps and the country sleeps,

The living sleep for their time, the dead sleep for their time,

The old husband sleeps by his wife and the young husband sleeps
by his wife;

And these tend inward to me, and I tend outward to them,

And such as it is to be of these more or less I am,

And of these one and all I weave the song of myself.

16

I am of old and young, of the foolish as much as the wise,

Regardless of others, ever regardful of others,

Maternal as well as paternal, a child as well as a man,

Stuff'd with the stuff that is coarse and stuff'd with the stuff that
is fine,

One of the Nation of many nations, the smallest the same and the
largest the same,

A Southerner soon as a Northerner, a planter nonchalant and
    hospitable down by the Oconee I live,
A Yankee bound my own way ready for trade, my joints the
    limberest joints on earth and the sternest joints on
    earth,
A Kentuckian walking the vale of the Elkhorn in my deer-skin
    leggings, a Louisianian or Georgian,
A boatman over lakes or bays or along coasts, a Hoosier, Badger,
    Buckeye;
At home on Kanadian snow-shoes or up in the bush, or with
    fishermen off Newfoundland,
At home in the fleet of ice-boats, sailing with the rest and tack-
    ing,
At home on the hills of Vermont or in the woods of Maine, or the
    Texan ranch,
Comrade of Californians, comrade of free North-Westerners, (lov-
    ing their big proportions,)
Comrade of raftsmen and coalmen, comrade of all who shake
    hands and welcome to drink and meat,
A learner with the simplest, a teacher of the thoughtfullest,
A novice beginning yet experient of myriads of seasons,
Of every hue and caste am I, of every rank and religion,
A farmer, mechanic, artist, gentleman, sailor, quaker,
Prisoner, fancy-man, rowdy, lawyer, physician, priest.

I resist any thing better than my own diversity,
Breathe the air but leave plenty after me,
And am not stuck up, and am in my place.

(The moth and the fish-eggs are in their place,
The bright suns I see and the dark suns I cannot see are in their
    place,
The palpable is in its place and the impalpable is in its place.)

17

These are really the thoughts of all men in all ages and lands, they
    are not original with me,
If they are not yours as much as mine they are nothing, or next
    to nothing,

If they are not the riddle and the untying of the riddle they are
     nothing,
If they are not just as close as they are distant they are nothing.

This is the grass that grows wherever the land is and the water is,
This the common air that bathes the globe.

18

With music strong I come, with my cornets and my drums,
I play not marches for accepted victors only, I play marches for
     conquer'd and slain persons.

Have you heard that it was good to gain the day?
I also say it is good to fall, battles are lost in the same spirit in
     which they are won.

I beat and pound for the dead,
I blow through my embouchures my loudest and gayest for them.

Vivas to those who have fail'd!
And to those whose war-vessels sank in the sea!
And to those themselves who sank in the sea!
And to all generals that lost engagements, and all overcome heroes!
And the numberless unknown heroes equal to the greatest heroes
     known!

19

This is the meal equally set, this the meat for natural hunger,
It is for the wicked just the same as the righteous, I make appoint-
     ments with all,
I will not have a single person slighted or left away,
The kept-woman, sponger, thief, are hereby invited,
The heavy-lipp'd slave is invited, the venerealee is invited;
There shall be no difference between them and the rest.

This is the press of a bashful hand, this the float and odor of hair,
This the touch of my lips to yours, this the murmur of yearning,
This the far-off depth and height reflecting my own face,
This the thoughtful merge of myself, and the outlet again.

Do you guess I have some intricate purpose?
Well I have, for the Fourth-month showers have, and the mica on
    the side of a rock has.

Do you take it I would astonish?
Does the daylight astonish? does the early redstart twittering
    through the woods?
Do I astonish more than they?

This hour I tell things in confidence,
I might not tell everybody, but I will tell you.

20

Who goes there? hankering, gross, mystical, nude;
How is it I extract strength from the beef I eat?

What is a man anyhow? what am I? what are you?

All I mark as my own you shall offset it with your own,
Else it were time lost listening to me.

I do not snivel that snivel the world over,
That months are vacuums and the ground but wallow and filth.

Whimpering and truckling fold with powders for invalids, con-
    formity goes to the fourth-remov'd,
I wear my hat as I please indoors or out.

Why should I pray? why should I venerate and be ceremonious?

Having pried through the strata, analyzed to a hair, counsel'd with
    doctors and calculated close,
I find no sweeter fat than sticks to my own bones.

In all people I see myself, none more and not one a barley-corn
    less,
And the good or bad I say of myself I say of them.

I know I am solid and sound,
To me the converging objects of the universe perpetually flow,
All are written to me, and I must get what the writing means.

I know I am deathless,
I know this orbit of mine cannot be swept by a carpenter's
    compass,
I know I shall not pass like a child's carlacue cut with a burnt
    stick at night.

I know I am august,
I do not trouble my spirit to vindicate itself or be understood,
I see that the elementary laws never apologize,
(I reckon I behave no prouder than the level I plant my house by,
    after all.)

I exist as I am, that is enough,
If no other in the world be aware I sit content,
And if each and all be aware I sit content.

One world is aware and by far the largest to me, and that is my-
    self,
And whether I come to my own to-day or in ten thousand or ten
    million years,
I can cheerfully take it now, or with equal cheerfulness I can
    wait.

My foothold is tenon'd and mortis'd in granite,
I laugh at what you call dissolution,
And I know the amplitude of time.

21

I am the poet of the Body and I am the poet of the Soul,
The pleasures of heaven are with me and the pains of hell are
    with me,
The first I graft and increase upon myself, the latter I translate
    into a new tongue.

I am the poet of the woman the same as the man,
And I say it is as great to be a woman as to be a man,
And I say there is nothing greater than the mother of men.

I chant the chant of dilation or pride,
We have had ducking and deprecating about enough,
I show that size is only development.

Have you outstript the rest? are you the President?
It is a trifle, they will more than arrive there every one, and still
    pass on.

I am he that walks with the tender and growing night,
I call to the earth and sea half-held by the night.

Press close bare-bosom'd night—press close magnetic nourishing
    night!
Night of south winds—night of the large few stars!
Still nodding night—mad naked summer night.

Smile O voluptuous cool-breath'd earth!
Earth of the slumbering and liquid trees!
Earth of departed sunset—earth of the mountains misty-topt!
Earth of the vitreous pour of the full moon just tinged with blue!
Earth of shine and dark mottling the tide of the river!
Earth of the limpid gray of clouds brighter and clearer for my
    sake!
Far-swooping elbow'd earth—rich apple-blossom'd earth!
Smile, for your lover comes.

Prodigal, you have given me love—therefore I to you give love!
O unspeakable passionate love.

22

You sea! I resign myself to you also—I guess what you mean,
I behold from the beach your crooked inviting fingers,
I believe you refuse to go back without feeling of me,
We must have a turn together, I undress, hurry me out of sight of
    the land,
Cushion me soft, rock me in billowy drowse,
Dash me with amorous wet, I can repay you.

Sea of stretch'd ground-swells,
Sea breathing broad and convulsive breaths,
Sea of the brine of life and of unshovell'd yet always-ready graves,
Howler and scooper of storms, capricious and dainty sea,
I am integral with you, I too am of one phase and of all phases.

Partaker of influx and efflux I, extoller of hate and conciliation,
Extoller of amies and those that sleep in each others' arms.

I am he attesting sympathy,
(Shall I make my list of things in the house and skip the house
    that supports them?)

I am not the poet of goodness only, I do not decline to be the
    poet of wickedness also.

What blurt is this about virtue and about vice?
Evil propels me and reform of evil propels me, I stand indifferent,
My gait is no fault-finder's or rejecter's gait,
I moisten the roots of all that has grown.

Did you fear some scrofula out of the unflagging pregnancy?
Did you guess the celestial laws are yet to be work'd over and
    rectified?

I find one side a balance and the antipodal side a balance,
Soft doctrine as steady help as stable doctrine,
Thoughts and deeds of the present our rouse and early start.

This minute that comes to me over the past decillions,
There is no better than it and now.

What behaved well in the past or behaves well to-day is not such a
    wonder,
The wonder is always and always how there can be a mean man
    or an infidel.

23

Endless unfolding of words of ages!
And mine a word of the modern, the word En-Masse.

A word of the faith that never balks,
Here or henceforward it is all the same to me, I accept Time abso-
    lutely.

It alone is without flaw, it alone rounds and completes all,
That mystic baffling wonder alone completes all.

I accept Reality and dare not question it,
Materialism first and last imbuing.

Hurrah for positive science! long live exact demonstration!
Fetch stonecrop mixt with cedar and branches of lilac,
This is the lexicographer, this the chemist, this made a grammar
    of the old cartouches,
These mariners put the ship through dangerous unknown seas.
This is the geologist, this works with the scalpel, and this is a
    mathematician.

Gentlemen, to you the first honors always!
Your facts are useful, and yet they are not my dwelling,
I but enter by them to an area of my dwelling.

Less the reminders of properties told my words,
And more the reminders they of life untold, and of freedom and
    extrication,
And make short account of neuters and geldings, and favor men
    and women fully equipt,
And beat the gong of revolt, and stop with fugitives and them that
    plot and conspire.

24

Walt Whitman, a kosmos, of Manhattan the son,
Turbulent, fleshy, sensual, eating, drinking and breeding,
No sentimentalist, no stander above men and women or apart from
    them,
No more modest than immodest.

Unscrew the locks from the doors!
Unscrew the doors themselves from their jambs!

Whoever degrades another degrades me,
And whatever is done or said returns at last to me.

Through me the afflatus surging and surging, through me the cur-
rent and index.

I speak the pass-word primeval, I give the sign of democracy,
By God! I will accept nothing which all cannot have their coun-
terpart of on the same terms.

Through me many long dumb voices,
Voices of the interminable generations of prisoners and slaves,
Voices of the diseas'd and despairing and of thieves and dwarfs,
Voices of cycles of preparation and accretion,
And of the threads that connect the stars, and of wombs and of
the father-stuff,
And of the rights of them the others are down upon,
Of the deform'd, trivial, flat, foolish, despised,
Fog in the air, beetles rolling balls of dung.

Through me forbidden voices,
Voices of sexes and lusts, voices veil'd and I remove the veil,
Voices indecent by me clarified and transfigur'd.

I do not press my fingers across my mouth,
I keep as delicate around the bowels as around the head and heart,
Copulation is no more rank to me than death is.

I believe in the flesh and the appetites,
Seeing, hearing, feeling, are miracles, and each part and tag of me
is a miracle.

Divine am I inside and out, and I make holy whatever I touch or
am touch'd from,
The scent of these arm-pits aroma finer than prayer,
This head more than churches, bibles, and all the creeds.

If I worship one thing more than another it shall be the spread of
my own body, or any part of it,
Translucent mould of me it shall be you!
Shaded ledges and rests it shall be you!
Firm masculine colter it shall be you!

Whatever goes to the tilth of me it shall be you!
You my rich blood! your milky stream pale strippings of my life!
Breast that presses against other breasts it shall be you!
My brain it shall be your occult convolutions!
Root of wash'd sweet-flag! timorous pond-snipe! nest of guarded
    duplicate eggs! it shall be you!
Mix'd tussled hay of head, beard, brawn, it shall be you!
Trickling sap of maple, fibre of manly wheat, it shall be you!
Sun so generous it shall be you!
Vapors lighting and shading my face it shall be you!
You sweaty brooks and dews it shall be you!
Winds whose soft-tickling genitals rub against me it shall be you!
Broad muscular fields, branches of live oak, loving lounger in my
    winding paths, it shall be you!
Hands I have taken, face I have kiss'd, mortal I have ever
    touch'd, it shall be you.

I dote on myself, there is that lot of me and all so luscious,
Each moment and whatever happens thrills me with joy,
I cannot tell how my ankles bend, nor whence the cause of my
    faintest wish,
Nor the cause of the friendship I emit, nor the cause of the friend-
    ship I take again.

That I walk up my stoop, I pause to consider if it really be,
A morning-glory at my window satisfies me more than the meta-
    physics of books.

To behold the day-break!
The little light fades the immense and diaphanous shadows,
The air tastes good to my palate.

Hefts of the moving world at innocent gambols silently rising
    freshly exuding,
Scooting obliquely high and low.

Something I cannot see puts upward libidinous prongs,
Seas of bright juice suffuse heaven.

The earth by the sky staid with, the daily close of their junction,
The heav'd challenge from the east that moment over my head,
The mocking taunt, See then whether you shall be master!

25

Dazzling and tremendous how quick the sun-rise would kill me,
If I could not now and always send sun-rise out of me.

We also ascend dazzling and tremendous as the sun,
We found our own O my soul in the calm and cool of the day-
    break.

My voice goes after what my eyes cannot reach,
With the twirl of my tongue I encompass worlds and volumes of
    worlds.

Speech is the twin of my vision, it is unequal to measure itself,
It provokes me forever, it says sarcastically,
Walt you contain enough, why don't you let it out then?

Come now I will not be tantalized, you conceive too much of
    articulation,
Do you not know O speech how the buds beneath you are folded?
Waiting in gloom, protected by frost,
The dirt receding before my prophetical screams,
I underlying causes to balance them at last,
My knowledge my live parts, it keeping tally with the meaning of
    all things,
Happiness, (which whoever hears me let him or her set out in
    search of this day.)

My final merit I refuse you, I refuse putting from me what I really
    am,
Encompass worlds, but never try to encompass me,
I crowd your sleekest and best by simply looking toward you.

Writing and talk do not prove me,
I carry the plenum of proof and every thing else in my face,
With the hush of my lips I wholly confound the skeptic.

26

Now I will do nothing but listen,
To accrue what I hear into this song, to let sounds contribute
    toward it.

I hear bravuras of birds, bustle of growing wheat, gossip of flames,
    clack of sticks cooking my meals,
I hear the sound I love, the sound of the human voice,
I hear all sounds running together, combined, fused or following,
Sounds of the city and sounds out of the city, sounds of the day
    and night,
Talkative young ones to those that like them, the loud laugh of
    work-people at their meals,
The angry base of disjointed friendship, the faint tones of the sick,
The judge with hands tight to the desk, his pallid lips pronoun-
    cing a death-sentence,
The heave'e'yo of stevedores unlading ships by the wharves, the
    refrain of the anchor-lifters,
The ring of alarm-bells, the cry of fire, the whirr of swift-streak-
    ing engines and hose-carts with premonitory tinkles and
    color'd lights,
The steam-whistle, the solid roll of the train of approaching cars,
The slow march play'd at the head of the association marching
    two and two,
(They go to guard some corpse, the flag-tops are draped with
    black muslin.)

I hear the violoncello, ('tis the young man's heart's complaint,)
I hear the key'd cornet, it glides quickly in through my ears,
It shakes mad-sweet pangs through my belly and breast.

I hear the chorus, it is a grand opera,
Ah this indeed is music—this suits me.

A tenor large and fresh as the creation fills me,
The orbic flex of his mouth is pouring and filling me full.

I hear the train'd soprano (what work with hers is this?)
The orchestra whirls me wider than Uranus flies,

It wrenches such ardors from me I did not know I possess'd
    them,
It sails me, I dab with bare feet, they are lick'd by the indolent
    waves,
I am cut by bitter and angry hail, I lose my breath,
Steep'd amid honey'd morphine, my windpipe throttled in fakes
    of death,
At length let up again to feel the puzzle of puzzles,
And that we call Being.

27

To be in any form, what is that?
(Round and round we go, all of us, and ever come back thither,)
If nothing lay more develop'd the quahaug in its callous shell were
    enough.

Mine is no callous shell,
I have instant conductors all over me whether I pass or stop,
They seize every object and lead it harmlessly through me.

I merely stir, press, feel with my fingers, and am happy,
To touch my person to some one else's is about as much as I can
    stand.

28

Is this then a touch? quivering me to a new identity,
Flames and ether making a rush for my veins,
Treacherous tip of me reaching and crowding to help them,
My flesh and blood playing out lightning to strike what is hardly
    different from myself,
On all sides prurient provokers stiffening my limbs,
Straining the udder of my heart for its withheld drip,
Behaving licentious toward me, taking no denial,
Depriving me of my best as for a purpose,
Unbuttoning my clothes, holding me by the bare waist,
Deluding my confusion with the calm of the sunlight and pasture-
    fields,
Immodestly sliding the fellow-senses away,

They bribed to swap off with touch and go and graze at the edges
   of me,
No consideration, no regard for my draining strength or my anger,
Fetching the rest of the herd around to enjoy them a while,
Then all uniting to stand on a headland and worry me.

The sentries desert every other part of me,
They have left me helpless to a red marauder,
They all come to the headland to witness and assist against me.

I am given up by traitors,
I talk wildly, I have lost my wits, I and nobody else am the
   greatest traitor,
I went myself first to the headland, my own hands carried me
   there.

You villain touch! what are you doing? my breath is tight in its
   throat,
Unclench your floodgates, you are too much for me.

29

Blind loving wrestling touch, sheath'd hooded sharp-tooth'd
   touch!
Did it make you ache so, leaving me?

Parting track'd by arriving, perpetual payment of perpetual loan,
Rich showering rain, and recompense richer afterward.

Sprouts take and accumulate, stand by the curb prolific and vital,
Landscapes projected masculine, full-sized and golden.

30

All truths wait in all things,
They neither hasten their own delivery nor resist it,
They do not need the obstetric forceps of the surgeon,
The insignificant is as big to me as any,
(What is less or more than a touch?)

Logic and sermons never convince,
The damp of the night drives deeper into my soul.

(Only what proves itself to every man and woman is so,
Only what nobody denies is so.)

A minute and a drop of me settle my brain,
I believe the soggy clods shall become lovers and lamps,
And a compend of compends is the meat of a man or woman,
And a summit and flower there is the feeling they have for each
    other,
And they are to branch boundlessly out of that lesson until it
    becomes omnific,
And until one and all shall delight us, and we them.

31

I believe a leaf of grass is no less than the journey-work of the stars,
And the pismire is equally perfect, and a grain of sand, and the
    egg of the wren,
And the tree-toad is a chef-d'oeuvre for the highest,
And the running blackberry would adorn the parlors of heaven,
And the narrowest hinge in my hand puts to scorn all machinery,
And the cow crunching with depress'd head surpasses any statue,
And a mouse is miracle enough to stagger sextillions of infidels.

I find I incorporate gneiss, coal, long-threaded moss, fruits, grains,
    esculent roots,
And am stucco'd with quadrupeds and birds all over,
And have distanced what is behind me for good reasons,
But call any thing back again when I desire it.

In vain the speeding or shyness,
In vain the plutonic rocks send their old heat against my approach,
In vain the mastodon retreats beneath its own powder'd bones,
In vain objects stand leagues off and assume manifold shapes,
In vain the ocean settling in hollows and the great monsters lying
    low,
In vain the buzzard houses herself with the sky,
In vain the snake slides through the creepers and logs,
In vain the elk takes to the inner passes of the woods,
In vain the razor-bill'd auk sails far north to Labrador,
I follow quickly, I ascend to the nest in the fissure of the cliff.

32

I think I could turn and live with animals, they are so placid and
    self-contain'd,
I stand and look at them long and long.

They do not sweat and whine about their condition,
They do not lie awake in the dark and weep for their sins,
They do not make me sick discussing their duty to God,
Not one is dissatisfied, not one is demented with the mania of
    owning things,
Not one kneels to another, nor to his kind that lived thousands of
    years ago,
Not one is respectable or unhappy over the whole earth.

So they show their relations to me and I accept them,
They bring me tokens of myself, they evince them plainly in their
    possession.

I wonder where they get those tokens,
Did I pass that way huge times ago and negligently drop them?

Myself moving forward then and now and forever,
Gathering and showing more always and with velocity,
Infinite and omnigenous, and the like of these among them,
Not too exclusive toward the reachers of my remembrancers,
Picking out here one that I love, and now go with him on brotherly
    terms.

A gigantic beauty of a stallion, fresh and responsive to my caresses,
Head high in the forehead, wide between the ears,
Limbs glossy and supple, tail dusting the ground,
Eyes full of sparkling wickedness, ears finely cut, flexibly moving.

His nostrils dilate as my heels embrace him,
His well-built limbs tremble with pleasure as we race around and
    return.

I but use you a minute, then I resign you, stallion,
Why do I need your paces when I myself out-gallop them?
Even as I stand or sit passing faster than you.

33

Space and Time! now I see it is true, what I guess'd at,
What I guess'd when I loaf'd on the grass,
What I guess'd while I lay alone in my bed,
And again as I walk'd the beach under the paling stars of the
     morning.

My ties and ballasts leave me, my elbows rest in sea-gaps,
I skirt sierras, my palms cover continents,
I am afoot with my vision.

By the city's quadrangular houses—in log huts, camping with
     lumbermen,
Along the ruts of the turnpike, along the dry gulch and rivulet bed,
Weeding my onion-patch or hoeing rows of carrots and parsnips,
     crossing savannas, trailing in forests,
Prospecting, gold-digging, girdling the trees of a new purchase,
Scorch'd ankle-deep by the hot sand, hauling my boat down the
     shallow river,
Where the panther walks to and fro on a limb overhead, where
     the buck turns furiously at the hunter,
Where the rattlesnake suns his flabby length on a rock, where the
     otter is feeding on fish,
Where the alligator in his tough pimples sleeps by the bayou,
Where the black bear is searching for roots or honey, where the
     beaver pats the mud with his paddle-shaped tail;
Over the growing sugar, over the yellow-flower'd cotton plant, over
     the rice in its low moist field,
Over the sharp-peak'd farm house, with its scallop'd scum and
     slender shoots from the gutters,
Over the western persimmon, over the long-leav'd corn, over the
     delicate blue-flower flax,
Over the white and brown buckwheat, a hummer and buzzer there
     with the rest,
Over the dusky green of the rye as it ripples and shades in the
     breeze;
Scaling mountains, pulling myself cautiously up, holding on by low
     scragged limbs,

Walking the path worn in the grass and beat through the leaves of
   the brush,
Where the quail is whistling betwixt the woods and the wheat-lot,
Where the bat flies in the Seventh-month eve, where the great gold-
   bug drops through the dark,
Where the brook puts out of the roots of the old tree and flows to
   the meadow,
Where cattle stand and shake away flies with the tremulous shud-
   dering of their hides,
Where the cheese-cloth hangs in the kitchen, where andirons
   straddle the hearth-slab, where cobwebs fall in festoons
   from the rafters;
Where trip-hammers crash, where the press is whirling its cylinders,
Wherever the human heart beats with terrible throes under its
   ribs,
Where the pear-shaped balloon is floating aloft, (floating in it my-
   self and looking composedly down,)
Where the life-car is drawn on the slip-noose, where the heat
   hatches pale-green eggs in the dented sand,
Where the she-whale swims with her calf and never forsakes it,
Where the steam-ship trails hind-ways its long pennant of smoke,
Where the fin of the shark cuts like a black chip out of the water,
Where the half-burn'd brig is riding on unknown currents,
Where shells grow to her slimy deck, where the dead are corrupt-
   ing below;
Where the dense-starr'd flag is borne at the head of the regiments,
Approaching Manhattan up by the long-stretching island,
Under Niagara, the cataract falling like a veil over my countenance,
Upon a door-step, upon the horse-block of hard wood outside,
Upon the race-course, or enjoying picnics or jigs or a good game of
   base-ball,
At he-festivals, with blackguard gibes, ironical license, bull-dances,
   drinking, laughter,
At the cider-mill tasting the sweets of the brown mash, sucking
   the juice through a straw,
At apple-peelings wanting kisses for all the red fruit I find,
At musters, beach-parties, friendly bees, huskings, house-raisings;
Where the mocking-bird sounds his delicious gurgles, cackles,
   screams, weeps,

Where the hay-rick stands in the barn-yard, where the dry-stalks
    are scatter'd, where the brood-cow waits in the hovel,
Where the bull advances to do his masculine work, where the stud
    to the mare, where the cock is treading the hen,
Where the heifers browse, where geese nip their food with short
    jerks,
Where sun-down shadows lengthen over the limitless and lonesome
    prairie,
Where herds of buffalo make a crawling spread of the square
    miles far and near,
Where the humming-bird shimmers, where the neck of the long-
    lived swan is curving and winding,
Where the laughing-gull scoots by the shore, where she laughs her
    near-human laugh,
Where bee-hives range on a gray bench in the garden half hid by
    the high weeds,
Where band-neck'd partridges roost in a ring on the ground with
    their heads out,
Where burial coaches enter the arch'd gates of a cemetery,
Where winter wolves bark amid wastes of snow and icicled trees,
Where the yellow-crown'd heron comes to the edge of the marsh
    at night and feeds upon small crabs,
Where the splash of swimmers and divers cools the warm noon,
Where the katy-did works her chromatic reed on the walnut-tree
    over the well,
Through patches of citrons and cucumbers with silver-wired leaves,
Through the salt-lick or orange glade, or under conical firs,
Through the gymnasium, through the curtain'd saloon, through the
    office or public hall;
Pleas'd with the native and pleas'd with the foreign, pleas'd with
    the new and old,
Pleas'd with the homely woman as well as the handsome,
Pleas'd with the quakeress as she puts off her bonnet and talks
    melodiously,
Pleas'd with the tune of the choir of the whitewash'd church,
Pleas'd with the earnest words of the sweating Methodist preach-
    er, impress'd seriously at the camp-meeting;
Looking in at the shop-windows of Broadway the whole forenoon,
    flatting the flesh of my nose on the thick plate glass,

Wandering the same afternoon with my face turn'd up to the
   clouds, or down a lane or along the beach,
My right and left arms round the sides of two friends, and I in the
   middle;
Coming home with the silent and dark-cheek'd bush-boy, (behind
   me he rides at the drape of the day,)
Far from the settlements studying the print of animals' feet, or
   the moccasin print,
By the cot in the hospital reaching lemonade to a feverish patient,
Nigh the coffin'd corpse when all is still, examining with a candle;
Voyaging to every port to dicker and adventure,
Hurrying with the modern crowd as eager and fickle as any,
Hot toward one I hate, ready in my madness to knife him,
Solitary at midnight in my back yard, my thoughts gone from me
   a long while,
Walking the old hills of Judæa with the beautiful gentle God by
   my side,
Speeding through space, speeding through heaven and the stars,
Speeding amid the seven satellites and the broad ring, and the
   diameter of eighty thousand miles,
Speeding with tail'd meteors, throwing fire-balls like the rest,
Carrying the crescent child that carries its own full mother in
   its belly,
Storming, enjoying, planning, loving, cautioning,
Backing and filling, appearing and disappearing,
I tread day and night such roads.

I visit the orchards of spheres and look at the product,
And look at quintillions ripen'd and look at quintillions green.

I fly those flights of a fluid and swallowing soul,
My course runs below the soundings of plummets.

I help myself to material and immaterial,
No guard can shut me off, no law prevent me.

I anchor my ship for a little while only,
My messengers continually cruise away or bring their returns to me.

I go hunting polar furs and the seal, leaping chasms with a pike-
   pointed staff, clinging to topples of brittle and blue.

I ascend to the foretruck,
I take my place late at night in the crow's-nest,
We sail the arctic sea, it is plenty light enough,
Through the clear atmosphere I stretch around on the wonderful
    beauty,
The enormous masses of ice pass me and I pass them, the scenery
    is plain in all directions,
The white-topt mountains show in the distance, I fling out my
    fancies toward them,
We are approaching some great battle-field in which we are soon
    to be engaged,
We pass the colossal outposts of the encampment, we pass with
    still feet and caution,
Or we are entering by the suburbs some vast and ruin'd city,
The blocks and fallen architecture more than all the living cities
    of the globe.

I am a free companion, I bivouac by invading watchfires,
I turn the bridegroom out of bed and stay with the bride myself,
I tighten her all night to my thighs and lips.

My voice is the wife's voice, the screech by the rail of the stairs,
They fetch my man's body up dripping and drown'd.

I understand the large hearts of heroes,
The courage of present times and all times,
How the skipper saw the crowded and rudderless wreck of the
    steam-ship, and Death chasing it up and down the storm,
How he knuckled tight and gave not back an inch, and was faith-
    ful of days and faithful of nights,
And chalk'd in large letters on a board, *Be of good cheer, we will
    not desert you;*
How he follow'd with them and tack'd with them three days and
    would not give it up,
How he saved the drifting company at last,
How the lank loose-gown'd women look'd when boated from the
    side of their prepared graves,
How the silent old-faced infants and the lifted sick, and the sharp-
    lipp'd unshaved men;

All this I swallow, it tastes good, I like it well, it becomes mine,
I am the man, I suffer'd, I was there.

The disdain and calmness of martyrs,
The mother of old, condemn'd for a witch, burnt with dry wood,
    her children gazing on,
The hounded slave that flags in the race, leans by the fence, blow-
    ing, cover'd with sweat,
The twinges that sting like needles his legs and neck, the mur-
    derous buckshot and the bullets,
All these I feel or am.

I am the hounded slave, I wince at the bite of the dogs,
Hell and despair are upon me, crack and again crack the marks-
    men,
I clutch the rails of the fence, my gore dribs, thinn'd with the
    ooze of my skin,
I fall on the weeds and stones,
The riders spur their unwilling horses, haul close,
Taunt my dizzy ears and beat me violently over the head with
    whip-stocks.

Agonies are one of my changes of garments,
I do not ask the wounded person how he feels, I myself become
    the wounded person,
My hurts turn livid upon me as I lean on a cane and observe.

I am the mash'd fireman with breast-bone broken,
Tumbling walls buried me in their debris,
Heat and smoke I inspired, I heard the yelling shouts of my com-
    rades,
I heard the distant click of their picks and shovels,
They have clear'd the beams away, they tenderly lift me forth.

I lie in the night air in my red shirt, the pervading hush is for my
    sake,
Painless after all I lie exhausted but not so unhappy,
White and beautiful are the faces around me, the heads are bared
    of their fire-caps,
The kneeling crowd fades with the light of the torches.

Distant and dead resuscitate,
They show as the dial or move as the hands of me, I am the clock
  myself.

I am an old artillerist, I tell of my fort's bombardment,
I am there again.

Again the long roll of the drummers,
Again the attacking cannon, mortars,
Again to my listening ears the cannon responsive.

I take part, I see and hear the whole,
The cries, curses, roar, the plaudits for well-aim'd shots,
The ambulanza slowly passing trailing its red drip,
Workmen searching after damages, making indispensable repairs,
The fall of grenades through the rent roof, the fan-shaped explo-
  sion,
The whizz of limbs, heads, stone, wood, iron, high in the air.

Again gurgles the mouth of my dying general, he furiously waves
  with his hand,
He gasps through the clot *Mind not me—mind—the entrench-
  ments.*

34

Now I tell what I knew in Texas in my early youth,
(I tell not the fall of Alamo,
Not one escaped to tell the fall of Alamo,
The hundred and fifty are dumb yet at Alamo,)
'Tis the tale of the murder in cold blood of four hundred and
  twelve young men.

Retreating they had form'd in a hollow square with their baggage
  for breastworks,
Nine hundred lives out of the surrounding enemy's, nine times
  their number, was the price they took in advance,
Their colonel was wounded and their ammunition gone,
They treated for an honorable capitulation, receiv'd writing and
  seal, gave up their arms and march'd back prisoners of war.

They were the glory of the race of rangers,
Matchless with horse, rifle, song, supper, courtship,
Large, turbulent, generous, handsome, proud, and affectionate,
Bearded, sunburnt, drest in the free costume of hunters,
Not a single one over thirty years of age.

The second First-day morning they were brought out in squads
    and massacred, it was beautiful early summer,
The work commenced about five o'clock and was over by eight.

None obey'd the command to kneel,
Some made a mad and helpless rush, some stood stark and
    straight,
A few fell at once, shot in the temple or heart, the living and dead
    lay together,
The maim'd and mangled dug in the dirt, the new-comers saw
    them there,
Some half-kill'd attempted to crawl away,
These were despatch'd with bayonets or batter'd with the blunts
    of muskets,
A youth not seventeen years old seiz'd his assassin till two more
    came to release him,
The three were all torn and cover'd with the boy's blood.

At eleven o'clock began the burning of the bodies;
That is the tale of the murder of the four hundred and twelve
    young men.

35

Would you hear of an old-time sea-fight?
Would you learn who won by the light of the moon and stars?
List to the yarn, as my grandmother's father the sailor told it to me.

Our foe was no skulk in his ship I tell you, (said he,)
His was the surly English pluck, and there is no tougher or truer,
    and never was, and never will be;
Along the lower'd eve he came horribly raking us.

We closed with him, the yards entangled, the cannon touch'd,
My captain lash'd fast with his own hands.

We had receiv'd some eighteen pound shots under the water,
On our lower-gun-deck two large pieces had burst at the first fire,
      killing all around and blowing up overhead.

Fighting at sun-down, fighting at dark,
Ten o'clock at night, the full moon well up, our leaks on the gain,
      and five feet of water reported,
The master-at-arms loosing the prisoners confined in the after-hold
      to give them a chance for themselves.

The transit to and from the magazine is now stopt by the sentinels,
They see so many strange faces they do not know whom to trust.

Our frigate takes fire,
The other asks if we demand quarter?
If our colors are struck and the fighting done?

Now I laugh content, for I hear the voice of my little captain,
We have not struck, he composedly cries, *we have just begun our
      part of the fighting.*

Only three guns are in use,
One is directed by the captain himself against the enemy's main-
      mast,
Two well serv'd with grape and canister silence his musketry and
      clear his decks.

The tops alone second the fire of this little battery, especially the
      main-top,
They hold out bravely during the whole of the action.

Not a moment's cease,
The leaks gain fast on the pumps, the fire eats toward the powder-
      magazine.

One of the pumps has been shot away, it is generally thought we
      are sinking.

Serene stands the little captain,
He is not hurried, his voice is neither high nor low,
His eyes give more light to us than our battle-lanterns.

Toward twelve there in the beams of the moon they surrender to
    us.

36

Stretch'd and still lies the midnight,
Two great hulls motionless on the breast of the darkness,
Our vessel riddled and slowly sinking, preparations to pass to the
    one we have conquer'd,
The captain on the quarter-deck coldly giving his orders through
    a countenance white as a sheet,
Near by the corpse of the child that serv'd in the cabin,
The dead face of an old salt with long white hair and carefully
    curl'd whiskers,
The flames spite of all that can be done flickering aloft and below,
The husky voices of the two or three officers yet fit for duty,
Formless stacks of bodies and bodies by themselves, dabs of flesh
    upon the masts and spars,
Cut of cordage, dangle of rigging, slight shock of the soothe of
    waves,
Black and impassive guns, litter of powder-parcels, strong scent,
A few large stars overhead, silent and mournful shining,
Delicate sniffs of sea-breeze, smells of sedgy grass and fields by the
    shore, death-messages given in charge to survivors,
The hiss of the surgeon's knife, the gnawing teeth of his saw,
Wheeze, cluck, swash of falling blood, short wild scream, and long,
    dull, tapering groan,
These so, these irretrievable.

37

You laggards there on guard! look to your arms!
In at the conquer'd doors they crowd! I am possess'd!
Embody all presences outlaw'd or suffering,
See myself in prison shaped like another man,
And feel the dull unintermitted pain.

For me the keepers of convicts shoulder their carbines and keep
    watch,
It is I let out in the morning and barr'd at night.

Not a mutineer walks handcuff'd to jail but I am handcuff'd to
    him and walk by his side,
(I am less the jolly one there, and more the silent one with sweat
    on my twitching lips.)

Not a youngster is taken for larceny but I go up too, and am tried
    and sentenced.

Not a cholera patient lies at the last gasp but I also lie at the last
    gasp,
My face is ash-color'd, my sinews gnarl, away from me people
    retreat.

Askers embody themselves in me and I am embodied in them,
I project my hat, sit shame-faced, and beg.

38

Enough! enough! enough!
Somehow I have been stunn'd. Stand back!
Give me a little time beyond my cuff'd head, slumbers, dreams,
    gaping,
I discover myself on the verge of a usual mistake.

That I could forget the mockers and insults!
That I could forget the trickling tears and the blows of the bludg-
    eons and hammers!
That I could look with a separate look on my own crucifixion and
    bloody crowning.

I remember now,
I resume the overstaid fraction,
The grave of rock multiplies what has been confided to it, or to
    any graves,
Corpses rise, gashes heal, fastenings roll from me.

I troop forth replenish'd with supreme power, one of an average
    unending procession,
Inland and sea-coast we go, and pass all boundary lines,

Our swift ordinances on their way over the whole earth,
The blossoms we wear in our hats the growth of thousands of
    years.

Eleves, I salute you! come forward!
Continue your annotations, continue your questionings.

39

The friendly and flowing savage, who is he?
Is he waiting for civilization, or past it and mastering it?

Is he some Southwesterner rais'd out-doors? is he Kanadian?
Is he from the Mississippi country? Iowa, Oregon, California?
The mountains? prairie-life, bush-life? or sailor from the sea?

Wherever he goes men and women accept and desire him,
They desire he should like them, touch them, speak to them, stay
    with them.

Behavior lawless as snow-flakes, words simple as grass, uncomb'd
    head, laughter, and naivetè,
Slow-stepping feet, common features, common modes and ema-
    nations,
They descend in new forms from the tips of his fingers,
They are wafted with the odor of his body or breath, they fly out
    of the glance of his eyes.

40

Flaunt of the sunshine I need not your bask—lie over!
You light surfaces only, I force surfaces and depths also.

Earth! you seem to look for something at my hands,
Say, old top-knot, what do you want?

Man or woman, I might tell how I like you, but cannot,
And might tell what it is in me and what it is in you, but cannot,
And might tell that pining I have, that pulse of my nights and
    days.

Behold, I do not give lectures or a little charity,
When I give I give myself.

You there, impotent, loose in the knees,
Open your scarf'd chops till I blow grit within you,
Spread your palms and lift the flaps of your pockets,
I am not to be denied, I compel, I have stores plenty and to spare,
And any thing I have I bestow.

I do not ask who you are, that is not important to me,
You can do nothing and be nothing but what I will infold you.

To cotton-field drudge or cleaner of privies I lean,
On his right cheek I put the family kiss,
And in my soul I swear I never will deny him.

On women fit for conception I start bigger and nimbler babes,
(This day I am jetting the stuff of far more arrogant republics.)

To any one dying, thither I speed and twist the knob of the door,
Turn the bed-clothes toward the foot of the bed,
Let the physician and the priest go home.

I seize the descending man and raise him with resistless will,
O despairer, here is my neck,
By God, you shall not go down! hang your whole weight upon me.

I dilate you with tremendous breath, I buoy you up,
Every room of the house do I fill with an arm'd force,
Lovers of me, bafflers of graves.

Sleep—I and they keep guard all night,
Not doubt, not decease shall dare to lay finger upon you,
I have embraced you, and henceforth possess you to myself,
And when you rise in the morning you will find what I tell you is so.

41

I am he bringing help for the sick as they pant on their backs,
And for strong upright men I bring yet more needed help.

I heard what was said of the universe,
Heard it and heard it of several thousand years;
It is middling well as far as it goes—but is that all?

Magnifying and applying come I,
Outbidding at the start the old cautious hucksters,
Taking myself the exact dimensions of Jehovah,
Lithographing Kronos, Zeus his son, and Hercules his grandson,
Buying drafts of Osiris, Isis, Belus, Brahma, Buddha,
In my portfolio placing Manito loose, Allah on a leaf, the crucifix
    engraved,
With Odin and the hideous-faced Mexitli and every idol and image,
Taking them all for what they are worth and not a cent more,
Admitting they were alive and did the work of their days,
(They bore mites as for unfledg'd birds who have now to rise and
    fly and sing for themselves,)
Accepting the rough deific sketches to fill out better in myself,
    bestowing them freely on each man and woman I see,
Discovering as much or more in a framer framing a house,
Putting higher claims for him there with his roll'd-up sleeves driving
    the mallet and chisel,
Not objecting to special revelations, considering a curl of smoke
    or a hair on the back of my hand just as curious as any
    revelation,
Lads ahold of fire-engines and hook-and-ladder ropes no less to
    me than the gods of the antique wars,
Minding their voices peal through the crash of destruction,
Their brawny limbs passing safe over charr'd laths, their white
    foreheads whole and unhurt out of the flames;
By the mechanic's wife with her babe at her nipple interceding for
    every person born,
Three scythes at harvest whizzing in a row from three lusty angels
    with shirts bagg'd out at their waists,
The snag-tooth'd hostler with red hair redeeming sins past and to
    come,
Selling all he possesses, traveling on foot to fee lawyers for his
    brother and sit by him while he is tried for forgery;
What was strewn in the amplest strewing the square rod about
    me, and not filling the square rod then,

The bull and the bug never worshipp'd half enough,
Dung and dirt more admirable than was dream'd,
The supernatural of no account, myself waiting my time to be one
    of the supremes,
The day getting ready for me when I shall do as much good as
    the best, and be as prodigious;
By my life-lumps! becoming already a creator,
Putting myself here and now to the ambush'd womb of the shadows.

42

A call in the midst of the crowd,
My own voice, orotund sweeping and final.

Come my children,
Come my boys and girls, my women, household and intimates,
Now the performer launches his nerve, he has pass'd his prelude
    on the reeds within.

Easily written loose-finger'd chords—I feel the thrum of your
    climax and close.

My head slues round on my neck,
Music rolls, but not from the organ,
Folks are around me, but they are no household of mine.

Ever the hard unsunk ground,
Ever the eaters and drinkers, ever the upward and downward sun,
    ever the air and the ceaseless tides,
Ever myself and my neighbors, refreshing, wicked, real,
Ever the old inexplicable query, ever that thorn'd thumb, that
    breath of itches and thirsts,
Ever the vexer's *hoot! hoot!* till we find where the sly one hides
    and bring him forth,
Ever love, ever the sobbing liquid of life,
Ever the bandage under the chin, ever the trestles of death.

Here and there with dimes on the eyes walking,
To feed the greed of the belly the brains liberally spooning,

Tickets buying, taking, selling, but in to the feast never once going.
Many sweating, ploughing, thrashing, and then the chaff for pay-
   ment receiving,
A few idly owning, and they the wheat continually claiming.

This is the city and I am one of the citizens,
Whatever interests the rest interests me, politics, wars, markets,
   newspapers, schools,
The mayor and councils, banks, tariffs, steamships, factories, stocks,
   stores, real estate and personal estate.

The little plentiful manikins skipping around in collars and tail'd
   coats,
I am aware who they are, (they are positively not worms or fleas,)
I acknowledge the duplicates of myself, the weakest and shallowest
   is deathless with me,
What I do and say the same waits for them,
Every thought that flounders in me the same flounders in them.

I know perfectly well my own egotism,
Know my omnivorous lines and must not write any less,
And would fetch you whoever you are flush with myself.

Not words of routine this song of mine,
But abruptly to question, to leap beyond yet nearer bring;
This printed and bound book—but the printer and the printing-
   office boy?
The well-taken photographs—but your wife or friend close and
   solid in your arms?
The black ship mail'd with iron, her mighty guns in her turrets—
   but the pluck of the captain and engineers?
In the houses the dishes and fare and furniture—but the host and
   hostess, and the look out of their eyes?
The sky up there—yet here or next door, or across the way?
The saints and sages in history—but you yourself?
Sermons, creeds, theology—but the fathomless human brain,
And what is reason? and what is love? and what is life?

43

I do not despise you priests, all time, the world over,
My faith is the greatest of faiths and the least of faiths,
Enclosing worship ancient and modern and all between ancient
and modern,
Believing I shall come again upon the earth after five thousand
years,
Waiting responses from oracles, honoring the gods, saluting the
sun,
Making a fetich of the first rock or stump, powowing with sticks in
the circle of obis,
Helping the llama or brahmin as he trims the lamps of the idols,
Dancing yet through the streets in a phallic procession, rapt and
austere in the woods a gymnosophist,
Drinking mead from the skull-cup, to Shastas and Vedas admirant,
minding the Koran,
Walking the teokallis, spotted with gore from the stone and knife,
beating the serpent-skin drum,
Accepting the Gospels, accepting him that was crucified, knowing
assuredly that he is divine,
To the mass kneeling or the puritan's prayer rising, or sitting
patiently in a pew,
Ranting and frothing in my insane crisis, or waiting dead-like till
my spirit arouses me,
Looking forth on pavement and land, or outside of pavement and
land,
Belonging to the winders of the circuit of circuits.

One of that centripetal and centrifugal gang I turn and talk like a
man leaving charges before a journey.

Down-hearted doubters dull and excluded,
Frivolous, sullen, moping, angry, affected, dishearten'd, atheistical,
I know every one of you, I know the sea of torment, doubt,
despair and unbelief.

How the flukes splash!
How they contort rapid as lightning, with spasms and spouts of
blood!

Be at peace bloody flukes of doubters and sullen mopers,
I take my place among you as much as among any,
The past is the push of you, me, all, precisely the same,
And what is yet untried and afterward is for you, me, all, precisely
    the same.

I do not know what is untried and afterward,
But I know it will in its turn prove sufficient, and cannot fail.

Each who passes is consider'd, each who stops is consider'd, not
    a single one can it fail.

It cannot fail the young man who died and was buried,
Nor the young woman who died and was put by his side,
Nor the little child that peep'd in at the door, and then drew back
    and was never seen again,
Nor the old man who has lived without purpose, and feels it with
    bitterness worse than gall,
Nor him in the poor house tubercled by rum and the bad dis-
    order,
Nor the numberless slaughter'd and wreck'd, nor the brutish koboo
    call'd the ordure of humanity,
Nor the sacs merely floating with open mouths for food to slip in,
Nor any thing in the earth, or down in the oldest graves of the
    earth,
Nor any thing in the myriads of spheres, nor the myriads of
    myriads that inhabit them,
Nor the present, nor the least wisp that is known.

44

It is time to explain myself—let us stand up.

What is known I strip away,
I launch all men and women forward with me into the Unknown.

The clock indicates the moment—but what does eternity indicate?

We have thus far exhausted trillions of winters and summers,
There are trillions ahead, and trillions ahead of them.

Births have brought us richness and variety,
And other births will bring us richness and variety.

I do not call one greater and one smaller,
That which fills its period and place is equal to any.

Were mankind murderous or jealous upon you, my brother, my
     sister?
I am sorry for you, they are not murderous or jealous upon me,
All has been gentle with me, I keep no account with lamentation,
(What have I to do with lamentation?)

I am an acme of things accomplish'd, and I an encloser of things
     to be.

My feet strike an apex of the apices of the stairs,
On every step bunches of ages, and larger bunches between the
     steps,
All below duly travel'd, and still I mount and mount.

Rise after rise bow the phantoms behind me,
Afar down I see the huge first Nothing, I know I was even there,
I waited unseen and always, and slept through the lethargic mist,
And took my time, and took no hurt from the fetid carbon.

Long I was hugg'd close—long and long.

Immense have been the preparations for me,
Faithful and friendly the arms that have help'd me.

Cycles ferried my cradle, rowing and rowing like cheerful boatmen,
For room to me stars kept aside in their own rings,
They sent influences to look after what was to hold me.

Before I was born out of my mother generations guided me,
My embryo has never been torpid, nothing could overlay it.

For it the nebula cohered to an orb,
The long slow strata piled to rest it on,

Vast vegetables gave it sustenance,
Monstrous sauroids transported it in their mouths and deposited
    it with care.

All forces have been steadily employ'd to complete and delight me,
Now on this spot I stand with my robust soul.

45

O span of youth! ever-push'd elasticity!
O manhood, balanced, florid and full.

My lovers suffocate me,
Crowding my lips, thick in the pores of my skin,
Jostling me through streets and public halls, coming naked to me
    at night,
Crying by day *Ahoy!* from the rocks of the river, swinging and
    chirping over my head,
Calling my name from flower-beds, vines, tangled underbrush,
Lighting on every moment of my life,
Bussing my body with soft balsamic busses,
Noiselessly passing handfuls out of their hearts and giving them
    to be mine.

Old age superbly rising! O welcome, ineffable grace of dying
    days!

Every condition promulges not only itself, it promulges what grows
    after and out of itself,
And the dark hush promulges as much as any.

I open my scuttle at night and see the far-sprinkled systems,
And all I see multiplied as high as I can cipher edge but the rim
    of the farther systems.

Wider and wider they spread, expanding, always expanding,
Outward and outward and forever outward.

My sun has his sun and round him obediently wheels,
He joins with his partners a group of superior circuit,
And greater sets follow, making specks of the greatest inside them.

There is no stoppage and never can be stoppage,
If I, you, and the worlds, and all beneath or upon their surfaces,
    were this moment reduced back to a pallid float, it would
    not avail in the long run,
We should surely bring up again where we now stand,
And surely go as much farther, and then farther and farther.

A few quadrillions of eras, a few octillions of cubic leagues, do not
    hazard the span or make it impatient,
They are but parts, any thing is but a part.

See ever so far, there is limitless space outside of that,
Count ever so much, there is limitless time around that.

My rendezvous is appointed, it is certain,
The Lord will be there and wait till I come on perfect terms,
The great Camerado, the lover true for whom I pine will be there.

46

I know I have the best of time and space, and was never measured
    and never will be measured.

I tramp a perpetual journey, (come listen all!)
My signs are a rain-proof coat, good shoes, and a staff cut from
    the woods,
No friend of mine takes his ease in my chair,
I have no chair, no church, no philosophy,
I lead no man to a dinner-table, library, exchange,
But each man and each woman of you I lead upon a knoll,
My left hand hooking you round the waist,
My right hand pointing to landscapes of continents and the public
    road.

Not I, not any one else can travel that road for you,
You must travel it for yourself.

It is not far, it is within reach,
Perhaps you have been on it since you were born and did not
    know,
Perhaps it is everywhere on water and on land.

Shoulder your duds dear son, and I will mine, and let us hasten
forth,
Wonderful cities and free nations we shall fetch as we go.

If you tire, give me both burdens, and rest the chuff of your hand
on my hip,
And in due time you shall repay the same service to me,
For after we start we never lie by again.

This day before dawn I ascended a hill and look'd at the crowded
heaven,
And I said to my spirit *When we become the enfolders of those*
orbs, and the pleasure and knowledge of every thing in
them, shall we be fill'd and satisfied then?
And my spirit said *No, we but level that lift to pass and continue*
beyond.

You are also asking me questions and I hear you,
I answer that I cannot answer, you must find out for yourself.

Sit a while dear son,
Here are biscuits to eat and here is milk to drink,
But as soon as you sleep and renew yourself in sweet clothes, I
kiss you with a good-by kiss and open the gate for your
egress hence.

Long enough have you dream'd contemptible dreams,
Now I wash the gum from your eyes,
You must habit yourself to the dazzle of the light and of every
moment of your life.

Long have you timidly waded holding a plank by the shore,
Now I will you to be a bold swimmer,
To jump off in the midst of the sea, rise again, nod to me, shout,
and laughingly dash with your hair.

47

I am the teacher of athletes,
He that by me spreads a wider breast than my own proves the
width of my own,

He most honors my style who learns under it to destroy the
    teacher.

The boy I love, the same becomes a man not through derived
    power, but in his own right,
Wicked rather than virtuous out of conformity or fear,
Fond of his sweetheart, relishing well his steak,
Unrequited love or a slight cutting him worse than sharp steel
    cuts,
First-rate to ride, to fight, to hit the bull's eye, to sail a skiff, to
    sing a song or play on the banjo,
Preferring scars and the beard and faces pitted with small-pox
    over all latherers,
And those well-tann'd to those that keep out of the sun.

I teach straying from me, yet who can stray from me?
I follow you whoever you are from the present hour,
My words itch at your ears till you understand them.

I do not say these things for a dollar or to fill up the time while
    I wait for a boat,
(It is you talking just as much as myself, I act as the tongue of
    you,
Tied in your mouth, in mine it begins to be loosen'd.)

I swear I will never again mention love or death inside a house,
And I swear I will never translate myself at all, only to him or her
    who privately stays with me in the open air.

If you would understand me go to the heights or water-shore,
The nearest gnat is an explanation, and a drop or motion of waves
    a key,
The maul, the oar, the hand-saw, second my words.

No shutter'd room or school can commune with me,
But roughs and little children better than they.

The young mechanic is closest to me, he knows me well,
The woodman that takes his axe and jug with him shall take me
    with him all day,

The farm-boy ploughing in the field feels good at the sound of my
  voice,
In vessels that sail my words sail, I go with fishermen and seamen
  and love them.

The soldier camp'd or upon the march is mine,
On the night ere the pending battle many seek me, and I do not
  fail them,
On that solemn night (it may be their last) those that know me
  seek me.

My face rubs to the hunter's face when he lies down alone in his
  blanket,
The driver thinking of me does not mind the jolt of his wagon,
The young mother and old mother comprehend me,
The girl and the wife rest the needle a moment and forget where
  they are,
They and all would resume what I have told them.

48

I have said that the soul is not more than the body,
And I have said that the body is not more than the soul,
And nothing, not God, is greater to one than one's self is,
And whoever walks a furlong without sympathy walks to his own
  funeral drest in his shroud,
And I or you pocketless of a dime may purchase the pick of the
  earth,
And to glance with an eye or show a bean in its pod confounds
  the learning of all times,
And there is no trade or employment but the young man following
  it may become a hero,
And there is no object so soft but it makes a hub for the wheel'd
  universe,
And I say to any man or woman, Let your soul stand cool and
  composed before a million universes.

And I say to mankind, Be not curious about God,
For I who am curious about each am not curious about God,

(No array of terms can say how much I am at peace about God
  and about death.)

I hear and behold God in every object, yet understand God not
  in the least,
Nor do I understand who there can be more wonderful than
  myself.

Why should I wish to see God better than this day?
I see something of God each hour of the twenty-four, and each
  moment then,
In the faces of men and women I see God, and in my own face in
  the glass,
I find letters from God dropt in the street, and every one is sign'd
  by God's name,
And I leave them where they are, for I know that wheresoe'er I go,
Others will punctually come for ever and ever.

49

And as to you Death, and you bitter hug of mortality, it is idle to
  try to alarm me.

To his work without flinching the accoucheur comes,
I see the elder-hand pressing receiving supporting,
I recline by the sills of the exquisite flexible doors,
And mark the outlet, and mark the relief and escape.

And as to you Corpse I think you are good manure, but that does
  not offend me,
I smell the white roses sweet-scented and growing,
I reach to the leafy lips, I reach to the polish'd breasts of melons.

And as to you Life I reckon you are the leavings of many deaths,
(No doubt I have died myself ten thousand times before.)

I hear you whispering there O stars of heaven,
O suns—O grass of graves—O perpetual transfers and pro-
  motions,
If you do not say any thing how can I say any thing?

Of the turbid pool that lies in the autumn forest,
Of the moon that descends the steeps of the soughing twilight,
Toss, sparkles of day and dusk—toss on the black stems that
    decay in the muck,
Toss to the moaning gibberish of the dry limbs.

I ascend from the moon, I ascend from the night,
I perceive that the ghastly glimmer is noonday sunbeams reflected,
And debouch to the steady and central from the offspring great or
    small.

50

There is that in me—I do not know what it is—but I know it is
    in me.

Wrench'd and sweaty—calm and cool then my body becomes,
I sleep—I sleep long.

I do not know it—it is without name—it is a word unsaid,
It is not in any dictionary, utterance, symbol.

Something it swings on more than the earth I swing on,
To it the creation is the friend whose embracing awakes me.

Perhaps I might tell more. Outlines! I plead for my brothers
    and sisters.

Do you see O my brothers and sisters?
It is not chaos or death—it is form, union, plan—it is eternal
    life—it is Happiness.

51

The past and present wilt—I have fill'd them, emptied them,
And proceed to fill my next fold of the future.

Listener up there! what have you to confide to me?
Look in my face while I snuff the sidle of evening,
(Talk honestly, no one else hears you, and I stay only a minute
    longer.)

Do I contradict myself?
Very well then I contradict myself,
(I am large, I contain multitudes.)

I concentrate toward them that are nigh, I wait on the door-slab.

Who has done his day's work? who will soonest be through with
    his supper?
Who wishes to walk with me?

Will you speak before I am gone? will you prove already too late?

52

The spotted hawk swoops by and accuses me, he complains of my
    gab and my loitering.
I too am not a bit tamed, I too am untranslatable,
I sound my barbaric yawp over the roofs of the world.

The last scud of day holds back for me,
It flings my likeness after the rest and true as any on the shadow'd
    wilds,
It coaxes me to the vapor and the dusk.

I depart as air, I shake my white locks at the runaway sun,
I effuse my flesh in eddies, and drift it in lacy jags.

I bequeath myself to the dirt to grow from the grass I love,
If you want me again look for me under your boot-soles.

You will hardly know who I am or what I mean,
But I shall be good health to you nevertheless,
And filter and fibre your blood.

Failing to fetch me at first keep encouraged,
Missing me one place search another,
I stop somewhere waiting for you.

EXPLANATORY NOTES

LEAVES OF GRASS (1855)

[SONG OF MYSELF]

Untitled (or headed 'Leaves of Grass') in 1855, this poem was subject to numerous revisions over the course of Whitman's career. In 1856, it became 'Poem of Walt Whitman, an American'; in 1860, and up until 1881, it was 'Walt Whitman'. From 1881 on, it became 'Song of Myself'. See Appendix B for the poem's final 1892 'Deathbed' version.

18 *kelson*: Whitman's spelling of 'keelson', the reinforcing structural component on top of the keel inside the hull of a wooden ship.

19 *Cuff*: racist, now obsolete slang for African American.

24 *shuffle and breakdown*: types of dance.

 stringpiece: long piece of timber used for support in construction.

26 *king-pin*: part of the steering mechanism of a vehicle. In this case a boat.

 jour printer: journeyman printer.

29 *a Hoosier, a Badger, a Buckeye*: nicknames for residents of Indiana, Wisconsin, and Ohio respectively.

30 *embouchures*: the way a musician applies their mouth (their use of the facial muscles, lips, tongue and teeth) when playing a brass or wind instrument.

32 *carlacue*: Whitman's spelling of 'curlicue', a doodled spiral or flourish.

35 *stonecrop*: fleshy-leaved succulent that spreads like a mat.

 cartouches: a carved tablet or drawing representing a scroll bearing an inscription.

36 *afflatus*: divine or poetic inspiration; Latin for blowing or breathing.

37 *coulter*: blade fixed in front of the share in a plough that makes a vertical cut in the soil (which is then sliced horizontally by the share).

 sweet-flag: herbacious perennial plant also known as 'Calamus'. See related note on p. 515.

39 *plenum*: filled space; opposite of vacuum. Here, the 'complete' or 'whole' proof.

40 *fakes*: coils of rope.

42 *pismire*: ant.

 esculent: edible.

 plutonic rocks: igneous or volcanic rocks.

45 *life-car*: type of lifeboat.

46 *bull-dances*: all-male dances.

 sqush: Whitman's spelling of 'squash'.

48 *foretruck*: top of a ship's tallest mast.

49 *rudderless wreck of the steamship*: probably based on the much-publicized fate of the ship *San Francisco*, a vessel that lost its ability to navigate during a voyage between New York and South America (23 December 1853–5 January 1854).

51 *Hear now . . . young men*: this passage refers to a massacre that took place at Goliad, Texas, on 27 March 1836 during the Texas Revolution. Related to the massacre at Alamo a few weeks earlier.

52 *oldfashioned frigate-fight*: the 1779 single-vessel battle between the British warship *Serapis* and the *Bonhomme Richard*, captained by John Paul Jones.

55 *Eleves*: correctly *Élèves*, French for 'pupils'.

56 *scarfed chops*: jaws around which a scarf was tied during illness.

57 *Manito*: a variation of 'Manitou', a life force or spirit to the Algonquin peoples.

58 *hostler*: Whitman's spelling of 'hustler', a petty criminal, someone who hustles for cash.

59 *dimes on the eyes*: payment for the ferryman Charon in the afterlife. Sometimes used to keep the eyes of the dead shut.

60 *circle of obis*: Obeah; spell-casting and healing traditions of the African diaspora.

61 *gymnosophist*: member of an ancient Hindu sect given to asceticism and contemplation.

   teokallis: Aztec temples.

   waiting dead-like till my spirit arouses me: Quaker practice of passively waiting for the spirit.

62 *brutish koboo*: racist slur, possibly referring to people from Sumatra.

63 *sauroids*: dinosaurs.

68 *accoucheur*: French for 'male midwife'.

71 *I stop some where waiting for you*: the period (full point) is missing at the end of the final line in several copies of the first edition—an omission that sparked much critical debate. Was this a moment when Whitman also dispensed with the basic rules of punctuation? No, it turns out that this type block slipped and fell out during the print run, meaning that some copies have a full point, some don't, and in a few you can see the precise moment when the slip actually happened. Whitman either didn't notice the typo, or, sticking to a strict budget, he just went with it. See Ed Folsom's *Whitman Making Books/Books Making Whitman: A Catalog and Commentary* (Iowa City: Obermann Center for Advanced Studies, University of Iowa, 2005).

[A SONG FOR OCCUPATIONS]

Untitled (again headed 'Leaves of Grass') in 1855, this poem was also subject to multiple revisions over the years. In 1856, it became 'Poem of The Daily Work of the Workmen and Workwomen of These States'; in 1860, it was #3 of the 'Chants Democratic' cluster; in 1867 it was 'To Workingmen'; in 1871 and 1876: 'Carol of Occupations'. From 1881 on, it was 'A Song for Occupations'.

78 *frisket and tympan*: terms that showcase Whitman's detailed knowledge of the printing process.

[TO THINK OF TIME]

Untitled (or headed 'Leaves of Grass') in 1855; 'Burial Poem' in 1856, then 'Burial' in 1860. From 1871 on, 'To Think of Time'.

[THE SLEEPERS]

Untitled (headed 'Leaves of Grass') in 1855; 'Night Poem' in 1856; 'Sleep-Chasings' in 1860. From 1871 on, 'The Sleepers'.

88 *douceurs*: French for 'delights', 'pleasures' or 'sweetnesses'.

cache: French for 'hiding place'.

91 *defeat at Brooklyn*: Battle of Brooklyn Heights, 1776—a significant setback and near-disaster for the Continental Army during the American Revolutionary War.

93 *erysipalite*: someone who suffers from the skin disease erysipelas.

[I SING THE BODY ELECTRIC]

Untitled (headed 'Leaves of Grass') in 1855; 'Poem of the Body' in 1856; poem #3 of the 'Enfans d'Adam' cluster in 1860; then most famously, 'I Sing the Body Electric' from 1867 on.

[FACES]

Untitled (headed 'Leaves of Grass') in 1855; 'Poem of Faces' in 1856; 'Leaf of Faces' in 1860; 'A Leaf of Faces' in 1867; and from 1871 on, 'Faces'.

102 *wrig*: Whitman's abbreviation of 'wriggle'.

103 *caoutchouc*: natural or crude rubber.

agents that emptied and broke my brother: Whitman's youngest brother Eddie had multiple physical and mental disabilities, and was periodically institutionalized throughout his life.

104 *albescent*: a whitish shade; in this instance, the colour of semen.

[SONG OF THE ANSWERER]

This poem was untitled in 1855; 'Poem of The Poet' in 1856; #3 in the 'Leaves of Grass' cluster of 1860; 'Now List to My Morning Romanza' in 1867. In 1881, some of the poem became part of 'Song of the Answerer'.

107 *Cudge*: like 'Cuff', racist obsolete slang for African American.

[EUROPE THE 72D AND 73D YEARS OF THESE STATES]

The only poem included in the 1855 edition to have been previously published: an early version had appeared as 'Resurgemus' in the *New York Tribune* (June 1850). Untitled in 1855; 'Poem of The Dead Young Men of Europe, The 72d and 73d Years of These States' in 1856. From 1860 on, 'Europe, The 72d and 73d Years of These States'. The poem is partly a response to the 1848 revolutions.

[A BOSTON BALLAD]

Untitled in 1855, this poem became 'Poem of Apparitions in Boston, The 70th Year of These States' in 1856; in 1860, 'A Boston Ballad, The 70th Year of These States'; in 1867, 'To Get Betimes in Boston Town (1854)'; from 1871, it was simply 'A Boston Ballad'. Whitman likely wrote the poem in 1854, as a response to the political storm surrounding Anthony Burns, who had been captured under the hated Fugitive Slave Act of 1850, prosecuted in Boston, and then escorted under armed guard through the city to a waiting ship bound for Virginia.

110 *Jonathan*: New England nickname for your average Yankee.

112 *cute*: acute, shrewd, keen-witted.

[THERE WAS A CHILD WENT FORTH]

Untitled in 1855; 'Poem of the Child That Went Forth, and Always Goes Forth, Forever and Forever' in 1856; #9 in the 'Leaves of Grass' cluster in 1860 (#1 in 1867). From 1871 on, 'There Was a Child Went Forth'.

[WHO LEARNS MY LESSON COMPLETE?]

Untitled in 1855; 'Lesson Poem' in 1856; #11 in the 'Leaves of Grass' cluster in 1860 (#3 in 1867). From 1871 on, 'Who Learns My Lesson Complete?'.

[GREAT ARE THE MYTHS]

Untitled in 1855; 'Poem of a Few Greatnesses' in 1856; #2 in the 'Leaves of Grass' cluster in 1860; 'Great Are the Myths' in 1867. From 1881 on, only four lines were kept to make the poem 'Youth, Day, Old Age and Night'.

FROM LEAVES OF GRASS (1856)

2—POEM OF WOMEN

#14 and #2 of the 'Leaves of Grass' cluster in 1860 and 1867 respectively. From 1871 on, 'Unfolded Out of the Folds'.

3—POEM OF SALUTATION

From 1860 on, 'Salut au Monde!'.

126 *slave-coffle*: caravan or line of enslaved people.

129 *avatars*: incarnation of deity in human form connected with Hindu belief.

misletoe and vervain: plants associated with pagan ritual.

131 *Paumanok*: Long Island, Whitman's adaptation of an Algonquian name for the area.

132 *winrows*: beach debris left by the tide.

136 *koboo*: see note to p. 62.

5 — BROAD-AXE POEM

#2 of the 'Chants Democratic' cluster in 1860; from 1867 on, 'Song of the Broad-Axe'.

137 *helve*: handle of a tool.

140 *hod-men*: labourers who carry mortar and bricks to builders.

148 *knees*: naturally curved or bent pieces of wood, often used in shipbuilding.

9 — POEM OF WONDER AT THE RESURRECTION OF THE WHEAT

#4 of the 'Leaves of Grass' cluster in 1860; from 1867 on, 'This Compost'.

11 — SUN-DOWN POEM

This poem received its final title, 'Crossing Brooklyn Ferry', in 1860.

12 — POEM OF THE ROAD

From 1867 on, 'Song of the Open Road'.

167 *adhesiveness*: a term taken from the pseudoscience of phrenology, describing a propensity for forming and maintaining attachments to others. A physical sticking-together.

168 *Allons!*: French for 'Let's go!'

169 *thews*: muscles or sinews.

13 — POEM OF PROCREATION

In 1860, #4 of the 'Enfans d'Adam' cluster; from 1867 on, 'A Woman Waits for Me'. For a discussion of the more disturbing lines in this poem, particularly in relation to sexual consent, see Jay Grossman's 'Walt Whitman and Sexuality', in Edward Whitley and Joanna Levin (eds.), *Walt Whitman in Context* (Cambridge: Cambridge University Press, 2018), 231–2.

15 — CLEF POEM

#12 and #1 of the 'Leaves of Grass' cluster in 1860 and 1867 respectively; given its final title, 'On the Beach at Night Alone' in 1871.

177 *clef*: clue.

21 — LIBERTY POEM . . . OF THE SEA

'To a Foiled Revolter or Revoltress' in 1860 and 1867; from 1871 on, 'To a Foil'd European Revolutionaire'.

28—BUNCH POEM

#5 of the 'Enfans d'Adam' cluster in 1860; from 1867 on, 'Spontaneous Me'.

31—POEM OF THE SAYERS OF THE WORDS OF THE EARTH

'To the Sayers of Words' in 1860; 'Carol of Words' in 1871; from 1881 on, 'A Song of the Rolling Earth'.

185 *Accouche! Accouchez!*: a translation from the French might be, 'Come on then! Give birth!'

186 *sisters*: stars and planets.

cotillions: a ballroom dance.

beautiful sister: earth.

FROM LEAVES OF GRASS (1860–1861)

PROTO-LEAF

This significantly revised poem received its final title in 1867, 'Starting from Paumanok'.

193 *Mannahatta*: Whitman's adaptation of Algonquian name for Manhattan Island.

194 *Libertad!*: Spanish for 'Freedom!'

197 *comrades*: a central term for Whitman, which takes on new dimensions in the run-up to the Civil War and beyond, and particularly in the 1860 'Calamus' cluster. It carried associations of same-sex intimacy, solidarity, and love. See also his invention and use of 'camerado' in 1865: 'As I lay with my head in your lap, camerado' (p. 317).

198 *Omnes!*: Latin for 'Everyone!'

201 *Ma femme!*: French for 'My wife!'

205 *dolce affettuoso*: Italian musical direction, 'sweetly, with affection'. Whitman was an avid and knowledgeable fan of the opera. See, for example, the poem 'Proud Music of the Storm' from 1871.

FROM 'CHANTS DEMOCRATIC AND NATIVE AMERICAN'

208 *14*: Became the shorter poem #4 in the 1867 'Leaves of Grass' cluster; from 1871 on, 'Poets to Come'.

209 *18*: from 1867 on, 'Me Imperturbe'.

20: from 1867 on, 'I Hear America Singing'.

FROM LEAVES OF GRASS

210 *1*: First published as 'Bardic Symbols' in the *Atlantic Monthly* of April 1860; it became 'Elemental Drifts' in the 1867 edition of *Leaves*. From 1881 on, 'As I Ebb'd with the Ocean of Life'.

211 *winrows*: see note to p. 132.

214 *16*: #4 in the 'Leaves of Grass' cluster in 1867; takes on its final title, 'The World Below the Brine' in 1871. Included as part of *Passage to India*.

17: from 1871 on, 'I Sit and Look Out'.

POEM OF JOYS

'Poems of Joy' in 1867; reverts to 'Poem of Joys' in 1871; becomes 'A Song of Joys' in 1881.

A WORD OUT OF THE SEA

First published in the *New York Saturday Press* (24 December 1859) as 'A Child's Reminiscence'. The final title, and rewrite of the first line, 'Out of the Cradle Endlessly Rocking', appeared in 1871.

224 *Paumanok*: see note to p. 131.

FROM ENFANS D'ADAM

231 *1*: from 1867 on, 'To the Garden, the World'.

232 *2*: from 1867 on, 'From Pent-up Aching Rivers'.

234 *8*: from 1867 on, 'Native Moments'.

I take for my love some prostitute: Whitman deleted this line in 1881.

235 *9*: from 1867 on, 'Once I Pass'd through a Populous City'.

10: from 1867 on, 'Facing West from California's Shores'.

236 *14*: from 1867 on, 'I Am He that Aches with Love'.

15: from 1867 on, 'As Adam Early in the Morning'.

THE COMPLETE 'CALAMUS' CLUSTER

CALAMUS: herbacious perennial plant most commonly known as 'sweetflag', selected by Whitman because of its resemblance to an erect penis. See also 'Live Oak, with Moss', a group of manuscript poems, available at the Walt Whitman Archive, that form the basis of this cluster.

236 *1*: from 1867 on, 'In Paths Untrodden'.

237 *2*: from 1867 on, 'Scented Herbage of My Breast'.

239 *3*: from 1867 on, 'Whoever You Are Holding Me Now in Hand'.

241 *4*: 'These I, Singing in Spring' in 1867; Whitman eventually dropped the comma.

242 *5*: poem expunged from future editions, though particular sections of it became 'Over the Carnage Rose Prophetic a Voice' (1865) and the later 'For You O Democracy' (1881) respectively.

245 *ma femme*: see note to p. 201.

6: from 1867 on, 'Not Heaving From My Ribb'd Breast Only'.

7: from 1867 on, 'Of the Terrible Doubt of Appearances'.

246 *8*: Whitman excised this poem from future editions, and did not allow it to be republished.

247 *9*: Whitman also removed this poem from all future editions.

248 *10*: in 1867, Whitman redacted the first two lines and replaced them with the phrase that would also serve as the title of this poem: 'Recorders Ages Hence'.

249 *11*: from 1867 on, 'When I Heard at the Close of the Day'.

250 *12*: from 1867 on, 'Are You the New Person Drawn toward Me?'.

251 *13*: from 1867 on, 'Roots and Leaves Themselves Alone'.

14: from 1867 on, 'Not Heat Flames up and Consumes'.

252 *15*: from 1867 on, 'Trickle Drops'.

16: Whitman excised this poem from all future editions.

253 *17*: from 1867 on, 'Of Him I Love Day and Night'.

254 *18*: from 1867 on, 'City of Orgies'.

19: from 1867 on, 'Behold This Swarthy Face'.

255 *20*: from 1867 on, 'I Saw in Louisiana a Live-Oak Growing'.

256 *21*: from 1867 on, 'That Music Always Round Me'.

tutti: Italian for 'everyone'; musical term indicating a passage for the whole orchestra or chorus, usually after a passage for solo instruments or voices.

22: from 1867 on, 'To a Stranger'.

257 *23*: from 1867 on, 'This Moment Yearning and Thoughtful'.

24: from 1867 on, 'I Hear It Was Charged against Me'.

258 *25*: from 1867 on, 'The Prairie-Grass Dividing'.

26: from 1867 on, 'We Two Boys Together Clinging'.

259 *27*: from 1867 on, 'O Living Always, Always Dying'.

28: from 1867 on, 'When I Peruse the Conquered Fame'.

260 *29*: from 1867 on, 'A Glimpse'.

30: from 1867 on, 'A Promise to California'.

31: from 1867 on, the two separate stanzas became 'What Ship Puzzled at Sea' and 'What Place is Beseiged?' respectively.

261 *32*: from 1867 on, 'What Think You I Take My Pen in Hand?'.

33: from 1867 on, 'No Labor-Saving Machine'.

34: from 1867 on, 'I Dreamed in a Dream'.

262 *35*: from 1867 on, 'To the East and to the West'.

36: from 1867 on, 'Earth, My Likeness'.

37: from 1867 on, 'A Leaf for Hand in Hand'.

263 *38*: from 1867 on, 'Fast Anchor'd Eternal O Love!'.

39: from 1867 on, 'Sometimes with One I Love'.

40: from 1867 on, 'That Shadow My Likeness'.

264 *41*: from 1867 on, 'Among the Multitude'.

42: from 1867 on, 'To a Western Boy'.

élève: see note to p. 55; this time Whitman has correctly accented the word.

43: from 1867 on, 'O You Whom I Often and Silently Come'.

265 *44*: from 1867 on, 'Here the Frailest Leaves of Me'. The poem's first line was deleted in 1867.

45: from 1867 on, 'Full of Life Now'.

FROM MESSENGER LEAVES

267 Walt Whitman's Caution: From 1881 on, 'To the States'.

MANNAHATTA

269 *Trottoirs*: French for 'pavements'.

SO LONG!

This poem ended every edition of *Leaves* from 1860 on.

FROM DRUM-TAPS (1865)

DRUM-TAPS

From 1881 on, 'First O Songs For A Prelude'.

SHUT NOT YOUR DOORS TO ME PROUD LIBRARIES

Poem excised in the 1867 edition. Appears again as 'Shut not Your Doors' from 1871 on.

QUICKSAND YEARS THAT WHIRL ME I KNOW NOT WHITHER

From 1871 on, 'Quicksand Years'.

THE DRESSER

From 1876 on, 'The Wound-Dresser'.

YEAR OF METEORS (1859–60)

298 *19th Presidentiad*: presidential race that elected Abraham Lincoln in 1860.

old man: John Brown, radical abolitionist, executed in 1859 for his raid on Harper's Ferry.

sweet boy of England: then Prince of Wales, the future King Edward VII, visited America in 1860.

Great Eastern: then the largest steamship in the world.

FROM SEQUEL TO DRUM-TAPS (1865–1866)

WHEN LILACS LAST IN THE DOOR-YARD BLOOM'D

306 *flambeaus*: French for 'torches'.

CHANTING THE SQUARE DEIFIC

316 *sudra*: the lowest of the four varnas of the traditional Hindu social order. Refers to artisans, laborers, or servants.

317 *Santa SPIRITA*: 'The Holy Spirit' but gendered feminine by Whitman ('Spiritus Sanctus' in Latin).

AS I LAY WITH MY HEAD IN YOUR LAP, CAMERADO

317 *camerado*: see note to p. 197.

FROM LEAVES OF GRASS (1867)

INSCRIPTION

This poem appeared as the frontispiece of the 1867 edition, and then from 1881 on, 'Small the Theme of My Chant'. In 1871, an extended rewrite of the opening becomes 'One's-Self I Sing'. See p. 327.

2

321 *2*: from 1871 on, 'Tears'.

FROM LEAVES OF GRASS (1871–1872)

ONE'S SELF I SING

This poem has its beginnings in 'Inscription' of 1867, see p. 321.

TO THEE, OLD CAUSE!

327 *old Cause!*: democracy.

ETHIOPIA SALUTING THE COLORS (A REMINISCENCE OF 1864)

329 *guidons*: standards or flags specifically in the United States' military.

FROM PASSAGE TO INDIA (1871)

Companion volume to the 1871–2 edition of *Leaves*.

PASSAGE TO INDIA

333 *antique ponderous Seven*: Seven Wonders of the Ancient World.
eloquent gentle wires: the first transatlantic cable was laid in 1858.
Eclaircise: from the French 'to clarify'.

335 *Genoese*: Christopher Columbus.

339 *Admiral himself*: Columbus.

PROUD MUSIC OF THE STORM

344 *cantabile*: 'songlike' in Italian; a musical direction to instrumentalists to perform a passage in a singing style, and to music performed in that style.

346 *Norma*: the druidess Norma, title character of Bellini's opera (1831).

poor crazed Lucia's eyes' unnatural gleam: Lucia is the title character in Donizetti's opera *Lucia di Lammermoor* (1835); her 'mad scene' is one of the most famous in the repertoire.

347 *Ernani*: Ernani, leader of the bandits, title character of Verdi's opera (1844).

clear, electric base and baritone ... Libertad forever: the duet 'Suoni la tromba' for baritone and bass, in Bellini's opera *I Puritani* (1835), includes the line 'It is beautiful to face death shouting "Freedom!"'.

Fernando's heart is breaking: allusion to the novice Fernand, in love with the king's mistress, in Donizetti's opera *La Favorite* (1840). Whitman cites the name in its Italian form 'Fernando'; the opera was first given in the US as *La Favorita* in 1855.

Awaking ... retriev'd Amina sings: Amina is the sleepwalking title character of Bellini's opera *La Sonnambula* (1831).

Alboni's self I hear: Whitman saw the contralto Marietta Alboni (1826–94) when she toured the United States in 1852–3.

348 *king*: ancient Chinese instrument.

349 *Creation*: Haydn's oratorio (1799).

FROM AS A STRONG BIRD ON PINIONS FREE (1872)

ONE SONG, AMERICA, BEFORE I GO

The revised version of this poem became the first stanza of the 1881 'As a Strong Bird on Pinions Free'.

SOUVENIRS OF DEMOCRACRY

The revised version of this poem became 'My Legacy' in 1881.

AS A STRONG BIRD ON PINIONS FREE

From 1881 on, 'Thou Mother with Thy Equal Brood'.

363 *hectic*: relating to fever typically accompanying tuberculosis.

FROM TWO RIVULETS (1876)

Companion volume to the 'Centennial' or 'Author's Edition' of *Leaves*.

EIDÓLONS

371 *Eidólons*: spirits or apparitions; insubstantial images of objects or persons.

PRAYER OF COLUMBUS

373 *Prayer of Columbus*: the prose introduction was deleted from 1881 on.

FROM NOVEMBER BOUGHS (1888)

A FONT OF TYPE

385 *nonpareil, brevier, bourgeois, long primer*: traditional names for various type sizes used in printing (ascending here from smallest to largest).

BROADWAY

387 *parti-colored*: multicoloured.

THE DEAD TENOR

388 *Fernando's heart, Manrico's passionate call, Ernani's, sweet Gennaro's*: for Fernando and Ernani, see notes to p. 347. Manrico is the tenor role in Verdi's opera *Il Trovatore* (1853); Gennaro, the tenor role in Donizetti's opera *Lucrezia Borgia* (1833).

FROM LEAVES OF GRASS (1891–1892)

ON, ON THE SAME, YE JOCUND TWAIN!

393 *eclaircissement*: correctly *éclaircissement*; French for 'clarification'.

APPENDIX A

PREFACE TO *LEAVES OF GRASS* (1855)

400 *embouchure*: see note to p. 30.

PREFACE TO *TWO RIVULETS* (1876)

430 *Personalism*: a term Whitman introduced in his *Democratic Vistas* (1871).

432 *Memoranda*: Reference to Whitman's *Memoranda During the War* (1875–6).

PREFACE TO *NOVEMBER BOUGHS* (1888)

440 *William O'Connor and Dr. Bucke*: early friends and supporters of Whitman. See Chronology.

APPENDIX B

'SONG OF MYSELF' FROM *LEAVES OF GRASS* (1891–1892)

See also the explanatory notes on pp. 509–10 to the first version of this poem in *Leaves of Grass* (1855).

462 *sluing*: twisting.

464 *First-day loafe*: Sunday. Quaker terminology.

INDEX OF TITLES

After the Supper and Talk   390
America   386
Among the Multitude, *see* Calamus 41   264
Are You the New Person Drawn toward Me?, *see* Calamus 12   250
As Adam Early in the Morning, *see* Enfans d'Adam 15   236
As a Strong Bird on Pinions Free   358
As I Ebb'd with the Ocean of Life, *see* Leaves of Grass 1   210
As I lay with my head in your lap, Camerado   317
As I Sit Writing Here   385
Base of all Metaphysics, The   328
Beat! Beat! Drums!   290
Behold This Swarthy Face, *see* Calamus 19   254
Boston Ballad, A, *see* Untitled 'Clear the way there Jonathan!...' 110
Broad-Axe Poem   137
Broadway   387
Bunch Poem   181
Calamus   236–65
   1. 'In paths untrodden...'   236
   2. 'Scented herbage of my breast...'   237
   3. 'Whoever you are holding me now in hand...'   239
   4. 'These I, singing in spring, collect for lovers...' 241
   5. 'States!...'   242
   6. 'Not heaving from my ribbed breast only...'   245
   7. 'Of the terrible question of appearances'   245
   8. 'Long I thought that knowledge alone would suffice...' 246
   9. 'Hours continuing long, sore and heavy-hearted...' 247
  10. 'You bards of ages hence!...'   248
  11. 'When I heard at the close of day...'   249
  12. 'Are you the new person drawn toward me...'   250
  13. 'Calamus, taste...'   251
  14. 'Not heat flames up and consumes...'   251
  15. 'O drops of me...'   252
  16. 'Who is now reading this?...'   252
  17. 'Of him I love day and night...'   253
  18. 'City of my walks and joys...'   254
  19. 'Mind you the timid models of the rest...'   254
  20. 'I saw in Louisiana a live-oak growing...'   255
  21. 'Music always round me...'   256
  22. 'Passing stranger...'   256
  23. 'This moment as I sit alone...'   257
  24. 'I hear it is charged against me...'   257
  25. 'The prairie-grass dividing...'   258
  26. 'We two boys together clinging...'   258
  27. 'O love!...'   259
  28. 'When I peruse the conquered fame...'   259
  29. 'One flitting glimpse...'   260
  30. 'A promise and gift to California...'   260

31. 'What ship, puzzled at sea...'   260
32. 'What think you I take my pen in hand...'   261
33. 'No labor-saving machine...'   261
34. 'I dreamed in a dream...'   261
35. 'To you of New England...'   262
36. 'Earth! my likeness...'   262
37. 'A Leaf for hand in hand...'   262
38. 'Primeval my love for the woman I love...'   263
39. 'Sometimes with one I love...'   263
40. 'That shadow, my likeness...'   263
41. 'Among the men and women, the multitude...'   264
42. 'To the young man, many things to absorb...'   264
43. 'O you whom I often and silently come...'   264
44. 'Here my last words, and most baffling...'   265
45. 'Full of life, sweet-blooded, compact...'   265
Cavalry Crossing a Ford   280
Chanting the Square Deific   315
Chants Democratic 14   208
Chants Democratic 18   209
Chants Democratic 20   209
City Dead-House, The   322
City of Orgies, *see* Calamus 18   254
City of Ships   291
Clear Midnight, A   381
Clef Poem   177
Crossing Brooklyn Ferry, *see* Sun-Down Poem   154
Dalliance of the Eagles, The   381
Dead Tenor, The   387
Dismantled Ship, The   389
Dresser, The   286
Drum-Taps   277
Earth, My Likeness, *see* Calamus 36   262
Eidólons   371
from Enfans d'Adam   231–6
   1. 'To the garden, the world...'   231
   2. 'From that of myself...'   232
   8. 'Native moments...'   234
   9. 'Once I passed through a populous city...'   235
  10. 'Inquiring, tireless, seeking that yet unfound...'   235
  14. 'I am he that aches with love...'   236
  15. 'Early in the morning...'   236
Ethiopia Saluting The Colors   329
Europe the 72d and 73d Years of These States, *see* Untitled 'Suddenly
   out of its stale and drowsy lair...'   108
Faces, *see* Leaves of Grass 'Sauntering the pavement...'   102
Facing West from California's Shores, *see* Enfans d'Adam 10   235
Fast Anchor'd Eternal O Love!, *see* Calamus 38   263
First O Songs For A Prelude, *see* Drum-Taps   277
Font of Type, A   385
For Him I Sing   327
For You O Democracy, *see* Calamus 5   242
From Pent-up Aching Rivers, *see* Enfans d'Adam 2   232

Full of Life Now, *see* Calamus 45   265
Give me the splendid silent Sun   294
Glimpse, A, *see* Calamus 29   260
Gods   353
Good-Bye my Fancy   393
Good-Bye my Fancy!   397
Great Are the Myths, *see* Untitled 'Great are the myths...'   116
Halcyon Days   386
Hand-Mirror, A   269
Here the Frailest Leaves of Me, *see* Calamus 44   265
I Am He That Aches With Love, *see* Enfans d'Adam 14   236
I Dreamed in a Dream, *see* Calamus 34   261
I Hear America Singing, *see* Chants Democratic 20   209
I Hear it Was Charged against Me, *see* Calamus 24   257
I Saw in Louisiana a Live-Oak Growing, *see* Calamus 20   255
I saw old General at bay   300
I Sing the Body Electric, *see* Leaves of Grass 'The bodies of men and
     women engirth me...'   95
I Sit and Look Out, *see* Leaves of Grass 17   214
In Paths Untrodden, *see* Calamus 1   236
Inscription   321
L. of G.'s Purport   396
Leaf for Hand in Hand, A, *see* Calamus 37   262
Leaves of Grass 1 'Elemental drifts!...'   210
Leaves of Grass 16 'Sea-water, and all living below it...'   214
Leaves of Grass 17 'I sit and look out...'   214
Leaves of Grass 'I celebrate myself...'   15
Leaves of Grass 'Come closer to me...'   71
Leaves of Grass 'To think of time...'   80
Leaves of Grass 'I wander all night in my vision...'   86
Leaves of Grass 'The bodies of men and women engirth me...'   95
Leaves of Grass 'Sauntering the pavement...'   102
Liberty Poem ... of the Sea, *see* To a Foil'd European Revolutionaire   179
Life and Death   389
Look down fair moon   299
Mannahatta 'I was asking for something specific'   268
Mannahatta 'My city's fit and noble name resumed'   385
march in the ranks hard-prest, and the road unknown, A   293
Memories   386
Me Imperturbe, *see* Chants Democratic 18   209
My Canary Bird   385
My Legacy, *see* Souvenirs of Democracy   357
Mystic Trumpeter, The   364
Native Moments, *see* Enfans d'Adam 8   234
No Labor-Saving Machine, *see* Calamus 33   261
Noiseless, Patient Spider, A   351
Not Heat Flames up and Consumes, *see* Calamus 14   251
Not Heaving From My Ribb'd Breast Only, *see* Calamus 6   245
Not youth pertains to me   301
O Captain! my Captain!   314
O Living Always, Always Dying, *see* Calamus 27   259
O You Whom I Often and Silently Come, *see* Calamus 43   264

Of Him I Love Day and Night, *see* Calamus 17 — 253
Of the Terrible Doubt of Appearances, *see* Calamus 7 — 245
On, on the Same, ye Jocund Twain! — 393
On the Beach at Night Alone, *see* Clef Poem — 177
Once I Pass'd through a Populous City, *see* Enfans d'Adam 9 — 235
One song, America, before I go — 357
One's–Self I Sing — 327
Out of the Cradle Endlessly Rocking, *see* A Word Out of the Sea — 223
Out of the rolling ocean, the crowd — 300
Over the carnage rose prophetic a voice — 296
Ox Tamer, The — 377
Pallid Wreath, The — 394
Passage to India — 333
Pioneers! O Pioneers! — 280
Poem of Joys — 215
Poem of Procreation — 175
Poem of Salutation — 124
Poem of The Road — 162
Poem of The Sayers of The Words of The Earth — 183
Poem of Women — 123
Poem of Wonder at The Resurrection of The Wheat — 152
Poets to Come, *see* Chants Democratic 14 — 208
Prairie-Grass Dividing, The, *see* Calamus 25 — 258
Prayer of Columbus — 373
Promise to California, A, *see* Calamus 30 — 260
Proto–Leaf — 193
Proud Music of the Storm — 343
Quicksand years that whirl me I know not whither — 286
Queries to My Seventieth Year — 386
Reconciliation — 318
Recorders Ages Hence, *see* Calamus 10 — 248
Roots and Leaves Themselves Alone, *see* Calamus 13 — 251
Runner, The — 321
Salut au Monde!, *see* Poem of Salutation — 124
Scented Herbage of My Breast, *see* Calamus 2 — 237
Shut not your Doors to me proud Libraries — 279
Sleepers, The, *see* Leaves of Grass 'I wander all night in my vision...' — 86
Small the Theme of My Chant, *see* Inscription — 321
So long! — 270
Sometimes with One I Love, *see* Calamus 39 — 263
Song for Occupations, A, *see* Leaves of Grass 'Come closer to me...' — 71
Song of Joys, A, *see* Poem of Joys — 215
Song of Myself, *see* Leaves of Grass 'I celebrate myself...' — 15
Song of the Answerer, *see* Untitled 'A young man came to me...' — 105
Song of the Broad-Axe, *see* Broad-Axe Poem — 137
Song of the Open Road, *see* Poem of The Road — 162
Song of the Rolling Earth, A, *see* Poem of The Sayers of The Words of The Earth — 183
Souvenirs of Democracy — 357
Sparkles from the Wheel — 352
Spirit That Form'd This Scene — 381
Spontaneous Me, *see* Bunch Poem — 181

Starting from Paumanok, *see* Proto-Leaf 193
Sun-Down Poem 154
Tears, *see* 'Tears! tears! tears!...' 321
'Tears! tears! tears!...' 321
Thanks in Old Age 388
That Music Always Round Me, *see* Calamus 21 256
That Shadow My Likeness, *see* Calamus 40 263
There Was a Child Went Forth, *see* Untitled 'There was a child...' 112
These I Singing in Spring, *see* Calamus 4 241
This Compost, *see* Poem of Wonder at The Resurrection of The Wheat 152
This Moment Yearning and Thoughtful, *see* Calamus 23 257
Thou Mother with Thy Equal Brood, *see* As a Strong Bird on Pinions Free 358
To a Common Prostitute 267
To a Locomotive in Winter 376
To a Stranger, *see* Calamus 22 256
To a Western Boy, *see* Calamus 42 264
To Get the Final Lilt of Songs 387
To Him That Was Crucified 265
To One Shortly to Die 266
To the East and To the West, *see* Calamus 35 262
To the Garden, the World, *see* Enfans d'Adam 1 231
To the States, *see* Walt Whitman's Caution 267
To the Sun-Set Breeze 394
To Thee, Old Cause! 327
To Think of Time, *see* Leaves of Grass 'To think of time...' 80
To You 268
Trickle Drops, *see* Calamus 15 252
Twilight 389
Twilight Song, A 395
Unfolded Out of the Folds, *see* Poem of Women 123
Unseen Buds 396
Untitled 'A young man came to me...' 105
Untitled 'Clear the way there Jonathan!...' 110
Untitled 'Great are the myths...' 116
Untitled 'Suddenly out of its stale and drowsy lair...' 108
Untitled 'There was a child...' 112
Untitled 'Who learns my lesson complete?...' 114
Vigil strange I kept on the field one night 291
Walt Whitman's Caution 267
We Two Boys Together Clinging, *see* Calamus 26 258
What Place is Beseiged, *see* Calamus 31 260
What Think You I Take My Pen in Hand?, *see* Calamus 32 261
What Ship Puzzled at Sea, *see* Calamus 31 260
When I Heard at the Close of the Day, *see* Calamus 11 249
When I heard the learn'd Astronomer 289
When I Peruse the Conquered Fame, *see* Calamus 28 259
When I Read the Book 322
When Lilacs Last in the Door-Yard Bloom'd 305
Whispers of Heavenly Death 351
Who Learns My Lesson Complete?, *see* Untitled 'Who learns my lesson complete?...' 114

Whoever You Are Holding Me Now in Hand, *see* Calamus 3   239
Word Out of the Sea, A   223
World below the Brine, The, *see* Leaves of Grass 16   214
Woman Waits for Me, A, *see* Poem of Procreation   175
Wound-Dresser, The, *see* The Dresser   286
Year of Meteors (1859–60)   298
Year that trembled and reel'd beneath me   299
You Lingering Sparse Leaves of Me   389

American Literature

British and Irish Literature

Children's Literature

Classics and Ancient Literature

Colonial Literature

Eastern Literature

European Literature

Gothic Literature

History

Medieval Literature

Oxford English Drama

Philosophy

Poetry

Politics

Religion

The Oxford Shakespeare

A complete list of Oxford World's Classics, including Authors in Context, Oxford English Drama, and the Oxford Shakespeare, is available in the UK from the Marketing Services Department, Oxford University Press, Great Clarendon Street, Oxford OX2 6DP, or visit the website at www.oup.com/uk/worldsclassics.

In the USA, visit www.oup.com/us/owc for a complete title list.

Oxford World's Classics are available from all good bookshops.

A SELECTION OF   **OXFORD WORLD'S CLASSICS**

HENRY ADAMS	**The Education of Henry Adams**
LOUISA MAY ALCOTT	**Little Women**
SHERWOOD ANDERSON	**Winesburg, Ohio**
EDWARD BELLAMY	**Looking Backward 2000–1887**
CHARLES BROCKDEN BROWN	**Wieland; or The Transformation and Memoirs of Carwin, The Biloquist**
WILLA CATHER	**My Ántonia** **O Pioneers!**
KATE CHOPIN	**The Awakening and Other Stories**
JAMES FENIMORE COOPER	**The Last of the Mohicans**
STEPHEN CRANE	**The Red Badge of Courage**
J. HECTOR ST. JEAN DE CRÈVECŒUR	**Letters from an American Farmer**
FREDERICK DOUGLASS	**Narrative of the Life of Frederick Douglass, an American Slave**
THEODORE DREISER	**Sister Carrie**
F. SCOTT FITZGERALD	**The Great Gatsby** **The Beautiful and Damned** **Tales of the Jazz Age** **This Side of Paradise**
BENJAMIN FRANKLIN	**Autobiography and Other Writings**
CHARLOTTE PERKINS GILMAN	**The Yellow Wall-Paper and Other Stories**
ZANE GREY	**Riders of the Purple Sage**
NATHANIEL HAWTHORNE	**The Blithedale Romance** **The House of the Seven Gables** **The Marble Faun** **The Scarlet Letter** **Young Goodman Brown and Other Tales**

A SELECTION OF   **OXFORD WORLD'S CLASSICS**

WASHINGTON IRVING   **The Sketch-Book of Geoffrey Crayon, Gent**

HENRY JAMES   **The Ambassadors**
The American
The Aspern Papers and Other Stories
The Awkward Age
The Bostonians
Daisy Miller and Other Stories
The Europeans
The Golden Bowl
The Portrait of a Lady
The Spoils of Poynton
The Turn of the Screw and Other Stories
Washington Square
What Maisie Knew
The Wings of the Dove

JACK LONDON   **The Call of the Wild, White Fang and Other Stories**
John Barleycorn
The Sea-Wolf

HERMAN MELVILLE   **Billy Budd, Sailor and Selected Tales**
The Confidence-Man
Moby-Dick

FRANK NORRIS   **McTeague**

FRANCIS PARKMAN   **The Oregon Trail**

EDGAR ALLAN POE   **The Narrative of Arthur Gordon Pym of Nantucket and Related Tales**
Selected Tales

HARRIET BEECHER STOWE   **Uncle Tom's Cabin**

HENRY DAVID THOREAU   **Walden**

A SELECTION OF   **OXFORD WORLD'S CLASSICS**

MARK TWAIN   **Adventures of Huckleberry Finn**
                          The Adventures of Tom Sawyer
                          A Connecticut Yankee in King Arthur's
                              Court
                          Pudd'nhead Wilson

THORSTEIN VEBLEN   **The Theory of the Leisure Class**

BOOKER T. WASHINGTON   **Up from Slavery**

EDITH WHARTON   **The Age of Innocence**
                          The Custom of the Country
                          Ethan Frome
                          The House of Mirth

WALT WHITMAN   **Leaves of Grass**

OWEN WISTER   **The Virginian**

	Late Victorian Gothic Tales
	Literature and Science in the Nineteenth Century
JANE AUSTEN	Emma
	Mansfield Park
	Persuasion
	Pride and Prejudice
	Selected Letters
	Sense and Sensibility
MRS BEETON	Book of Household Management
MARY ELIZABETH BRADDON	Lady Audley's Secret
ANNE BRONTË	The Tenant of Wildfell Hall
CHARLOTTE BRONTË	Jane Eyre
	Shirley
	Villette
EMILY BRONTË	Wuthering Heights
ROBERT BROWNING	The Major Works
JOHN CLARE	The Major Works
SAMUEL TAYLOR COLERIDGE	The Major Works
WILKIE COLLINS	The Moonstone
	No Name
	The Woman in White
CHARLES DARWIN	The Origin of Species
THOMAS DE QUINCEY	The Confessions of an English Opium-Eater
	On Murder
CHARLES DICKENS	The Adventures of Oliver Twist
	Barnaby Rudge
	Bleak House
	David Copperfield
	Great Expectations
	Nicholas Nickleby

A SELECTION OF   **OXFORD WORLD'S CLASSICS**

CHARLES DICKENS
The Old Curiosity Shop
Our Mutual Friend
The Pickwick Papers

GEORGE DU MAURIER
Trilby

MARIA EDGEWORTH
Castle Rackrent

GEORGE ELIOT
Daniel Deronda
The Lifted Veil and Brother Jacob
Middlemarch
The Mill on the Floss
Silas Marner

EDWARD FITZGERALD
The Rubáiyát of Omar Khayyám

ELIZABETH GASKELL
Cranford
The Life of Charlotte Brontë
Mary Barton
North and South
Wives and Daughters

GEORGE GISSING
New Grub Street
The Nether World
The Odd Women

EDMUND GOSSE
Father and Son

THOMAS HARDY
Far from the Madding Crowd
Jude the Obscure
The Mayor of Casterbridge
The Return of the Native
Tess of the d'Urbervilles
The Woodlanders

JAMES HOGG
The Private Memoirs and Confessions of a Justified Sinner

JOHN KEATS
The Major Works
Selected Letters

CHARLES MATURIN
Melmoth the Wanderer

HENRY MAYHEW
London Labour and the London Poor